Spiro Agnew and the Rise of the Republican Right

Spiro Agnew and the Rise of the Republican Right

JUSTIN P. COFFEY

PRAEGER™

An Imprint of ABC-CLIO, LLC
Santa Barbara, California • Denver, Colorado

Library of Congress Cataloging-in-Publication Data

Coffey, Justin P., author.
Spiro Agnew and the rise of the Republican right / Justin P. Coffey.
pages cm
Includes bibliographical references and index.
ISBN 978–1–4408–4141–5 (hard copy : alk. paper) — ISBN 978–1–4408–4142–2 (ebook) 1. Agnew, Spiro T., 1918–1996. 2. Vice-Presidents—United States—Biography. 3. United States—Politics and government—1969–1974. I. Title.
E840.8.A34C55 2015
352.23′9092—dc23 2015024608
[B]

ISBN: 978–1–4408–4141–5
EISBN: 978–1–4408–4142–2

19 18 17 16 15 1 2 3 4 5

This book is also available on the World Wide Web as an eBook.
Visit www.abc-clio.com for details.

Praeger
An Imprint of ABC-CLIO, LLC

ABC-CLIO, LLC
130 Cremona Drive, P.O. Box 1911
Santa Barbara, California 93116-1911

This book is printed on acid-free paper ∞

Manufactured in the United States of America

Contents

Introduction

In his account of his fall from power, Spiro Agnew claimed that part of his problems arose from being a "conservative at a time when liberals captured the imagination and sympathy of the communications media."[1] When Agnew began his political career he fashioned himself as a pragmatic moderate. A Baltimore County executive, Agnew eschewed ideology and charted a middle path, one that he hoped the Republican Party would adopt. In 1964, Agnew opposed Senator Barry Goldwater's candidacy for the Republican presidential nomination. When he ran for governor of Maryland in 1966, Agnew continued to portray himself as a moderate, and during much of the 1960s, Agnew denounced political extremism and was particularly critical of the right-wing of the GOP. But as Agnew climbed up the political ladder, his views evolved and his political metamorphosis helped earn him a spot on the Republican presidential ticket in 1968.

Vice President Agnew continued to move to the right, as did the Republican Party. During the 1950s and into the 1960s ideologues battled for control of the GOP. Conservatives achieved a monumental triumph in 1964 when Barry Goldwater captured the Republican nomination for president. While the conservatives had won a battle, the fight for the future of the GOP was hardly over. Goldwater's crushing defeat caused soul-searching among the party's faithful. Two years after the Goldwater debacle, Republican moderates and liberals scored a number of victories, including Agnew taking the Maryland gubernatorial election.

Agnew took part in the struggle within the Republican Party. In the mid- to late-1960s it was by no means evident that the right-wing would take control of the GOP. For decades the Republicans had struggled to find a winning political strategy. Ever since the Great Depression, the Democrats had dominated the political landscape. Franklin D. Roosevelt's election in 1932 ushered in an era of Democratic control of the presidency and Congress. From 1932 through 1964 the Democrats controlled both houses of Congress for all but four years. The Republicans had won the presidency just twice, in 1952 and 1956 when Dwight Eisenhower was able to take enough votes from the Democratic coalition to win the presidency.

But in the early 1960s, the Republicans were still a minority party. Vice President Richard M. Nixon lost to Senator John F. Kennedy in the 1960 election, and afterward, the liberals, moderates, and conservatives in the party battled over the direction of the GOP. Many on the right blamed Nixon's defeat on his middle-of-the-road approach, arguing that the Republicans needed, for political and ideological reasons, to move rightward. The moderates, such as Nixon and Eisenhower, wanted to stay the course, while liberals pushed for a more progressive agenda.

At the time Agnew aligned himself with both the moderates and the liberals. His journey from moderation to conservatism mirrored that of the GOP. Eventually the Right took control of the GOP. The conservative revolution not only changed the makeup and direction of the GOP, but also fundamentally realigned the electoral map.

Race played the critical role in the transformation. Beginning with Harry S. Truman in the late 1940s, many leading Democrats began calling for an end to Jim Crow laws. In 1948 Truman issued an executive order desegregating the military and publicly endorsing an end to the poll tax. Truman's aggressive support of a civil rights agenda enraged segregationists and led to a revolt at the 1948 Democratic Convention. Delegates from five states walked out and nominated South Carolina governor Strom Thurmond and Mississippi's Fielding L. Wright on the Dixiecrat ticket. Thurmond and Wright took four states but their protest party ended as quickly as it appeared. As the Civil Rights Movement gained momentum during the 1950s, Southern Democrats reacted with dismay and sought to maintain segregation at all costs. Two years after the Supreme Court issued its ruling in *Brown v. Board of Education* in 1954, twenty senators and eighty-two representatives signed the "Southern Manifesto," calling for resistance to further attempts at desegregation.[2]

But the Southerners were fighting against their own party. The estrangement between the Southern wing and the rest of the party grew in the early 1960s as Kennedy and then Lyndon B. Johnson gradually embraced the civil rights cause. The ardent segregationists saw Johnson's signing of the 1964 Civil Rights Act as a betrayal. Goldwater's vote against the bill made him—and the Republican Party—an acceptable alternative to Johnson and the Democrats. For over a century the Democrats controlled much of the South and the Republicans stood almost no chance of winning any part of Dixie in presidential contests. In 1964, however, Goldwater became the first Republican since Reconstruction to win South Carolina, Georgia, Alabama, Mississippi, and Louisiana.[3]

The results marked the end of the solid South. Johnson's overwhelming victory overshadowed signs that the Roosevelt coalition was beginning to crack. Over the next few years the Republicans continued to make inroads in the states of the former Confederacy. By 1968 Blue Dog Democrats were deserting their party in droves. In that year's election, Democrat Hubert H. Humphrey won just 22 percent of the Southern vote and just one Southern state—Texas. Between them, Richard Nixon and George Wallace carried the rest of the South, with Wallace capturing the Deep South and Nixon the rest.[4]

A number of Nixon's critics contended that Agnew was on the ticket in 1968 as part of Nixon's "Southern Strategy." Agnew, the theory went, would offset Wallace's appeal to white voters, particularly in the South and in border-states. To Nixon, Agnew was an attractive running mate with his forceful denunciation of civil rights activists at a meeting in Maryland in the wake of Martin Luther King Jr.'s assassination in April 1968. Rioting broke out in Baltimore and Agnew blamed much of the disorder on Maryland's African American leaders. Ironically, Agnew's support from black voters helped make him governor of Maryland. In the 1966 gubernatorial contest, Agnew was viewed as a progressive on race, particularly when juxtaposed against his opponent. But by 1968 all the goodwill between Agnew and Maryland's African American community had evaporated.

The GOP largely abandoned civil rights as an issue and along with it African American voters. At the same time party insurgents took control, steering the Republicans to the right. When Nixon nominated Agnew as the vice presidential candidate in 1968, prominent conservatives knew little about Agnew. Four years later, they ensured that Agnew would stay on the ticket. How Agnew became the Right's champion is the focus of this work.

During the Nixon years, the Republican Party began to use social issues as a wedge to divide the electorate and attract the Democrats and independents disillusioned with the excesses of 1960s' liberalism. Crime became a bedrock issue, as did permissiveness, sexual liberation, and drugs. In 1972 Nixon used the phrase "acid, amnesty, and abortion" against Democratic senator George McGovern, as a way of painting him as out of touch with traditional American values.

Vice President Agnew gained notoriety for his fiery speeches blasting the "radiclibs" and "nattering nabobs of negativism" for being fundamentally unpatriotic. Conservatives loved his attacks and Agnew soon was the darling of the Right. After the 1972 election, Agnew had an excellent chance of earning the 1976 presidential nomination, as many conservatives in the GOP backed his potential candidacy.

But it was never to be. There is another part of the Agnew story, a more sordid tale of greed and corruption. Agnew quit the vice presidency because he was caught taking kickbacks. During his time as county executive, governor, and vice president, Agnew took money from contractors whom he helped land government contracts. As a politician, Agnew had always prided himself as being above reproach, but he was eventually exposed as a hypocrite who abused his power and broke the public trust.

Since he resigned the vice presidency in October1973, little has been written about Agnew. This work is the first scholarly study of Agnew's life and career. By drawing upon primary sources, archival papers, memoirs, and other sources, the book provides a look at the man and the politician. What emerges is a portrait of a political figure, often depicted in the media as a buffoon. Indeed, Richard Nixon, the president Agnew served under, once dismissed Agnew as a "clown," whereas Henry Kissinger claimed Agnew was smarter than he was usually given credit for. Agnew disliked the hand-shaking and glad-handing that came with politics, yet he never lost an election. He was ambivalent about his own background. Son of a Greek immigrant, Agnew was an Episcopalian, not Greek Orthodox, and he made sure that his children did not have "Greek" first names. Elected governor of Maryland in 1966 with the help of African American voters, Agnew quickly lost almost all the support he had in Maryland's black community. Agnew championed "law-and-order" but pled no contest to a charge of tax evasion.

After pleading guilty and resigning his office, Agnew went quietly, but his fall should not obscure his importance. He has a larger legacy than that of a fallen politician. This book also details Agnew's political career from the early days in Maryland through the vice presidency and charts his move to the right at the same time the Republican Party was going in that direction. It was not inevitable that the conservatives would come to dominate the GOP, but it did happen. Apart from strategic mobilizing and dedicated commitment from grassroots organizers, the conservatives wrested control because of issues that millions cared about. These ranged from a reaction against liberal Great Society programs, to a concern over the base and scope of civil rights, to law and order, and anti-communism.

In 1964, an overwhelming majority of Americans rejected Barry Goldwater's conservative message. Sixteen years later, the country elected Ronald Reagan, who ran on a Goldwater-esque platform promising to roll back the size and scope of government. Reagan also campaigned against what he argued was the result of the excesses of liberalism: waning patriotism, rising crime, increasing welfare rolls, and America's declining rank in the world. The "Reagan Revolution" ushered in an era of conservative government that outlasted Reagan. By the 1980s, the right wing of the Republican Party had seized control of the party, a situation that continues to this day.

In 1994, historian Leo P. Ribuffo asked in the pages of *The American Historical Review*, "Why Is There So Much Conservatism in the United States and Why Do So Few Historians Know Anything About It?"[5] Over the past two decades historians have examined how and when the conservatives emerged as the dominant faction in the GOP. One of the first analyses was Mary C. Brennan's *Turning Right in the Sixties: The Conservative Capture of the GOP*. Brennan details how the Right came to dominate the party. In her view, conservative activists outside the party helped shape the direction of the GOP, and by the late 1960s, the Republican Party was ideologically conservative.[6] Geoffrey Kabaservice argues that by the early 1960s, the moderates were doomed; while Rick Perlstein contends that in 1964 the Right had seized control of the GOP.[7] These three works are some of over a dozen books on the rise of the Right. Scholars differ not only on when the conservatives took over the party, but also, on why. A number of authors, including Perlstein, contend that race was the critical factor. The Civil Rights Movement, and the Democratic Party's embrace of it, alienated white Southerners, who fled the Democrats during the 1960s and 1970s. The "white backlash" also led many whites outside the South to begin voting Republican. Capitalizing on racial fear, Richard Nixon and Ronald Reagan rode to victory and established Republican hegemony in the South.

Race played a critical role in the conservative ascendancy, but there were other factors that were just as important. Here Agnew's career is very instructive in illuminating why the conservatism became the dominant ideology in the GOP. In the early part of his political career, Agnew was a moderate-to-liberal Republican. By the early 1970s, Agnew had turned to the right. He thought the liberalism of the 1960s had caused more harm than good. Further, Agnew remained an ardent Cold War warrior who wanted the Vietnam War fought more aggressively and rejected overtures to communist nations.

This work places Agnew's career in the context of the turbulent late 1960s and early 1970s. The issues that Agnew embraced and championed as he turned right were race, crime (and those two were directly related), anticommunism, and the reach of the federal government. Agnew came to believe that many of the country's crimes were the fault of liberal elites and their policies. As vice president Agnew spoke for so many who were disaffected by all the liberal programs of the 1960s, who were frightened by the rising crime rates in America, who were uneasy with integration, and who feared the spread of communism around the world. Today the Republican Party is ideologically conservative and the political career of Spiro Agnew helps explain why and how this is.

Chapter 1

The Rise of Spiro Agnew

Spiro Agnew's formative years do not provide much insight into the man who eventually stood a heartbeat away from the presidency. Throughout much of his early life Agnew was apolitical. Not until he reached his forties did Agnew delve into the world of politics. Even then his ideological framework differed greatly from the right-wing points he espoused as vice president.

Agnew came from a humble background. His father, Theofraste Anagnostopoulos (he later anglicized his name to Theodore Agnew), arrived in America from Greece in 1902. A native of Gargalianoi, Theofraste later told his son that there was "some sort of disaster in the olive industry and they were pretty well wiped out financially."[1] The elder Agnew settled in Schenectady, New York, and opened up a diner.[2] He spent six years in Schenectady and then moved south to Baltimore, Maryland. In 1914 he opened up a restaurant, the Piccadilly. There he met William Pollard, a trained veterinarian who was working as the U.S. meat inspector in Baltimore, and Pollard's wife, Margaret—a couple who were regulars at the restaurant. Agnew struck up a friendship with the Pollards, and he often paid social visits to their home. After William Pollard died of leukemia in April 1917, Margaret and Agnew began dating. Margaret Pollard, a native of Bristol, Virginia, was the youngest of ten children. Orphaned at an early age, she was raised by her older brother James Akers in Roanoke, Virginia. After working at a law firm in Bristol, Margaret moved to Washington and found employment in Cordell Hull's office. She married William Pollard in 1907 and was thirty-seven when her husband died. Her new suitor was thirty-nine and a bachelor with no children. After a very brief courtship they married on December 12, 1917.[3]

Spiro T. Agnew was born eleven months later, November 9, 1918. He was the couple's first and only child, though Margaret had a son, Roy, from her first marriage. Spiro enjoyed a mostly happy childhood. His father was clearly the dominant figure in his youth. "He was the authority in the family and when he indicated that he'd made a decision, I listened, and I was quite fearful of disobeying him," he later recalled.[4] During interviews Agnew invariably described his father as "stern."[5] Agnew's half-brother Roy agreed with that assessment, labeling his stepfather a "disciplinarian."[6] Still, Spiro respected his father. Years later, as a public figure, Agnew constantly harkened to the lessons he learned from his father. He spoke of his father in glowing terms and offered profuse praise; the admiration he had for his father was deep and genuine. When addressing a Greek American organization in 1969—the AHEPA, a group that was honoring Theodore Agnew by endowing a scholarship in his name—Spiro Agnew told the assembly, "I am proud to say that I grew up in the light of my father. My beliefs are his."[7]

But as a teenager, Agnew felt like an outsider because of his Greek heritage. Classmates picked on him because of his funny sounding name. His friends teased him about his father's thick accent, while neighbors referred to the Agnews as the "Greek family up the street."[8] Spiro resented the taunts and the embarrassment remained with him into his adulthood. He never liked his first name, and as he grew up he insisted on being called "Ted." When he had children of his own, he made sure they didn't have Greek surnames. His father offered him money to learn Greek and to attend a Greek school, but he refused. One disagreement his parents had was over where to baptize Spiro. The elder Agnew was Greek Orthodox, while his wife was an Episcopalian, and Spiro was baptized and raised an Episcopalian.[9]

At fourteen Agnew entered Forest Park High School. A tall and gangly youth (he was already over six feet by age thirteen), Agnew made few friends. He spent much of his free time during those years working. The Depression hit the Agnew family hard and Theodore Agnew closed the doors of his restaurant in 1929. A year later the bank where the family deposited their savings went under, leaving the family destitute. They eventually sold their Forest Park home and moved into a small apartment in downtown Baltimore.[10]

By Spiro's senior year his father had saved enough money to be able to send him to college, and in 1937, he enrolled at Johns Hopkins University where he majored in chemistry. However, Spiro spent most of his time partying. He drank a lot of beer and for a time smoked a pipe.[11] All the while he neglected his studies. Although he liked the theory involved in chemistry, he was less enthusiastic about the long hours that chemistry majors needed to spend in the lab.[12] During his three years Agnew ruefully acknowledged that, "my studies were pursued rather unsuccessfully because of a lack of application on my part." His laziness cost dearly, as after his junior year he had only completed one course in his major, another in French, one in economics, and several English courses.[13]

Agnew dropped out after his junior year. Believing that his strengths were "more compatible with the law than with the sciences," Agnew enrolled for classes at the University of Baltimore Night Law School.[14] Needing money to pay for law school, he went to work at the Maryland Casualty Company, a Baltimore-based insurance firm. The company hired him as an assistant underwriter at a starting salary of $11 a week. While there, Spiro came across Elinor "Judy" Judefind, a short, shy brunette who worked as a file clerk. A native of Baltimore, she lived in the Forest Park neighborhood and had attended the same high school as Spiro. When she saw Spiro she recognized him as a "familiar face," but they had never met before. Agnew asked her out and in just four months the couple became engaged.[15]

In 1940, in response to the gathering storm clouds overseas, the Congress passed the Selective Service Act, a draft that required all able-bodied men between the ages of eighteen and thirty-five to register with the government. Just a few months after leaving law school, Agnew received his draft notice.[16] Two weeks after Pearl Harbor, the army ordered Agnew to report for basic training at Camp Croft in South Carolina—a place he later described as a "quagmire of red clay."[17] The training exposed Agnew to different peoples and helped him mature; as he later explained, "I remember it (basic training) so well because we had all regular Army NCO's and they were real tough boys, and most of the draftees came from New York and Brooklyn and they were pretty rough boys too, and I'd led a very sheltered life. I became unsheltered very quickly."[18] After completing his training he moved to Officers Candidate School at Fort Knox, Kentucky.[19] On May 23, 1942, Spiro Agnew graduated with a second lieutenant's commission in the armored infantry.[20]

The draft interrupted Spiro and Judy's marriage plans. The couple had originally decided on a Christmastime wedding but they had to postpone their plans because the Officers Candidates School was not accepting married men. Four days after earning his commission, on May 27, 1942, Spiro and Judy were married in front of the fireplace at the bride's childhood home.[21] After a two-day honeymoon in Baltimore, he returned to Kentucky, where he was assigned to the 8th Armored Division, while Judy joined him in June. During his two years at Fort Knox, Agnew served as instructor in what were called "military subjects" and also was responsible for organizing athletic teams for Special Services.[22] On March 25, 1944, the army sent Agnew overseas to Birmingham, England. After D-Day the army dispatched Agnew to France, where he was assigned to the 54th Armored Infantry Battalion of the 11th Armored Division. Appointed a company commander of the 743rd Tank Battalion, Agnew and his troops arrived in Metz after General George Patton's forces liberated the town. When the Germans launched their massive counterattack in December 1944, Patton ordered Agnew's division, which had been split off and attached to the 101st Airborne Division, to Belgium. The company supplied fuel, rations, and other supplies to soldiers near the Bastogne area, where heavy fighting was taking place.[23]

The siege of Bastogne lasted over six weeks, and Agnew's company spent nearly forty days in the maelstrom. The war in Europe was winding down, but it was by no means over, and Agnew's company spent the next four months moving across the German countryside until the Nazis sued for peace in early May.[24] Agnew's military career was honorable and distinguished. His participation in the Battle of the Bulge earned him the Combat Infantryman's Badge and the Bronze Star. Agnew spent the remaining months of the war in France and Germany and returned to the United States on November 26, 1945. The army released Agnew from active duty a week later.[25]

As the conflict ended, Agnew worried about his immediate plans. In January 1945, he sent a letter to Johns Hopkins asking if he could resume his education. Determined to finish school, he asked how long it would take to earn his chemistry degree while taking night classes. The response from the school could not have heartened him. The registrar noted that although he left the school in good standing, fulfilling all the requirements would likely take at least eight years.[26]

With that avenue closed, Agnew had to make a quick decision. When he returned home in early Spiro Agnew was twenty-six, married, and a father. He decided to reenroll at the Baltimore Night Law School. "I returned immediately to law school," he recalled, "for now I had an insatiable desire to learn and get on with my education. I had much better scholastic ability than before and, of course, greater incentive, with a wife and children to support."[27] Agnew landed a job with one of Baltimore's most prominent law firms, Smith and Barrett. The firm hired him as a clerk and he worked in the office during the day while attending school at night. Although a small firm, it was one of the most powerful and respected in Baltimore's tight-knit legal community. Moreover, both partners were politically connected. Michael Paul Smith was one of the leading trial lawyers in the city, and a prominent member of Baltimore's Democratic Party. Lester Barrett, a Republican, eventually became the chief judge of the Baltimore County Circuit Court.[28]

Agnew often talked politics with Barrett. Years before, when he turned twenty-one he had registered as a Democrat, not because of any strong convictions, but because, as he later explained, "my father was a Democrat."[29] The senior partner, a staunch Republican, imparted his views to the impressionable Agnew. Agnew attributed his shift to the GOP to Barrett's influence.[30] Agnew's motives in switching parties were as practical as they were ideological. Agnew confided to Barrett that he wanted to run for political office. Barrett offered his encouragement and advice. If Agnew wanted to go anywhere in Baltimore County it would have be as a Republican since the county remained a Democratic stronghold, and there was no shortage of ambitious young men Democrats yearning to take office. At the time there was little separating the parties ideologically so Agnew took Barrett's advice and registered as a Republican.[31]

For the next decade, Agnew devoted most of his time to his legal career and to his growing family. Judy, who once happily admitted to having "majored in marriage," stayed at home with their four children—three girls, Pamela, Susan, and Kim, and one boy, Randy. Her husband helped as much as he could, as Judy later told an interviewer: "when the children were small and their mother was not feeling up to par, he would pitch in. He's washed diapers, made formulas, and done everything a wife and mother has to do . . . He never hesitated, when it was necessary to do any of those chores."[32]

Agnew also kept busy with his civic activities. He rose to the presidency of the Loch Raven Kiwanis Club (where he compiled a seven-year perfect attendance record), the presidency of the Loch Raven Intercommunity Council, and the presidency of the Dumbarton P.T.A.[33] He also became involved in local politics, stuffing envelopes and ringing doorbells for Republican candidates.

Agnew lived in Baltimore County, a rapidly growing area full of suburban families. The Republicans swept the county council elections that were held in November 1957. Republican leaders awarded Agnew with an appointment to the three-person zoning board of appeals. His original appointment was for one year at a salary of $3,600.[34] A year later, in May 1958, the chair stepped down and Agnew took his place. In this position Agnew experienced firsthand the enormous effect suburban life had on American politics. Baltimore County, like other suburban areas, was in the midst of a building boom, and the battles over what could be built, where something could be built, and who could build it were decided at weekly zoning board meetings. With so much at stake, the meetings often descended into shouting matches. As a biographer of Agnew noted,

> Few things arose the passions in suburban America that zoning does. There is a never-ending clash between developers and conservationists, traditionalists and modernists. Millions of dollars are involved, and some builders are not averse to spreading them around, particularly if they will influence the votes of those who decide what they can or cannot do.[35]

The answers to those questions were often found in envelopes stuffed with cash. Though money flowed freely in Baltimore County, Agnew, ironically, remained above reproach. While he angered both partisan Democrats and even a few Republicans with his overbearing manner, he earned the respect and admiration of nearly everyone with his fairness and his honesty. He often told his friends and supporters that he could have accepted money under the table, but his strict code of ethics prohibited from taking anything. This was not just bravado on his part. His reputation for honesty was well earned, as George Callcott, perhaps the preeminent historian of Maryland, wrote years later, "Agnew was superb and fair in the job: firm and fair, without a hint then or later of impropriety. From time to time others were tainted, but not Agnew."[36]

In 1962 the county GOP asked him to run for Baltimore County Executive. Party leaders assured him that he would face no opposition. Agnew mulled over the offer and accepted. Most political observers gave him little chance of winning. For over a century the Democratic Party had dominated Baltimore County. Democrats outnumbered Republicans in Baltimore County by a nearly four-to-one margin. The Democrats backed up those numbers with a strong machine that had allowed them to control the leadership of Baltimore County for seventy-seven consecutive years. But Agnew liked his chances in the race. He cast himself as a progressive reformer, playing down his party affiliation and stressing issues such as education and other public services. All throughout the campaign Agnew eschewed ideology in favor of pragmatism. He would govern, so he said, as an able and honest administrator who placed results in front of partisanship.

His strategy in the 1962 election was to attack the Democratic establishment as inefficient and corrupt. By the late 1950s, the county's Democratic machine was under assault and bitter factionalism began to undermine its grip on power. The strife resulted from the personal struggle between two power brokers, Michael Birmingham and Christian Kahl. From 1951 to 1958 Birmingham had ruled the organization, but he chose not to run for county executive in 1958, opening the way for Kahl, who easily won the Democratic nomination and the general election. Relations between Kahl and Birmingham slowly deteriorated and divisions spread throughout the machine. Birmingham eventually decided to challenge incumbent Kahl in the 1962 Democratic primary.[37]

Birmingham was not alone. Another Democrat, W. Brooks Bradley, threw his hat in the ring. An outsider, Bradley denounced the Democratic machine as corrupt. Bradley's accusations about malfeasance riled Kahl but attracted support from other county Democrats. The incumbent Kahl now faced two major opponents, Bradley and Birmingham. On top of that, a grand jury was investigating the county government's insurance practices. Though no indictments were handed down, the public airing of the grand jury proceedings, which should have remained sealed, damaged Kahl.[38]

With no opposition in the GOP primary, Agnew had the luxury of watching the Democrats destroy themselves. During the primary season, Kahl and Birmingham traded barbs that demonstrated the depths to which their former alliance had plunged. Birmingham accused Kahl of running a "dirty, underhanded, illegal and downright dishonest" campaign.[39] Kahl shot back, claiming that he was a far better executive than Birmingham, and arguing that Birmingham had left behind a mess that he had to clean up. As primary day approached the contest was too close to call. Voters went to the polls on May 15, 1962, and Michael Birmingham emerged as the victor, besting Kahl by some 3,000 votes.[40]

On the surface "Iron Mike" as he was also known, appeared to have scored a major triumph. He came out of retirement to defeat the incumbent county executive, and the seven candidates he backed for nomination to the county council all won. In an editorial on the primary elections, the *Baltimore Evening Sun*, certainly no friend of Birmingham, allowed that the "voters spoke unmistakably for the political organization led by Michael J. Birmingham."[41] The odds in the general election seemed to favor Birmingham against the green newcomer, but despite the daunting registration numbers, the power of the Democratic machine, and the name recognition of his opponent, Agnew remained confident. Baltimore County was changing and

Agnew was more in touch with the suburbanite voters than Birmingham was.

Like thousands of other residents, Agnew was a newcomer to Baltimore County, having arrived in 1946. He was part of a massive migration that dramatically altered the county's landscape. Surrounding the city of Baltimore like a horseshoe, 610-square-mile Baltimore County was (and remains) an entirely separate entity. Before 1945 the county was sparsely populated. Its population totaled 156,000 in 1940 and most of the residents lived in small towns made up of family farms, with a few genteel estates sprinkled throughout. The county had plenty of room to grow, and expand it did. During the 1940s its population increased 73 percent, while the city of Baltimore rose by just 10 percent. The enormous growth occurred mostly after World War II, when the county's population doubled between 1945 and 1950. Over the next decade the population exploded, reaching 492,000 by 1960. Between 1949 and 1956, contractors built some 32,573 dwelling units, and from 1953 onward, the county issued almost 10,000 permits for new houses a year.[42]

Along with the influx of residents came more services. The county's Director of Works, John B. Funk, reported that 550 miles of sanitary sewers and 170 miles of storm drain were completed during 1950–1955. During the 1950s, 50 miles of new roads were laid each year, and, on average, twenty-six new traffic lights went up (as compared to one in the 1930s). School construction also skyrocketed. In 1950 there were 69 elementary and secondary schools with 1,071 classrooms; fourteen years later the numbers were 126 schools and 3,355 classrooms. The county was unprepared for the huge number of students entering public schools, and many pupils were sent to churches and other temporary quarters. When Timonium Elementary school opened in 1958 it was already overcrowded.[43]

Many of the county's newer residents believed that the existing apparatus could not, or would not, solve all the pressing needs of the community. The battle over the new charter demonstrated that in the minds of many people, the government had failed because it was inextricably linked with the Baltimore County Democratic Party. The organization (the Democrats always referred to it as the "organization"), established during World War I, dominated the county for over forty years. George Callcott, the preeminent historian of Maryland, once described it as a "classic among machines." Beginning with the first boss, Harrison Rider, the machine determined the county's Democratic ticket, it doled out patronage jobs, and it received "campaign contributions" from contractors, engineers, and all others who were awarded government contracts.[44]

By 1962 many of the residents of Baltimore County were tired of the machine and were willing to vote Republican. After the primary Agnew began assembling a campaign staff. One of his first decisions was naming Arthur J. Sohmer as his campaign manager. Sohmer, a graduate of Lafayette College and a student at the University of Maryland Law School, worked as salesman for the Union Camp Corporation of Baltimore before entering politics. He ran unsuccessfully in the primary campaign for a seat in the Maryland House of Delegates in 1962, and afterward Agnew asked him to come aboard as campaign manager. Even though Sohmer "told him that I didn't know anything about it," he accepted Agnew's offer, thus starting a professional relationship that lasted until 1973. Sohmer proved to be an effective manager and excellent strategist.[45]

Shortly after taking over the reins, Sohmer drew up a paper that he called "A Preliminary Examination of the Campaign of Spiro T. Agnew." In the document, Sohmer listed Agnew's strengths and weaknesses, offered strategic plans, and analyzed Agnew's organization. Sohmer believed Agnew's advantages to be the fractured opposition, the corruption issue, and his personal assets, which included: "his age, his professional status, clean record, health, community service, war record, appearance, sincerity, family (and) ability to think quickly." Sohmer also came up a slogan for the campaign: "Agnew: The Man with a Plan."[46]

The campaign created an Agnew Bi-Partisan Committee in August.[47] Throughout the rest of the campaign Agnew's team worked to attract Democrats, which proved to be a simple task. On September 24, over 100 Democrats gathered for a bipartisan testimonial dinner for Agnew that reporter Frank DeFilippo described as more "like a United Nations roster than a Republican fundraising dinner."[48] In attendance were Walter Rasmussen, county register of wills, Edgar J. DeMoss, Baltimore Colt defensive end Gino Marchetti, former Republican governor Theodore McKeldin, and W. Brooks Bradley. Bradley told the assembly: "The Democratic machine must be broken up on November 6. Its greedy, antiquated leadership is so well organized that it is a threat to the county."[49]

That blast clearly wounded Birmingham. Political observers believed that Christian Kahl would have won the Democratic primary if Bradley had not run. Bradley's charges of cronyism resonated with reform-minded Democrats, as he received 18,000 votes. Perhaps even more damaging to Birmingham was Kahl's lack of support. After the primary Kahl pointedly refused to say if he would get behind the nominee and he kept his silence throughout the spring and summer. As the campaign began in earnest in September, Kahl's reticence threatened to doom any chances Birmingham had of winning. Kahl eventually decided to remain uncommitted, but he told his associates that he would not retaliate against anyone who voted Republican.[50]

In his stump speeches, Agnew stuck to several major themes. He portrayed Birmingham as head of a corrupt political machine that was out of touch and indifferent to the needs of the community. When discussing specific issues, Agnew demonstrated a pragmatic orientation. Agnew staked out a progressive platform, calling for an equal rights bill for the county, tougher pollution laws, and more spending on education, libraries, and internal improvements. Addressing a radio audience, Agnew attacked Birmingham for ignoring these matters. "Does he know, as you and I do, that children in Baltimore County are forced to walk narrow, heavily traveled roadways on their way to school?" On that same radio spot Agnew attacked Birmingham for caring more about the politics than people and assured that he would be different. "If I am elected to that post," Agnew promised, "I shall see to it that, during the next four years our county will progress free from bossism and political patronage." Agnew went on to stress that as executive he would serve the interests of all the people in the county regardless of their political affiliation.[51]

One advantage Agnew enjoyed over Birmingham was youth. Agnew was forty-three, while Birmingham was seventy. Agnew, unlike Birmingham, waged an energetic race. But Agnew was not a natural politician, and he wasn't really able to hide that he disliked the pressing of the flesh that comes with being a candidate. His detractors noticed his attitude. The staff of Maryland Democratic congressman Franklin Burdette compiled a "Fact Sheet on Spiro T. Agnew." Of Agnew the staff wrote: "Agnew is reputed to have an active distaste for the public functions and appearances required in politics, and to lack a genuine liking for mixing with the voters."[52] Even his staff and supporters admitted he just wasn't a glad hander. His secretary, Alice Fringer, admitted that he "can't stand cocktail parties and hates small talk."[53]

Several newspapers rallied to Agnew's candidacy, partially out of disgust for the Democratic machine, but also because they backed Agnew's planks. Agnew's calls for more spending on public schools, ending political patronage, and modernizing the county's government appealed to local newspapers. As an active participant in community affairs, Agnew grasped that the voters of the county wanted candidates who shared their concerns. When trying to get his message across, Agnew reached out to nonpartisan organizations such as the Parent-Teacher Association (PTA), the Kiwanis, and veterans' groups. In contrast, Birmingham never fully grasped how much the county had changed by 1962. The changing face of Baltimore County was neatly encapsulated in a 1962 *Baltimore Sun* election-day cartoon. "Modern Baltimore County" is represented by the quintessential organizational man, a sharply attired white-collar professional male, who holds a "Vote Agnew" placard in his right hand while pointing angrily with his left hand at the Baltimore County establishment, an old, smug, cigar-smoking dinosaur who carries several of the prominent Democratic figures on his hump. Wielding a club in his hand and donning a "Boss" hat is Michael Birmingham. Sitting behind him are other cavemen, including one red-nosed lush who drinks merrily from a bottle of "Olde Towson." The caption above the cartoon read: "They Seem Terribly Out of Date!"[54]

Election day fell on November 7, 1962. Defying historical trends, the Democratic Party fared quite well that day. Despite being the party in power nationally, the Democrats gained two Senate seats. They also did well in state-wide races, winning thirty-two of the forty gubernatorial elections. In the most closely watched race, Democrat Pat Brown trounced Richard Nixon for governor of California by nearly 300,000 votes. The Democrats finished strongly in Maryland, as Governor J. Millard Tawes coasted to reelection; Daniel Brewster easily won the open Senate seat; and six of Maryland's eight congressional seats went Democratic.

But it was not a good day for one Maryland Democrat. After forty years in politics, Michael Birmingham suffered an inglorious defeat. The voters of Baltimore County elected Spiro T. Agnew County Executive with 78,487 votes to 60,993. For the first time in the century, the people elected a Republican to govern Baltimore County. Agnew's call for a responsible government and his attacks on the old establishment's political complacency resounded with voters, who shared a different concept of the role of government and of the responsibilities of elected officials. Michael Birmingham simply did not understand this. He was a relic of a bygone era, and his machine, as the cartoon in the normally reliable Democratic *Baltimore Sun* portrayed it, was a dinosaur.

After his election, Agnew's circle of business associates and friends grew, and the associates often became friends. In this period Agnew also renewed his acquaintance with a childhood friend I. H. "Bud" Hammerman. In the 1962 campaign Hammerman, a wealthy real estate investor and mortgage banker, supported Michael Birmingham; but the day after the election Hammerman called Agnew to congratulate him. Arranging a conference at his office Hammerman told Agnew that he wanted to help settle Agnew's campaign deficit, allegedly offering Agnew $10,000. Agnew declined the money, but reportedly told Hammerman that if he ran for office again, he expected a contribution of $30,000.[55]

It would not have been unusual, though, if Agnew had taken the money. Graft, the use of a politician's power for personal benefit, was a staple of Maryland politics. Just a month after Agnew took office as county executive, a scandal of sorts exploded in the state capital. The speaker of the house, A. Gordon Boone, was enmeshed in a savings and loan scandal. Boone had been one of Baltimore County's delegates since 1947 and was one of the original investors in the Security Financial Insurance Corporation, which insured over a dozen of Maryland's savings and loan institutions. Michael Birmingham was also on the board, and the revelations about the bank damaged his reelection effort in 1962. Boone remained unscathed and he was overwhelmingly reelected. But in February 1963, a federal grand jury indicted Boone and five others on charges of mail fraud (Birmingham was not indicted.) Investigators swooped in and arrested Boone on the floor of the Maryland legislature. As he departed in handcuffs, Boone's fellow legislatures gave him a thirty-second standing ovation. After his conviction on mail fraud charges, Boone returned to Annapolis, where he was treated as something of a hero by legislators who viewed him as a victim, not a crook.[56]

Maryland had a well-earned reputation as the "Free and Easy State." The easygoing atmosphere that reigned in Annapolis also extended throughout the rest of the state. Baltimore County was no exception. Lester Matz learned this lesson the hard way. A partner in the firm of Matz, Childs and Associates, Matz received his engineering degree from the Johns Hopkins University. His credentials, however, carried very little weight in Baltimore County. He and Childs opened an office in Towson in 1956, but the next seven years proved to be very frustrating. Time and time again their firm was passed over for county projects. The majority of the contracts were rewarded to a small group of engineers who just happened to have close ties to the Democratic machine.[57]

As county executive, Agnew had the power to decide what companies or individuals were awarded county contracts, and when he took office, he had some in mind. During the campaign, Agnew received money from a number of contributors who hoped his election would pay dividends for them. One was Lester Matz; Matz gave $500, a relatively small amount, but one that paid Matz big dividends.[58] Shortly after Agnew's inauguration, Agnew, Matz, and Jerome Wolff, another engineer, agreed that Matz and Childs would soon be awarded county contracts. They agreed upon a system that would give the firm of Matz and Childs opportunities that it had previously been shut out of.[59] Also in on the scheme was J. Walter Jones, a Towson banker and real estate developer. Even though Jones was a registered Democrat, he supported Agnew in 1962, raising much-needed funds for the underdog Republican. According to Lester Matz, Jones believed that he and Matz stood to make a great deal of money in the next four years. Matz also claimed that Agnew told him that he had great "confidence" in Jones, which Matz inferred to mean that payments should go to Jones, who would then turn it over to Agnew.[60]

And so began Agnew's crimes. When investigators later uncovered evidence of his malfeasance, Agnew denied any wrongdoing. He always maintained that the money he received from the contractors was not a quid pro quo, but campaign donations. His denials rang hollow and eventually collapsed under the weight of the evidence. For whatever reason, possibly because he needed the money, Agnew took kickbacks, broke the law, betrayed the public trust, and ultimately cost himself the chance at the presidency.

In 1963, however, Agnew's future was very bright. At forty-four he was entering the prime of his life. Before taking over his new duties as county executive he had established a successful, if not thriving, law practice, making enough to purchase a five-bedroom colonial-style house on Concordia Street in the fashionable section of Chatterleigh in Towson. The family moved there in 1961. The eldest daughter Pamela was eighteen; Randy, fifteen; Susan, fourteen; and Kimberly, ten. At forty-one, Judy had settled comfortably into her role as housewife, a position she cherished. Her life centered around her husband and children. She learned to cook "real fast" during their stay at Fort Knox, and her husband loved her cooking. Over the years he frequently requested her crab cakes, spaghetti with meat sauce, and potato salad. Apart from raising the children, Judy served as president of the KI-WIVES of Loch Raven, volunteered at a local hospital, worked as a Girl Scout leader. Judy was the primary caretaker, and it was a role she cherished.[61]

Agnew had created a good life for himself and his family. His daughter Pamela recalled, "We were a normal suburban family."[62] Her father was a conventional suburbanite. He joined a country club and after one golf lesson was hooked. As county executive, he scheduled rounds of golf for every Tuesday and Thursday afternoons, and the business of Baltimore County was settled on the greens. Early in his term, Maryland National Bank president Tilton Dobbin called up Agnew and asked if he needed anything. Yes, Agnew replied, "Well, the one thing I'd like to do is get out of this office and onto the golf course," Dobbin recalled. Dobbin later became treasurer of Agnew's gubernatorial campaign.[63] Agnew was a rabid sports fan, particularly of the Baltimore Colts. He was a season-ticket holder and for fifteen years didn't miss a single home game. While he loved the game for its own sake, his devotion to the Colts helped his political career. Marchetti campaigned for Agnew in 1962, and four years later, when Agnew ran for governor, nearly half of the Colts' roster endorsed him.[64]

Agnew took office in January 1963, and one of the first issues he had to confront was civil rights. It seemed a strange issue for Agnew to become so involved with. Agnew certainly was not paying back any political IOUs. The black vote in Baltimore County, as opposed to the city, was negligible—blacks made up only 2 percent of the population—yet during the 1962 campaign Agnew forcefully called upon the County Council to pass a public accommodations law.[65]

Maryland, on the whole, had experienced little of the turmoil that other Jim Crow states had. There had been few demonstrations and almost none of the violence that racked the Deep South during the 1950s and 1960s. But the racial issue was increasingly a problem that the state's white politicians had to face. Millard Tawes, the state's septuagenarian governor, reluctantly confronted the issue only when left with no other choice. Tawes's motives were simple—the image of his beloved state was being dragged through the mud. The trouble centered mostly on the treatment of African diplomats who traveled through the state on Maryland's Highway 40. Most of the UN delegates took that road when coming and going to the United Nations and Washington, D.C. For the most part, the restaurant owners along on the highway simply refused to serve the blacks, and it made no difference to them whether the blacks were ambassadors of foreign nations. This discrimination grew in the early 1960s as African nations earned their independence. With new countries came new delegations to the United Nations, which meant more African diplomats in the United States going up and down Highway 40. As more of them were turned away, the media began to offer more coverage, which harmed Maryland's image both in the United States and around the world.[66]

President John F. Kennedy, initially, was not particularly indignant over the incidents. His first reaction was to blame the diplomats: "It's a hell of a road," he told his aides. "I used to drive it years ago, but why would anybody want to drive it today when you can fly? Tell the ambassadors I wouldn't think of driving from New York to Washington. Tell them to fly!"[67] Some of Kennedy's aides were more sensitive and intervened. Aware that if the problems along Highway 40 persisted the United States would stand to lose valuable support in the international community, the administration prevailed upon Governor Tawes to do something (the federal Civil Rights Bill, which would bar discrimination in public accommodations, would not be introduced until June 1963). Embarrassed by all the negative publicity, Tawes acted by helping push a civil rights bill through the Maryland legislature, which he signed into law in May 1963. The law prohibited discrimination in public facilities licensed by the state, including hotels, restaurants, recreational places, and theaters.

But the legislation that Tawes signed was not comprehensive. It targeted the very specific problem arising from incidents that occurred in places such as Route 40. Maryland legislators gutted many of the enforcement mechanisms, and the bill granted exemption to eleven of Maryland's twenty-three counties, principally the southern counties and those along the state's eastern shore. Taverns and bars were also exempt from the law. As a result, the final piece of legislation could hardly be called an equal rights bill. The *Washington Post* took the Maryland General Assembly to task for watering down the state's first effort to require hotels and restaurants to desegregate. In an editorial, "Timorous Gesture," the paper opined that,

> the Legislature has given Maryland 'half a loaf' in this performance.... Passed under a pretense of guaranteeing equal treatment to Negroes, it prescribes grossly unequal treatment to both patrons and owners of hotels and restaurants in different counties. A state policy that is effective in only about half of the counties in the state is a farce on its face.[68]

This halfway approach also angered Agnew. After the bill's passage he told reporters that the fight for equal rights would continue. For a man who was later denounced as a race-baiter, Agnew took a very strong line in support of civil rights early on in his career. A few weeks after taking office, Agnew requested that state legislators from Baltimore County sponsor enabling legislation, allowing the county to pass its own public accommodation bill. In this request Agnew forcefully asserted: "We would certainly prefer to see those actions taken at the State level. We seek only the privilege of being able to do something about those matters locally if there is no State-wide action."[69]

The delegation refused Agnew's request. The members argued that the county council already possessed the power to pass an equal rights bill because such a law was already being considered; there was no need to grant the petition. Agnew responded as he always did whenever things didn't go his way: he exploded. "I sincerely hope that action taken by the delegation is not indicative of a desire to throw the blanket of confusion over long needed public accommodations legislation."[70]

Agnew's rhetoric provides insight on how he felt about one of the great issues of the day. He had a genuine commitment to guaranteeing equal rights of all people, regardless of their race, creed, or national origin. At the time many Republicans were on the fence about civil rights, but Agnew was forthright about his views. He backed equal treatment even when it did him little good politically.

His feelings were put to the test in the first crisis of his tenure. The problem centered on Gwynn Amusement Park. Run by two brothers, the park had a policy of refusing to allow blacks into the grounds. For several summers local organizations had picketed the park, but the matter finally reached a boiling point in 1963. The public accommodations law did not include amusement parks, so when it opened in the summer of 1963, it could legally deny entry to blacks. The brothers' decision to continue segregation outraged civil rights groups, who held a huge demonstration on July 4, with over a thousand protestors at the county's fairgrounds. Even though the protest was nonviolent, the police arrested 283 demonstrators, including several prominent clergymen, on charges of violating the state's anti-trespass laws.[71]

The summary arrest of so many people simply fueled the fire, and three days later another 300 picketed the park. The scene turned ugly that day as a crowd estimated at several thousand jeered the protestors, taunting them with racial epithets. Some of the demonstrators managed to get inside the park, including a white woman who was struck in the head by a rock. A gang of white teenagers assaulted two black washroom attendants they mistook for demonstrators (the Price brothers allowed blacks to work in, but not visit, the park). While the police had cordoned off the picketers, the hostile crowd, including members of FAN (Fighting American Nationalists), an offshoot of the Ku Klux Klan, threw beer cans and stones and chanted "two, four, six, eight, we don't want to integrate" and "kill all of them Niggers." They became so unruly that police dogs were brought in to try to bring the situation under control.[72]

Agnew decided to intervene, announcing that he and the county council would create a Human Relations Commission. The long-term goals of the commission were to deal with "employment, housing, education, public accommodations and . . . any other field where intergroup (sic) are in question." In the short term, the Human Rights Commission was to find a way to end the standoff at Gwynn Oak, and its establishment was one small step. The creation of the commission eased some of the tension, and the Congress of Racial Equality (CORE) sent Agnew a telegram announcing that it had called off a planned march.[73]

CORE issued a statement commending Agnew's leadership, stating that Agnew and the county council "never at any time left any doubt" as to their good faith in trying to resolve the problem. The mass arrests led Senator Hubert Humphrey (D-MN), one of the Senate's leading civil rights proponents, to deliver what the *Baltimore Sun* described as a "long, angry speech" denouncing the treatment of the protestors. Humphrey called the trespass laws "anachronistic," and argued that the wrong persons had been arrested.[74]

Humphrey contended that the controversy exposed the need for a federal accommodations bill, an idea Agnew agreed with. Agnew moved decisively to try to find an end to the growing crisis. Acting as an honest broker between the two factions, Agnew arranged a meeting with both the Price brothers and members of CORE on July 9, and he also pledged to appoint members to the Human Rights Commission. The *Baltimore News Post* lauded Agnew's actions, describing them as a "clear-cut victory."[75]

The meetings, however, failed to produce the desired results. While Agnew had a "cordial" talk with James and David Price, the brothers remained steadfast; they would not allow blacks into the park. The three spent over an hour trying to find a solution, but to no avail. While the brothers impressed Agnew as sincere, and only concerned with keeping the status quo to save their business, Agnew failed to persuade them that integration would not harm their business. The discussion with the CORE representatives went a little better, as the group agreed to delay further protests for a few more days. Agnew also managed to convince both sides to sit down with the Human Relations Committee.[76]

After his meetings with the Price brothers and CORE, Agnew told reporters, "Morally I feel that the park should integrate." The problem, as Agnew saw it, was that the county lacked the power to legally compel the Price brothers to desegregate the park. Again Agnew brought up the county's delegation refusal to grant the county council enabling legislation. The delegation's refusal "handcuffed" the county, Agnew complained. He also contended that little could be accomplished until a ruling from the Supreme Court on a similar matter in nearby Montgomery County. There, the Glen Echo Amusement Park, which had a half-century segregationist policy, faced a sit-in in June 1960 over its policy. Five blacks were arrested for violating Maryland's trespass laws, which allowed private businesses that discriminated to enlist the aid of the state government. Several of those convicted appealed to the U.S. Supreme Court, which set oral arguments for the fall. Until the Supreme Court decided that case, Agnew argued, not he or anyone else in Baltimore County could do anything more than apply moral suasion.[77]

On July 10, Agnew fulfilled a promise he made to the civil rights activists by appointing members to the new Human Rights Commission. The eleven members were a diverse lot: three blacks; two attorneys, including Owen Hennegan, Agnew's former law partner; the general manager of the Baltimore Colts football team; a Lutheran minister; a Catholic priest; and a rabbi. Its first order of business was to attempt to end the stalemate at Gwynn Oak.[78]

Even before the commission could act, the Baltimore branch of CORE decided to renew the protests. Leo Burroughs, CORE's project director, dismissed the Human Rights Commission as a toothless organization, with "no power at all." The surprise announcement jolted Agnew, and in a telegram he warned CORE about the consequences: "Further law-breaking, whether technical or not, will enflame emotions and create new hostility that will lessen the chances of solving the problem."[79]

In an effort to quell any more violence, the Human Rights Commission called upon the Prices to desegregate the park by July 26, and recommended that all demonstrations cease. The Price brothers rejected that date, but after some discussion with the commission, they agreed to integrate the park in 1964. Agnew lauded this compromise, and he urged civil rights groups to accept the deal. He also made them further promise,

> If the civil rights groups will recognize and exercise the tremendous ameliorating force which they hold in this instance I shall not fail to follow through with my responsibilities in seeing that this Administration remains a vital force dedicated to the elimination of bias and bigotry in Baltimore County.[80]

Eventually all sides resolved their differences and reached an agreement. The Price brothers relented and announced that the park would be opened to everyone on August 28. They also stated that they would ask that all charges against the demonstrators be dropped. Agnew helped to broker the deal and he hailed the decision. The key figures on both sides lauded Agnew. Jervis Finney, the only Republican on the Baltimore County Council, told an interviewer: "He got the owners to agree to integrate the park. I can perfectly well remember being at one of those sessions, and I can perfectly well remember him thanking the Prices for not placing economics above principles."[81]

According to most observers, Agnew had acquitted himself quite well during the crisis. He fought for integration and helped win a battle for civil rights, acting as an honest broker and working with the Price brothers. His efforts defused any chance of violence. His sensible, pragmatic approach appealed to all sides and served as a model of how to champion equal rights for all without fanning the flames of racial discord.

Only eight months into his tenure, he had carried himself like a seasoned professional, not only during the Gwynn Oak affair, but in his other battles as well. His success did not go unnoticed. As early as January 1964 there were some rumblings that he would run for governor of Maryland. The incumbent governor Millard Tawes, a Democrat, was retiring, which presented the Maryland GOP with an opportunity to run against a nonincumbent. However, none of the state's elected Republicans were actively pursuing the nomination. This was not an unusual situation for the Republicans. Four years earlier the GOP had difficulty fielding a ticket at all, until the party finally settled on a former member of Congress, Frank Small, Jr. The popular incumbent easily defeated Small, but Tawes would not be on the ballot in 1966. Because the Democrats enjoyed such a large advantage in voter registration, the Republicans needed to be united in their effort to win the gubernatorial race. Instead of uniting, however, the Republicans in Maryland were engaged in ideological battles that threatened to divide them.[82]

Agnew took part in this battle as the future of the Republican Party was something he cared deeply about. At the time, Agnew was a moderate and he wanted the GOP to remain a centrist party. In the early 1960s it was not clear what direction the party would take. There were two factions battling for control. The first was the moderate liberal wing, represented by New York governor Nelson Rockefeller. Elected in 1958, Rockefeller had hoped to win the Republican nomination in 1960, but quickly realized that Vice President Nixon was the overwhelming favorite. Though Nixon did not need Rockefeller's endorsement to get the nomination, Rockefeller withheld his support until a meeting with Nixon in July 1960 at his home on Fifth Avenue. At the parley they agreed to a compact calling for the GOP platform to include a stronger civil rights plank and more federal spending for education and welfare benefits. Nixon's capitulation drew the ire of the party's right wing, with Arizona senator Barry Goldwater denouncing the pact as the "Munich of the Republican Party."[83]

Nixon's defeat in the general election emboldened conservatives. Many blamed the loss on Nixon's centrism, which they believed offered voters no clear choice. They hoped to take control of the party and nominate Goldwater in 1964. Goldwater had enunciated the right's convictions in his 1960 treatise *The Conscience of a Conservative*. Largely ghostwritten by L. Brent Bozell, the manifesto articulated the movement's goals. Goldwater called for cuts in federal spending, ending federal involvement in public education, and allowing the states to deal with questions of civil rights.[84]

As the battle brewed between the two wings, Agnew thrust himself into the debate. In the summer of 1963 he launched a movement to draft Senator Thomas H. Kuchel of California for the Republican nomination in 1964. The two first met in Kuchel's Senate office in June 1963, where they discussed the state of the party. Kuchel, a liberal Republican, who had first been appointed to the Senate by Governor Earl Warren in 1953 (to fill the vacancy created when Richard Nixon was elected vice president) made quite a favorable impression on Agnew. A few days after their meeting, Agnew wrote to Kuchel about his decision to back Kuchel for the presidential nomination in 1964: "In short, and in a rather presumptuous manner since I do not have your permission, I am aligning myself with you and will look to you for guidance in the national situation."[85]

On July 30, 1963, Agnew issued a press release announcing his support for Kuchel. The statement started out by attacking President John F. Kennedy, whom Agnew viewed as vulnerable in the 1964 contest. It criticized the Republicans over the liberal versus conservative battle, which Agnew called "an absurd ideological struggle—a blurred misunderstood, oversimplification, and a struggle which rivals in intensity the global contest of the East and West." After that bit of hyperbole, Agnew urged his party to drop its cold war and unite in 1964 behind Kuchel, "the courageous enemy of all political extremists."[86]

The problem for Agnew was that Kuchel had no presidential ambitions. Two days after Agnew issued his statement, Kuchel sent a letter to Agnew, politely but firmly asking Agnew to halt the draft movement. A somewhat chagrined Agnew waited two weeks to write back. While accepting Kuchel's decision not to run in 1964, Agnew seemed unable to get it through his mind that Kuchel was not running. "Obviously, we must now begin grooming you for 1968," Agnew wrote, adding, "Let's get started at your earliest convenience."[87]

Agnew's delusions about making Kuchel the Republican presidential nominee did not mask his very serious concerns about his party. It is interesting to note his reasons for backing Kuchel. His primary concern reflected that of any politician—he wanted to go with a winner. What made Agnew believe Kuchel could be elected president was Kuchel's ideological stands on the issues, or perhaps, more accurately, his nonideological positions. At the time, Agnew evinced a deep distrust, if not disdain, for ideology-driven politics. In letters, speeches, and press releases Agnew condemned Republicans ideologues, be they on the left or right, as extremists who would destroy the GOP. Whenever he was queried about his own views, Agnew would reply with the stock answer: "It's possible to be conservative on some issues and liberal on others."[88]

In January 1964, Agnew issued a press release concerning his own political philosophy. As he often did before making a statement, Agnew jotted down some notes on index cards. On one of these cards he wrote out his "Political Philosophy" consisting of five key elements, the first being that the "moderate course of progressive Republicanism represented by the successful Eisenhower administration" was the path the party should take. Next, Agnew stated the party needed a presidential candidate in 1964 who "shuns the liberal and/or conservative label." Agnew also took a shot at Goldwater, the front-runner for the GOP nomination in 1964, declaring that a "candidate should reserve [*sic*] right to satisfy *own* conscience on each issue without predetermined set of directives and presuppositions." Such candidates, he believed, stood the best chance of commanding widespread support from the electorate.[89]

Agnew often referred to himself as an "Eisenhower Republican," believing the GOP should adopt the former president's middle-of-the-road mentality, because Eisenhower had been a successful candidate (he attempted to enlist Eisenhower's support for Kuchel in 1964 but that went nowhere). Agnew worried the party was developing a deep ideological cleavage that threatened to destroy any chance of winning the White House in 1964. Beginning in 1963 Agnew told anyone who would listen—and very few did—that the GOP had to put aside its differences and unite behind a moderate candidate who could appeal to the broadest number of Americans.[90]

It would be wrong, however, to assume that Agnew's sole concern was with winning elections. His suspicion of ideologically driven candidates was genuine, as was his aversion of ideology. Agnew placed an emphasis on practicality, not theory. Nostrums had no appeal to a man elected to oversee the building of roads, schools, and bridges. Agnew approached issues (or liked to think he did) from a reasoned, not ideological, viewpoint, allowing him to have views on issues that were not dogmatic. To bolster his argument that such an approach not only behooved the Republicans but also was a tradition in the GOP, Agnew noted that Robert Taft, the late senator from Ohio and hero to the right, supported federal aid to education and housing.[91]

Although Agnew was no Bob Taft, he nonetheless staked out positions on issues that did not lead to easy categorization. On the more liberal side, Agnew supported gun control, aid to education, and tough environmental legislation. He did not have much, if anything, in common with Goldwater. In fact, Agnew disliked the man and distrusted his politics. Agnew did not hide his feelings, as Goldwater supporters found out. In November 1963, John W. Steffey, who had recently been named chair of the Maryland Draft

Goldwater Committee, wrote Agnew informing him of the progress of the movement in Maryland (though he did not ask Agnew for support). Writing back the following week and, thanking him for the update, Agnew made clear that the chair knew he opposed Goldwater's nomination. "Although I have a high respect for Senator Goldwater," Agnew wrote, "I would much prefer a candidate of a more moderate viewpoint."[92]

In reality, however, Agnew had little, if any, personal regard for the Arizona senator. As the battle over the Republican nomination heated up in 1964, Agnew tried to do what he could to block Goldwater's path to the nomination. The Maryland Republicans did not have a contested primary, so the real battle over the Republican delegation was fought at the state convention in June. The normally staid affair took on a heated atmosphere when Pennsylvania governor William Scranton arrived on the second day to address the convention. For months moderates in the GOP had urged Scranton to enter the presidential race. Scranton, however, was content in his job and refused the entreaties. The pressure built and Scranton eventually yielded. He arrived in Baltimore, Maryland, on Friday, June 12. Addressing the Republican delegates, Scranton announced he was running in order to "save the true spirit of the Party."[93]

Those words must have heartened Agnew, who was on the platform while Scranton delivered his speech. During the state convention, Agnew was elected as a large delegate, leaving the convention pledged as a Scranton supporter.[94] Agnew also became chairman of the Maryland for Scranton Committee. A month later, in July 1964, Agnew attended the Republican National Convention in San Francisco. This was his first convention and he was one of twenty Maryland delegates. The Marylanders who arrived at the Cow Palace were a divided group and the chasm only deepened during the week. On the second day of the convention Scranton visited the Maryland delegates on the floor, an event the *Washington Post* reported "reopened the bickering among Maryland delegates."[95] The squabbling centered on Goldwater's civil rights views, in particular about his no vote on the 1964 Civil Rights Act. From beginning to end the delegates battled over the platform, especially the civil rights plank. The same battle was taking place all over the convention floor. On the second night of the convention the Maryland delegates, including Agnew, voted seventeen to three to liberalize the plank. Taking its lead from the Goldwater campaign, the Platform Committee wrote a short sixty-six-word statement that did not include an endorsement of the 1964 Civil Rights Act. Members of the Maryland delegation fought to include such an endorsement. That movement failed, as did their effort to nominate Scranton, who had entered the race just four weeks before the convention and received just 214 delegates to Goldwater's 883.[96]

After the Scranton bubble burst, Agnew and other disappointed Marylanders had to face the harsh reality of Goldwater's nomination. Against Scranton's wishes a few delegates chose to campaign against their party's nominee. Enraged by Goldwater's refusal to vote against cloture in the

Senate debate on the 1964 Civil Rights Act, two African American delegates, along with four alternates, pledged not to support him.[97]

Agnew wrestled with the decision to back Goldwater, but finally on July 24, 1964, a week after the convention, he endorsed the Republican nominee. But as his notes demonstrate, he harbored serious reservations about the Arizona senator. In his endorsement, Agnew made it clear that he strongly opposed "Au H2O's (Goldwater's) brinksmanship" on foreign policy issues and his "reluctance to support legislation to remove discrimination in public accommodations." Agnew criticized Goldwater's famous clarion, "Extremism in the defense of liberty is no vice; moderation in the pursuit of justice is no virtue." But unlike so many others in the party who bolted after the performance at the Cow Palace, Agnew stuck with his party, if only because he found the alternative even more distasteful. He wrote down that he decided he would "take chance with forthrightness [and] integrity even if mixed with naivete [*sic*], stubbornness, oversimplification of Goldwater."[98]

With the convention over, Agnew turned back to local affairs. In July 1964 he became embroiled in another civil rights issue—open housing—the second major battle in his two years as county executive. That civil rights should become a prominent issue was a curious development in an area with a negligible black population. Yet the battles over equal rights that were raging across the country also took place in Baltimore County, forcing its executive to make difficult decisions.

Given that Agnew later rose to national power partially because of his attack on civil rights leaders, it is interesting to note that he compiled a very good record on the issue as county executive. He certainly was more liberal on racial issues than most in his party. Agnew always maintained that his views on the subject were consistent and he expressed those views both privately and publicly. Before making a speech on civil rights at a testimonial dinner in his honor in May 1964, Agnew, as was his custom, jotted down some notes. He had nine key points to make. In point number one Agnew wrote, "freedom, as established by our Constitution, is not compatible with discrimination in the use of facilities either privately owned but open to the general public, or publicly owned." However, in point four Agnew argued, "Privately owned facilities to which the general public not invited are sacrosanct & secured . . . discrimination long practiced here is legal, proper and the basis for unjustified Negro complaint." Agnew ended with these thoughts, "For first class citizenship for all Americans," but "It should not be expected to social compatibility among all Americans."[99]

In point five Agnew urged the "need for calm & moderation to replace militant antagonists of both races."[100] Although not mentioning him by name, it is likely Agnew was referring to Alabama governor George Wallace. At the time Agnew was writing down his thoughts, Wallace was campaigning across Maryland. The renegade Democrat decided to challenge for his party's presidential nomination in 1964, and Maryland was one of the few states with an open Democratic primary. A one-time moderate on civil rights, Wallace won the governor's office in 1962 with a slogan of "Segregation now, segregation tomorrow, segregation forever." He traveled north in 1964, entered the Wisconsin and Indiana presidential primaries, and surprised political pundits by taking at least 30 percent in each primary.[101]

Wallace then announced his plans to enter the Maryland primary, a decision that shocked the state's Democratic leaders who believed they would deliver the vote to Lyndon Johnson without any problem. Governor J. Millard Tawes even went so far as to claim that Wallace would "be smothered."[102] Tawes and other top Democrats were soon disabused of that notion when Wallace began touring Maryland. He drew tremendous crowds wherever he went, and more ominously, officials noticed that large numbers were registering to vote, many of those people openly admitting they were planning to vote for Wallace.[103]

Even though Wallace had created problems in the Democratic Party that could have created a Republican advantage, Agnew had no time for the Alabama governor.[104] During the campaign Agnew spoke at an event honoring Maryland senator Daniel Brewster. Because Lyndon Johnson did not officially enter the primaries, the Democrats needed a stand-in on the ballot. At the time, Governor Millard Tawes was considered a risk after pushing through a tax hike; so the Democrats, especially President Johnson, leaned heavily on Brewster to place his name on the ballot. Agnew urged the Democrats to reject Wallace, telling them "Please, my Democratic friends, do not encourage hatred and bigotry by supporting Mr. Wallace."[105]

In a huge turnout Wallace won 43 percent of the vote. Wallace's impressive tally might have been partially a result of his position on open housing. This had become a hot button issue, so highly charged that an open housing provision had not been included in the 1964 Civil Rights Act. During the Maryland primary Wallace had stoked fears over open-housing legislation, warning that such a law would mean homeowners would even have to sell to a man with "green eyes and blue teeth."[106]

During 1964 Agnew continued to push for a county-wide public accommodations bill, even though the 1964 Civil Rights Act would have seemingly abrogated the need for such a law. When Agnew presented his proposal for the bill before the council, opponents made that case, but Agnew countered that the Civil Rights Act allowed for municipalities to craft their own legislation. Agnew also argued that it was needed because "we don't want a federal police state in Baltimore County."[107]

The push for a law went nowhere and Agnew's own political prospects were cloudy. Agnew certainly must have recognized that he faced an uphill battle should he run for reelection. By early 1965 he was known to be entertaining the notion of seeking the GOP gubernatorial nomination. Publicly at least Agnew remained noncommittal when asked about his plans for 1966, but some of his friends and supporters were urging him to run.[108] Even though the incumbent governor J. Millard Tawes was not running again, the GOP had no one ready to get the nomination, leaving Agnew in a good position to become the front-runner. In October 1965 twenty-three of the thirty-two Republican members of the Maryland General Assembly were polled about their leading preference for governor. Eleven delegates listed their first choice as Representative Rogers B. Morton, while Agnew and House Minority Leader J. Glenn Beall came in second with three votes each.[109]

By late 1965 Agnew had decided not to seek reelection for county executive. He remained circumspect about his future plans, but at the same time he quietly explored the possibility of running for governor. His chances of winning improved as a number of prominent Republicans decided not to seek the office. The favorite, at least among some of Maryland's elected Republicans, Rogers Morton, preferred to remain as a member of the House of Representatives. Baltimore mayor Theodore McKeldin, who had served two terms as governor, contemplated joining the race before deciding against it, so Agnew essentially had a clear path to the nomination.[110] For a year, Agnew toured the state speaking to leading Republicans to gauge support for a run at the office, receiving mostly positive feedback. Just as helpful was that no other prominent Republican stepped forward. By February 1966 Agnew made his final decision—he would seek the Republican nomination for governor.[111]

Since Agnew wanted to continue his career in public office, he had little elsewhere to turn. There were no open Senate seats and Agnew never entertained the idea of running for the House of Representatives. Running for the Maryland Assembly would have been a step down, so that left only the governorship. Just how much Agnew actually wanted to run for governor is a matter of some debate. Some political colleagues believed that Agnew really aspired to be a judge. Historian George Callcott argues that Agnew was a reluctant candidate who only ran at the behest of his friends Lester Matz, Bud Hammerman, and J. Walter Jones, men who stood to rake in cash if Agnew became governor.[112]

It is unlikely, however, that anyone pushed Agnew into entering the campaign. No one as proud and stubborn as him could be forced into making such a monumental decision. In all likelihood, Agnew carefully weighed the odds and jumped into the fray. With no serious competition for the nomination, it was not a foolish decision. Before formally declaring his candidacy, Maryland's Republican leaders touted Agnew as "the party's best hope for capturing the urban voters needed to elect a GOP governor in Maryland this fall."[113]

As county executive Agnew did not employ a pollster, so there is no sure way of judging just where he stood in terms of an approval rating, but there certainly was no clamor for him to run for reelection. When he was sworn in Agnew made a dramatic gesture by asking Dale Anderson, the Democratic leader of the County Council, to join him on the platform in a spirit of bipartisanship. During the first half of his tenure, Agnew and the Democrats worked well together, but these good feelings eventually dissipated. Agnew battled with the opposition over a number of issues, which Agnew invariably lost. One of these fights was over pinball machines. For nearly two decades opponents railed against the machines a corrupting influence on the younger generation, and they waged a battle to outlaw them. The owners and operators of the machines were not without friends in the right places and almost all local and state efforts to ban them were beaten back. Agnew launched a crusade to rid Baltimore County of them. A month into office he requested that the state allow Baltimore County the right to ban the machines. His request was ignored. Agnew also tried to get the county council to help in his fight, but with no better results. Over the next four years Agnew continued to wage a campaign against the gambling interest, including several proposals to raise the license for the machines to $2,000. All of his efforts were wasted, as the Democrats in the state legislature and on the county council simply refused to in any way regulate the pinball machines. Their intransigence led to a lecture. The members of the council, Agnew railed, were under "complete domination . . . by the gambling fraternity." When the councilmen protested that Agnew's call for a 2,000 percent increase was irrational and that a tax increase of that magnitude should not be based on "the obsession of one man or his personal vendettas," Agnew shot back with a venom-laced diatribe that impugned the integrity of his opponents: "The petulance displayed by the Council in its message . . . can be mostly overlooked. Indeed I do have and will continue to have a personal vendetta with the unsavory elements who prey upon those least able to protect themselves and thereby embarrass all the citizens of Baltimore County."[114]

The episode sheds light on Agnew the man and the politician. Throughout his political career Agnew never shied away from a fight, even when he had little chance of winning. Agnew showed courage in taking on the gambling industry. Yet Agnew also impugned the integrity of his adversaries, and he would do the same repeatedly over the next decade. Anyone who opposed him was not just wrong but dishonest or corrupt. When he served on the zoning board of Baltimore County, he charged fellow board members with corruption. As county executive he did the same. Later as governor he attacked "extremists" whom he claimed were inciting violence. And as vice president, when he was involved in the fight of his life, he claimed prosecutors and others were plotting to drive him from office.

When Agnew was being self-righteous, he was, of course, being extraordinarily hypocritical. For decades, if not longer, politicians awarded contracts to developers based not upon merit but on "campaign contributions." If anything the amount of malfeasance in Maryland expanded after World War II, particularly in the suburbs. The suburbs needed roads, streetlights, public schools, town halls, and the like. Savvy contractors learned that the best-prepared plans stood little chance of getting approval without an envelope stuffed with cash. Agnew took part in the malfeasance. He took kickbacks and in so doing laid the groundwork for his own fall from grace.

Agnew's legacy as county executive would later be tarred by his criminality, but he did have a list of accomplishments. During his term Agnew modernized the mechanisms of government. When he entered office, the police and fire departments were almost extensions of the Democratic organization. Agnew stepped in and rid those important safety bureaus of patronage, as he instituted a merit system for county hires. He created a Human Rights Commission to combat racial issues, and successfully pushed through a reluctant county council an equal rights bill. The former president of the PTA made education a top priority and in his four years in office reduced student-to-teacher ratio and established a county-funded kindergarten program. Agnew also initiated programs to combat the problems caused by the rapid population growth.[115]

These were not laws that would have come to pass anyway. Neither Michael Birmingham nor Chris Kahl would have supported, let alone fought for, an equal accommodations bill for Baltimore County. The men, steeped as they were in old-time politics, never would have dared to end patronage in the fire or police departments. Agnew did.

Shortly after Agnew announced that he was seeking the Republican nomination for governor, the *Central Maryland News* published a glowing portrait of the candidate, one that claimed that Agnew had "masterfully handled one of the state's most challenging jobs."[116] Agnew had performed well enough to earn the Republican nomination for governor. He faced an uphill battle to reach the governor's mansion, but Agnew was ready for fight.

Chapter 2

Agnew and the Politics of Race

As Baltimore County Executive, Spiro Agnew practiced the politics of moderation. His middle-road approach resulted from both conviction and circumstances. Essentially a manager of a large and growing country, Agnew had to deal with nuts and bolts issues such as education and other public services. He was a man who thought a pragmatic approach to issues was the correct course. When he decided to run for governor of Maryland in 1966 he presented himself as a candidate who could appeal to Democrats and Republicans alike, hoping his brand of centrism would catapult him to the governor's mansion.

On April 16, 1966, Agnew formally announced he was running for governor of Maryland. His announcement ended months of speculation about his plans. Two days later Agnew traveled to Annapolis to fill out the required paperwork. His wife Judy joined him, as did a number of prominent Maryland Republicans, including Representative Rogers Morton, Anne Arundel County executive Joseph Alton, and Baltimore mayor Theodore J. McKeldin.[1]

The *Baltimore Sun*, a paper that usually endorsed Democrats, lauded Agnew's decision to run as a step toward bipartisanship elections, a rarity in Maryland. "Formal announcement of Spiro T. Agnew's candidacy for Governor is good news for Marylanders of whatever political persuasion. In politics as in other forms of human activity, competition is a healthy safeguard against complacency and stagnation," the paper editorialized the day after Agnew made public his plans. The *Sun* also praised Agnew as an effective administrator who would force the Democrats to nominate a man with equally strong credentials.[2]

As the *Sun* noted, the Democratic candidates were usually in a position of fighting Republicans who stood little chance of winning. For a century the Democrats had dominated the governor's office. Only four Republicans had been elected governor since the end of the Civil War (including

Theodore McKeldin, who remains the only Republican ever to be reelected governor). Astute political observers believed that the stranglehold the Democrats had in the office would continue in 1966. McKeldin, Morton, J. Glenn Beall Jr., and Charles Mathias had all passed on the opportunity to run for the office to no small extent because they had no desire to be their party's sacrificial lamb. With the exception of McKeldin, those men were up for reelection in 1966, and were poised to breeze to victory.[3]

Not so Agnew, but he had a better chance than most Republican gubernatorial candidates. As a candidate Agnew had much to offer. In a television era, Agnew was a telegenic figure. Tall with a solid frame, Agnew impressed many observers with his looks. Agnew inherited from his parents a near obsession about his appearance and took great pains to always be presentable. He was a family man and had a solid record to run on. Friends and associates expressed amazement that they never saw Agnew sweat, no matter what the temperature. When he traveled in cars he never crossed his legs, so as to not get any wrinkles in his pants.[4]

But Agnew also had weaknesses. He was a remarkably poor orator. On the stump Agnew spoke in a monotone, never changing his inflection and rarely deviating from his prepared text. His speeches were much like the man—meticulous and deliberate. Agnew was not, and never could be, a firebrand speaker, and to his credit, he never tried to be one. Agnew could deliver a one-liner but usually lacked the pizazz to make audiences jump to their feet in applause. He had a measured cadence that proved to be a liability when he started touring the state as a political candidate. By no means a natural politician, Agnew disliked the glad-handing and backslapping that more outgoing personalities thrived upon. As county executive he had developed a not underserved reputation for aloofness. While Agnew was quite good in small settings with friendly audiences, he was not comfortable plunging into crowds and speaking before large groups.[5]

As the campaign kicked off, Agnew needed publicity, but in July Agnew garnered some that he didn't want and that threatened to eliminate one his positives: his reputation as an honest man. Three months after making his candidacy official, Agnew released a personal financial statement. For the first time Agnew's investment in the Chesapeake Bay Bridge became public, which caused a minor furor. His Democratic critics pounced on the issue, and even some of Agnew's allies raised concern about the deal. For his part Agnew dug in and lashed out at anyone who dared question his propriety. But as Agnew discovered, a gubernatorial candidate could not make scandal disappear through righteous indignation. The matter of the Bay Bridge, as far as Agnew was concerned, was neither a secret nor in any way unethical. He had engaged in what the famous nineteenth-century Tammany Hall politician Thomas Plunkitt called "honest graft." A year earlier, Agnew's close friend J. Walter Jones invited Agnew to join him in a real estate venture. Jones, Agnew, and seven others put up an estimated $267,000 to purchase land near the Chesapeake Bay Bridge in Anne Arundel County. At the time the state of Maryland was weighing building a bridge that ran parallel to the existing bridge. Agnew never made his stake in the matter public, and the uproar that ensued after the release of the information caught him off guard. Independent candidate Hyman Pressman called on Agnew to immediately dispose of his interest or drop out of the race, while Congressman Clarence Long blasted Agnew for keeping the deal a secret. The *Baltimore Sun* also weighed in on the brewing scandal. Describing the matter as a "self-inflicted wound" the paper warned that Democrats would exploit the issue throughout the campaign.[6]

Agnew angrily dismissed the charges against him as nothing more than crass political partisanship. Nevertheless Agnew admitted that he was contemplating disposing of his shares in the deal, though not of course because he was guilty of any malfeasance. Such a proud and vain man could never admit to any wrongdoing, and he stubbornly denied that he had kept the speculation a secret and denied that there was any conflict of interest since the land was not located in Baltimore County: "The mere fact that a public official has made a personal investment in land, as opposed to stocks and bonds, does not automatically create a conflict of interest," Agnew told reporters.[7] Agnew's less-than-forthright explanations failed to squelch the story, and on July 11, he announced that he was selling his shares in the deal. He asked that a Maryland bank sell his $34,200 investment at auction and donate the proceeds to the Children's Rehabilitation Institute in Reisterstown, Maryland.[8]

Three days later, Agnew released a financial statement. His assets included three different properties: his Chatterleigh home, which had a $15,000 equity and a $23,000 mortgage; a row house left to him by his parents, estimated at $15,500 (his mother died in January 1966); and property in the Virgin Islands valued at $1,650. Agnew's bank account stood at $21,200, and he owned over $14,000 in stocks. He did not list any income outside his official salary.[9]

The disposal of his stake in the investment ended any further damage and Agnew got on with the campaign. During the summer Agnew concentrated on touring the state, while the Democrats flayed at each other. To the dismay of the Democratic leadership, the campaign was turning out to be a divisive affair. There were five major candidates vying for the nomination, and from the spring through the summer, they wasted few opportunities to attack each other. The one lone exception to the fratricide tactics was George P. Mahoney, Maryland's eternal candidate.

George Mahoney deserves a work all his own, for he just might be the biggest loser in American political history. Lyndon Johnson once caustically dismissed Richard Nixon as a "chronic campaigner," but Nixon had nothing on Mahoney.[10] Beginning in 1950 and running through 1962, George P. Mahoney sought elected office six times. He lost six times. The 1966 race would be his fifth attempt for the governor's office.[11] Part of Mahoney's campaign was to ignore his opponents and concentrate on his message. By August, his opponents could no longer ignore Mahoney, mostly because of his message. In his previous six attempts at office, George Mahoney had never evinced any clear convictions. He might not have had any real principles, and might well have been running only for the sake of power. Regardless, in 1966, he happened across an issue that resonated with a large segment of the population, especially white Democratic voters: open housing.

Open housing was an issue that white politicians, including the most ardent civil rights proponents, had dared not touch. The question of open housing cut deeply at the core of property rights and home ownership. The 1964 Civil Rights Act did not end racial discrimination in housing, and two years later, Congress had still not taken up a bill to end that type of discrimination. By 1966 there was little chance that an open housing bill would make it through Congress. The mood of the country had changed by that time, mostly in response to the violence that broke out in largely black urban areas. In August 1965, just five days after the landmark Voting Rights Bill was signed into law, Watts, a largely African American section of Los Angeles, exploded. The spark that set off the blaze was the arrest of a black teenager for a traffic violation. Witnesses to the arrest claimed the police used excessive force, even by the usual tough standards of the Los Angeles Police Department. Clashes between residents and the police immediately ensued. The National Guard was called in to quell the disturbances. The riots lasted seven days, leaving thirty-four dead and over a thousand injured. Property damage was estimated at $35 million.[12]

Watts shocked the country. Many white Americans watched in horror as African Americans went on a rampage, burning, looting, and tangling with the police and the National Guard. These images, broadcast daily on the national news, frightened many white Americans. A number of prominent blacks also expressed fear, including Martin Luther King Jr., who warned that the "more there are riots, the more repression will take place, and the more we face the danger of a right-wing take-over, and eventually a fascist society."[13] President Johnson, the man who had just signed the Voting Rights Act, the man who believed, with justification, that he had done more for blacks than any president since Abraham Lincoln, expressed similar reactions asking, "How is it possible after all we've accomplished?"[14]

According to a few commentators, the true cause of the rioting lay in the 1964 California statewide referendum on fair housing. Nine months earlier voters overwhelmingly approved an initiative overturning a fair housing law the state legislature passed in 1963. That law sent a clear message that there was a limit to what many whites would accept in terms of civil rights. It was one thing for blacks in Montgomery, Alabama, to be able to sit anywhere on a bus, or for an African American in Charlotte, North Carolina, to be able to vote; but it was quite another to have a black family move next door in San Bernardino. So it was that Californians could, in the same election, overwhelmingly reject Barry Goldwater—a man who had voted against the 1964 Civil Rights Act—but cast their ballots against fair housing. A similar result occurred in Akron, Ohio, where, in the summer of

1964, the city council enacted a fair housing bill. In November the voters overturned the ordinance.[15]

Open housing was a hot-button issue that the civil rights laws of 1964 and 1965 did not address. For decades activists had been pushing for state and federal legislation to make housing available to people of all colors, only to see their efforts consistently stymied. These proponents cheered John F. Kennedy's promise in the 1960 campaign that he would, with a stroke of the pen, integrate public housing, but they expressed disappointment when Kennedy failed to make good on that promise.[16] For eighteen months they pressured the president to sign the executive order, but Kennedy hesitated. Kennedy proved unwilling to sacrifice what little support he had in the Southern congressional delegation by signing the order. But it was not just Southern Democrats who warned the president to shelve the issue until after November 1962. Democratic candidates in the Northeast urged Kennedy to delay until the midterm elections.[17]

When Kennedy finally signed the executive order, its limited scope disheartened fair housing supporters. The directive covered only housing owned or financed by the federal government, it exempted federal lending institutions, and it was not retroactive.[18] Even one of Kennedy aides, Burke Marshall, admitted the order was not "very meaningful."[19] Over the next several years housing discrimination persisted. After Kennedy's order the struggle for open housing shifted to the state and local levels, but fair housing advocates encountered fierce resistance. Only a minority of states had open housing laws, and efforts by state legislatures to enact laws often met with fierce resistance—as the 1964 referendum in California demonstrated.[20] Localities were no more amenable to legislation or ordinances than the legislatures, so by 1966 the battle for an end to discrimination in housing had reached a stalemate.

Finally in the spring of 1966, President Lyndon B. Johnson intervened. In two separate messages to Congress, Johnson called for an end to discrimination in both the sale and renting of housing. Later that year the administration sent to Capitol Hill a bill that would effectively end discrimination in the sale and rental of homes. Southern Democrats immediately announced their opposition, as did some moderate Republicans. A fight ensued, but Johnson's supporters were able to fashion a compromise, and a bill passed in the House. The bill moved to the Senate. The Southern bloc reflexively initiated a filibuster. Those same Southerners had failed to kill the 1964 Civil Rights Act and the 1965 Voting Rights Act, but in 1966 the mood in the Senate had shifted, and the issue of open housing was a touchy subject for northern legislators.[21] In a dramatic move that illustrated this change, Senate Minority Leader Everett Dirksen (R-IL), announced his opposition to the open housing provision of the 1966 Civil Rights Bill.[22]

Events in Dirksen's home state exposed just how inflammatory the issue was. Early in 1966 Martin Luther King Jr. moved his base of operations to Chicago. The civil rights leader's first concern was to help clear, and eventually end, the city's slums; but when that effort foundered, King set his sights on the racially segregated housing districts. King aimed specifically at neighborhoods in Chicago's northwest and southwest sides, areas populated by white ethnics. For years the middle-class residents of those enclaves had refused to sell their homes to blacks. They were aided by real estate agents who openly ignored the city's fair housing ordinance. The bungalows in Gage Park, Bogan, and Marquette Park housed whites only—and the homeowners were determined to keep it that way. Reverend King was equally determined to break down the barriers. He organized a series of marches that took protestors directly into the neighborhoods to call attention to the problem. What occurred shocked King, a man who had been beaten, jailed, and attacked in the Deep South. The whites of Chicago exploded in a rage that King had never experienced. At one point King was struck in the head by a brick thrown by one of the white protestors.[23]

It was in this atmosphere that the Maryland gubernatorial election was fought. At a time when the nation was in the throes of racial unrest, little was needed to stoke tensions between blacks and whites; yet in that election Agnew's Democratic rival fanned the flames. George Mahoney picked up a slogan that he hoped would finally lead him to victory: "Your Home Is Your Castle: Protect It."[24]

There was nothing subtle about this slogan. Mahoney based his entire campaign on a single issue—open housing. And unlike his Democratic primary opponents, Mahoney took a nonnegotiable stance on fair housing legislation: he opposed it. The other Democrats all tried to finesse or ignore the issue, which left Mahoney as the only candidate who appealed to voters opposed to open housing. Fortunately for Mahoney, many voters were opposed.

Mahoney rode the fear of open housing to victory in the Democratic primary in September. After the results were in, Mahoney called for party unity. He might as well have asked for world peace. Before the vote was even finalized Maryland Democrats were deserting their nominee. A host of Maryland Democrats decided not to back Mahoney. Former governor William Preston Lane, who defeated Mahoney in the 1950 gubernatorial primary, refused to endorse Mahoney. Mahoney's defeated rivals were no more charitable. Clarence Miles announced: "any candidate who sought victory by a route chartered to inflame racial prejudice was not fit to be governor."[25] Despite his protestations, "I have no desire to prolong the election," Carlton Sickles was determined to drag out the recount. Thomas Finan refused to say who he would endorse in the campaign. Governor Tawes stated that he would wait until the final canvass to make any comment, but was reported to be "disturbed over the prospect of Mahoney's moving into the statehouse." The state's two Democratic senators, Tydings and Brewster, remained uncharacteristically silent.[26]

In analyzing the vote, the *Washington Post* found that Mahoney drew much of his strength from the same regions that went for George Wallace in the 1964 presidential primary. Mahoney won twelve of Maryland's twenty-three counties. They were the southern and eastern shore areas, regions with high concentrations of working-class whites. Mahoney also fared well in Baltimore's white ethnic neighborhoods. That was to be expected. But Mahoney also captured Baltimore County.[27]

Mahoney's strong showing in that suburban enclave demonstrated that his message had an appeal outside the blue-collar areas. The result also showed the unease that white middle-class suburbanites had about the direction of the civil rights movement. In the 1950s most Americans outside the South supported an end to the legal barriers that relegated blacks to second-class citizenship. A year after the 1954 Supreme Court *Brown v. Board of Education* decision, according to a Gallup Poll, Americans were critical of President Dwight Eisenhower's leadership in the civil rights arena, believing that he "encouraged segregation."[28] The violent methods employed by segregationists, including many law enforcement officials, offended Americans outside the South and made the pursuit of simple justice for African Americans a moral issue that a majority rallied behind.

The struggle for justice culminated in the 1964 Civil Rights Act and the 1965 Voting Rights Act, measures that effectively removed the legal barriers that denied blacks and others their equal rights under the law. After 1965, pollsters picked up on a trend in white attitudes toward the civil rights issue. In February 1964 the Gallup Poll asked Americans, "Do you think the Johnson administration is pushing racial integration too fast, or not fast enough?" Only 30 percent responded too fast, but in May 1965, the figure jumped to 45 percent, and in September 1966, it climbed to 58 percent.[29]

The 1966 elections were an ugly affair and many contests boiled down to one issue: race. Georgia Democrats nominated Lester Maddox, a business owner who threatened to take an ax handle to any black who tried to enter his restaurant. Other white politicians also capitalized on the growing backlash against civil rights. Both major parties were divided on the issue. Northern Republicans, such as Charles Percy who was running for the Senate in Illinois, were strong supporters of civil rights, but Republicans across the country were finding out that opposing any further civil rights legislation played well with voters. The GOP was beginning to make inroads in Dixie, almost exclusively because of the race issue. For over a century the Democrats had ruled the South, but white voters were growing increasingly disenchanted with the national party. In the 1964 election, Barry Goldwater took the deepest Southern states—Mississippi, Alabama, Louisiana, Georgia, and South Carolina. But it was not inevitable that disaffected Southern whites would abandon the Democratic Party for the Republicans. Many recognized that Jim Crow was abolished and there was no going back.[30]

For his part Agnew struggled with the issue of open housing. Mahoney's shocking upset win in the Democratic primary meant that no longer could he dodge the issue. Open housing catapulted Mahoney to victory and he had every reason to make it the central topic in the general campaign. Voters knew where he stood; but not so Agnew, who had consistently danced around the question. Agnew decided to ignore the problem. On the advice of his campaign staff he tried initially to concentrate on other issues while ignoring open housing. His Opposition Research Committee prepared an eight-page memorandum on the "significance of a Symbol in relation to a Political Campaign." The memo dealt with open housing and discussed why the concept of home ownership was so central to Americans. The Research Committee even delved into the history of the slogan, "A Man's Home Is Your Castle." The authors of the report issued a recommendation: "That Mr. Agnew avoid political exchanges with Mr. Mahoney regarding the issue involving the Symbol 'Open Housing.' "[31]

A speech Agnew delivered at the Maryland GOP candidates meeting on September 17, 1966, typified his approach. As the leading Republican in the state Agnew gave the keynote address. In a remarkably dull talk, Agnew urged his fellow Republicans to "unite together as a team," around several key issues, among them education, stricter environmental controls, and an office of local affairs. Although Agnew claimed that he wasn't "going to evade the issue of fair housing" he mentioned it only in passing and offered some milquetoast statements on the question that was bound to dominate the campaign.[32]

The chance that "Your Home Is Your Castle: Protect It" might carry Mahoney to victory drove liberals crazy. For years editorialists had ridiculed Mahoney as a clownish figure. Party stalwarts distanced themselves from him. They all saw him as a loser, and there are no lovable losers in politics. The personal attacks might have hurt Mahoney but they certainly did not deter him. At sixty-four, a time when some are giving thought to retiring, Mahoney kept running. By all accounts he loved being out on the campaign trail and found pressing the flesh exhilarating. In that regard he was the opposite of Agnew, who considered having to actually campaign a nasty requisite for holding office. Mahoney contracted the political bug in his late forties and from that point onward he never stopped campaigning. Running for office became a way of life, though not a profession since he could never get himself elected. Still, his determination never wavered. During his failed 1956 bid for the U.S. Senate, a reporter visited his office and noticed on the wall a framed parchment that listed each of Abraham Lincoln's election losses. Lincoln lost eight contests; in 1954 Mahoney had lost three. Mahoney probably did not want to pass Lincoln, but by 1966 he was getting close.[33]

In 1966 Mahoney decided to throw away the African American vote. He told an audience that he did not care if his open housing stand cost him support in Baltimore's black wards.[34] Speaking before a group of Democrats at the opening of his headquarters in Anne Arundel County, Mahoney announced that he would not modify his opposition to any state or federal fair housing legislation.[35] His fight against any fair housing legislation struck a chord with many Marylanders. At one campaign event a woman went up to Mahoney and told him, "I believe in you 100 per cent and my husband does too. We are not prejudiced but we don't think it's American to be forced to se(ll) our home." Another said, "the people can be pushed only so far. I've had it up to here with these (pro-Civil Rights) Supreme Court decisions and someone's got to draw the line."[36]

That someone was George Mahoney. His slogan articulated the frustration that so many white Marylanders, and perhaps so many Americans, felt about their status in America. While those feelings are often dismissed as simply racism, to apply such reductionism does not fully explain the deep-seated grievances that so many felt at that time. Many of those voters were Democrats, and their support for Mahoney demonstrated the severe split in the Democratic Party in Maryland and across the country. The Democratic coalition was cracking up. Across the South many conservative "blue dog" Democrats were deserting the party of their ancestors.[37]

Those fissures were evident in Maryland, as the state's Democratic Party was fiercely divided. Attempts to unite the party proved futile. A meeting with some of the state's top Democrats at the Maryland Inn in Annapolis on October 13 failed to help. At the conclave Mahoney and a host of Democrats, including Speaker of the House and chairman of the state Democratic Party Marvin Mandel, gathered in the hotel room in an effort to draft a platform. Mandel, who believed the issue "would kill" Mahoney, urged him to get rid of the slogan, and after a long session that dragged on past 2:00 A.M., Mandel and the others seemingly prevailed as Mahoney agreed to drop the slogan from the platform. Later that day Mahoney reneged on his promise and persuaded the rank and file to include a slightly modified version of his slogan: "A Man's Home Is His Castle" in the party plank. Addressing the convention, Mahoney defiantly announced, "I say a man's home is his castle and I say it proudly."[38]

Then Mahoney engaged his opponent. For the most part Mahoney had conspicuously avoided talking about Agnew. Still, Mahoney could not pass up the chance to impugn an opponent and he tore into Agnew. Mahoney's attack portended that the race might descend into a name-calling contest. Unfortunately for Agnew, Mahoney excelled at mudslinging. Agnew fired back. Using language that the *Baltimore Sun* described as "the most caustic Mr. Agnew has used so far in the campaign," he ripped into Mahoney, describing him a "vulgar opportunist."[39]

At that same event Agnew claimed that his campaign was gaining momentum. Certainly, if endorsements from Democrats, labor unions, and newspapers were any indication, Agnew was picking up steam. Democrats for Agnew popped across Maryland, in what the *Cumberland Evening Times* described as "an action unprecedented since labor became a political force ... the AFL-CIO's political education committee backed a Republican."[40] The liberal organization Americans for Democratic Action announced its support for Agnew.[41] Former secretary of state, Dean Acheson, wrote to the *Baltimore Sun*: Because "the Democratic convention under the leadership of Mr. Mahoney has seceded from the national party to join the Wallace confederacy" Acheson wrote, "I shall vote for Mr. Agnew."[42] And in the space of four days, from October 12 to October 16, Agnew received the endorsements of the *Baltimore News American*, the *Aegis*, a paper in Hartford County, and the *New York Times*.[43]

Despite all the positive news, Agnew was in serious trouble. His calm, measured speeches about roads, bridges, pollution, taxes, and schools had gotten him nowhere, as the results of a poll commissioned by the Agnew campaign in the middle of October showed. "The Political Picture in Maryland," prepared by a Pennsylvania public opinion research firm, had Agnew trailing Mahoney by 14 percentage points, 50 to 36 percent, with independent Hyman Pressman getting 9 percent, and 5 percent undecided. According to the study, Agnew's strategy discussing "all issues of importance to the State of Maryland" had been for nothing because Mahoney had "set the tone of the campaign, and his ground rules have dominated." The authors of the poll detailed why and how Mahoney had taken such a decisive lead: "First is his personality and style. . . . He has a personality, a background as a successful self-made businessman, and a manner of speaking which have become familiar and are appreciated by many voters." All of the newspaper editorials and the denunciations by labor unions and groups like the ADA and the AFL-CIO, mattered not since, "Whether objective observers view him as totally undesirable Governor material, he has made an impact on the people."[44]

Yet Mahoney's name recognition and charisma were not the primary reason for his popularity: "The second and probably far more important reason for Mahoney's strength, despite its mention by fewer voters than his personality, is his opposition to proposed open housing legislation in Maryland." The reason that those polled cared less about personality, the study concluded, was because many Mahoney supporters were embarrassed about *why* they were backing him. Mahoney's view on his issue was in accord with theirs. The study found that, "Fifty-six per cent of all our respondents indicate that they are definitely, absolutely, and irrevocably against any open housing legislation."[45]

The visceral reaction to that question explained Mahoney's strong position. At the same time Agnew drew much of his support from those turned off by "A Man's Home Is Castle." Few of his potential voters knew much about him or had positive feelings about him; they were simply opposed to Mahoney. As the authors wrote, "Agnew, then, is the alternative to Mahoney. Just as Johnson reaped anti-Goldwater votes by the bushelful [*sic*], so Agnew reaps anti-Mahoney votes. But in Maryland, unlike the nation in 1964, the Mahoney creed—anti-civil rights, anti-open housing—appears to be the dominant mood, and so he may win."[46]

The study predicted that Mahoney would win with 48 percent of the vote.[47] Realizing that he had failed to connect with voters, Agnew abruptly switched tactics and strategy. Agnew hired the Boston-based firm Campaign Consultants Incorporated (CCI). Founded in January 1966, the firm worked with over twenty Republican candidates in 1966. With a few weeks to go in the election the Agnew team turned to CCI to help turn the tide. Five of the company's members, including Robert Ellsworth, a Kansas congressman, spent a day in Baltimore analyzing the race. Instead of ignoring Mahoney, and his slogan, Agnew should tackle them both head-on in the hopes this might turn the tide.[48]

First Agnew had to articulate a consistent policy. When he did brave to mention the housing issue, Agnew issued opaque statements that only obscured his position. The *Baltimore Sun* ran an editorial on October 6 criticizing Agnew's posturing and flip-flopping. Four days earlier Agnew told an audience he would veto any bill that restricted the rights of individual homeowners to sell to whomever they desired, including new housing units, which Agnew previously stated should not be exempt. On October 7, his campaign wired a statement to the Baltimore NAACP (National Association for the Advancement of Colored People) that Agnew was on record promising to introduce legislation that would guarantee open housing in new developments. Then, on October 12, Agnew recanted his earlier pledge to veto such a bill.[49]

According to some, Agnew backtracked on the veto threat because at the time he was speaking to a crowd in Montgomery County, perhaps the most liberal area of the state, yet even there the debate over fair housing legislation raged. In the summer of 1966 the Montgomery County Board of Realtors conducted a telephone poll of 500 residents. Although unscientific, the results showed that 60 percent opposed nondiscrimination in housing. William Raspberry, a young columnist for the *Washington Post*, found these numbers disturbing, especially since they were taken from Montgomery County, "where the residents are among the most enlightened (or at any rate, best educated) in the Nation."[50] Other more scientific polls taken around the same time showed the similar attitudes across the country. A poll by the National Research Council in October 1966 revealed 51 percent of whites opposed a federal law prohibiting discrimination in housing. Another study by the Miami Valley Regional Planning Commission suggested that white suburbanites were even more opposed to such a law than the general white population.[51]

Agnew shared the same misgivings about open housing and his concerns were a large part of the reason he struggled to offer a consistent position. During his political career, Agnew often jotted down notes about issues, including civil rights and open housing. In October 1965, when thinking about open housing Agnew made two points: "In principle, strongly oppose existing legislation," he wrote. However, he also believed "no legislation to abridge individual discretion in right of sale justified."[52]

Agnew's internal struggle regarding open housing was part of a larger battle. Like many other white Americans, Agnew had conflicting feelings over civil rights. He supported civil rights and equal opportunity just as strongly as he deplored racism and discrimination. Still, there were limits, and laws inhibiting the rights of homeowners to sell to whomever they liked struck him as unfair. After all, he owned a home. While he attacked Mahoney's race-baiting, not once during the campaign did Agnew ever say a man's home was not his castle.[53]

As a candidate, Agnew was clearly in his element when campaigning among white, middle-class voters. The same could not be said when he went to urban centers looking for votes in predominantly black areas. Given the strange dynamics of the race, Agnew needed all the black votes he could get, but he struck observers as reluctant to push hard for that vote. When Agnew finally made an appearance in Baltimore on October 23, he seemed ill at ease, particularly compared to the city's mayor, and former two-term governor, the progressive Republican Theodore McKeldin. Although McKeldin resented having to campaign for Agnew, he nonetheless waded into the crowds, enthusiastically shaking hands with "my brother" and "my people," while Agnew held back, waving, more grimacing than smiling.[54]

As the campaign entered the final stretch, Agnew stepped up his attacks. With election day falling on November 8, Agnew had short time to make up what he and most observers believed was a sizable Mahoney lead. In an Associated Press story that ran on October 26, Agnew admitted to Annapolis Bureau chief Herb Thompson he was "running very, very scared."[55] That same day Agnew leveled a serious and reckless charge against his Democratic opponent. Addressing group of Republican precinct workers at a Baltimore hotel, Agnew tied Mahoney to the Ku Klux Klan. "Why" Agnew wanted to know, "were those Ku Klux Klaners wearing Mahoney hats at their rally two weeks ago." Because, Agnew claimed, "It is nothing but bigotry that this man (Mahoney) is appealing to."[56]

Angry over Agnew's charges, Mahoney hit back hard, threatening to expose some dirt he claimed to have on Agnew. Although Mahoney would not elaborate on just what damaging information he possessed, he hinted that it had something to do with a meeting Agnew had in New York with several Greek Americans. "The Greeks in New York and some of the worst characters in the world sit around (together). If he gets too nasty I will be compelled to talk about it."[57]

In a harbinger of how he would react when far more serious and substantive charges were made against him, Agnew defended himself as a man with nothing to hide: "There is nothing I'm ashamed of during my political career, or during my life." Apparently taking kickbacks from engineers in return for government contracts wasn't something Agnew was ashamed of. Agnew made integrity one of the hallmarks of his campaign. Entering the race he issued a personal statement "embodying my philosophy of government." One of part of that philosophy included "the right of people to expect, and get, public servants who, in the performance of their public trust, are above reproach."[58]

As the election entered its last ten days, the chances of Agnew getting elected seemed remote. The *New York Times* ran a story about the race under the headline "Mahoney Given Edge in Maryland: Coalition for Rival Doubted." The *Times* detailed Agnew's problems, among them Comptroller Hyman Pressman's surprisingly strong showing (he was running as an independent). The *Times* reckoned that Pressman might get enough votes from

Baltimore City to preclude any chance of victory for Agnew. The only glimmer of hope for Agnew was that Mahoney might have peaked too early.[59]

By this time Agnew had given up any sense of civility. At an address in the town of Essex, Agnew delivered a venomous attack on his rival. He called Mahoney a "devil" and told the crowd his only goal in life was to "expose George P. Mahoney for the fraud that he is."[60] A day later Agnew retreated a bit, claiming that while Mahoney was not a devil, his slogan was "devilish." Mahoney, Agnew lectured, was not a "force of evil" but a man with terribly misguided views who was "trying to tempt mankind to yield to its baser impulses."[61]

Mahoney shot back, denouncing Agnew's appeals to the state's African American voters as racist. It was an odd charge, even stranger given the other remarks Mahoney gave that same day. Addressing an all-white audience in Baltimore, Mahoney thundered about the breakdown of law and order. He told the cheering crowd that as governor he would allow police to take back the streets from the criminals. Without identifying specifically to whom he was referring Mahoney claimed the police were hamstrung since they "have been told to treat certain people with kid gloves." These criminals Mahoney screamed were running wild, raping with impunity, but Mahoney had a plan: "I'll take care of those birds."[62]

Throughout the race Mahoney denied being a racist and even his critics allowed that he was not.[63] But whatever he really felt, there is no excuse for the racially tinged rhetoric he delivered in the final week of the campaign. By that time he was pitting whites against blacks. Claiming that rapists ran free on the city streets raised the old specter of black men violating white women, which all too often had once led to the lynching of blacks even in border states like Maryland. As though he had not fanned the flames enough already, Mahoney's next target was busing—hardly a pressing issue since there was not any busing of children going on at the time. Again, Mahoney blamed "certain people" for the problem, or in this case the nonexistent problem.[64]

On Monday, November 7, Agnew and Mahoney concluded their campaigns. After sixteen years and six failed campaigns, Mahoney believed his time had finally come. Before one of his final appearances, Mahoney, tasting victory, predicted that the election was as "good as won." During the day Mahoney appeared ebullient, and his statements reflected his upbeat mood. The same could not be said of Agnew. In a paid fifteen-minute television address Agnew claimed Mahoney was employing the "big lie" that the Nazis used.[65]

On election day Agnew voted early in the morning and then hit the links for a round of golf. Early in the evening he went to his hotel headquarters at the Lord Baltimore Hotel. After enjoying a steak dinner with his family, Agnew went upstairs to his suite to wait for the results. The first television reports were discouraging. Around 8:00 P.M. CBS reported that based upon early returns, George Mahoney was the probable winner, estimating that

Mahoney would win with 57.5 percent of the vote. The local news stations reported the figures, and the Baltimore *News American* published an early election special with a headline: "Mahoney Elected Governor."[66]

The results were premature, and as more votes poured in, it became clear that the election was turning into a rout for Spiro Agnew. The winner made his appearance shortly before midnight. Smiling broadly Agnew accepted the well-wishes of his supporters. He then held a news conference, during which he told reporters he won because "The people want to hear candidates talk about issues out of their own mouths." For the most part Agnew was gracious and modest, perhaps even too modest. When asked if his election had any national significance Agnew said no, since "I have difficulty imagining myself as a national leader and I sometimes have difficulty imagining myself as a State leader."[67]

But he was a leader. In a record turnout, where 64.7 percent of eligible voters cast ballots, the people of Maryland provided Agnew with a resounding victory. Agnew polled 455,318 votes to Mahoney's 373,538 and Pressman's 90,899. Agnew won 49 percent, Mahoney 41 percent, and Pressman 9 percent. African American voters made the difference in the race. Agnew carried Baltimore City by some 24,000 votes and won 80 percent of the black vote.[68] Mahoney's overtly racist appeal failed, but elsewhere around the country the results were more mixed. Just across the border in Delaware a Republican candidate for the House scored a stunning upset based largely on his strident opposition to open housing. The open housing question helped elect Charles Percy to the Senate in Illinois. Running against liberal incumbent Paul Douglass, Percy made major inroads in suburban Chicago areas, where tensions from the summer demonstrations still ran high. In other states the backlash issue backfired, including in Arkansas, where for the first time since Reconstruction a Republican was elected governor. There, Winthrop Rockefeller defeated an arch-segregationist who tried to ride an anti-Washington, anti-civil rights plank to victory.

Rockefeller's politics of moderation attracted more voters than his opponent's extremist positions. Such was also the case for Agnew. Agnew won thanks to the votes of African Americans and liberal Washington suburbanites. The results showed that moderate Republicans could attract black voters. And 1966 was the year of the GOP moderates. The year 1966 is often remembered as the year Ronald Reagan won in California and that race supposedly marked a turning point. The GOP, scholars argue, was now controlled by conservatives, and the party turned its back on African Americans. The truth is more complicated. While it is true that Reagan was a rising star, moderate and liberal Republicans fared very well in the Northeast and New England. Massachusetts Republican Edward Brooke became the first African American elected to the Senate since Reconstruction. The direction of the party was still in question.[69]

Meanwhile, for the time being, Agnew could bask in his accomplishment. Agnew won an election in a state where Democrats outnumbered Republicans three to one. He became only the fifth Republican elected governor in the state's history. A relatively unknown figure, he defeated two veteran political opponents with far greater name recognition. The governor-elect ascribed his victory to the sensibility of his fellow Marylanders. In a remark that perfectly captured his own thinking, Agnew claimed the election signaled that "the people of Maryland want to remain in the mainstream of the American tradition." Agnew certainly saw himself in the mainstream of American politics. During his brief political career, Agnew, in both word and deed, staked out a moderate course on the pressing issues of the day. A product of his environment, Agnew adopted a middle-of-the-road mentality that guarded against rigid ideological stands. This served him well enough to get elected county executive and governor. But Agnew's moderation did not last.

Chapter 3

Governor Agnew

On November 9, 1966, Spiro Agnew celebrated his forty-eighth birthday. He had much cause to celebrate. Just a week earlier he had been elected governor of Maryland, becoming only the fourth Republican elected governor of Maryland in the twentieth century, and the fifth in its history. He was also the first Greek American ever elected governor of any state. He won over 50 percent of the vote and garnered a great deal of praise for running a forward-looking campaign against an opponent who sought to exploit racial tensions in an effort to get elected.

As he prepared to take on his new duties, Agnew had good reason to take pride in his accomplishments. He had achieved much in his life. He was a war veteran, attorney, and successful politician, and he had the loving support of his family. On election night, a *Baltimore Sun* photographer snapped an image of a beaming Agnew being kissed on the head by his wife, Judy. She supported her husband's political ambition and campaigned tirelessly for him. Their four children were nonplussed by their father's new job. The eldest child, Pamela, stayed on her own. Pamela, twenty-three, became the first member of the Agnew family to earn a college degree when she graduated from Towson State College in 1965. She taught history at Franklin Junior High School in Reisterstown, Maryland, and wanted to stay close to her job. Her siblings, Randy, Susan, and Kim, moved to Annapolis with their parents. Randy, twenty, had never been much of a student, and like his father he struggled in college. After graduating from Towson High School in 1964 Randy enrolled at Valley Forge Military Academy and then the University of Baltimore. After a year of college he decided not to return. Although Randy had hopes of becoming a physical education teacher, he decided to put off a career and instead volunteered for service in the Naval Reserves. The third child Susan, nineteen, worked as a secretary for Westinghouse.[1] The youngest daughter, Kim, ten, had to change schools when the family moved to Annapolis.[2]

For a few months, Judy and the children lived in a cottage they owned in Ocean City as they waited for renovations to the Governor's Mansion to be completed. Spiro spent the week on the state yacht and spent weekends with the family in Ocean City. Repairs began in March on the Government House, a red-brick Georgian mansion located in the heart of downtown Annapolis, home to Maryland's governors since 1870, which was in dire need of repair (on inauguration day a shower in the mansion failed to turn off). When the Government House reopened it came equipped with a sauna bath on the second floor and a recreation room in the basement. The sauna was Agnew's "gift" to the House and was constructed to alleviate Agnew's arthritis.[3] Downstairs there was a new wine cellar and a recreation room equipped with a ping pong table, a chess set, a dartboard, and a pool table. It was the room where Agnew escaped the pressures of the office, as he explained in an interview:

> We have a table tennis setup in the basement, and in the evening if I don't have anything to do I'll go down there and lose myself banging that thing around for a couple of hours. It's not so much what I'm doing—it's the fact that it has absolutely no connection with being governor.[4]

Agnew often escaped the pressures of his office. He was not, as he readily admitted, a workaholic. As governor, a typical workday began sometime after nine and ended by five. Two afternoons a week were set aside for golf, and he took weekends off.[5]

Although he might not have been a very hardworking governor, Agnew was, at least in 1967, a fairly successful one, particularly given that the Democrats overwhelmingly controlled both houses of the Maryland legislature. They had a commanding 35–8 control in the state Senate, and had a 177–25 majority in the House of Delegates. These overwhelming numbers failed to daunt Agnew since so many of the Democrats had endorsed him. "I'll be dealing with many Democrats who either openly or quietly worked for Mr. Mahoney's defeat. I'm going to go more than half way with them. I think I will get excellent cooperation," Agnew told the press the day after the election.[6]

Agnew began his tenure as governor hoping to work across party aisles and espousing a progressive program of reform for the state. At the time he still considered himself a centrist and wanted to govern from the middle. Averse to ideology, Agnew was not looking to bring about an ideological transformation of Maryland. Unlike California's new governor, Ronald Reagan, Agnew had not gained a political following by calling for a conservative revolution. He was a moderate to progressive Republican who believed that pragmatism should outweigh ideology.

When he was sworn in as governor the *New York Times* predicted that "although the legislature is dominated by the Democrats, Mr. Agnew is expected to have little difficulty in making a progressive legislative record in civil rights, education and crime prevention."[7] It was an accurate forecast.

In his first three months in office Agnew not only successfully pushed through the largest tax increase in Maryland's history and engineered a radical overhaul in the state's education financing, but also steered several other important measures through the House and Senate. As governor, Agnew worked well with the Democrats, forging strong ties with Marvin Mandel, the Speaker of the House (and the man who succeeded him as governor), and other key Democrats.

These bonds served Agnew well, as they aided him immeasurably in his quest to modernize Maryland. Agnew wanted to remake both the structure of the state government and its image. Agnew, for example, advocated the repeal of an anti-Miscegenation Law passed in 1661, and still remaining on the books in 1967. Incredibly, the statute was still being enforced. In January 1967, Marine Ensign Manuel R. Lopez applied for a marriage license. When he arrived to pick up the document two days before his wedding at Prince George's County Courthouse, the clerk informed Lopez that he did not qualify. Lopez, as it turned out, was in violation of Article 27, Section 398, of the Annotated Code of Maryland, which barred marriage not only between blacks and whites, but also between whites and "members of the Malay race." The Naval Academy graduate failed to qualify for the license because his father was Filipino. The story made the front page of the *Washington Post*, and became an embarrassment for the entire state.[8] Soon after taking office Agnew prevailed upon the legislators to rectify this lamentable remnant of a bygone era. In June 1967 the law was finally repealed; the *Baltimore Afro-American* reported, "thanks to the enlightened leadership of Gov. Spiro T. Agnew."[9]

For a while Agnew continued to receive high marks from civil rights leaders. Before his inauguration Agnew created an Advisory Committee on Human Rights. Black leaders praised his selection of Gilbert Ware, an African American, as his advisor on health, welfare, and human relations. Agnew also named a special assistant for race relations and in his first year alone appointed twenty-two African Americans to positions in the state judiciary, education, and other executive posts. With the Vietnam War raging, Agnew showed his sensitivity to the concerns that a disproportionate number of blacks were being drafted by requesting that the draft boards increase their membership from three to five members so Agnew could expand the numbers of African Americans on the local boards. He also signed an extension of the public accommodations law, and established a fair employment practice code.[10]

And what of the issue that dominated the campaign? Although he considered it a problem best handled on the federal level, he recognized that given the election results and the strong support he received from Maryland's African American voters—support that was the decisive factor in his victory—he needed to do something. A bill sponsored by Senator Royal Hart, a Democrat from Prince George's County, called for an end to discrimination in the sale or rental of all houses and apartment units with over five rentals. During the campaign Agnew endorsed legislation prohibiting discrimination in new homes and apartments with over twelve rentals, but now he announced that he would sign any fair housing act the legislature passed. In early March Agnew met with several legislators and members of Maryland's National Association for the Advancement of Colored People (NAACP). After the meeting state senator Clarence Mitchell claimed that the governor had accepted a deal in which liberal representatives would agree to a weak housing bill in 1967 in return for a promise by the governor to push for a stronger more comprehensive law in 1968.[11] While the new law was not what fair housing proponents hoped for, it was nonetheless a historic piece of legislation. On April 21, 1967, Agnew signed Senate Bill 237—the first open housing law below the Mason-Dixon Line.[12]

The governor reorganized the executive department, modernized the state's antiquated business tax structure, and proposed creating a state ombudsman. In establishing a "People's Advocate," Agnew fulfilled one of his major campaign promises. Agnew hoped the advocate would combat the rampant malfeasance in the notoriously corrupt state. The plan gave the advocate the power to investigate "preferential treatment and influence peddling," and "payoffs and kickbacks in state contracts."[13] The *Baltimore News American* ran an editorial lauding the proposal, arguing that it "is a bellwether of the progressive thinking that promises the Free State one of its most alert administrations in years."[14]

The *Baltimore News American* was not alone in applauding Agnew. The state's opinion makers seemed to be in competition to lavish praise on the governor. The *Baltimore Sun* trumpeted "Maryland's New Image." The *Hagerstown Herald* lauded him as "Our Kind of Man," while the *Afro-American* praised his "enlightened leadership." Maryland's premier political journalist Bradford Jacobs devoted a column to Agnew's "first remarkably successful session."[15]

After the 1967 legislative session wrapped up, Agnew took a vacation. But his respite was interrupted by events in the small coastal town of Cambridge. Because he subsequently made a name for himself by attacking rioters and those he believed condoned their behavior, it seems incongruous that Agnew played, or tried to play, the role of racial conciliator. Still the evidence of Agnew's commitment to ensuring racial justice in Maryland is overwhelming, as state senator Clarence Mitchell, himself an African American, pointed out two years after Agnew moved on to the vice presidency:

> To be perfectly fair, in Agnew's first few months in office he did more in moving the state in the direction of bettering black-white relations than any governor in the state's history. He helped us remove a chairman of the Board of Electrical Examiners who had for years been practicing discrimination. He elevated two black judges to the Supreme bench and put another on the Municipal Court. He gave us our first black representative on the Workmen's Compensation Commission, the key commission for black workers. He put a black member on the Board of Engineering Examiners.[16]

Harry A. Cole, the first African American ever appointed to Maryland's Court of Appeals, remembered Agnew as a man dedicated to the cause of civil rights. Cole recalled Agnew as a man of "principles and commitment." Cole contrasted Agnew very favorably to Theodore McKeldin, whom Cole dismissed as an opportunist who had to be reminded to do anything, whereas, "Agnew called you."[17]

As governor Agnew made it a point to call upon state and national civil rights leaders. In June 1967 Agnew asked if Roy Wilkins Jr., the NAACP's executive director, would meet with him in Annapolis. Wilkins agreed and they arranged to talk on July 17. Before the talk Agnew sent Gilbert Ware, his assistant on civil rights, a memo stating, "I want to do everything possible to assure maximum executive efforts in Civil Rights."[18]

During the session Agnew informed Wilkins that he was going to establish a code of fair practices to insure equal opportunity in state hiring. Afterward, the pair held a joint press conference at which Agnew forcefully stated his goal of removing "all discrimination in Maryland, and I mean all discrimination." The words pleased Wilkins, who praised the governor for work on behalf of civil rights. A reporter inquired of Wilkins if the governor had asked him about "riot control." Wilkins said "no" since "this conference was not in the context of preventing riots." The question was in reference to the disorder that had broken out in Newark, New Jersey, following the assault of a black cabdriver by two police officers. That event sparked five days of rioting. Agnew and Wilkins briefly discussed Newark; most of their talk was about racial problems Maryland.[19]

The question over rioting arose out of unrest in Newark and Plainfield, New Jersey. Less than a week later violence erupted in Cambridge, Maryland. Located on Maryland's Eastern Shore, Cambridge had experienced racial unrest all throughout the 1960s with *Time* magazine describing the city as "the most violent place in America. . . . A cauldron of hate." Rioting so fierce broke out in June 1963 that the National Guard was called in and martial law declared. Whites and blacks continued to battle each other over the next year. When George Wallace delivered a campaign speech in Cambridge in May 1964 before an overflowing crowd in the local Veterans of Foreign Walls hall, he was interrupted by applause thirty-five times and mobbed by the crowd afterward.[20]

After 1964 there was a significant cooling off period. That changed in July 1967 when Cambridge exploded. By the summer, tensions were simmering in the city. Unemployment in the African American community was in the double digits. Racial divisions had merely abated, not disappeared. These tensions were exacerbated by the appearance of white and black radicals who served, quite deliberately, to stoke the flame of discontent. In early July 1967, several members of the National States Rights' Party showed up in Cambridge for no other reason than to foment discord. A few weeks later, a young black radical, H. Rap Brown, arrived in Cambridge in response to the National States Rights' Party demonstration. Brown had recently been appointed national chairman of the Student Non-Violent

Coordinating Committee (SNCC). Given Brown's advocacy of violence, it seemed a rather strange choice, but by that time SNCC was but a shadow organization, and many of its dwindling members were attracted to the ideas on black power and the race consciousness of black militants. Although they might not have caused the rebellions (as Agnew came to believe), these men, according to historian Clayborne Carson, "did formulate a political vocabulary that expressed the previously unarticulated anger of many blacks, particularly the young and urban poor."[21]

That rally only stoked the simmering racial turmoil in the city. In between the States Rights' Party rally and Brown's arrival, a fight between a black youth and white youth heightened the tensions. The white boy unleashed his dog upon the black child, leaving him badly injured. The wounded child's father went to the authorities but the States' Attorney of Dorchester County refused to file charges.[22] A later study of the Cambridge riot described the fight and the prosecutors' inaction as the "precipitating incident."[23] The report also discussed the host of grievances in Cambridge's African American community. The sense of anger and resentment boiled over when H. Rap Brown visited the city. On the night of July 24, Brown, in what one paper described as a "white-baiting harangue of about three hours," exhorted a crowd of roughly four hundred to burn Cambridge down. In his address Brown told the crowd, "It's time for Cambridge to explode" and goaded the crowd to "take your violence to the honkies."[24]

A few dozen followed his orders and started burning parts of the city down. The flames started late that night, with several shops looted and one school destroyed by fire. Things could have been worse, as the violence was largely confined to a few areas, and the total damage paled in comparison to the destruction in other cities that summer.[25] In his work, *Civil War on Race Street: The Civil War in Cambridge, Maryland*, Peter Levy argues "a riot never really took place" in Cambridge.[26]

Whatever it might be called, the outbreak incensed Agnew. Learning of these events, he broke off his vacation and arrived in Cambridge in the early hours of July 25. Accompanied by a police escort he toured the city, at times stopping to talk to its black residents. His words sounded somewhat conciliatory, as he suggested that he understood why people felt aggrieved enough to resort to violence. But he demanded an immediate end to the violence and the capture of Brown, who had fled Maryland soon after his speech. After the National Guard quelled the rioting, Agnew focused all of his considerable ire on Brown. Upon learning that an arrest warrant had been issued for Brown, Agnew commented, "I hope they pick him up soon and throw away the key." Brown's fiery words were caught on tape. Agnew obtained a copy and he played it again and again. The contents convinced Agnew that his initial reaction against Brown was entirely justified. Over the next several weeks Agnew invited others to hear the contents, including a group of Maryland civil rights leaders, who were not as perturbed by what they heard as Agnew.[27]

A host of observers, including some of Agnew's biographers, pointed to the Cambridge incident as a turning point in Agnew's career. Here Agnew jumped ideological ship. Some ascribed the change to sheer opportunism; while others claimed Brown's words and the crowd's reaction stunned him enough to move him from the liberal to the conservative camp. Whatever the reason, it was and remains today a generally accepted view that after Cambridge Spiro Agnew became a different man.[28]

The evidence supports this conclusion, even though Agnew wrote, "those who accuse me of becoming increasingly conservative are not in possession of all the facts."[29] The Cambridge riot was a defining moment in his career. He began to move to the right and was increasingly critical of not just the civil rights movement but liberalism in general, which he blamed for much of the unrest in Maryland and across the country. Like many white Americans, Agnew believed that the civil rights movement had taken a radical and even dangerous course. The urban rioting of the late 1960s turned Agnew and others against that movement. And for Agnew, there was no going back. The events in Cambridge remained seared in his mind for the rest of his political career.[30]

As tough as Agnew talked, his language resembled that of many Democratic politicians, including a few prominent liberals. These included New Jersey governor Richard J. Hughes, a man with a reputation as a strong advocate of civil rights. During his two terms the state poured tens of millions into New Jersey's poorest cities. Further, Hughes prided himself as having good relations with his minority constituents. The eruptions in Newark shocked him and Hughes reacted in a manner strikingly similar to Agnew. Like Agnew, Hughes toured the devastated areas and talked to some residents. Like Agnew, Hughes said he didn't blame them; instead he placed the onus on militants who had attended a Black Power conference in Newark days prior to the rioting. Like Agnew, Hughes blamed "outsiders" for fomenting trouble, and he also singled out H. Rap Brown as a particular danger.[31]

In the midst of all the violence, the *New York Times*, hardly a bastion of conservatism, published an editorial that read like an Agnew speech. The *Times* allowed that urban residents had grievances but nonetheless "the looters and arsonists have to be dealt with as the criminals that they are." The editors blasted the extremist elements in the black community—a small group that "prevailed at the National Conference on Black Power in Newark—and sent forth a drumbeat of hostility around the country. The violent elements there preached hatred, separatism and revolution."[32]

What the *Times* editorial demonstrates is the widespread revulsion at urban rioting across the ideological spectrum. Politicians could be expected to denounce the violence, and indeed almost all did. After all, even New York senator Robert F. Kennedy, perhaps the most popular white figure among African Americans, condemned the disorders.[33] The near universal response was not just a reaction against the burning and looting; it expressed a fear over the growing militancy in the Civil Rights Movement. That movement was splintering, as younger members were eschewing Martin Luther King Jr.'s nonviolent methods. Increasingly H. Rap Brown, Stokely Carmichael, and LeRoi Jones were the face, and the voice of black America.

Carmichael, who had worked with SNCC, came to reject nonviolence and coined the term "Black Power." Jones was a black activist who was arrested in the wake of the Newark riots. Many white Americans were frightened by the likes of Brown and the Black Panthers, Agnew included. Shortly after Cambridge, Agnew lashed out at the trio, claiming that they threatened America's security as much as any foreign enemy. Agnew took a consistent stand against those who went beyond civil disobedience. As violence became more commonplace, Agnew grew more vocal in his denunciations, and his rhetoric began to attract notice across the country. Agnew had been elected as a moderate Republican, with significant African American support. By the end of 1967, Agnew's politics had changed, as had his base of support. Agnew did not become a racist, nor did he ever stoop to the level of George Wallace or other race-baiters. His own feelings mirrored that of millions of white Americans uncomfortable with the urban riots and with the idea that once all segregation laws had ended, there was no real further need of Civil Rights Movement. Agnew shared those beliefs and began forcefully enunciating them.[34]

When Agnew next confronted a civil rights issue, he reacted in a manner that showed he remembered Cambridge. In late March 1968, a group of students from the small, traditionally all-black Bowie State College, located eighteen miles north of Washington, DC, initiated a boycott of classes. The students had a host of grievances, most of which centered on the dilapidated state of the campus. Agnew initially expressed concern about the situation, enough to dispatch his aide Charles Bressler to the college, but he also made clear that he had little time for the students' complaints. Bressler's indifferent attitude inflamed the already smoldering situation.[35]

Unable to persuade the governor or the legislature to take their concerns seriously enough, on April 4, the students moved their campaign to Annapolis, staging what they termed a "wait-in." For several hours neatly attired young men and women peacefully demonstrated inside Maryland's statehouse. The demonstrators repeatedly asked to meet with the governor, but Melvin Cole, his aide on educational matter, informed them that the governor was not in Annapolis. Finally, after 5:00 P.M., Agnew ordered the campus closed until "conditions returned to normal."[36]

The protestors refused to disperse, so the state police arrested 228 picketers. The arrests proceeded in an orderly manner, but the situation remained tense and a potential clash between the students and the authorities loomed. Agnew's actions drew praise from some quarters, condemnation in others. The Annapolis *Evening Capital* published an editorial lauding the governor's toughness: "Agnew has handled the situation at Bowie State well. . . . Agnew is made of stern stuff and knows about warfare having been a captain in the airborne branch of the Army during World War II. He isn't about to encourage disorder and worse within Maryland by being wishy washy."[37] The *Washington Post* disagreed, calling Agnew's response "overkill," while the Anne Arundel branch of the NAACP castigated Agnew for his "failure to carry out your official obligation" to meet with the students and address the poor conditions at the Bowie campus.[38]

An assassin's bullet relegated the protest, along with almost everything in the country, to the background. On April 4, 1968, an hour after Agnew ordered the arrest of the demonstrators, James Earl Ray, a career criminal, shot and killed Martin Luther King Jr. The murder of America's most prominent civil rights leader shocked much of the nation. A distraught Agnew sent his condolences to Coretta Scott King. "Words at a time like this," Agnew wrote, were "inadequate to express the overwhelming horror of this senseless act. I can only say that I extend my deepest sympathy." The governor ordered the state's flags to fly at half-mast, and also took a more concrete action to demonstrate his outrage and his commitment to seeing King's dream of an integrated society achieved. At time of the murder the U.S. House and Senate were debating an open housing bill. The bill was stalled in committee, and two days after the assassination Agnew released a statement calling upon the Maryland delegation to support the legislation.[39]

The delegation did, as did a majority in both houses. After years of acrimonious debate, a federal fair housing bill passed on April 10, 1968.[40] Unfortunately for the country, that was one of the few positive reactions following the slaying. Ray's terrible deed touched off a wave of violence in the nation's cities. The problems exploded first in Washington, D.C., forcing President Johnson to call out the National Guard, but it took the Guardsmen several days to quell the rioting. Eventually the violence spread to over 130 American cities.[41]

Maryland's cities initially stayed peaceful, but a month earlier Agnew's aide on racial issues, Gilbert Ware, sent a prophetic memo to the governor entitled, "Your Image in the Negro Community," warning him potential trouble loomed in state's urban areas, especially in Baltimore. "Cohesion is catching on in the Negro community in Baltimore and, I think, will spread to other parts of the state," Ware wrote, "which is pregnant with the potential for the kind of social unrest which we deplore." At the present time, the Negro community "has considered you a foe," Ware contended, in part because "you have overstated the case against Rap Brown."[42]

In the margins of the paper Agnew wrote, "There is absolutely no way to overstate the case against Rap Brown."[43] Following the Cambridge riots in July 1967, Agnew developed a near obsession with black militants, in particular Rap Brown, Stokely Carmichael, and LeRoi Jones, whom he believed fomented rebellion and anarchy. Agnew pestered New York governor Nelson Rockefeller about the Ford Foundation's apparent funding of "democratic institutions which in turn embraces such non-worthies as Stokely Carmichael" (a frustrated Rockefeller wrote back that he had investigated the matter, found nothing to back up Agnew's charges and told Agnew, "I really don't know what else I can do").[44] During the Bowie State incident, Agnew refused to meet with the students in part because he believed that they had been "inflamed by outside influences."[45]

In an ominous development, at least for relations between the governor and much of the state's black population, Stokely Carmichael visited Baltimore on April 2. No violence erupted that night, and all was quiet in

Maryland on April 4 and April 5. The calm ended around 5:30 P.M. on Saturday night, April 6. Fires broke out across the city and by 10:00 P.M. the Baltimore police "declared the situation out of control."[46] Police from surrounding areas were called in, and on April 7, Agnew asked President Lyndon B. Johnson to send in the National Guard. Even with the presence of the National Guard the looting continued, and the *Washington Post* reported on April 9 that the mood of the rioters had turned more hostile. Finally, on Thursday, April 11, the burning and looting came to an end.[47]

In the wake of the riots, Agnew took steps to help rebuild the city and provide assistance to poor blacks, such as trying to find them employment.[48] Those measures, however, were overshadowed by a speech Agnew delivered on April 11. Agnew was at the Baltimore State Office Building for a prearranged meeting with many of Maryland's prominent civil rights leaders. Agnew clearly was expecting fireworks, while most of the estimated 150 invitees expected the governor to ask for their aid in calming racial tensions. Agnew quickly disabused them of that idea, instead delivering a stern rebuke. His manner was deliberate, and his demeanor calm. His words were not. The words shocked the guests but an unfazed Agnew pressed on with his lecture. Under the glare of television cameras the governor of Maryland told them that black civil rights leaders bore some, if not most, of the responsibility for the wave of violence in that state.

As Agnew saw it, the match that lit the flame was Stokely Carmichael, one of the two "twin priests of violence" (the other being Agnew's bête noire H. Rap Brown). Carmichael, according to Agnew, met surreptitiously with "local black power advocates and known criminals" in Baltimore three days prior to the riots. This was crucial, since it preceded King's murder by a day. While most attributed the riots to that event, Agnew pointed to Carmichael's visit as the real cause.

And why were these civil rights leaders, those Agnew complimented as not being part of the "caterwauling, riot-inciting, burn-America-down type of leader," to blame? Because when confronted with demagoguery, when facing threats from extremists, they "ran." Agnew argued: "You met in secret with that demagogue and others like him—and you agreed . . . that you would not publicly criticize any black spokesman, regardless of the contents of his remarks."

Though Agnew told them he was not there to pass blame, his diatribe seemed to be placing the onus squarely on the civil rights leaders:

> Now, parts of many our cities lie in ruins. You need not leave these City limits to verify the destruction and the resulting hardship to our citizens. And you know whom the fires burned out just as you know who lit the fires. They were not lit in honor of your great fallen leader. Nor were they lit from an overwhelming sense of frustration and despair. These fires were kindled at the suggestion and with the instruction of the advocates of violence. It was no accident that one such advocate appeared at eight separate fires before the fire chief could get there.[49]

By this point nearly half of the guests had walked out. Agnew ignored their protests and continued:

> I am sure that these remarks come as somewhat of a surprise to you; that you expected nebulous promises and rationalizations and possibly a light endorsement of the Kerner report. This I could not do. Some hard things needed to be said. The desperate need to confront the problem squarely justified the political risk in saying them.[50]

These remarks predictably caused a furor and Agnew's already deteriorating relations with the black community declined further. Across the state civil rights leaders rushed to censure the governor. Some of the attendees refuted Agnew's charges and condemned his words as "more in keeping with the slave system of a bygone era." Many resented the condescending tone. "Talk to us like we are ladies and gentleman," the Reverend Sidney Daniels snapped at Agnew before walking out.[51] Baltimore mayor Thomas D'Alesandro, who had called on the black leadership for help during the riots joined in, blasted Agnew for the content and timing of the speech. A member of Baltimore's Interdenominational Ministerial Alliance called Agnew "as sick as any bigot in America." Denunciations poured in from around the country, as men like Roy Wilkins who had earlier praised Agnew, now fiercely criticized him for being insensitive and even racist.[52]

At the same time, however, his hard-line approach garnered praise. Letters and telegrams poured into the governor's office, and they were overwhelmingly favorable.[53] Over the next several weeks the governor's office received thousands of letters in support. Among those who wrote Agnew were his childhood neighbor Mary Muzette who thanked Agnew for "being the one man in both state and federal government to stand up for law and order"; John S. Hunter, an army buddy at the OCS (Officer Candidate School) in Fort Know with Agnew, thanked Agnew for "the strong-stand you took with the so-called Negro leaders in this state"; Jesse Helms, a commentator for a television station in North Carolina; the president and publisher of the *Suburban Record*, a local Montgomery County paper; and Republican senator Gordon Allott of Colorado.[54]

For his part Agnew refused to back down, refused to recant anything. A day after the speech his press secretary Herb Thompson told reporters that the governor, "read the speech over again this morning and is convinced everything he said is right."[55] Agnew actually thought his remarks were conciliatory, or at least were intended as such. If only Maryland's black leadership could join him in denouncing H. Rap Brown and Stokely Carmichael—"the apostles of anarchy"—then Agnew believed, racial tensions would wane. Only then could their respective goal of "the elimination of all prejudice against Negroes in America" be achieved. The fires, Agnew claimed, were not lit "from an overwhelming sense of frustration or despair." According to Agnew, decades of oppression and discrimination contributed nothing to the riots; nor did being forced to live in decaying neighborhoods or being denied opportunities available to white Americans.[56]

Few African Americans agreed with him. A number of the invitees expressed their anger at being talked down to by the governor, and were justifiably angry. According to William Adams, a prominent Baltimore African American, Agnew fell into the trap of believing that black Americans had spokesmen who controlled their community.[57] As the *Baltimore Afro-American* noted in a searing editorial, Agnew acted out of "sheer stupidity" when he claimed that the attendees bore some accountability for the actions of their race.[58]

Agnew's speech and the reaction in the black community demonstrated the widening gulf between white and black Americans over the state of race relations, poverty, equality, and justice. Like many Americans, Agnew had deplored the violent attacks on civil rights activists while supporting the end of Jim Crow. To Agnew and others, blacks seemed ungrateful after the passage of the 1964 Civil Rights Act and 1965 Voting Rights Act. That these laws did not abolish racism or bring about economic gains did not seem to occur to many whites, including Agnew.

In 1967, President Lyndon Johnson appointed a commission to study the urban disorders. Chaired by Republican governor Otto Kerner of Illinois, the committee issued its report in March 1968. The National Advisory Commission on Civil Disorders, or "Kerner Report" as it was called, argued the underlying causes of the riots on white racism, inequality, and poverty. Unless action was taken to improve the status of black Americans, the commission warned, the county would move inexorably "toward two societies, one black, one white—separate and unequal."[59] When the commission published its report in March 1968, Agnew quickly and fiercely attacked it. In a prepared statement Agnew contended the commission blamed "everyone but the people who did it." A "masochistic group guilt of white racism" pervaded the report, leading the members to excuse the violence and ignore the true reasons behind the disorders. Showing how much the Cambridge riots influenced his mind-set, Agnew claimed "inflammatory" statements by the likes of H. Rap Brown "have created an aura of belief that rioting is the inalienable right of the ghetto resident." Agnew dismissed the commission's recommendation and argued the "Ultimate resolution rests with our system of free enterprise, good old American capitalism. I don't apologize for our materialistic success; it is the source of our strength."[60]

Polls showed that most Americans disagreed with the committee's findings. Other polls ranked crime as one of the public's main concern and there was simmering anger toward politicians who excused or even condoned the violence. When Agnew hit the demonstrators and refused to accept the "root causes" of crime he struck a chord with Americans who were worried about the violence. His rhetoric mirrored the public mood. That did not, however, make Agnew a racist. It was possible to support racial equality while denouncing rioting. This distinction is critical for understanding Agnew's rise and the transformation of the American electorate during the late

1960s and early 1970s. However, too often the rise of the right and the success of politicians such as Nixon, Agnew, and Ronald Reagan are simply reduced to how they used racial appeals to gain votes. The GOP, it is argued, benefited from the "white backlash."[61] Besides being too simplistic, that argument essentially states that a majority of American voters were racist. Race has always played a role in American politics but arguing a conservative majority arose because of race is not a nuanced argument. Never did Agnew, Nixon, or Reagan ever argue that the civil rights gains of the 1960s should be rolled back. Nixon and Agnew both had supported civil rights legislation. They drew votes by expressing—and sharing—the concerns of middle-class whites who backed racial equality but believed that civil rights movement had gone astray. Many voters also came to believe that the Democratic Party either ignored or abandoned them. By 1968 they were in a position to end the Democratic coalition that Franklin Roosevelt had built three decades earlier. Disgruntled with the Great Society's excesses, worried that crime might spread, and believing that they had been forgotten, these Americans started voting Republican in increasing numbers.[62]

Because he knew as well as any politician the hopes and anxieties of middle-class Americans, Agnew rose to the pinnacle of American politics. His response to the Baltimore riots attracted attention across the nation. Agnew shared with millions of white Americans a belief that with civil rights enough was enough. While not racist, this message resonated with what Nixon called the "Forgotten Americans." By 1968 the United States was as divided politically as it had been since the Civil War. The fissures ran along generational, sectional, and racial lines. Leading Republicans such as Nixon, Reagan, and Agnew did little to bring the country together. They did not create the divisions in America but they did capitalize on them.

Chapter 4

Nixon, Agnew, and the 1968 Campaign

On January 31, 1968, over 70,000 North Vietnamese and Vietcong forces launched a surprise offensive in South Vietnam. The Tet Offensive, so named after the Vietnamese lunar new year, was aimed at overthrowing the South Vietnamese government. The communist North and the South Vietnamese rebels in the South had been trying for a decade to unite Vietnam and saw an opportunity in late January to accomplish that goal. Each new year both the North and South Vietnamese had observed a truce, but the South Vietnamese and the United States ignored warnings that the North Vietnamese and their Vietcong allies were marshaling forces for an offensive against the South.[1]

American and South Vietnamese troops eventually repelled the attack but the scale of the operation came as a shock to many Americans. For over a decade the United States had been aiding the South Vietnamese, and by the end of 1967, the United States had over 500,000 troops in Vietnam. President Lyndon B. Johnson had been telling the American people the United States was winning the war but Tet exposed that the claim was untrue.

Johnson's handling of the war, and the war itself, fractured an increasingly divided America. The war helped split the Democratic Party and shatter the anti-communist Cold War consensus that had existed since the late 1940s. Everywhere Johnson went he was hounded by the chant of "Hey! Hey! LB! How many kids did you kill today?" Antiwar protests grew larger every year, and in November 1967, Senator Eugene McCarthy of Minnesota announced he would challenge LBJ for the Democratic nomination. For three months, McCarthy volunteers flooded New Hampshire, working tirelessly to round up support for the senator. On March 12, 1968, New Hampshire held its primary. The results shocked the political world; Johnson failed to carry a majority of the vote, winning 49.6 percent to McCarthy's 41.9 percent.[2]

Five days later, Robert F. Kennedy entered the race. After his brother's assassination, RFK left his cabinet post as attorney general to challenge New York senator Kenneth Keating in 1964. Kennedy won in a landslide, though he actually polled 2,000,000 fewer votes than LBJ. Although Kennedy hated Johnson, he did support the Vietnam War well into 1967. Kennedy's entry into the race demonstrated the depths of LBJ's standing the Democratic Party. On March 31, 1968, Johnson went on national television to talk about a partial bombing halt and new peace proposals between the United States and North Vietnam. At the end of the speech, Johnson announced he would neither seek nor accept the Democratic nomination for president.

Johnson told the country he would not run because, as president, he needed to devote all his time to the "awesome duties" of his office. Left unsaid was that Johnson's own party might deny him the nomination. Vietnam had fractured the Democratic Party, leaving Johnson a weakened candidate if he chose to run. Recognizing his reelection efforts were poor at best, he bowed out. McCarthy and Kennedy were soon joined by Vice President Hubert Humphrey. Kennedy and McCarthy were both outspoken critics of the war, but Humphrey was not. Being LBJ's vice president placed Humphrey in an awkward position. He couldn't come out as an opponent of the war for fear of alienating Johnson, but backing the war would hurt his chances to get the nomination, so Humphrey largely said nothing.

While Vietnam had split the Democratic Party, the same was not true of the Republican Party. Most Republicans supported the war, and much of the criticism among Republicans was that Johnson was not fighting the war aggressively enough.

Agnew, himself, supported Johnson's handling of the war. His son, Randy, was serving in Vietnam. After dropping out of college in 1967, Randy enlisted in the navy. He completed his basic training in January 1967, and for a time was stationed in California before being sent to Vietnam in February 1968. He served in Mobile Construction Battalion 8, repairing roads and bridges.[3]

His father consistently backed President Lyndon Johnson's handling of war. Asked his opinion of the Vietnam War in April 1967, Agnew responded forcefully, "The President has my full support in what he is doing in Vietnam, and until somebody gives me some good information, reliable information based upon personal observation of experts in that area, I'm going to stick with the President of the United States."[4] A few months later, Agnew reiterated his approval of the war, this time in even stronger terms. He attacked Democrats and Republicans who criticized the conflict since, Agnew believed, they lacked the facts on which to base their conclusions:

> "It just makes me a little bit ill to see candidates of both parties who have no information whatsoever, except what they're imaging and conjecturing and receiving secondhand, taking positions on whether we should escalate or deescalate, or where we should bomb, or how we should run this war." As for

> himself, Agnew still stood behind Lyndon Johnson and the war: "I support the President 100 percent."[5]

Agnew was a cold warrior and staunch anti-communist. While his views on domestic issues modified, his foreign policy opinions did not. He was a hawk on Vietnam from beginning to end. Over time, as he became a national figure, Agnew began to attack opponents of Vietnam as soft on communism. In the late 1960s, the Democratic Party was fracturing over Vietnam and Agnew found himself much more in tune LBJ than many Democrats. Agnew described Johnson as a "conscientious person who has the interest of the United States at heart."[6] Republican Agnew never shied away from praising the Democratic Johnson and the two men developed a good relationship. Johnson invited Agnew to the White House on several occasions, and Agnew told friends that he was LBJ's "favorite Republican." It must have been heady stuff for Agnew to be courted by the president of the United States, and he apparently became transfixed by Johnson's attentions. Agnew believed he just might be in line for a cabinet appointment if LBJ was reelected.[7]

As much he liked and admired LBJ, Agnew's real love was for Nelson Rockefeller, New York's Republican governor, considered by many to be a pillar of the liberal wing of the party. Agnew first met Rockefeller in November 1963. Rockefeller invited Maryland's elected Republicans to discuss the upcoming campaign and perhaps gain their support for his presidential candidacy. While Agnew came away impressed with the Rockefeller, he withheld an endorsement and went to the 1964 Republican National Convention pledged as a delegate to Pennsylvania governor William Scranton. After the 1964 Goldwater debacle Agnew quickly chose Rockefeller as his candidate for 1968.[8]

The only snag was that Rockefeller was not running. That mere fact did not bother the stubborn Agnew, who persisted in pushing for a Rockefeller candidacy. Rockefeller refused to budge. Aboard a governor's cruise in October 1967, Rockefeller, according to a news account, "came closer than ever today to ruling out the possibility of his becoming the Republican Presidential candidate next year." Still, the news failed to deter Agnew, who the *New York Times* described as Rockefeller's "chief gubernatorial backer." "If he is drafted," Agnew told the press corps on the ship, "it would take a pretty emphatic individual to turn it down. Indeed, I can't conceive of it."[9]

The press speculated on Agnew's goals. In April 1967, a reporter asked if Agnew might be interested in being vice president. Agnew replied, "I have no ambition to move into national politics."[10] At that point in time, just three months into his governorship, Agnew was probably telling the truth. His motives for supporting Nelson Rockefeller were sincere—Agnew genuinely believed that the New York governor was "the best administrator in the country."[11] It is worth noting that Nelson Rockefeller was not much of a "Rockefeller Republican." That phrase—mostly used in a pejorative tone by modern conservative Republicans—describes, or really derides, Republicans whose views on major social issues lean in the liberal direction. Nelson earned that label mostly for his vocal support of civil rights and lavish spending policies. The myth of Nelson Rockefeller's liberalism persists, but Agnew, even after he left office, correctly pointed out that the reality was quite different. Agnew and Rockefeller agreed on many of the major issues of the day. They were both ardent Cold War warriors. Agnew later wrote of Rockefeller's views: "A lot of people considered Rockefeller very liberal and very dovish on foreign policy, but he was not. He was harder than Nixon, and a lot more hawkish about the mission of America in the world."[12]

As the 1968 primary season approached, Rockefeller remained steadfast in his stance as a noncandidate but Agnew continued to be hopeful that the "tremendous amount of public pressure that is being put on the Governor to revise his position" would help change Rockefeller's mind.[13] On January 9 Agnew announced that he had agreed to assist a draft Rockefeller committee being formed by Maryland Republicans (the members included a number of Agnew's friends and key financial contributors, including J. Walter Jones and I. H. Hammerman).[14]

The first presidential primary was scheduled for March 12 in New Hampshire. Though too late to get Rockefeller's name on the ballot, his supporters hoped to organize a write-in campaign. For his part Rockefeller wanted nothing to do with the draft and he stuck by his candidate, Michigan governor George Romney. However, by mid-February Romney's campaign was in shambles. His own polling showed him trailing Richard Nixon by a six to one margin. Once pegged as the inevitable nominee, Romney had imploded like few candidates in history. Romney showed a remarkable ability to stick his foot in his mouth. After returning from a tour of Vietnam, Romney told an interviewer "he had the greatest brainwashing that anybody can get," meaning that U.S. military officials were trying to convince him the war was being won. The remark buried Romney and he bowed out of the race on February 28, 1968.[15]

Romney's decision left Richard Nixon as the last man standing. The former vice president had risen from the ashes and stood poised to achieve the most remarkable comeback in political history. After suffering a narrow defeat for the presidency in 1960 and a bitter loss in California's gubernatorial contest two years later, Nixon seemed finished. But on March 1, 1968, Nixon appeared well on his way to winning the Republican presidential nomination. With Romney out and with Nelson Rockefeller not in, Nixon stood poised to sail to the nomination.

The thought of Nixon as their party's nominee energized Rockefeller's supporters. These moderately liberal Republicans hated Nixon even more than Barry Goldwater. Even though Nixon was himself a centrist who disdained the party's right-wing, most liberal Republicans simply detested him. The patrician Nelson Rockefeller was too kind a man to hate Nixon, but he certainly looked down on him (the historian Arthur Schlesinger later wrote that Henry Kissinger told him that Rockefeller loathed Nixon).[16] So after his favorite Romney dropped, Rockefeller stepped in—sort of. Rockefeller released a poll to the media showing him easily defeating President

Lyndon Johnson. He announced: "I am not going to create dissension within the Republican Party by contending for the nomination but I am ready and willing to serve the American people if called."[17]

To demonstrate his willingness to run if asked, Rockefeller summoned three dozen national Republican leaders to his Fifth Avenue apartment on March 10, 1968. The powerbrokers included Senator Hugh Scott of Pennsylvania, Arkansas's governor and Nelson's younger brother Winthrop, William Miller, the 1964 Republican vice presidential nominee Congressman Charles Goodell, New York Mayor John Lindsay, and Spiro Agnew. The guests tried to convince Rockefeller to enter the ring, an effort that went well, as the *Washington Post* reported the session "brought Rockefeller to the brink of a formal candidacy."[18]

The startling turn of events heartened Agnew. On March 14 he announced the establishment of a "National Rockefeller '68 Committee" headquartered in Annapolis, with Agnew serving as temporary chair. Two days later Agnew and Rockefeller met in Washington, DC. In his memoir, *Go Quietly . . . or else*, Agnew wrote that he had inside information:

> Many admirers expected Rockefeller to announce his candidacy for the presidency when he called a New York press conference on March 21, 1968. I was even more confident that he would announce because he had personally assured me that he had made up his mind to run. We had talked when I introduced him at the *Ahepa* (a Greek lodge) convention in Washington only a few days before.[19]

On Thursday morning, March 21, all of Agnew's tireless work looked to be rewarded. But nothing is ever simple in American politics, and certainly not in that volatile year. By "pure happenstance" Agnew was hosting his regularly scheduled news conference in Annapolis. An aide suggested that a television set be brought into the room so the assembled could watch the announcement, and Agnew could presumably bask in the limelight. At 2:00 P.M. Agnew, his staff, and the press corps watched as Rockefeller strode to his platform in the Hilton Hotel and began reading a prepared statement. It began: "I have decided today to reiterate unequivocally that I am not a candidate campaigning, directly or indirectly, for the Presidency of the United States."[20]

Back in Annapolis all eyes immediately turned to Agnew. A man who prided himself on always keeping cool (literally in most cases; aides marveled at how they never saw him sweat), Agnew went back to his podium and managed to keep his composure. The only thing he could do was put the best spin on an awkward situation. Rockefeller, he argued, still had not definitively closed the door on accepting a draft: "I confess I am tremendously surprised . . . and greatly disappointed."[21] When asked if he would continue his efforts to get Rockefeller to enter the race, he said, "No, I want time to analyze the situation as it has developed. As I indicated to you," he went on, "this comes as a complete surprise to me. As I said during my press conference in response to a question before the Governor's statement came on, I had scrupulously avoided being a confidant in the decision and I knew no more than anyone else." That statement is in contradiction to his later claim that Rockefeller told him he was running. Time dulls memory and pride can evaporate it. Agnew can perhaps be excused for putting himself in the best possible light. It was a terribly embarrassing moment, and at the time Agnew did his best to conceal his pain. When out of sight Agnew let loose his real feelings. "I feel like I've been hit in the stomach by a sledgehammer," he told his secretary Alice Fringer.[22]

Years later Agnew confessed to feeling "furious and humiliated" since Rockefeller "had not even shown me the courtesy of informing me of his intentions in advance. He finally telephoned me hours afterward but only when word had gone out on the wires that I was as mad as a hornet."[23] What exactly happened that morning is still not exactly clear. Apparently the people in Rockefeller's camp thought Agnew had been informed. George Hinman, one of Rockefeller's closest advisors, was apparently tasked with calling Agnew and letting him know Rockefeller was not running. There are several different versions of whether any call was placed to Agnew or his aides. Regardless of what actually occurred, Agnew was not aware of Rockefeller's intention. And he never forgave Rockefeller for the slight.[24]

After Rockefeller made his stunning announcement, a reporter asked Agnew if he would now support Nixon. "Yes," Agnew replied, "I have indicated that Mr. Nixon is a very acceptable candidate to me."[25] After Rockefeller's announcement, Nixon and Agnew began courting each other. Their first substantive talk took place at the Fifth Avenue apartment of Louise Gore in January 1968. Gore, a wealthy native Marylander and state senator, asked the men to stop by her apartment during a party she was hosting. The two men talked in depth for the first time, and they both, according to one Agnew biographer, came away "impressed with the other."[26]

Not every Republican felt the same way. Milton Eisenhower, the younger brother of President Dwight Eisenhower and himself the former president of Penn State and Johns Hopkins University, did not believe Richard Nixon was an acceptable candidate. Like his older brother, Milton Eisenhower harbored reservations about Nixon's suitability for the presidency. Unlike Dwight, who remained scrupulously neutral throughout the primary season, Milton acted upon his qualms, and not for the first time tried to stymie Nixon's career. Twelve years earlier, when President Eisenhower was weighing whether to keep Nixon on the ticket Milton urged that he be dumped and wondered why Nixon could not take a hint and gracefully step aside.[27] Disclaiming any personal dislike of Nixon, Milton Eisenhower wrote Agnew, urging the governor "to become a favorite-son candidate from Maryland as a means of holding the State delegation together at least during the early balloting at the Miami convention." Eisenhower believed that this maneuver would help derail Nixon from getting the nomination on the first ballot, thereby assuring "a wiser decision can be made at Miami than can be made at this stage."[28]

Agnew responded on April 1, appearing receptive to the idea of stopping Nixon. "I would very much like the opportunity to discuss with you the subject of your March 26th letter," Agnew wrote Eisenhower.[29] The night before Agnew responded, the political world received yet another jolt as President Lyndon Johnson announced to a national television audience he would not seek nor accept the Democratic nomination. That shock only heightened Eisenhower's concerns. Fearing that the "egocentric, power-hungry, immature, and dangerous" Bobby Kennedy might now become the Democratic nominee, Eisenhower again urged Agnew to become a favorite-son candidate.[30]

Agnew's letter to Eisenhower contained only cryptic references to Milton Eisenhower's goal. Agnew was not a paranoid man, but there was no downside to being careful. Public exposure would have derailed any chance Agnew would have of landing a cabinet job, a federal appeal court appointment, or possibly even being Richard Nixon's vice presidential candidate. Nixon was a man with a long memory and he did not easily bury the hatchet.

One can only speculate about what might have been without Spiro Agnew on the ticket. If Nixon ever caught wind of the intrigue between Eisenhower and Agnew there would have been no Nixon-Agnew team in 1968. A different running mate would have meant a different vice president in August 1974, hence, no President Gerald Ford. Or perhaps Nixon might not have been elected and the nation might have been spared the Watergate scandal.

But Richard Nixon never learned of Agnew's machinations. A week after Rockefeller made his decision not to run, Nixon and Agnew met again on March 29—this time at Nixon's Fifth Avenue apartment. Nixon later wrote that he came away "impressed by his intelligence and poise."[31] Over the next few weeks Nixon continued to woo Agnew. He dispatched Martin Anderson, his key advisor on domestic affairs, down to Annapolis to sound out Agnew on urban problems. The encounter left Anderson decidedly nonplussed by the Maryland governor and his staff. The people around Agnew, Anderson complained to another Nixon aide Richard Whalen, were political neophytes. Whether Anderson shared this assessment with his boss is not clear but Anderson's conclusion was in marked contrast with Nixon's opinion of Agnew.[32]

By that point Nixon was confident he would be the Republican nominee. His only serious competition seemed to be the long-shot candidacy of California governor Ronald Reagan. Ever suspicious of Nixon, the conservative wing wanted an alternative and it focused on the former B-movie actor and first-term governor. For his part Reagan carefully avoided entering the race but did allow that he would be available if drafted. Nixon, who detested the Right, feared Reagan more so than any other rival, including Nelson Rockefeller, who changed his mind and on April 30 Rockefeller declared his candidacy.[33]

When asked if he remained as enthusiastic about his former favorite, Agnew obfuscated: "No. I'm not a bit less enthusiastic for Governor

Rockefeller's candidacy but I'm much more enthusiastic for Mr. Nixon's candidacy than I was before."[34] Agnew refused the overtures Rockefeller made when he jumped in the race. Agnew refused to take calls from the Rockefeller people. At a "chance encounter at Baltimore's airport" Rockefeller apologized to Agnew but there was nothing Rockefeller could do win back Agnew.[35] His unintentional insult virtually insured that there would be no reconciliation. Further, Agnew always displayed a remarkable political antenna. He must have recognized that by early May, Rockefeller had no chance of derailing Nixon. By waiting until then Rockefeller cost himself any chance of defeating Nixon in the remaining primaries. (Oregon held its primary on May 4. Nixon took 73 percent of the vote, Rockefeller 4 percent.)[36]

The nomination was not wrapped up but Nixon was clearly the front-runner. Between the Oregon primary and the Republican National Convention in early August, Nixon could afford the opportunity to think about potential running mates. On May 17, 1968, *Washington Post* reporter David Broder wrote that Nixon was considering Agnew for the number two slot. Broder had an impeccable source for the information—Nixon himself—and he discussed why Nixon was weighing the Maryland governor. Agnew's high standing among his fellow governors impressed Nixon and he liked Agnew's views on a host of major issues.[37]

It must have been a heady moment for Agnew. He was being considered for the vice presidency. His rise occurred during one of the most turbulent years in American history. Johnson's withdrawal did nothing to stem the discord across the country. On April 4, Martin Luther King, Jr., was struck down in Memphis. Two months later Robert F. Kennedy was assassinated in Los Angeles. At the Democratic National Convention in Chicago, police clashed in the streets with anti-war protestors. The Vietnam War dragged on, killing thousands of American GIs, and many more Vietnamese.

The 1968 presidential election, fought in the backdrop of all these events, was an ugly affair that underscored the nation's deep fissures. Divisions existed on almost every level of American society: geographic, racial, and generational. Toward the end of the presidential campaign a teenager held up a sign pleading for the candidates to "Bring Us Together."[38] That would prove to be an almost insurmountable task.

By July, Nixon had come to think of Agnew as the likely vice presidential choice. But Nixon could not let the matter rest. He gave insight into his decision making: "But like most important decisions, this one would not be final until it was announced. I still wanted to test it, to weigh alternatives, to hear other views. It was a tentative choice, and still reversible."[39]

Richard Nixon had devoted the previous four years in running for the presidency, beginning after Barry Goldwater's nomination in 1964, who Nixon believed would lose to Lyndon Johnson. Unlike some Republicans, especially Nelson Rockefeller, Nixon endorsed the Arizona senator and vigorously campaigned for him. His vocal support of the hopeless cause earned him Goldwater's gratitude. After the race Goldwater told Nixon, "Dick, I will never forget it."[40] Earning Goldwater's support was a critical part of

Nixon's strategy for capturing the nomination. The plan was thought through. A meticulous man, obsessed with the presidency, Nixon cultivated supporters, wooed potential delegates, traveled everywhere, and probed every issue.

For a man who left nothing to chance, who weighed every angle before uttering the most innocuous statement, Nixon strangely dedicated little thought to the vice presidency. Nixon himself had served as vice president for eight years. Further, when he first ran for the presidency in 1960 Nixon almost cavalierly selected Henry Cabot Lodge Jr. of Massachusetts for the number two position. Lodge was a disaster. A former senator from Massachusetts, and grandson of Henry Cabot Lodge, the senator who helped derail Woodrow Wilson's League of Nations Treaty, Lodge Jr. added nothing of value to the Nixon campaign. Lodge did not help Nixon carry his home state of Massachusetts, while John F. Kennedy's running mate, Lyndon B. Johnson, made a crucial difference in his home state of Texas and other Southern states. Lodge was a poor campaigner and a lazy one. He took naps every day and watched television at night.[41]

Given how poor his selection had been eight years earlier, Nixon might have spent more time contemplating who his running mate would be. Instead Nixon pushed the matter to the background and waited until almost the last minute to make his choice. The whole process seemed to irk him. According to his own private polling, Nixon ran better in trial heats by himself than with any vice president.[42] Nixon also had cause to think his candidate might hurt him especially with members of his own party. While Nixon was on the way to capturing the GOP nomination, he had not, nor would he ever, captured the hearts of his fellow Republicans. The right wing of the party distrusted him; the liberal wing disdained him. After 1964 the conservatives controlled the party, but the progressives were still a force to be reckoned with. Both sides, for the most part, reluctantly accepted the inevitability of Nixon (Rockefeller and Reagan's campaigns notwithstanding). Both wings were making noises about the vice presidential selection, and Nixon could not afford to alienate either faction.

Finally, in 1968 Nixon had to contend with one more variable: the South. The 1964 presidential contest was a catastrophe for the Republican Party in all but one regard—for the first time since Reconstruction, the GOP won South Carolina, Georgia, Mississippi, Alabama, and Louisiana. Even though those states would not be in play in 1968—George Wallace was all but certain to carry them except for South Carolina, a fact Nixon conceded—they were vitally important to Nixon as he sought to sew up the nomination and solidify control of the party. The rules of the party dictated that states that went Republican four years earlier had larger delegations. Therefore, the five deep Southern states had a disproportionate share of the votes at the convention. And since none of the states had primaries their delegates went to the convention uncommitted to any candidate. Many of the delegates took their cue from South Carolina's Strom Thurmond. The sixty-eight-year-old Thurmond, himself a presidential candidate in

1948, left the Democratic Party in 1964 for the GOP. An arch foe of integration and a fierce anti-communist, Thurmond exerted tremendous influence over much of the Republican South. Aware of Thurmond's power, Nixon assiduously courted him, meeting with South Carolinian several times in early 1968. In June they parlayed in Georgia. According to legend Thurmond wrestled a concession out of Nixon. The story goes that Nixon agreed to appoint a vice presidential nominee acceptable to Thurmond. All Thurmond asked of Nixon, however, was that Nixon not go soft on the communists.[43]

The choice was Nixon's to make. He played it close to the vest. His secretiveness failed to prevent political journalists from speculating about potential running mates. The pundits bandied around dozens of names, though Agnew often failed to garner a mention. On July 21, for example, the *New York Post* cited eight likely choices, including Ronald Reagan and George Romney. Agnew did not make the list. For his part, Agnew maintained his status as the favorite son candidate. He refused to endorse any candidate and he pledged to go the convention uncommitted.[44]

The Republican National Convention opened on Monday, August 5. That morning the *New York Times* ran a front-page story proclaiming, "Nixon Said to Want Rockefeller (New York Mayor John) Lindsay or (Illinois Senator Charles) Percy for 2nd Place." According to "authoritative sources," Nixon had narrowed down his choices to three members of the liberal wing—Rockefeller, Lindsay and Percy.[45] The pair represented the progressive wing of the party, suggesting that Nixon might be tilting in a liberal direction. The leak of these names sent shockwaves through the Southern delegations. Even though some of Nixon's campaign team scurried around to control the damage and deny the crux of the story, the controversy simmered. Two days later the columnists Rowland Evans and Robert Novak reported that the story was essentially true and Nixon was leaning toward Lindsay.[46]

That, of course, would have excluded Agnew. He had been in Miami since the Friday before the convention, working diligently on the nomination speech. In the meantime the Rockefeller people tried one last time to lure him back, but to no avail.[47] The convention opened on Monday, August 5. Early in the afternoon Agnew dropped all pretenses and announced that "after months of soul searching" he was dropping his favorite son stance and declaring his support for Nixon. Herb Klein, Nixon's communications chief, helped time the event for the network evening broadcasts.[48] The development strengthened Nixon's position, but also angered a few members of the Maryland delegation. Several of the members remained loyal to Representative Charles Mathias, who continued to support Nelson Rockefeller. A series of "bitter debates" followed among the Maryland delegation, with one member, George Beall, the younger brother of Senator Glenn Beall, remaining particularly obstinate. In the end the delegation voted eighteen to eight for Nixon.[49]

As it turned out Nixon did not need the entire Maryland delegation. Neither Rockefeller's desperate maneuverings nor Ronald Reagan's entry had cut into Nixon's numbers. When he arrived at his hotel suite on Monday he asked his campaign manager and law partner John Mitchell about the count. "We've got everything under control," Mitchell assured him.[50] Later that night Mitchell paid a secret visit to Agnew's suite. Agnew was chatting with his press secretary Herb Thompson when Mitchell knocked at the door. Agnew later wrote that Mitchell "told me it was 90 percent certain that I was going to be the vice-presidential nominee." Mitchell looked at Agnew and said, "I'm looking for a vice president." Thompson quickly departed and waited for a half an hour to return. Afterward, when Thompson returned he found his boss in a glum mood. Agnew informed Thompson that he had been offered and accepted the vice presidential nomination. Instead of reveling in the moment Agnew forlornly told Thompson, "We've got trouble." A puzzled Thompson asked why. "Because I've accepted the offer," Agnew replied. Still unclear on the problem, Thompson pressed his boss. "We've got trouble," Agnew wailed, "political trouble at home. I've stated publicly that I'm not interested in national office." Thompson laughed and told his boss, "I'm sure the people of Maryland will forgive you."[51] Mitchell swore Agnew to secrecy, in part because both he and Nixon wanted to see how Agnew's nominating speech went.[52]

As directed, Agnew kept silent. On Wednesday night he delivered the nominating address. It was not his finest hour. It began:

> A nation torn by war wants a restoration of peace. A nation plagued by disorder wants a renewal of order. A nation haunted by crime wants respect for law. A nation wrenched by division wants a rebirth of national unity. If there is one great cry that rings clear, it is a cry for a leader. At this moment of history the Republican Party has the duty to put forward a man—a man to not only match this moment but to master it.
>
> "We have that man!"[53]

Throughout the thirteen-minute address the conventioneers applauded sporadically, though Agnew gave them little to cheer about. Although he had spent the weekend working on the speech, the best Agnew could do was offer a short, cliché-ridden talk that failed to inspire any enthusiasm among the delegates. To be fair, the setting was all wrong for Agnew. Partisans at a political convention want to hear stirring screeds with catch lines that spark audience eruptions. That was not Agnew's style. As always, Agnew spoke in a monotone, never changed his inflection and kept to the text without any deviations. Instead of rousing the crowd he almost sedated them.[54]

But the delegates were not Agnew's real audience. He had to impress Richard Nixon. If silence speaks volumes, Agnew failed his first big test. A decade later Nixon wrote of that Wednesday night: "Ted Agnew placed my name in nomination. Mitchell had asked him if he would like to have the assignment and had suggested that, if he did a good job, he would be among those considered for the second spot on the ticket. To that extent, at least, Agnew's speech was an audition."[55] Significantly, Nixon makes no mention of how the audition went over.

The balloting began after Agnew's speech. Nixon won on the first ballot, capturing 692 votes. With the nomination secure Nixon concentrated on finally picking his running mate. Doubts about Agnew, always there, seemingly increased after the nominating address. Nixon convened a series of meetings to discuss the vice presidential candidate. The conclaves were held at Nixon's penthouse suite in the 18th floor of the Miami Hilton Plaza and lasted until 5:00 A.M. Nixon decided to solicit, or appear to solicit, the advice of national Republicans. The list of names included two former Republican presidential nominees Thomas Dewey and Barry Goldwater; Senators Hiram Fong, Strom Thurmond, and Karl Mundt; and the Reverend Billy Graham. These stalwarts offered their choices, with most suggesting Lindsay, Oregon senator Mark Hatfield, and Massachusetts governor John Volpe as the top choices. Not a single person—except Nixon—mentioned Agnew.[56]

It was all a charade since "Nixon wasn't interested" in any of the names put forth. After the meetings adjourned, Nixon offered the vice presidential post to his friend and political confidant Robert Finch. A former aide to Nixon, and the current lieutenant governor of California, who actually outpolled Ronald Reagan in 1966, Finch had political experience and political skills. Finch declined the offer, citing fears that the move from lieutenant governor to the vice presidency was too big a leap.[57] Instead of going to Agnew, Nixon next turned to another Marylander, Congressman Rogers B. Morton. A native of Kentucky (and younger brother of Senator Thurston Morton of Kentucky) Morton moved to Maryland in 1953 and quickly became active in Maryland politics. Elected to Congress in 1958, Morton earned a reputation as a skilled political operator who could work with Democrats. The chair of the Maryland State Republican Party, Morton endorsed Nixon when Agnew was still touting Rockefeller. Nixon respected Morton and quizzed him about Agnew. According to Nixon, Morton said Agnew was somewhat lazy and that must be considered since, as the candidate, Agnew would have a heavy campaign schedule. After that not-so-slight dig Nixon surprised Morton by offering him the slot. "Had Morton said that he wanted it, even at that late moment," Nixon later wrote, "I might well have picked him. Politically he had the same border-state advantage as Agnew. I knew him far better than I knew Agnew, and I considered him one of the best campaigners, one of ablest individuals, and one of the most astute politicians in the party."[58]

Like Finch, Morton turned down the offer, telling Nixon, "If it's between me and Ted Agnew, Ted would be the stronger candidate." Morton's assessment "pretty well cinched it" for Nixon.[59] He told Morton to call Agnew and deliver the news. Morton placed the call to Agnew and asked, "Are you sitting down?" Nixon got on the line and informed Agnew, who admitted being "overwhelmed."[60]

This was hardly a way to choose a vice president. The process had an almost surreal quality to it. Nixon procrastinated about picking a running mate. He called together the Republican establishment and then proceeded to ignore their advice. He first offered the choice to Morton and Finch. Nixon never admitted to having doubts about Agnew but the manner in which he settled on Agnew indicates that he harbored serious, if not grave, reservations concerning the man he chose to be a heartbeat away from the presidency. By his own admission he barely knew Agnew. While Nixon liked Agnew's views on domestic issues, there is no evidence that he ever asked Agnew about foreign affairs. Even though Nixon wanted someone in good health he never saw Agnew's medical files. He wanted a vigorous campaigner but found someone even his friend Rogers Morton described as lazy.[61] And of course, Nixon never thought to conduct a background check on Agnew.

In retrospect, it is easy to criticize Nixon for not probing into Agnew's past; but it was only after Watergate that candidates' backgrounds have been subject to intense media scrutiny. At the time, investigations were not commonplace, nor had they ever been. In 1944 when advisors urged Franklin Roosevelt to replace Vice President Henry Wallace with Senator Harry Truman of Missouri, Roosevelt replied that he barely knew Truman. Eight years later Dwight Eisenhower failed to look into Richard Nixon's past. Estes Kefauver, the 1956 Democratic vice presidential candidate, had a serious drinking problem that went overlooked. When John F. Kennedy approached Lyndon B. Johnson in 1960, Kennedy never quizzed Johnson about his contested 1948 senate primary race, nor about Lady Bird Johnson's supposed directorship of radio and television stations in Texas. By 1960 the Johnsons were millionaires thanks to the purchase of the station, KTBC, in the early 1940s. At that time the Federal Communications Commission (FCC) was in danger of being abolished, but Congressman Lyndon Johnson saved the agency. Over the next decade the FCC issued a number of favorable rulings that helped the station expand and enrich the Johnsons. Although LBJ steadfastly maintained he had no involvement in KTBC, his biographer Robert Caro has demonstrated that was false.[62]

Further, Nixon could not rely on the Secret Service and the FBI for a background check. Since he waited until the last day of the convention to pick Agnew he had left no time to launch an investigation. Nixon, many have said, should have asked Agnew whether he had anything to hide. But such an approach would have yielded nothing, as the answer from Agnew would have been "No." In his own mind Agnew sincerely believed that he was a man above reproach. He never would have admitted to taking kickbacks since he had managed to convince himself that he was not accepting bribes.[63]

But a full enquiry was never made and Spiro T. Agnew became Richard Nixon's vice presidential nominee. The Nixon campaign scheduled the formal pronouncement for 1:00 P.M. In the meanwhile Agnew was quickly ushered from his suite at the Eden Roc Hotel to Nixon's suite. There he huddled with the staff about the press conference that would follow the official announcement. At the appointed time Nixon walked into the ballroom of the Hilton Hotel. At the podium he informed the nation of his choice:

Governor Spiro T. Agnew of Maryland. With that Nixon abruptly walked out, leaving Agnew in the room to face a stunned, shocked, and hostile press corps. Nixon's press secretary Herbert Klein introduced "Spyro Agnew" to the media. That pronunciation gaffe turned out to the first of many during the 1968 campaign. Agnew took the podium, where he made some desultory comments and then fielded a barrage of rapid-fire questions from a startled and aggressive press corps. Most of the questions centered on Agnew's response to the Baltimore riots, while others focused on Agnew's relative anonymity. In response to the latter query from CBS's Mike Wallace, Agnew remarked, "I'm not a household word, but I certainly hope that it will become one within the next couple of months."[64]

Agnew's first press conference with the national media set the tone for the rest of the campaign. He got off to a rocky start with the press and the relationship thereafter only deteriorated. At the time, though, the press was the least of his worries. Immediately after Nixon selected him, a small cadre of liberals launched a stop-Agnew movement. Led by New York senator Charles Goodell and Rhode Island's John Chafee, the disgruntled cabal made a last-minute push for someone besides Agnew. They first turned to John Lindsay, who rejected the overtures and even agreed to place Agnew's name in nomination. Next up was George Romney, whose name was placed in opposition to Agnew. An angry Nixon ordered John Mitchell to halt the insurrection. The brief uprising fizzled, and Agnew received 1,128 delegate votes to Romney's 168.[65]

Agnew's selection came as a shock to many delegates, the media, and the public. He had little, if any, name recognition, and no national following. Cries of "Spiro Who?" swept through the convention hall. In Atlanta a television reporter asked pedestrians if they know who, or what, Spiro Agnew was. "It's some kind of disease," one replied, "It's some kind of egg," another answered, and "He's a Greek who owns that shipbuilding firm," guessed a third.[66]

A number of prominent Republicans were equally taken aback by the choice. When he learned that Agnew was the choice, Gerald Ford later wrote, "I shook my head in disbelief."[67] When told that Nixon had consulted one hundred leading Republicans about Agnew, Nelson Rockefeller caustically remarked, "I must be the one-hundred first." At least Rockefeller knew Agnew. Some delegates admitted they had never heard of him. Those who were aware of Agnew were not especially charitable in their comments. An Iowa delegate sarcastically quipped, "Boy, this is just great. We'll get every Greek vote in Iowa—all eight or nine of them."[68]

While many reacted with surprise and dismay at the selection, GOP conservatives welcomed the pick. Barry Goldwater had told Nixon the choice was acceptable to him, while Ronald Reagan expressed his approval. Nixon had hoped that Agnew would appeal to a broad spectrum but clearly the liberals mostly opposed Agnew while the Right embraced him.[69]

After the selection Nixon summoned speechwriter William Safire to his suite. It was late in the night, and Nixon, after talking for a while, closed his eyes. Safire got up to leave, but Nixon perked up and delivered a blunt and devastating critique of those he passed over for the vice presidential nomination. He then issued a harsh assessment of his new running mate: "He can't give a speech worth a damn, but he's not going to fall apart."[70] Nixon's comment was the first indication of the doubts he harbored about Agnew. From that point on, Nixon kept a distance from Agnew. Agnew never became a member of Nixon's inner circle, and Nixon rarely sought Agnew's advice on anything. In many ways, Nixon's treatment of Agnew mirrored Dwight Eisenhower's treatment of Nixon. Eisenhower was always ambivalent and he expressed his doubts about Nixon privately and publicly. In 1960, when Nixon was running to succeed him, Eisenhower delivered a rebuke that stung Nixon for the rest of his life. During the 1960 campaign, Nixon was heralding his foreign policy experience, claiming his eight years as vice president gave him an edge over John Kennedy. At a press conference Eisenhower was asked by a reporter if he could name a time that he had "adopted" one of Nixon's ideas. Eisenhower's response demonstrated his uncertainty about Nixon. And the answer neutralized whatever advantage Nixon had over Kennedy in terms of foreign policy experience. "If you give me a week, I might think of one. I don't remember," Ike answered. Although Eisenhower later claimed he meant no disrespect, the line revealed the fissures between Eisenhower and Nixon and showed that Nixon was never part of the administration's inner circle. Nixon never forgot how Eisenhower treated him and it does not stretch the imagination to suggest that Nixon was exacting a measure of revenge by treating Agnew even worse than Ike treated him.[71]

Agnew learned of Nixon's opinions of him and Agnew's view of Nixon eventually changed for the worse, but in 1968 he remained a loyal soldier. For most of his political career Agnew had enjoyed good relations with the media, but that changed overnight. The attacks stung Agnew, and he took criticism personally—too personally at times. However, his reaction to the condemnation following the nomination was hardly out of line given the barrage of attacks from almost every quarter. On Friday, August 9, the morning after the convention, Agnew sat down with the editors of the *New York Times* where he admitted that he was angry over "being made to appear that I'm a little to the right of King Lear."[72]

A few years later, Agnew spoke with his aide David Keene about his sudden transformation in the media. "He told me," Keene related:

> I was the darling of the *Washington Post* and all this. I was the greatest, the smartest governor, the best governor. Then I'm nominated to be vice president and the next day I'm the dumbest son of a bitch that they ever imagined. I can't do anything right, I've never done anything right. I may not be the smartest guy, but I do know one thing: I didn't change from that day to the next. So it wasn't me. It had to be them.[73]

Agnew departed from Miami on Friday, August 9. Over the weekend he met with Nixon in California for a strategy session. At the conference Nixon spelled out Agnew's role in the campaign. Polls taken after the Republican Convention gave Nixon a double-digit lead over his likely Democratic challenger Vice President Hubert Humphrey.[74] With the presence of third-party candidate George Wallace, the election was going to be very close. Nixon, who did not lack for boldness, played it conservative in 1968. Instead of going on the attack, Nixon (who loved employing sports metaphors, especially football ones) went into a prevent defense. With the election less than three months away Nixon did not want to do anything to jeopardize his lead. He refused to say how he would end the Vietnam War, he refused to debate his opponents, and he refused to stray from his stump speeches that obscured his views on the pressing issues of the day.

Nixon wanted Agnew to adopt a low-key approach in the campaign. In California, Agnew, accompanied by his friend, attorney, and campaign aide George White, huddled with Nixon and campaign manager John Mitchell. Nixon assigned Agnew the task of visiting traditional Republican areas while Nixon himself would court the swing voters. He also informed Agnew that he was assigning several staff members to help with scheduling, but not to monitor Agnew. For the most part Agnew was going to be on his own.[75]

During the parley there was talk of having Agnew serve as the point man against George Wallace. Many commentators concluded that Nixon selected Agnew in large measure to either neutralize or outflank Wallace. Over the next three months, Democrats, hostile journalists, and even George Wallace himself claimed that Agnew was Nixon's answer to Wallace. *New York Times* columnist James Reston speculated to the same effect in a column shortly after the convention. Larry O'Brien, the Democratic National Chairman, charged that the Agnew selection was a direct message to potential Wallace voters that they could feel at home with the Republican ticket. Shortly after the convention Wallace held a news conference where he took credit for Agnew's selection. Wallace bragged that his tough rhetoric against the "anarchists" influenced the Republicans to choose a vice presidential nominee with a similar outlook.[76]

Wallace reached this conclusion upon reading Agnew's hard-line screed against the Baltimore rioters. While Agnew denounced the rioters, most of whom were black, he was no George Wallace. A distinction must be made between Wallace's racial demagoguery and Agnew's denunciations of the riots. While Agnew condemned violence, so too did nearly all politicians of both parties. There were some dissonant voices who talked about the "root causes" of the problems, and there were even a few, such as former black congressman Adam Clayton Powell, who celebrated the uprisings.[77] Most of the country's leaders denounced the riots. During his brief presidential campaign even Robert F. Kennedy peppered his speeches with calls for "law and order."[78]

Conservatives, liberals, Republicans, and Democrats all talked tough, in no small part because of the public's anxiety about crime. According to a May 1968 Gallup Poll, violence in America's inner cities ranked as the third most pressing problem of the day. Racial issues came in at second, and the Vietnam War ranked first. A Harris Poll taken in the summer of 1968 showed that 81 percent of Americans believed that the "system of law and order had broken down."[79] Americans, these polls demonstrated, were dissatisfied with the course of race relations and anxious over all the urban violence. The situation in the nation's urban areas deteriorated to the point where Mayor Richard J. Daley of Chicago ordered the police to shoot looters on sight. A Gallup Poll asked respondents if they agreed with that solution. Forty-seven percent answered yes.[80]

This "backlash" sentiment, if it can be called that, found its most forceful outlet in the campaign of George Wallace. The former Alabama governor, running as an independent, played upon people's fears. Wallace got elected governor by promising to block integration in Alabama. He infamously stood in the doorway of the University of Alabama's registrar to prevent black students from enrolling. George Wallace was a racist. He not only played upon fear, but also stoked racial tensions.

Spiro Agnew never got in the gutter like Wallace. While the Democrats and much of the press portrayed him as Wallace in a white collar—just as Nixon was described as Joe McCarthy in a white collar in 1954—Agnew shared little in common with the Alabama governor. For one thing, Agnew rarely dwelled upon racial matters, and his views on race were far more enlightened. Second, Agnew and Wallace appealed to vastly different audiences. In his third study of presidential campaigns, journalist Theodore H. White vividly described a Wallace rally in Cicero, Illinois, a "solidly working-class suburb." Wallace talked about the concerns of blue-collar workers, something the white-collar Republican rarely mentioned. After attacking the usual suspects, intellectuals, and anarchists, Wallace turned his attention to an issue Agnew was quite familiar with: open housing. At the end of his diatribe against open housing Wallace employed a phrase Agnew had come to know well in 1966: "One of the first things I'm going to ask the Congress to do is to repeal this law about the sale of your own property and then let them know that a man's home is still his castle."[81]

Two years earlier Agnew had defeated a candidate who ran on that very slogan. George Mahoney's appeal to the voter's basest instinct disgusted him. As governor, Agnew moved tepidly on the matter at first, but after Martin Luther King Jr.'s assassination he publicly urged the Maryland congressional delegation to support the law that Wallace promised to repeal. So, on the question of race, a wide gulf separated George Wallace and Spiro Agnew.

Wallace drew his strength from the ardent racists and segregationists in the Deep South. He also had support outside that area, as his trip to Cicero amply demonstrated. Theodore White correctly described Cicero as a suburb, but it differed from the towns in Washington, Baltimore, or Montgomery County. Those upscale bedroom communities were comprised mostly of white-collar professionals; Cicero was a declining blue-collar, industrial town made up of lower and middle-class ethnics. These voters opposed open housing and were terrified of busing and so responded to Wallace's attacks.

Critics have long accused Richard Nixon of employing a "Southern Strategy" in 1968. Picking Agnew, supposedly a racist, is viewed as part of that strategy. However, there is no evidence suggesting Nixon devised this strategy. In *Nixon's Civil Rights: Politics, Principle, and Policy*, Dean Kotlowski challenges the idea that Nixon devised a plan to gain votes from white Southerners. During the 1968 campaign, Kotlowski contends, Nixon ceded the Deep South to Wallace. Nixon did not use "code words" to lure white voters to his side. Nixon did talk about "law and order" and those words are taken as evidence that he used code words to appeal to whites. But there was nothing sinister, or implicitly racist, about addressing an issue that worried so many Americans. Liberal Democrats used the same language. Kotlowski also notes that contrary to popular perception, Nixon had been a strong supporter of civil right and never did he promise to turn back the clock on civil rights.[82] Finally, there is nothing in the record suggesting Nixon picked Agnew because he thought Agnew could steal away votes from Wallace.[83]

Wallace was going to take most of the Deep South, giving him about 45 electoral votes, leaving Nixon and his opponent Vice President Hubert Humphrey battling over 493, with 270 needed for a majority. In early September Nixon had a solid lead. The 1968 Democratic National Convention turned out to be a disaster for the Democrats, as activists took to the streets of Chicago to protest the Vietnam War. The demonstrators clashed with the Chicago police and the delegates inside fought over the nomination and the party's Vietnam plank. When it was over Hubert Humphrey emerged as the nominee of a badly divided party.[84]

About the only thing that the Democrats did not fight about was the vice presidential selection. Humphrey picked Maine senator Edmund Muskie. While most of the news during and after the Convention was negative, Humphrey received high marks for his vice presidential choice.[85] Both the print and electronic media lauded Muskie as a competent, pragmatic legislator. The fifty-four-year-old Muskie had served as governor of the traditionally Republican Maine and then in 1958 became the first popularly elected Democrat senator in the state's history. A Polish-American Catholic, Muskie, analysts believed, would deliver votes in pivotal swing states such as Ohio, Michigan, Illinois, and Pennsylvania.[86]

From mid-September through the end of October Nixon's lead dwindled. Nixon ran a defensive campaign designed to minimize any mistakes and hold on long enough to beat Humphrey. Nixon was determined to avoid the mistakes he made eight years earlier, ones he thought cost him the election, including debating John F. Kennedy. Humphrey challenged Nixon to debate but he flatly refused. Believing the media was hostile to him, Nixon avoided the press. Throughout the campaign Nixon made guarded statements and stayed on message.[87]

Agnew did not. Thrust onto the national scene, Agnew made a number of mistakes that marred the campaign and left him embittered. A series of misstatements in the campaign, along with the nearly relentless hostile press coverage, hurt his image. The Humphrey campaign's decision to focus their attacks on Agnew and a *New York Times* investigation questioning his business dealings compounded his travails. The negative coverage, partisan attacks, and general ridicule so rocked Agnew that according to a later report, he contemplated quitting the race.[88]

Some, though by no means all, of Agnew's wounds were self-inflicted. His problems began in early September. On September 6 he held a news conference in New York City where he suggested that communists might be behind the anti-war protests. "I think we have a tendency to play down to some extent the communist influence because it was played up too highly in some of our past years," Agnew told reporters. Nonetheless, Agnew asserted a "definite link" between all the unrest and the Communist Party.[89] That naïve statement made headlines the next day and also elicited more criticism of Agnew, but he brushed it off and went even further two days later. Appearing on NBC's "Meet the Press" Agnew claimed that there was an organized conspiracy among some of the young radicals to "overthrow the free enterprise system as we know it."[90] At a breakfast with reporters on September 9, Agnew alleged that Hubert Humphrey was soft on law and order and soft on communism. When asked later that day to clarify his remarks, or repudiate them, Agnew stood by his statements.[91]

The comments caused a predictable avalanche of condemnation and rightly so. The charge was as misguided as it was indefensible. If anything Humphrey might have been tougher on communism than Agnew—or Nixon. As a young politician in Minnesota, Humphrey drove out communists from the Democrat-Farmer-Labor Party. As a senator, Humphrey consistently advocated bigger military budgets and sponsored legislation that would have outlawed the Communist Party in America. And as vice president Humphrey vocally supported the Vietnam War. While many Democrats had deserted Lyndon Johnson and denounced American involvement in Southeast Asia as a mistake, if not criminal act, Humphrey loyally backed the president, and the troops. His refusal to distance himself from the war or to take a stance in opposition to LBJ (such as calling for a bombing halt in North Vietnam) earned him the wrath of protestors who hounded his every public appearance. Maybe Agnew was unaware of all of this when he labeled Humphrey "soft on communism." But, said many commentators, he should have known better than to even utter the words, let alone believe them to be true.

Agnew's charge brought forth a bipartisan chorus of denunciation. The statement "indicates clearly a revival of McCarthyism," Lawrence O'Brien, Hubert Humphrey's campaign manager charged.[92] When asked about the statement Senate minority leader Everett Dirksen and House minority leader Gerald Ford seemed embarrassed by the matter. Ford stated, "I don't think that this is an issue that should be pushed at this time."[93] In a biting editorial, the *Washington Post* mocked Agnew's explanation that he did not hear the echoes of McCarthyism. "We do not know where Governor Agnew has been, lo these eighteen years, but it could not have been in the United States. Did the Governor think his statement would invite comparison with St. Francis of Assisi?"[94] Many of Nixon's critics labeled Agnew as "Nixon's Nixon," a red-baiter who did Nixon's dirty work. No one encapsulated that feeling better than Nixon's old nemesis, Herblock, the *Washington Post's* editorial cartoonist, and he could not pass up the opportunity to paint Agnew as Nixon's "Apt Pupil."[95]

The story refused to go away. At a news conference on September 11, 1968, in Annapolis, the questioning lasted for about ten minutes and centered mainly on the Third Red Scare. The next day the *Baltimore Sun*, a paper that had championed Agnew's political career since his days on the Baltimore County Zoning Board of Appeals, reported on its front page that Agnew claimed he had a list of "62 members of political dissent movements in the United States who allegedly have Communist leanings."[96]

If Agnew actually had made that claim he deserved all the opprobrium heaped upon him, and probably should have been kicked off the ticket. But Agnew never said that he had sixty-two names. On September 14 the *Sun* ran an editorial admitting its story was incorrect: "Governor Agnew denies having used the figure 62, or any other figure whatever. We now believe that on that point *The Sun* was in error." Although the paper acknowledged its mistake, it offered no apology to Agnew.[97]

Still, there were gaffes and Agnew had himself to blame for those. For all of his political experience Agnew remained a remarkably provincial man. Agnew claimed that some of his best friends were Jews. When campaigning in Chicago on September 20, the city with largest population of Poles next to Warsaw, he referred to Polish-Americans as "Polacks." Just two days later Agnew stuck his foot further in his mouth. As the campaign plane *The Kim* (named after Agnew's youngest daughter) made its way from Las Vegas to Reno, Agnew strolled to the back of the plane to chat with some of the dozen reporters assigned to cover him. On board a plane he spotted Gene Oishi, the *Baltimore Sun* correspondent, taking a nap. Walking by, Agnew asked, "What's the matter with that fat Jap?"[98]

Oishi accepted it as a joke. Herb Thompson, who witnessed the incident, claimed that Agnew only intended the comment for Oishi to hear and that "Gene opened his eyes and smiled."[99] The quip, or slur, did not make the papers until three days later when Richard Homan of the *Washington Post* included it in a story that ran on September 22. After seeing the story Representative Spark Matsunaga (D-HI) took to the floor of the House to denounce Agnew. "Even the disadvantaged in education among our citizens know that to win the peace in the world, we need friends among Europeans and Asians," Matsunaga began. "Every American—yes, every American indeed—knows this except one—that one is running as Vice Presidential candidate on the Republican ticket."[100] Matsunaga's fiery condemnation made headlines in Hawaii, the state with the highest percentage of Japanese Americans. By coincidence Agnew was in Hawaii that very day. With the controversy over his remarks hitting a fever pitch Agnew had to address it. Although he was not rattled he was clearly taken back by all the fuss. In an attempt to deflect any further criticism Agnew decided to play the Greek card:

> A funny thing happened on the way to Hawaii. Maybe it wasn't so funny after all. Those of you who read your local papers are going to find that this Vice Presidential candidate, the son of a Greek immigrant, is being accused of insensitivity to the national pride and heritage of other peoples. I submit to you that this is a rather ridiculous charge to make to a man who grew up in a neighborhood where his family was the only Greek family, a man who saw his father come home dead tired in the afternoon and climb down off a vegetable truck to be ridiculed by certain people who referred to us as "those Greeks on the block."[101]

After insulating himself against charges of bigotry, Agnew defiantly announced that he would not apologize to Oishi because "I don't think I said anything quite that harmful to my friend."[102] The problem, as Agnew saw it, was that he had "inadvertently" used two slang words in less than a week without realizing the import of his words, as he explained: "I confess ignorance because my Polish friends have never apprised me of the fact that when they call each other by this appellation it was not in the friendliest context." He ended by offering a blanket nonapology that placed the blame more on those who took offense than himself: "To those of you who have misread my words I only say you've misread my heart."[103] The audience, which included many Japanese Americans, heartily applauded his words, though some of Hawaii's political analysts believed that the "fat Jap" slur might ultimately cost the Nixon-Agnew ticket the state's four electoral votes.[104]

The race clearly took a toll on Agnew. The insular world of Maryland politics had not prepared him for the rough and tumble of the national scene. The three other major candidates, Nixon, Humphrey, and Muskie were all familiar with national politics and for the most part avoided the pitfalls that bedeviled Agnew. George Wallace's outrageous statements—threatening to run over protestors—were deliberately provocative; they were Wallace being Wallace. Anyway, there were few shrewder politicians than the former Alabama governor. Not so his running mate, General Curtis LeMay. The former chief of staff of the Air Force, LeMay proved to be no benefit to Wallace's insurgent campaign. Wallace introduced LeMay as his running mate at a press conference on October 3. LeMay immediately put his foot in his mouth when he said that if he found it necessary he would drop nuclear bombs on North Vietnam. Although he did not, as famously reported, call for bombing North Vietnam back into the Stone Age, his cavalier attitude toward the use of nuclear weapons demonstrated his lack of political experience.[105]

LeMay at least had foreign policy experience; Agnew had none. That might have actually helped get Agnew on the ticket since Nixon planned to control foreign policy by himself. To help Agnew, Nixon dispatched a Republican policy advisor Kent Crane, a former State Department foreign affairs officer.[106] Crane was one of a number of Nixon aides assigned to work with, or handle, the vice presidential candidate. Over the course of the campaign Agnew grew increasingly suspicious of the Nixon people, whom he came to view not as helpmates but spies. According to one story Agnew warned his staff not to trust anyone:

> A close advisor boarded the campaign plane in New York, took the seat across from the 1968 GOP vice presidential candidate and started talking. 'Look out the window while you talk,' Spiro T. Agnew snapped. 'No one can hear us—there's too much plane noise,' the advisor said. 'No, that guy can read lips,' said Agnew, nodding toward a man in a nearby staff seat. 'But Ted, he's from Nixon's staff—to help us,' the advisor said. 'We don't know who are friends are,' said Agnew, looking out the window.[107]

The anecdote might be apocryphal but it does speak to the level of Agnew's bitterness about the campaign. Agnew was not by nature a cynic but the 1968 campaign left scars on him that never healed. He felt abandoned by the Nixon team, whom he believed, did not come to his defense and even might have been feeding negative stories to the media. And it was the press that Agnew developed a visceral distrust of. His attacks on the media were borne out of what happened in the campaign. The depths of Agnew's distrust of the media is evident in a story David Keene, today one of the country's most prominent conservative activists, related to the author. In the late spring of 1970 speechwriter Pat Buchanan brought Keene, the national chairman of the conservative organization Young Americans for Freedom, to an Oval Office meeting with President Nixon. Later that day Keene interviewed with Agnew for a position on the vice president's staff. Soon afterward syndicated columnists Rowland Evans and Bob Novak wrote that Keene requested that Nixon muzzle Agnew. Evans and Novak got the story wrong. An irate and justly worried Keene asked the columnists for a retraction, and then called Agnew and told him the story was not true. An unperturbed Agnew laughed it off, telling Keene that he never believed anything he read in the newspapers. And he added Keene to his staff.[108]

About the only Nixon aide that Agnew trusted was Patrick J. Buchanan: Nixon's firebrand speechwriter and in-house conservative. Buchanan had pushed for Agnew to be on the ticket and his admiration for Agnew increased as he observed Agnew in action, so much so that in early October Buchanan volunteered to transfer to Agnew's staff. It is too much to say that Buchanan helped turn Agnew into a conservative, but in Buchanan he found a soul mate who shared his disdain of the media. The campaign was clearly a turning point for Agnew in his ideological transformation. He came to believe that the broadcast networks and major newspapers such as the *New York Times* and the *Washington Post* were bastions of liberalism, which never gave Republicans a fair shake. Nixon had felt the same way; his "Last Press Conference" after his defeat six years earlier in the California gubernatorial contest spoke to his anger at the Fourth Estate. Agnew would express his feelings about the media later on and his ideas dovetailed with many who thought the media to have a liberal bias.[109]

But Buchanan stayed for only a short while, and Agnew relied almost entirely on the Marylanders whom he had worked with over the years. The Agnew people were unseasoned in national politics. The *Washington Star* reported that they were "often tense, harried and somewhat apprehensive about what may happen at the next stop."[110] His friend and attorney George White served as campaign manager. Herb Thompson continued his duties as press secretary. Dr. William Prendergast, a professor of political science at Johns Hopkins University, served as Director of Research. Two very old friends also joined the candidate. Dr. Emmett Queen, who had known Agnew since a teenager, was Agnew's doctor, and Colonel James O'Hara, Agnew's battalion commander in 11th Armored Division, worked as liaison with veterans and military organizations.[111]

September had been a terrible month for Agnew, and October was not faring much better. In September his opponents, in the Democratic Party and in the media, asked questions about his competency, his sensitivity, and his intelligence. Those questions paled in comparison to allegations raised by the *New York Times* concerning Agnew's probity. The charges came in late October, as polls showed Nixon's lead over Humphrey was below five points. Nixon's strategy of playing it safe allowed him to maintain a lead, but the number of people likely to vote for him stayed stuck at around 43 percent. Wallace's numbers, as high as twenty in early October, were sliding, while Hubert Humphrey was finally making inroads. With his lead narrowing Nixon did not need any surprises that could derail his candidacy. He got several.[112]

Since the "fat Jap" remark Agnew had tried to steer clear of any controversy. He stopped holding press conferences and in his speeches he stuck carefully to the script. By October Agnew had settled into a routine, one that the *Washington Star* described as "leisurely."[113] Agnew generally made two appearances a day along with a taped television interview. His campaign stops typically drew moderate-sized crowds, ranging from 1,000 to 5,000. The stops were mostly in moderate-sized cities in important swing states, such as Jacksonville, Florida; Youngstown, Ohio; Portland, Oregon; and Spokane, Washington. His speeches included substantive policy proposals, such as eliminating the draft and supporting the Equal Rights Amendment. But on Vietnam Agnew was as opaque as Nixon. Apart from some mild criticism of the Johnson administration's handling of the war, Agnew offered almost nothing of substance about what a new administration would do to bring about an end to the war.[114]

On October 17, after a period of hiding from the media, Agnew fielded questions from journalists covering him. A relaxed Agnew provided frank answers to the questions. During the give-and-take session Agnew discoursed on his role as Baltimore County executive and how it helped prepare him to deal with urban problems. That experience, Agnew argued, gave him a better understanding of the ills confronting the nation's cities than Muskie. The day before Muskie had stopped in Harlem, the poorest section of Manhattan, and a reporter asked Agnew why he was not spending time in

America's cities. Because, "I've been in many of them, and to some extent I would have to say this, if you've seen one city slum you've seen them all."[115]

The Democrats jumped on this remark as further evidence of Agnew's ignorance and insensitivity. But *New York Times* reporter Thomas Johnson, himself African American, wrote that Agnew was merely responding to the question at hand.[116] The rest of Agnew's answer, "I don't think it's imperative that that I conduct showboat appearances through ghetto areas to prove I know something about the problems of the cities," shows that Agnew was trying to make a larger point about political grandstanding, but that part of the answer was ignored. His "Fat Jap" remark and his "if you've seen one city slum you've seen them all," demonstrated a remarkable insensitivity about race and ethnicity.

The Humphrey campaign made the Agnew-isms a major campaign issue. Capitalizing on Agnew's supposed verbal gaffes, the Democrats ran a television commercial that began silently with the words "Agnew for Vice President" on the screen. Gradually a chuckling sound was heard, that turned into full-fledged laughter. Finally, the spot ended with an announcer solemnly intoning: "This would be funny if it weren't so serious."[117]

The Democrats also took out full-page advertisements in newspapers that highlighted some of the more infamous statements. The full-page ads included a photo of Agnew underneath a bold headline that read: President Agnew said: "You can't look to gun control to cure violence and lawlessness"; "While there is hunger and poverty in this country, much of it is exaggerated"; "it is not evil conditions that cause riots, but evil men"; and of course, "If you've seen one slum you've seen them all."

Agnew mostly ignored these attacks, though mostly because he was too consumed with another battle. On October 22 the *New York Times* published a story on page 29, under the headline, "Old Issues Revived as Investigators Study Agnew's Past." The story, published from Towson, Maryland, began with: "People who notice 'outsiders' in this bustling suburban county seat say that a person can hardly throw a stone around here nowadays without hitting someone investigating Gov. Spiro T. Agnew." The newsmen and political operatives were looking for any dirt on Agnew, who had not undergone any real vetting by the Nixon team before his selection. The "tradition of easygoing political ethics in Maryland" led some to believe that perhaps Agnew might not be above suspicion like Caesar's wife.[118]

Up to that point none of the investigations had yielded any results. In fact, the *Times* shed no new night but merely rehashed old stories about Agnew's stake in the Bay Bridge property, the Executive Assembly Club, and his directorship of a Towson-based bank. The paper talked with many Agnew associates, including J. Walter Jones, Agnew's close friend and business partner. Jones assured the *Times* that "neither he nor any of his business associates had sought or obtained favors from Mr. Agnew or rewarded him in any way for favors unsolicited but received." As for Agnew, he "indignantly rejected as untrue and unfounded suggestions that he had ever received personal loans or payments from any person."[119]

Whenever confronted about his ethics Agnew always flew into a rage. Agnew either always believed or managed to convince himself that he was above reproach, that he was cleaner than a hound's tooth. But Agnew had accepted payments. Over the course of six years he had taken kickbacks from contractors and engineers and would continue to do so even after the investigation into his finances.

Agnew's cries of innocence were as brazen as they were mendacious, but at the time no one uncovered any evidence of wrongdoing. Still, the lack of solid information failed to deter the *Times*'s editors from calling into question Agnew's ethics and suitability for the vice presidency. In an editorial "Fitness for Office," published on October 26, the paper chided Richard Nixon for failing to conduct a proper background check of his running mate. Turning to Agnew, the *Times* went through the litany of charges and concluded that "Mr. Agnew has demonstrated that he is not fit to stand one step away from the Presidency."[120]

The next day, October 27, Nixon defended his running mate. Appearing on the CBS Sunday morning network show "Face the Nation," Nixon angrily dismissed the allegations as "the lowest kind of gutter politics that a great newspaper could possibly engage in." He also issued a warning to the paper: "A retraction will be demanded at The Times legally tomorrow." After the publication of the editorial, Agnew consulted with his lawyer George White and John Mitchell about filing a libel suit against the *Times*. But the paper refused to recant anything. In response to Nixon's "gutter politics" charge, the *Times* actually reprinted its original October 26 editorial. On Monday, October 28, Everett I. Williams, an attorney hired by the Nixon-Agnew campaign, met with the *Times*'s legal counsel to ask the paper to retract charges of malfeasance leveled against Agnew. No retraction was forthcoming.[121]

The final volley was fired on October 30. The lead editorial that day reiterated the charge that Agnew, while not guilty of any criminal violations, had proven himself unfit to be vice president because "he failed to act with a sufficient sense of propriety in maintaining the essential difference between public office and the very possibility of any private gain that might be derived therefrom."[122]

Despite all of the *Times*'s coverage and Agnew's heated denials, the accusations never generated much public interest. The charges were not new, and they involved some intricate financial matters that were not sufficiently explosive to arouse much public interest. Further, the stories appeared just as the peace talks between the Americans and the North Vietnamese were heating up. With Nixon's lead dwindling, with Hubert Humphrey finally having put distance between himself and Lyndon Johnson, and with a settlement in Vietnam potentially on the horizon, Agnew's troubles were largely confined to the back pages.

Vietnam continued to dominate the headlines. On September 30 in Salt Lake City, Humphrey called for an immediate bombing halt. With that declaration Humphrey changed the dynamics of the campaign. The swarms of protestors who harassed his every stop disappeared. Finally freed of being LBJ's lap dog, Humphrey's campaign gathered momentum and by late October the polls showed him within striking distance of Nixon.[123]

Nixon continued to prevaricate about his plans for ending the war. Publicly and privately he supported LBJ, but he also let the president know he would not back any cessation of the bombing in Vietnam.[124] But Nixon worried that LBJ just might strike a deal with the North Vietnamese before the elections, an agreement Nixon feared would cost him the election.[125]

On March 31, the night Johnson dropped out of the presidential contest, he also announced that he was sending a delegation to Paris to negotiate with the North Vietnamese. The talks began in May but quickly stalled, with the North demanding an immediate end to the bombing. But Humphrey's statement helped break the impasse, as the North Vietnamese recognized that a settlement aided their cause. On October 11, the North Vietnamese delegates approached the Americans with a proposal: if the United States halted the bombing, they would sit down with the South Vietnamese. After agreeing on the shape of the negotiating table (one of the arguments over process that had held up the talks for months) peace seemed to be at hand, if only the South Vietnamese could be persuaded to go along with the deal.[126]

Such an arrangement was not at all in the best interests of the beleaguered South Vietnamese government. President Nguyen Van Thieu, while not a strong man, was not a dumb one either. While initially giving tacit approval to the peace talks, Thieu recognized any agreement that left the Viet Cong forces intact in the South would ultimately lead to the destruction of South Vietnam. He wanted no part in the downfall of his country and he realized that he might get a better deal with a new administration, particularly a Nixon administration.

The story that Nixon convinced Thieu to hold out for a better deal is one that historians continue to debate. Although Thieu and Nixon had a back channel in the person of Anna Chennault, the widow of a World War II flying ace and herself Co-Chair of Republican Women for Nixon, and Nixon had Chennault relay messages to Thieu urging him to holdout, it was Thieu who ultimately decided to back out. Nixon biographer Stephen Ambrose argues: "Insofar as the charges imply that Nixon prevented peace in November 1968, they are false. Not that Nixon did not want to, or try to, but he did not have to. Nixon did not need Mrs. Chennault to persuade Thieu to refuse to go to Paris. Thieu had no trouble figuring that one out for himself."[127] Other historians contend Nixon sabotaged the peace deal and in the process came close to committing treason.[128]

Agnew figured into all this chicanery in a bizarre way. On Saturday, November 2—the same day Thieu announced that his government would not participate in the peace talks—Chennault placed a call to the American embassy in Saigon. The FBI wiretap on the phone recorded Chennault urging "Saigon to hold firm; they'd get a better deal with Nixon." The embassy official enquired if Nixon knew about Chennault's call. No, she replied, but "our friend in New Mexico does."[129]

FBI officials interpreted Chennault's cryptic remark as referring to Spiro Agnew, who made a campaign stop in Albuquerque, New Mexico, on November 2. Later, however, Chennault told an interviewer that a mistake had been made. The "friend" referred to John Mitchell, who was in New Hampshire that day. Whether Mitchell actually knew any of this is highly questionable; but certainly Agnew knew nothing.[130] When Agnew later learned that Johnson had him wiretapped because of his supposed contact with Chennault, he wrote that it did not bother him since Johnson was acting out of concern for national security.[131]

Nixon never thought of discussing the Vietnam settlement with his running mate, or anything else for that matter. In the last weekend of the campaign, Agnew made stops in New Mexico, Texas, Ohio, Michigan, West Virginia, and Virginia. On Monday, November 4, he flew back to Annapolis. Early in the morning Agnew cast his ballot in Annapolis, played a round of golf with a friend, and then returned to the governor's mansion. Later that night Agnew hosted a party for his campaign staff. During the night Agnew tried to get in contact with Nixon, but Nixon only returned his call at 3:15 A.M. "Well, Ted, we've won," Nixon informed his running mate.[132] The next morning, at around 10:30 A.M. the networks announced that Richard Nixon and Spiro Agnew were elected the next president and vice president of the United States.[133] In the popular vote the Nixon-Agnew ticket took 31,770,376 votes to Humphrey-Muskie's 31,270,533, while George Wallace and Curtis LeMay finished with 9,906,141. Nixon won the Electoral College, with 301 to Humphrey's 191 and Wallace's 46.[134]

What role did Spiro Agnew play in this election? Given all the misstatements and controversy, it seems incongruous that Agnew might have actually helped Nixon in 1968. Some of the shrewder politicos gave Agnew credit for helping swing the election to Nixon. David Stolberg of the *Washington Daily News*, wrote on November 8: "In the cold dawn of post-election second guessing, the pundits and pollsters are beginning to see the light—maybe Maryland's Spiro Agnew wasn't Richard Nixon's big mistake of the campaign. Maybe, instead, he was actually the keystone in Mr. Nixon's carefully architectured arch of triumph."[135] One pollster, Lou Harris, whom the Nixon campaign accused of slanting his polls in Humphrey's favor, spoke to the National Press Club two days after the election. Harris told the assembly that his firm picked up a late drop for Wallace in the outer South, and the wavering voters ultimately cast their ballots for Nixon-Agnew, because the Democrats "whipped up Southern sympathy by the vehemence of their anti-Agnew scorn in the campaign's closing weeks." The *Dallas Morning News* argued Agnew helped Nixon not only in the border regions but also in the Southwest and the Far West. "In a big sense," the paper concluded, "Agnew was to Nixon what Lyndon Johnson was to John F. Kennedy."[136]

He may well have helped Nixon carry several border states Nixon lost in 1960. On inauguration day, as Johnson and Nixon rode from the White House to Capitol Hill, Lyndon Johnson, Nixon later wrote:

> spoke with very strong feeling with regard to Muskie and Agnew. He said that a dinner the night before, a group of people were talking about how much Muskie had contributed to the campaign. He, Johnson, had replied that all the press had slobbered over Muskie, but when it came down to votes Muskie had delivered Maine with four votes, whereas Agnew could take credit or at least a great deal of the credit on South Carolina, North Carolina, Virginia, Tennessee, and Kentucky. Obviously, he liked Agnew and had very little use for Muskie.[137]

Agnew helped make Nixon president. Despite all the gaffes in the campaign, real and imagined, Agnew delivered votes to Nixon in some of the key swing states. The victory was narrow and Nixon needed all the votes he could get. Almost from the moment he picked Agnew, Nixon expressed reservations about him, but Agnew was an asset to Nixon in 1968. He remains one of the few vice presidential candidates to make a difference in an election.

Chapter 5

Becoming "Nixon's Nixon"

The 1968 election did not bring about an end to ideological division in the United States. After his election Nixon had told the nation he would try to "bring us together." At times, Nixon tried to heal the fissures; at other times he exploited the differences for his political benefit. One of his political weapons would be his vice president, who would use the office to attack the administration's opponents. Over the next four years Agnew built a solid base of his support, mostly among the Republican Party's right wing. While many of Nixon's policies—such as issuing wage and price controls, creating the Environmental Protection Agency, opening diplomatic relations with China, and pursuing arms control with the Soviet Union—alienated the conservatives in the GOP, those same conservatives came to admire Agnew.[1] Agnew would continue his rightward drift and by 1972 he rivaled Ronald Reagan as the party's most popular conservative. In 1972, the American Conservative Union endorsed Agnew for redenomination as vice president but would not endorse Nixon.[2]

But that was four years away. In the aftermath of the 1968 election Agnew was unclear of what his role would be and Agnew had no clear idea of what Nixon expected of him. When Nixon announced Agnew as the vice presidential candidate, Nixon made some nebulous statement about Agnew handling urban and federal affairs but never offered any concrete proposals. Much more concerned with winning than governing, Nixon gave little thought to what Agnew would actually do in his administration.

Nixon provided some help to Agnew immediately after the election. After taking a much-needed vacation, Nixon met shortly with Agnew on November 9 at Nixon's vacation spot in Key Biscayne, Florida. With Agnew at his side, Nixon told reporters that his vice president would not be burdened with traditional ceremonial roles (as had Nixon in his eight years under Dwight Eisenhower) but instead would have "new duties beyond what any Vice President has previously assumed." In a further gesture of goodwill

Nixon announced that Agnew would have an office in the southwest corner of the West Wing of the White House, a first for a vice president.[3]

Two days later Nixon returned home and set up his transition office in New York's Pierre Hotel, where he closeted himself with his closest aides. The men began assembling the cabinet and staff, but no one thought to have Agnew in New York until November 27, three weeks after the election. The hour-long meeting went well, and Agnew told reporters afterward he felt "exhilarated" with his upcoming responsibilities. Agnew announced that he would "have all the staff that Vice President Humphrey and other Vice Presidents have had including an administrative assistant." However, there was no mention of exactly what Agnew's role would be.[4]

Although Agnew had the trappings of power, he never made it into Nixon's inner circle. That Agnew would not be an insider in the administration reflected less upon his abilities, or lack thereof, than the office itself. For well over 150 years, occupants of the vice presidency exercised almost no influence in any administration. Presidents rarely consulted their underling, and potential successor, on matters of state, with the only real exception being William McKinley's reliance on his first vice president Garrett A. Hobart. Not until after 1933 did vice presidents regularly attend cabinet meetings. Before 1949 no vice president had an office in the White House complex; instead they worked down Pennsylvania Avenue at the Capitol.[5]

After World War II, the vice presidency grew in importance, both in law and in practical politics. Under the 1947 National Security Act, the vice president was made a member of the National Security Council. After the assassination of John F. Kennedy in 1963, Congress passed and the states ratified the 25th Amendment, which required that the new president choose a vice president who would be ratified by the House and Senate. Still, for all its development, the vice presidency remained an institution dependent upon the presidency. While Dwight Eisenhower used Nixon as his partisan spokesman and, at times, hatchet man, he rarely, if ever, leaned upon Nixon for advice on foreign policy or important state issues. John Kennedy mostly ignored Lyndon Johnson, who in turn snubbed and humiliated his vice president, Hubert Humphrey.[6]

Agnew's role in the Nixon White House was up to Nixon, not Agnew. Nixon had expressed his displeasure with Agnew and planned to keep Agnew away from his inner circle. Agnew grew frustrated with his status, but over time he carved out a role for himself, one that created a power base for him. Although Agnew lacked power within the Nixon administration, he developed influence outside the White House with the Republican Party's conservatives. It was the GOP's right wing that ensured that Nixon could not rid himself of Agnew, as previous presidents had dumped vice presidents.

Although Agnew was unclear what role, if any, he would play in the Nixon White House, he was excited about the future. As he prepared to take up his new responsibilities, Agnew was in the prime of his life. A week after the election Agnew celebrated his fiftieth birthday at the Governor's Mansion. After staying in bed on Sunday, November 10, nursing a cold and catching his beloved Baltimore Colts on television, Agnew took his family to St. Croix, Virgin Islands, for a vacation (he and his friend J. Walter Jones were partners in a condominium venture there). Agnew used the respite to hit the links, and in act of bipartisanship, he invited Vice President Hubert Humphrey and Senator Edmund Muskie to join him for a round. The transition period was a heady time for Agnew and he took advantage of his new status, along with lull in work, to have some fun before taking on his new position. Apart from his vacation in St. Croix, Agnew traveled around the country, including a stop in Memphis for the Liberty Bowl between Mississippi State and Virginia Tech. He and Judy attended the New York nuptials of Julie Nixon and David Eisenhower in December. Later that month, Agnew visited Capitol Hill where he toured his office suite and sat in the rostrum where was to preside over the U.S. Senate. In early January he flew out to Miami to attend Super Bowl III, which pitted his beloved Baltimore Colts against the AFC's New York Jets. At the game Agnew sat in the owner's box with his friend Carroll Rosenbaum. They watched as the Jets, led by quarterback Joe Namath, shocked the heavily favored Colts, sixteen to seven.[7]

Agnew spent a lot of his time preparing for life in Washington, DC. His first order of business was finding living quarters. At the time, the government provided no permanent residence for the vice president. (In 1966 Congress authorized that a vice presidential residence be located at the unused Naval Observatory in Washington DC, but President Johnson asked that no funds be appropriated for the house.)[8] He and Judy decided upon an apartment suite at the Sheraton Hotel, the same suite occupied by Vice President Hubert Humphrey and his family. Judy busied herself preparing for the move to Washington and the upcoming inaugural festivities. As always she took on every task with equanimity. Although she preferred to live in Maryland "simply for the reason that I'm a Marylander," finances dictated that the family move into the Sheraton. Unsure as to the role she would play, Judy mentioned that she planned to ask Pat Nixon about her upcoming responsibilities. When informed that Mrs. Nixon had already picked her inaugural dress, Judy admitted that she had not yet shopped for one and was considering wearing the "lovely one left over" from the gubernatorial inaugural ball.[9]

Only Kim, their youngest daughter, moved with them to Washington. Their two eldest daughters, Pamela and Susan, decided to stay in Maryland, as did Randy and his wife. Spiro was still financially supporting all his children, which was a burden since the vice presidency offered little to its occupants. It paid a salary of just $43,000 a year, along with a $10,000 allowance to defray costs incurred in his official duties. It was not a lot for a married man with four children to take care of. But Agnew had additional sources of income and was determined to keep them. Shortly after the election Agnew met Jerry Wolff, an engineer, whom Agnew appointed as head of the State Roads Commissioner. Agnew asked him to compile a list of the state contracts awarded to the engineering firm of Allen Green. Wolff then called Green and the two wrote up a list of the contracts. According to the agreement

Agnew made with Green, the latter owed 10 percent of the contract fees to Agnew. Agnew then arranged a sit-down with Green at the governor's office in Baltimore where the talk, as it usually did, revolved around Agnew's poor financial status. Green alleged that Agnew "went on to state expressly that he hoped to be able to be helpful to Green with respect to the awarding of federal engineering contracts to Green's company."[10]

When investigators first began probing malfeasance in early 1973 in Baltimore County and the state of Maryland, Agnew's potential involvement was discounted as either hearsay or immaterial since the five-year statute of limitations covering any crimes would have made him immune from prosecution. But Agnew continued to receive monies while vice president, which left him vulnerable when the U.S. attorneys uncovered corruption in 1973. He was placing himself in a dangerous position for a relatively small amount of money. In all Agnew took about $200,000 over a ten-year period, not enough to make him a wealthy man but just enough to ruin him. Whether it was hubris, small-time greed, or stupidity, he risked his entire political career.

During the transition period, Agnew worked on building a staff and he hired many of his aides from Annapolis. As his chief of staff, Agnew turned to C. Stanley Blair.[11] Born in 1927, in Kingsville, Maryland, Blair earned a B.A. and law degrees from the University of Maryland. After a three-year stint in the army, he worked in private practice before successfully winning a seat in Maryland's House of Delegates in 1962. In 1967 Agnew asked Blair to serve as secretary of state. Blair moved with Agnew to Washington and served with him for seventeen months.[12]

Arthur Sohmer, who had been with Agnew since 1962, was put in charge of political affairs. A graduate of Lafayette College and a student of the University of Maryland Law School, Sohmer worked as salesman for the Union Camp Corporation of Baltimore before entering politics. He ran unsuccessfully in the primary campaign for a seat in the Maryland House of Delegates in 1962, and afterward Agnew asked him to come aboard as campaign manager. Even though Sohmer "told him that I didn't know anything about it," he accepted Agnew's offer, thus starting a professional relationship that lasted until 1973. Sohmer proved to be an effective manager, excellent strategist, and close confidant. He was with Agnew from beginning to end.[13] Alice Fringer served as his secretary (she was the only member of the staff to actually work in the West Wing; all the rest worked out of the Old Executive Office Building).[14] Herb Thompson, the former AP Annapolis bureau chief, had gone to work for Agnew in 1967 and served as his press secretary. He held the same job when he moved with Agnew to Washington, while his wife Ann performed the same duties for Judy Agnew.[15] Agnew's trusted aide Cynthia Rosenwald came aboard as his chief speechwriter. The press often dubbed her as a "Baltimore County housewife," which she was.[16] For his director of research, Agnew turned to Dr. Jean Spencer. In 1967, Agnew named her the assistant director of the Governor's Task Force on Modern Management. To help out with his duties in federal and state relations,

Agnew turned to a Nelson Rockefeller aide C. D. Ward as an administrative assistant on local relations.[17] Ward earned the reputation as the house liberal on the Agnew staff.[18] Fran DeCosta, like Thompson, a Democrat, served as the vice president's legislative assistant.[19] Finally, Agnew turned to his friend Jerome Wolff to be his advisor on science and technology.[20]

Despite Nixon's promise that he and Agnew would share staff, for the most part the Agnew and Nixon staff had little contact. Problems between Nixon staff members and Agnew's team arose almost immediately. Nixon aides viewed many of Agnew's assistants as incompetent. [21] They also didn't trust some of Agnew's staff. White House Chief of Staff H. R. "Bob" Haldeman was angered when he learned that Agnew hired Lyndon Johnson's former advance man, whom Haldeman described as a "total spy." On February 5 Haldeman wrote in his diary:

> E (John Ehrlichman) and I had a knock-down with the VP, about his staff and his office facilities. Hard to get anywhere. Afraid we made things worse, and that it will have to go the P. VP has no concept of P's view of how he should handle the role, and I don't think he ever will. Real problem about his hiring LBJ advance man. He sees no reason not to, and apparently intends to buck us all the way.[22]

Very early on Agnew learned he would have no say in foreign policy decisions. At one cabinet meeting early in the administration, Agnew vocally shared his opinions. An angry Nixon dispatched Haldeman to put the vice president in his place. Keep quiet from now on, the brusque Haldeman told Agnew.[23] Agnew believed the genesis of his problems with Nixon centered on his forthrightness in stating his opinions. He later wrote,

> Looking back, I now believe that Mr. Nixon's dissatisfaction with me had its roots in my outspoken criticism at N.S.C. and cabinet meetings. I felt that a Vice President should contribute, not just observe. Since I was given no chance to contribute in private, I had to do it in front of my family. The President did not have the confidence to take even implied criticisms of his predetermined decisions.[24]

Needing something for Agnew to do, Nixon put him in charge of the newly created Office of Intergovernmental Relations. In the executive order, issued February 14, Nixon stated the "office shall be under the immediate supervision of the Vice President," and shall "serve as the clearinghouse for the prompt handling of federal-state-local problems."[25] The president also placed Agnew in charge of Indian Affairs, named him the Chair of the National Space Council and, in February, directed Agnew to discuss with the nation's governors "what, action, consistent with the vital importance of maintaining the traditional independence of American universities, might be taken at the state and federal levels to cope with the growing lawlessness and violence on our campuses."[26]

The office and the responsibilities were unglamorous and unrewarding, but Nixon was determined to keep Agnew out of his inner circle. In a meeting with

Haldeman Nixon ranted, "Burns should explain to Agnew how the Vice Presidency works."[27] This was a strange order since the man designated to carry out the assignment, Arthur Burns, the chairman of the Economic Council, had not been vice president, and did not have any great insights into how the vice presidency operated. It is entirely probable that the mission was never carried out. As it happened, Agnew soon made another blunder that effectively damned him in Nixon's eyes. On Friday, April 25, Nixon flew to Camp David and just before he sat down to dinner Agnew called, saying the he desperately needed to speak with the president. Nixon took the call, but the conversation did not go well; in fact it sent Nixon into a rage. Later Nixon called Haldeman into his room and fumed about Agnew. The urgent matter Agnew wanted to talk about was appointing a friend to be director of the Space Council. As Haldeman recounted in his diary, the call, "May turn out to be the straw that breaks the camel's back. He [Agnew] just has *no* sensitivity, or judgment about his relationship with the P[resident]."[28]

Eventually, Nixon and Haldeman decided to bequeath the Agnew problem to John Ehrlichman, Nixon's Domestic Policy Director and the other half of the so-called palace guard. Ehrlichman did not relish his new duties. He later related:

> At first, in 1969, I was sent to see Agnew when Haldeman realized he and the Vice President did not get along well. The President's idea was that a high-level staff person should listen to Agnew (when an appointment with the President had been requested) and try to deflect his imprudent demands; I was expected to arrange for the ministerial tasks to be done by our staff, and I was supposed to show Agnew why his other demands ought not to be pressed in talks with the President. None of that worked, of course.[29]

For the next five years Agnew remained away from the center of power. When it came to the major decisions he was simply frozen out. Nixon never consulted Agnew about domestic policies. Agnew never had the chance to weigh in with his thoughts about Vietnam. The situation left Agnew angry and demoralized. Later describing himself as the "number-one hawk on Vietnam in the administration," Agnew recounted his frustration with administration policies he viewed as appeasement.[30] His first sense that Nixon and his advisors were not going to pursue tough anti-communist policies occurred in the wake of a major incident off the Korean peninsula. In mid-April the North Koreans shot down an American reconnaissance plane, making a routine mission near the North Korean coast, killing all thirty-one Americans aboard. Nixon promptly convened a meeting of the National Security Council, where Secretary of State William Rogers and Secretary of Defense Melvin Laird urged caution. Their advice irked Agnew, who, in clear frustration asked, "Why do we always take the other guy's position?"[31]

Agnew came to loathe Rogers and Laird. He thought them doves who undercut Nixon's ability to respond forcefully, later writing, "Every time Nixon leaned against a (that is, toward) forceful action against Communist power, Rogers and Laird in effect would say, 'Oh, you can't do that, Mr. President, the Russians would misunderstand it. We would be risking nuclear war.' "[32] In this crisis Nixon reluctantly accepted "the other guy's views" and took no military action against the North Koreans.

By the summer of 1969 Spiro Agnew had been moved from his office in the West Wing to a new suite on the second floor of the Old Executive Office Building. This move served a symbolic function—Agnew was being removed from the corridors of power. A few months into the presidency as Agnew related, "Bob Haldeman came to me and said they needed more space in the West Wing; would I give up my office there, since I rarely used it anyway?"[33] Agnew cooperated but the move had to be humiliating. The first eight months in office were a trying period for him and by the time autumn rolled around Agnew began searching for a role that would bring him more responsibility and enhance his status. So too did some of his advisors. In September his chief of staff Stanley Blair gathered several members of the vice presidential staff to formulate some ideas, including an attack on anti-war protestors, intellectuals, and their supposed apologists in the Democratic Party.[34]

Meanwhile, President Nixon continued to find fault with Agnew. On September 5, the president met with Haldeman and Ehrlichman. Nixon discussed how to work with the country's governors, both Republicans and Democrats. Since Agnew had served as a governor it might have made sense to seek his input, but according to Ehrlichman's notes, Nixon thought the "VP doesn't play them well." The president especially wanted to cultivate New York governor Nelson Rockefeller, but emphasized "never with Agnew."[35]

Agnew was not the only issue was Nixon was dealing with. When he came to office in January 1969, Nixon believed he could end the war within a year. That proved far too optimistic, and by the fall of 1969, there was no end in sight. Although a majority of Americans backed the war effort, by fall 1969, that support was eroding and the North Vietnamese shrewdly capitalized on public discontent on the course and conduct of the war. On October 14, the new premier of North Vietnam, Pham Van Dong (Ho Chi Minh died in September), released a letter broadcast on Radio Hanoi. The letter, directed at the American public, read in part:

> This fall, large sectors of the U.S. people, encouraged and supported by many peace- and justice-loving American personages, are launching a broad and powerful offensive throughout the United States to demand that Nixon administration put an end to the Vietnam aggressive war. . . . May your fall offensive succeed splendidly.[36]

Pham issued this on October 14, a day before the scheduled anti-war Moratorium. Nixon resented the North Vietnam's meddling in American politics, but he kept quiet on the urging of several aides. In a precursor of things to come, Nixon dispatched his vice president to hit the North: "To indicate the seriousness with which I viewed this blatant intervention in our domestic affairs, I asked Agnew to hold a press conference at the

White House."[37] The president and Bob Haldeman enlisted speechwriter Patrick Buchanan to write a brief opening statement for Agnew and then "frantically got him into a review with P."[38] In the hastily drawn up statement, Agnew called on the Moratorium leaders to "repudiate the support of a totalitarian government which has on its hands the blood of 40,000 Americans." After finishing his remarks Agnew fielded questions from the White House press corps. The reporters, who rarely had the chance to ask questions of the president—Nixon held only two formal news conferences in his first ten months in office—were eager to go on the attack. Undaunted, Agnew refused to yield an inch. When asked just how the antiwar protestors could "disassociate themselves from a letter written from Hanoi," Agnew replied, "That's up to them. They organized the demonstration. Let them figure out how to explain it."[39]

Agnew performed his task quite ably. Hoping to appear presidential and above the fray, Nixon began using Agnew as his point man. The episode marked the beginning of Agnew's role as "Nixon's Nixon." During his eight years as vice president, Nixon essentially served as the political spokesman of the Eisenhower White House. A gifted politician with an innate instinct for the jugular, Nixon proved, via Agnew, very adroit at attacking the Democrats. Time had not dulled Nixon's rhetorical knives, but he chose (publicly at least) to use those skills sparingly. The job went to Agnew. Since the vice president lacked any true responsibilities, and because he employed strong rhetoric, Nixon quite naturally designated his vice president to be the administration's point man. Agnew finally found a role and discovered he loved it.

Agnew's first shot in his war on the antiwar protestors and the media was fired on Sunday, October 19, in New Orleans. Cynthia Rosenwald, Agnew's chief speechwriter wrote a rough draft Agnew considered too tepid. The final remarks were entirely Agnew's own, and they predictably created a firestorm. In the broadside Agnew added catch phrases that remain part of political lore, none more so than this line "A spirit of national masochism prevails, encouraged by an effete corps of impudent snobs who characterize themselves as intellectuals."[40]

That line garnered headlines, obscuring, in Agnew's opinion, his larger point. According to Agnew, this "effete corps" essentially duped well-intentioned young people to march in a protest that was a "massive outpouring of sentiment against the foreign policy of the President of the United States. Most did not care to be reminded that the leaders of the Moratorium refused to disassociate themselves from the objectives enunciated by the enemy in Hanoi."[41]

Agnew's volleys made headlines and generated intense reaction across the political spectrum. Democratic Senate majority leader Mike Mansfield described himself as being embarrassed by the speech. His counterpart, Republican minority leader Hugh Scott of Pennsylvania, also rebuked Agnew, though not by name. Claiming that the public had "enough of invective against Americans who feel a different way," Scott called for an end to name-calling.[42] The *New York Times* intoned, "Vice President Agnew demonstrated a truly monumental insensitivity to the most profound concern of millions of Americans—and particularly the nation's youth—when he described last week's Vietnam Moratorium as the creation of 'an effete corps of impudent snobs who characterize themselves as intellectuals.' " The editors then went on to compare the youth favorably with Agnew's World War II generation: "In the same speech," the editorial continued, "he lambasted the nation's youth in sweeping and ignorant generalizations, when it is clear to all perceptive observers that American youth today is far more imbued with idealism, a sense of service and a deep humanitarianism than any generation in recent history, including particularly Mr. Agnew's." The title of the editorial was "Mr. Agnew Doesn't Understand."[43]

As Agnew saw it, it was the *Times*'s editorial writers who did not understand. Looking back on the speech a couple of years later, Agnew complained that his conclusions had been deliberately distorted.

> I do find that one has to be very specific in one's comments, because if not, the press immediately shreds away all the qualifications that you put in. For instance, I said originally that those who *encouraged* the student riots were 'effete snobs.' Within two or three days it had become, in the press, not the people who had *encouraged* the students, but the students themselves. Then presently it became *all* students. Then presently it became *all* youth. And that is the way it goes.[44]

October 1969 was a crucial moment in Agnew's career. He found himself as the spokesman of middle America and he became a darling of the GOP's conservatives. The ideological Right had never liked nor trusted Nixon. William F. Buckley in particular disliked Nixon, a feeling Nixon reciprocated.[45] In 1972, Buckley's *National Review* published an article by M. Stanton Evans. Entitled "The Political Odyssey of Spiro T. Agnew: How Come a Nice Liberal Protestant from Maryland Turned Out to Be Mr. Conservative of '72? A Study of How the Vice President Operates and Why the Left Is Right to Fear Him," the piece was a detailed and insightful examination of Agnew's record and rhetoric. When discussing Agnew's fall 1969 addresses, Evans wrote: "The thing that strikes one in reading these speeches is that they actually *say something*, and say it with a reflective subtlety that one would never guess from the manner in which they are treated. Consider for example, the opening passages of the 'impudent snobs' address." Evans quoted the first three paragraphs of the speech and concluded that:

> Whatever one thinks of this particular mentality or Agnew's distaste for it, there can be little question that he has described it correctly. . . . This is hardly the stump speech of a Neanderthal. I doubt very much if anything of comparable substance and discernment has been uttered in recent years by any major spokesman for the political left, almost all of whom themselves use the repetition of clichés and not to their analysis.[46]

Agnew's New Orleans speech was only the beginning of his verbal volleys. The following day, Monday, October 20, Agnew was the keynote speaker at a $100-a-plate Republican fund-raiser in Jackson, Mississippi. Organizers of the dinner expected a crowd of 1,500. Nearly 2,600 jammed the Mississippi Coliseum, many of them not Republicans, including Mississippi governor John Bell Williams and Jackson mayor Russell Davis.[47] Again Agnew zeroed in on intellectuals, but added a different twist to suit his audience. Speaking in the heart of the Deep South, a state that had in 1964 gave Barry Goldwater 87 percent of the vote, Agnew delivered a searing assault on those who mocked Dixie. In the speech, entitled "Racism, the South and the New Left," Agnew lectured:[48]

> For too long the South has been the punching bag for those who characterize themselves as intellectuals. Actually they are consistently demonstrating the antithesis of intelligence. Their reactions are visceral, not intellectual; and they seem to believe that truth is revealed rather than systematically proved. These arrogant ones and their admirers in the Congress, who reach almost for equal arrogance at times, are bringing this nation to the most important decision it will ever have to make. They are asking us to repudiate principles that have made this country great. Their course is one of applause for our enemies and condemnation for our leaders. Their course is a course that will ultimately weaken and erode the very fiber of America. They have a masochistic compulsion to destroy the country's strength whether or not that strength is exercised constructively. And they rouse themselves into a continual emotional crescendo—substituting disruptive demonstration for reason and precipitate action for persuasion.[49]

The crowd cheered Agnew's defense of Dixie. Tired of being uniformly derided by the northern liberal intelligentsia, Southerners welcomed this ringing defense of their land and traditions. But Agnew stressed that his words were not part of a "Southern Strategy": "This administration," Agnew told the all-white audience, "will never appeal to a racist philosophy." Instead, Agnew argued, the administration—in concert with the GOP—was trying to develop a "national strategy."[50]

The intellectuals Agnew denounced attributed the applause as an indication Agnew was playing to the basest instincts of white Southerners. These critics were quick to accuse Agnew of playing the race card. Still, some of the establishment grudgingly admitted that Agnew was not entirely out of line. *Time* allowed that Agnew "had a point about the South."[51]

Publicly Nixon remained silent about Agnew, but published reports indicated his dissatisfaction with the vice president. But to his aides, Nixon dismissed those as rumors. Meeting with Ehrlichman on October 27, Nixon recounted that during his years as vice president, "for 8 years (the) press tried to divide him and Ike without success—same game. Never criticize the VP."[52]

Nixon liked the tone and content of Agnew's speeches and he looked for a way to make use of Agnew. The opportunity presented itself in the aftermath of Richard Nixon's "Silent Majority" speech. The "Silent Majority" speech, as it became known, grew out of two separate but related events: the Moratorium and North Vietnam's rejection of Nixon's peace overtures. Fearing that a loss of domestic support would undercut his ability to negotiate with Hanoi, Nixon decided his only option was to deliver a message to the country in early November.[53]

For days on end Nixon closeted himself—working away at, what he contended would be, one of the few speeches to actually change the course of history. The contents of the address were kept a secret, and anticipation about it ran high. But Nixon offered few concrete proposals to divest America from its longest war. Instead, he asked for time. And he ended the speech with a plea: "And so tonight, to you, the great silent majority of my fellow Americans, I ask for your support. Let us be united for peace. Let us also be united against defeat. Because let us understand: North Vietnam cannot defeat or humiliate the United States. Only Americans can do that."[54]

The administration's anger toward the media reached a boiling point after the so-called Silent Majority speech. Supporters deluged the White House with calls, telegrams, and letters. Polls taken in the aftermath showed overwhelming approval of Nixon's Vietnam policies. But the reaction in many of the major media outlets was critical, if not hostile.[55]

Shortly after November 3, Pat Buchanan began work on a response to the media's assessment of the Silent Majority speech.[56] Agnew and Haldeman went over the proposal on Monday, November 10. Haldeman found Agnew intrigued about it, but thought the remarks a "bit too abrasive." The next day Haldeman talked with Nixon. "Considerable discussion of Buchanan's idea of VP doing a major speech blasting network commentators. P (Nixon) feels it's a good idea," Haldeman recorded in his diary on November 11.[57] The next day Agnew, Nixon, and Buchanan hashed out a final draft. Agnew later described the process as a "labor of love."[58] However, not everyone on his staff was on board. Agnew's chief of staff Stanley Blair expressed his misgivings to Agnew's chief speechwriter Cynthia Rosenwald, who had helped draft parts of the speech. "I have great respect for Pat Buchanan and you," Blair began, but "Neither of these, however, can keep me from saying that I think the Des Moines speech is basically unsound." Rosenwald concurred: "Stan—I agree. What is more I would play it even more conservatively than you! And I am willing to do anything to aid and abet you."[59] For his part Nixon loved the result: "P really pleased and highly amused by Agnew speech for tomorrow night," Haldeman noted. "(Nixon) Worked over some changes with Buchanan and couldn't contain his mirth as he thought about it. Will be a bombshell and the repercussions may be enormous, but it says what people think."[60]

The speech was set for Thursday, November 13, 1969. A few hours before the scheduled address, the White House released the text. The content sent shockwaves through the media. The networks scrambled to get their technical equipment ready in time to televise the speech live in prime time. They preempted their regularly scheduled programs to carry Agnew's address.

Although they were targets, the three broadcast networks recognized the news value of the blast and carried it live.

Agnew launched an unprecedented attack against the three broadcast networks. "Tonight I want to discuss the importance of the television news medium to the American people," Agnew began. "No nation," he continued,

> depends more on the intelligent judgment of its citizens. No medium has a more profound over public opinion. Nowhere in our system are there fewer checks on vast power. So, nowhere should there be more conscientious responsibility exercised than by the news media. The question is, Are we demanding enough of our television news presentations? And are the men of this medium demanding enough of themselves?[61]

The rhetorical questions needed no answer, at least for an audience composed of Midwestern Republicans, so Agnew continued:

> Monday night a week ago, President Nixon delivered the most important address of his Administration, one of the most important of our decade. ... When the President completed his address—an address, incidentally, that he spent weeks in the preparation of—his words and policies were subjected to instant analysis and querulous criticism ... by a small band of network commentators and self-appointed analysts, the majority of whom expressed in one way or another their hostility to what he had to say ... It was obvious that their minds were made up in advance.

According to Agnew, "a tiny and closed fraternity of privileged men, elected by no one, and enjoying a monopoly sanctioned and licensed by government," wielded a power so strong that they could determine the course of the Vietnam War. Tired of this "small group of men" determining what and what was not newsworthy, Agnew challenged their hegemony and their right to dictate to Americans what was and was not newsworthy. Agnew concluded by asking whether "it is time that the networks were made more responsive to the views of the nation and more responsible to the people they serve."[62]

Agnew's address that night had been a year in coming. Vic Gold, who served as Agnew's press secretary from 1972 to 1973, remarked that taking on the media was something Agnew "relished."[63] During the 1968 campaign, Agnew developed an animosity toward the media that never went away. He believed that media treated him unfairly and that journalists did so because they had a liberal bias. Agnew did not invent the theory of bias; he enunciated the bitterness and suspicion that many on the Right harbored about the media. The partisan crowd roared its approval. For decades Republicans held as an article of faith that the major media outlets were hopelessly biased against the GOP and conservative causes. The positive reaction among the crowd that night in Des Moines and the outpouring of support after November 13 illuminated the depth of hostility that so many

Americans felt toward the networks. The morning after the address Pat Buchanan boarded *Air Force Two*, the vice president's plane. Spotting the young firebrand, Agnew triumphantly chortled "Gangbusters."[64] Four decades later, Buchanan looked back at the Des Moines speech as a turning point, arguing that after Agnew's speech many media outlets hired conservatives in an effort to provide ideological balance to their papers and news networks.[65]

Agnew looked upon his Des Moines address as one of his finest moments. A decade later he wrote, "I believe the reaction to my speech was even greater than the November 3 speech, not because I made it, but because the average America had been frustrated for so long about the proselytizing of some network commentators. The number of favorable responses was overwhelming."[66]

Others in the administration agreed—including President Nixon. "(P) was really pleased with VP talk last night," Haldeman noted in his diary, "and feels he's now become a really good property, and we should keep building and using him."[67] Clark Mollenhoff, a former investigative reporter for the *Des Moines and Tribune* and the *Washington Post* who worked in the White House Communications Office, told the White House press corps the talk reflected the views of the Nixon administration.[68]

Reaction from the three networks was defensive. Leonard H. Goldenson of ABC defended his network's coverage: "In our judgment, the performance of ABC has always been and will continue to be fair and objective." CBS president Frank Stanton stated, "No American institution, including the network news organization, should be immune to public criticism or to public discussion of its performance. In a democracy that is entirely proper." Stanton admitted that there were "bound to be occasions when their (anchors and reporters) judgments is questioned," but also warned, "Whatever their deficiencies, they are minor compared to those of a press which would be subservient to the executive power of Government." NBC's Julian Goodman went even further. Agnew's speech, according to Goldman, was an "appeal to prejudice." He went on: "It is regrettable that the Vice President of the United States would deny to television freedom of the press."[69] Goodman further claimed that Agnew wanted "a different kind of television reporting—one that would be subservient to whatever group was in authority at the time."[70]

Agnew was not calling for an end to the First Amendment nor a state-run media. The First Amendment simply prohibits Congress from passing legislation restricting the freedom of the press. The Constitution also guarantees freedom of speech, including the right to criticize the press. Agnew was exercising his First Amendment rights; the charge of censorship was overwrought.

The network anchors responded the next day and all three men stressed that their respective networks provided fair and balanced news coverage. ABC's Howard K. Smith told a reporter that Agnew had made several good points, but was incorrect that any mistakes stemmed from any ideological bias. According to a published report, Walter Cronkite of CBS planned to deliver a strong retort to Agnew but was dissuaded by the president of the news division. NBC's Chet Huntley compared Agnew's showing to Richard Nixon's famous or infamous "Last Press Conference," and claimed that Nixon approved of the content.[71]

Certainly the remarks reflected Nixon's long-standing grudge against the media. The speech also reverberated with millions of Americans who believed that while the networks spoke to Americans, they did not speak for Americans. Republicans, especially the conservative wing, harbored a deep distrust of the press. They believed then, as the right-wing still believes today, that most members of the networks, the major American newspapers, and weekly magazines were to the left of the political center. Further, the conservatives maintained these views seeped into coverage of events and campaigns, putting Republicans and conservatives in a disadvantageous position. A few days after Des Moines, the godfather of the Conservative movement, Senator Barry Goldwater, said in a news conference that he was in full agreement with Agnew.[72]

The question of bias is a tricky one. Viewers see and hear and what they choose. Quantifying slanted news coverage is difficult. Yet one prominent member of the Fourth Estate admitted that the national news media leaned left. Howard K. Smith, an ABC news anchor, told a Republican newsletter that most of his colleagues were liberal and that their ideological bent shaped and distorted news coverage.[73] Edith Efron, a staff writer for *TV Guide*, published a work in 1972, *The News Twisters*, that documented liberal bias among the networks. Efron's careful examination of how ABC, CBS, and NBC covered the 1968 presidential campaign led her to conclude: "The networks actively favored the Democratic candidate, Hubert Humphrey, for the Presidency over his Republican opponent. The Networks actively opposed the Republican candidate, Richard Nixon, in his run for the presidency."[74]

Efron also analyzed Agnew's Des Moines speech and concluded her findings "generally support Mr. Agnew's charges." She presented some anecdotal evidence that the public agreed with Agnew. In the week after Des Moines, the *New York Times* received 40,428 letters; 38,736 were supportive of Agnew. The results were similar, Efron claimed, at the networks: "The mail and telephone responses as tailed by the networks and their affiliated stations across the country confirmed these results: Mr. Agnew's speech had triggered a national explosion."[75]

According to some Agnew detractors, the vice president's remarks fomented anti-Semitism, playing to perceptions among some Americans that the media was controlled by elite Jews. James Reston, the *Times*'s venerable columnist, charged both Agnew and Nixon (perhaps inadvertently) with playing upon the deep-seated prejudices of the Silent Majority:

> One doubts that (Mr. Nixon) intended to arouse the old back lash extremists on the right, but with the help of the Vice President he has apparently done so. For the crusade against the 'Eastern Snobs' has not only aroused support for his Vietnam policy but revived the always latent anti-New York feelings

in this country, and this in turn has produced some ugly anti-Negro and anti-Semitic and anti-Communist reactions.[76]

In retrospect, the charge of anti-Semitism gains more credence given some of the statements Nixon and Agnew had made over the years. Some twenty years later, in a review of the Agnew phenomenon, William F. Safire, who served as a Nixon speechwriter, explored the charges of anti-Semitism leveled against Agnew—the man whom Safire both admired and deplored. "His bitterness at witnesses who turned him in—mainly Jewish—along with the Arab business dealings, earned him a blast here for anti-Semitism, though this was not exhibited before or since his travail" (the scandal that brought Agnew's resignation), Safire wrote.[77]

Nearly four decades after Des Moines, some of Agnew's assessment of the three networks holds up. There was, for example, Cronkite, CBS's long-time anchor, and the "most trusted man in America," who admitted after his retirement that he had always been a liberal. So too did Eric Severaid, who served as the CBS's nightly news commentator for twenty years. A study published in the 1980s by social scientists Stanley Rothman and Robert Lichter demonstrated the liberal persuasion of the major networks' anchors and correspondents. The study revealed that among those eligible to vote in 1972, more than 80 percent voted for Democrat George McGovern. More than half of those surveyed described themselves as politically liberal, and a majority claimed not to believe in God. The results prompted *Washington Post* publisher Katherine Graham to wonder if, "Spiro Agnew *had* something with all that media-conspiracy business."[78]

Graham's comment is even more remarkable in light of Agnew's assault on her newspaper. Agnew followed his broadside against the networks with a scathing assault on the *New York Times* and the *Washington Post*. A year earlier, the *Times* published a series of articles questioning Agnew's business dealings. The *Times*'s stories represented, in Agnew's mind, another example of how the liberal media distorted the news. The *Post* earned his wrath when the editors ridiculed his selection as running mate by claiming Nixon's choice was "the strangest political move since the Emperor Caligula named his horse a consul."[79]

These accusations and ridicule seared Agnew and he savored the opportunity to take them on. Three years earlier both the *New York Times* and the *Washington Post* enthusiastically endorsed Agnew for governor of Maryland. The papers depicted the candidate as a sensible, moderate, even mildly progressive politician who would represent Maryland well, especially compared to his Democratic opponent, George P. Mahoney. In the 1968 campaign, the two newspapers portrayed him as unfit for the vice presidency. As he told aide David Keene, "I didn't become an idiot overnight."[80]

The assault against the two major national papers of record originated with Pat Buchanan.[81] A former newsman himself, Buchanan wrote editorials for the conservative *St. Louis Globe Democrat*. A true conservative believer if there ever was one, Buchanan viewed his former media colleagues as enemies. His views nicely dovetailed with Nixon's. Every morning Nixon read the news summary of major events from the previous day prepared by Buchanan and White House special assistant Mort Allin.[82]

Nixon's paranoia is, of course, legendary; but in the case of media it was not entirely unjustified. Most of the reporters, anchors, producers, and editors of the three networks, two major newsweeklies, and two major newspapers disliked, if not hated, Nixon. For two decades the *Washington Post* had waged an unremitting campaign against him. The battle between Nixon and the *Post* was joined during the Alger Hiss case when Nixon, as a young congressman, pursued claims that Hiss, a former State Department employee, had lied about his involvement in espionage. The *Post* aggressively defended Hiss and stridently attacked his dogged pursuer. After a drawn-out battle, including one mistrial, a jury convicted Hiss on two counts of perjury. In Nixon's view the paper never forgave him for being right about Hiss and longed for the opportunity to settle the score. During Nixon's vice presidential years, Herblock, the *Post*'s editorial cartoonist, so infuriated the Nixons with his biting cartoons that the family canceled their subscription to the paper. Benjamin Bradlee, the paper's editor, had been a close friend and confidant of John Kennedy.[83]

The Washington establishment disdained Nixon and Agnew. Nixon and Agnew felt the disdain and reciprocated the feelings. On November 20, 1969, before a standing room only crowd at the Jefferson Davis Hotel in Montgomery, Alabama, Agnew let loose with a broadside against the *New York Times* and the *Washington Post*. He claimed the two newspapers, along with *Newsweek* (owned by the Washington Post Company), carved out editorial stances that reflected a narrow view of the world, a vantage point that Agnew stressed was markedly different than the majority of Americans. After stressing his opposition to censorship, Agnew warned the audience of a creeping media monopoly. "The American people should be aware," Agnew declared, "of the trend toward monopolization of the great vehicles and the concentration of power over public opinion in fewer and fewer hands."[84]

Agnew cited examples of how that concentrated power harmed the public interest: "When 300 Congressmen and 59 Senators signed a letter endorsing the President's policy in Vietnam it was news—it was big news. Even the *Washington Post* and the *Baltimore Sun*—scarcely house organs of the Nixon administration—placed it prominently on their front page. Yet the next morning the *New York Times*, which considers itself America's paper of record, did not carry a word."[85]

Next Agnew critiqued the nation's youth, who burned their draft cards and "deserted to Canada and Sweden to sit out the war." But Agnew stressed he was not lumping all of America's younger generation together—a view he believed resulted because the newspapers had deliberately distorted his message. "How can you ask the man in the street in this country to stand up for what he believes if his own elected leaders weasel and cringe?" Agnew asked.

"It is not an easy thing to wake up each morning to learn that some prominent man or institution has implied that you are a bigot, a racist, or a fool?"[86]

Toward the end Agnew issued a declaration that sounded very much like a threat to the media: "The day when the network commentators and even the gentleman of the *New York Times* enjoyed a form of diplomatic immunity from comment and criticism of what they said is over. Yes gentleman that day is past."[87]

The *Post* and the *Times* were quick to defend their reporting. Arthur Ochs Sulzberger, the *Times*'s publisher and president, criticized Agnew for getting his facts wrong. "Vice President Agnew is entitled to express his point of view, but he is in error when he implies that The New York Times ever sought or enjoyed immunity from comment and criticism. … It would be wise, however," Sulzberger continued, "for those involving themselves in such a discussion to be certain of their facts. Some of Mr. Agnew's statements are inaccurate." Sulzberger noted that while his paper's Washington edition did not carry the letter of support from the senators and house members, its final edition did.[88] Katherine Graham also knocked Agnew for getting his facts wrong. The Washington Post Corporation, which owned *Newsweek*, several newspapers, and radio stations, did not, Graham contended, churn "out the same editorial line." In fact, "It is a longstanding policy of The Washington Post Company to enlist in each of its enterprises the best professional journalists we can find and to give them a maximum freedom in which to work."[89]

Overall, Nixon was pleased with Agnew's verbal volleys, but he expressed one note of disappointment with the November 20 speech. A day after the address, Haldeman sent a memo to Buchanan. "One other note the President had regarding the Vice President's speech last night," Haldeman wrote, "he (Agnew) didn't use the term 'Silent Majority' at any point in the speech. This phrase should be used at every possible opportunity and, obviously, there were some in the Vice President's speech last night."[90] Still, that was only a minor critique.

On November 24, Nixon sent Haldeman a memo laying out how questions about his own involvement should be addressed in the speeches.

> You might point out to (Communications Director Herb) Klein, (White House Press Secretary Ronald) Ziegler, (Deputy Assistant Lyn) Nofzinger et al if the question is raised with regard to the Vice President receiving assistance on his speeches that I covered that point when I made the announcement in Key Biscayne about the Vice President having an office in the White House and having the White House staff available to him. It is a good subtle way to answer the question without getting into the specific controversy as to whether the President approved the speeches. In other words, the Vice President *always* has the White House staff available to him for research and assistance on speeches subject to their first responsibility to prepare items for the President.[91]

Three days later the president received an update on Agnew—courtesy of his daily news summary. All the attacks, according to Buchanan and Allin, had boosted Agnew's political status. "As the *New York Times* admits," the summary reported, "the Vice President has become a 'formidable political asset' to the Administration. Those who were laughing three weeks ago are now writing columns about the danger of 'Agnewism' and 'Agnewsticism' to the American body politic." Within a brief period, "he has become the acknowledged spokesman of the Middle American, the Robespierre of the Great Silent Majority. The magazines which ripped him in pieces several weeks ago now write with concern and alarm over recent developments."[92]

Nixon, Buchanan, and Allin welcomed the angst felt among the papers and magazines. Agnew's broadsides had clearly rattled the establishment media, who, as the summary correctly pointed out, could no longer summarily dismiss Agnew. Still, Buchanan and Allin had some concerns: "First, there is no squaring of the Vice Presidential speeches with the 'lowering of voices,' the President called for. Second, should the Vice President continue solely on the attack, he risks being classified as wholly non-constructive—and a hatchet man." "I agree," Nixon wrote on the margins. "Third," the summary read, "there is a general mood among the responsible middle that the time has come to 'wind down the rhetoric.' " Nixon apparently conceded the point, underlining most of the sentence. The report continued:

> A temporary armistice on this issue is more in our interest now than theirs (the media.) The reason would simply be that we have discovered an issue on which we can rally a majority of the country and the South—why waste it now piling up our poll results. The Vice President, in our view, should move on to other issues, where he can be strong and positive.[93]

"Right," Nixon wrote. And so ended the attacks on the Fourth Estate—for the time being; the controversy temporarily raised Agnew's standing with his boss. Pleased with the speeches and the ensuing political lift, Nixon recognized that his vice president could be an asset. A report by Gordfrey Sperling in the *Christian Science Monitor* that a "source close to RN said that the VP had not helped with RN's opposition," duly noted in the Daily News Summary, elicited a sharp rebuke from the president. "H (Haldeman)—who in Hell on staff puts this out?" an angry Nixon asked.[94] In fact, Agnew's popularity increased. A poll taken in late November showed that Agnew's approval rating was at 64 percent. On the side of the News Summary, Nixon scribbled "good job!"[95]

Many conservatives agreed with Nixon's assessment. Agnew's speeches increased his profile, demonstrated that he could give as good as he got, and boosted his standing among conservatives. Agnew articulated what many Republicans believed and he initiated a debate about the role of the networks and the monopoly in the media and concentrations of power. The attacks were not that of a demagogue trying to stifle administration critics or destroy the First Amendment. While the rhetoric may have been a bit overheated, Agnew's concerns were not, at least among many Americans.

The issue of media bias still resonates today, especially among conservatives who believe the mainstream media continue to lean left. Many conservatives argue Rush Limbaugh and Fox News are so popular because they offer a different ideological viewpoint from the "mainstream media." How much merit there is to the charge of a liberal bias is debatable. But part of Spiro Agnew's legacy is that he gave a voice to those on the Right who were suspicious of the networks, the major newsweeklies, and the leading newspapers. His legacy continues long after he left office.

Chapter 6

"Nattering Nabobs of Negativism": Agnew and the Politics of Division

When Richard Nixon took office in January 1969, over 500,000 Americans were serving in Vietnam. Hoping to wind down the war but maintain the viability of South Vietnam, Nixon created a policy he called "Vietnamization." Under this plan, the United States would furnish the South Vietnamese with the weapons to fight the war, but it would be the South Vietnamese doing the fighting, not the American military. The spring of 1970 was a crucial time for the administration's Vietnamization plans. Negotiations with the North Vietnamese yielded no results. By April 1970 the administration had scaled down America's troop levels, yet the South Vietnamese army was faring poorly in its efforts to combat the Viet Cong. Then, in March 1970, a mini crisis erupted in neighboring Cambodia when General Lon Nol overthrew Cambodia's head of state, Prince Sihanouk.

Caught entirely by surprise, Nixon initially wanted to provide support for the anti-communist Lon Nol, but backed away on the advice of Secretary of State William Rogers and Defense Secretary Bill Laird. Taking advantage of the disorder in Cambodia, the Viet Cong and North Vietnamese had captured nearly a third of Cambodia's territory and, by April 1970, were on the verge of overtaking the capital city of Phnom Penh. The infiltration violated Cambodian neutrality and also threatened South Vietnamese survival. Both Nixon and Henry Kissinger believed the United States needed to intervene. At an April 22 national security meeting, Nixon proposed an attack on two communist sanctuaries in Cambodia. The proposal split the council, with Rogers and Laird urging restraint. After Rogers and Laird made their case, an angry Agnew interjected. The session invariably frustrated him. He usually sat silently throughout the meetings, ever since Haldeman told him to keep his mouth shut. That forced Agnew to sit and listen as Rogers and Laird offered their dovish advice. Agnew mocked the pair in his memoirs, claiming that every time Nixon advocated firm action against communists, Rogers and Laird piped in with the same refrain: "Oh, you can't do that Mr. President, the Russians would misunderstand it. We would be risking nuclear war."[1]

But this time Agnew was not going to let Rodgers and Lair have their way. According to Kissinger, Agnew thought the whole debate unnecessary. If the sanctuaries were a threat, he argued, take them both out. Kissinger concurred. "Agnew was right," Kissinger later stated.[2] Regardless of the merits of Agnew's argument, the advice might well have swayed Nixon, who authorized an attack on the Parrot's Beak sanctuary. At the same time Agnew's conduct infuriated Nixon. After the National Security Council meeting, Nixon conferred with Kissinger and proceeded to berate Kissinger for not warning him of Agnew's views. In his memoirs, Kissinger pleaded ignorance; but he never mentioned that, a day earlier, he briefed Agnew and asked the vice president to "work on the hawks."[3]

Soon after the meeting, American and South Vietnamese troops amassed upon the Cambodian border. For the next week, Nixon crafted the plans, and on April 30, 1970, he went on national television to announce them. During the Oval Office address, Nixon pointed to a map of Cambodia showing the country where the military operations would take place. Most of the speech was measured, but near the conclusion Nixon issued an apocryphal warning. "If, when the chips are down, the world's most powerful nation, the United States of America" he intoned, "acts like a pitiful, helpless giant, the forces of totalitarianism and anarchy will threaten free nations and free institutions throughout the world."[4]

After Nixon discussed the plans with his cabinet, a "proud" Agnew stopped the president in a corridor and praised Nixon's decision. After leaving the White House Agnew became a fierce critic of Richard Nixon; but a decade after the incursion, Agnew remained steadfast in his support of the action—a move he viewed as necessary and just. He attacked critics who charged that Nixon had violated international law: "The American incursion was to prevent attacks by the Communists from protected Cambodian bases, but the celebrity-led left-wingers in the United States labeled it an 'invasion' of a helpless country and another exhibition of American 'imperialism.' "[5]

American and South Vietnamese troops entered Cambodia on May 1. Early that morning Nixon visited the Pentagon for a briefing by the Joint Chiefs of Staff. The early reports indicated success; the Viet Cong offered little resistance and the sanctuaries were hit hard. As Nixon left the room, Pentagon employees rushed to greet him. They cheered enthusiastically as he walked through the halls. Before leaving Nixon paused to shake the hand of a woman whose husband was in Vietnam. The greeting moved Nixon, and as he thought of the soldiers fighting in Southeast Asia, he told the crowd, "I have seen them. They're the greatest. You see these bums, you know, blowing up the campuses. . . . here they are burning up books. . . . Then out there, we have kids who are just doing their duty. And I have seen them. They stand tall, and they are proud."[6]

The media quickly but inaccurately reported that Nixon called all antiwar protestors "bums." During the month of April 1970, radicals set fires to several campus buildings in Kansas, Connecticut, and California. The fires caused millions of dollars in damage, and one visiting foreign scholar at Stanford University had his entire scholarly files destroyed. Bums was not a harsh enough condemnation; to many Americans, these perpetrators of violence were just criminals.[7]

Nixon's critics ignored the distinction and charged him with being cruel and callous. Similar charges had recently been leveled at Agnew. In mid-April, 1970, Agnew called for the dismissal of Yale University president Kingman Brewster after Brewster stated that the Black Panthers could not receive a fair trial in the United States. Agnew disagreed. Dating back to Cambridge and H. Rap Brown in 1967, the Black Panthers were an obsession of Agnew's. Six months into the vice presidency he mailed a letter to members of Congress and newspapers about the dangers of the Black Panther movement. "There has been a great amount of publicity recently about the eleemosynary activities of a completely irresponsible, anarchistic group of criminals, the Black Panther Society," Agnew wrote. "Don't believe the hype," he warned: "Unfortunately, what is served at these breakfasts is more than food. I am enclosing a copy of the Black Panther Coloring Book." The "inflammatory propaganda," Agnew thought, was so dangerous that he needed help "waging war" on the Black Panthers.[8]

Nixon thought Agnew's attack on Brewster was over the top. He told John Ehrlichman that the "Brewster speech was a mistake," and that Agnew should "stay more on prin."[9] When Nixon took office he told the nation, "We cannot learn from another until we stop shouting at one another." However, by May 1970, the country was as divided as it had been in January 1969, and a lot of Americans blamed Nixon and Agnew. Appearing on CBS's "Face the Nation," on Sunday, May 3, Agnew was asked if he bore responsibility for exacerbating tensions. No, he replied: "When a fire takes place, a man doesn't run into the room and whisper, 'Would somebody please get the water?'; he yells, 'Fire!' and I am yelling, 'Fire!' because I think 'Fire' needs to be called here."[10]

The next day fire indeed broke out at Kent State University in Ohio. For three days students at the college demonstrated against the incursion. Governor James Rhodes sent out the National Guard in order to prevent any violence. On Monday, May 4, some of the protestors hurled rocks and stones at the Guardsmen. The Guardsmen panicked and fired into the crowd, killing four and wounding seven. The incident called for sympathy and restraint, but Agnew showed little of either. Just a little while after Kent State, Agnew delivered a prepared address attacking those who committed "philosophical violence." Given that four young men and women had been gunned down, Agnew might have demonstrated more sensitivity by striking the references to violence, but he persisted in delivering the original remarks. The shootings, Agnew claimed, were "predictable."[11]

During a May 8 press conference Nixon tried to cool emotions by offering conciliatory words toward the anti-war movement. Agnew had planned on taking a different approach. He was scheduled to give a speech in Boise, Idaho, that night. The words were harsh even by Agnew's standards.[12] After viewing Nixon's press conference, Agnew scrapped the text in favor of a more subdued speech. Agnew denied that Nixon "muzzled" him; instead, he said his more restrained rhetoric represented part of the administration's effort to calm the political waters.[13]

In fact, Nixon did temporarily silence Agnew. For two straight days Nixon told Haldeman that he wanted Agnew to "stop saying anything about students."[14] Over the next few weeks Agnew kept a low profile. A few weeks after Kent State, Pat Buchanan proposed a new Agnew speech, one that would slam prominent Democratic critics of the Cambodian incursion. Haldeman, acting at Nixon's command, told Agnew the speech was off. "P feels this is not the right time for it," Haldeman noted.[15] Yet less than a week later Nixon changed his mind. The day after Nixon's televised press conference, which Nixon followed with a bizarre early morning trek to the capitol's Mall, where he met with student protestors, he made three lengthy tape recordings. At the end of the second tape Nixon instructed Haldeman:

> Another item I would like for you to follow through on ... is with regard to Agnew. I believe that the next Agnew attack—one that would come with great responsibility and could have enormous effect—would be one on the three turncoats, (Clark) Clifford, (Averill) Harriman and (Cyrus) Vance, or call them the three Monday-morning quarterbacks or what have you.[16]

Nixon had a long and bitter history with Averill Harriman. Nixon's first confrontation with the Democratic scion came soon after his 1950 senatorial victory over Helen Gahagan Douglas. That campaign was marked by heavy mudslinging on both sides, with Nixon infamously saying that Douglas was "pink right down to her underwear." Alleging Douglas was soft on communism helped propel Nixon to the Senate but earned him the undying enmity of millions, including Harriman. At a dinner party in Washington DC, Harriman spotted Nixon. "I will not break bread with that man!" Harriman loudly announced as he walked out.[17] Nixon exacted some revenge via Agnew nineteen years later. On the night of Nixon's 1969 "Silent Majority Speech," CBS invited Harriman on as a commentator. During the Johnson administration Harriman served as a negotiator in the Vietnam peace talks. When asked about Nixon's speech Harriman offered some mild criticism, but Agnew reacted as if Harriman's comments provided aid and comfort to the enemy. In his Des Moines address, he offered a harsh rejoinder:

> A word about Mr. Harriman. For ten years he was America's chief negotiator at the Paris peace talks—a period in which the United States swapped some of the greatest military concessions in the history of warfare for an enemy agreement in the shape of a bargaining table. Like Coleridge's Ancient Mariner,

> Mr. Harriman seems to be under some heavy compulsion to justify his failures to anyone who will listen.[18]

However much Nixon and Agnew would have liked to slam Harriman, the attack went undelivered. Perhaps Nixon relied on his first instinct to quiet Agnew. Still, Agnew was not one to remain silent for long. "So long as I am Vice President," Agnew told a former law school classmate, "I must speak out against the policies which I consider to be emasculating."[19]

While Nixon might have worried about Agnew's rhetoric, and while liberals feared and despised both the man and the message, Agnew's popularity with his party continued to grow. "Agnew May Be the Hottest Fund Raiser in GOP History," gushed the Republican National Committee's March 16, 1970, newsletter.[20] The newsletter noted Agnew's frequent travels on behalf of the GOP (already 25,000 miles in the first three months of 1970), his prodigious fund-raising abilities (Agnew helped raise over $1 million at a Minnesota event), and the enormous number of requests the vice president received on a weekly basis. Partisans loved Agnew's righteousness and combativeness. There were no sacred cows with Agnew and he enthusiastically attacked Democrats, liberals, protestors, and other Republican banes. Georgia State Republican chairman Wiley Wadsen said of Agnew: "I thought he was great. People really liked him and what he had to say. He's a very striking speaker and people down here like his outspokenness and strength."[21] Following a Lincoln Day dinner in Chicago, where Agnew denounced racial quotas and delivered a scathing critique of the nation's universities, Illinois State chair Victor Smith told the press that the speech was one that Republicans wanted to hear, "a real wowser."[22]

Agnew did more than just launch verbal volleys at the opposition. He also defended Nixon's administration policies, although without the same gusto as when slashing Nixon's opponents. When he became vice president, Agnew hoped for a substantive role. Since that never happened, Agnew made the best of his situation. While he liked to speak of himself as the spokesman for Middle America, Agnew also could not have been unaware of the effect his speeches had on the rank and file of the Republican Party. His popularity with the party soared, and his willingness to campaign for GOP candidates added to his appeal. Although Agnew never mentioned if he harbored presidential ambitions, his efforts on behalf of the party were earning him the gratitude of those who would decide Nixon's successor. As president, Nixon largely avoided heavy campaigning—a void that Agnew filled. With the 1970 off-year elections approaching, Agnew had more opportunities to burnish his partisan credentials. He jumped eagerly at the chance.

As the 1970 off-year elections approached, the Nixon White House had high hopes for Republican gains in the House and in the Senate. The White House harbored no illusions, however, of capturing both houses. Realizing that the Democrats had a solid majority in the Senate and an insurmountable hold of the House, Nixon wanted a working majority in Congress. Frustrated that Senate Democrats and liberal Republican senators had blocked two of his Supreme Court nominees, and angry over having to fight tooth-and-nail for major legislative goals, Nixon hoped to craft an alliance of conservative Southern Democrats with sufficient numbers of Republicans to realign the balance in Congress; the president told staffers "we are not out for a Republican Senate." Instead he aimed for a "New Majority. Nixon viewed the elections as a crucial test for his presidency, one that he was determined to pass."[23]

Yet Nixon would not be front and center in 1970. Taking a page from Dwight Eisenhower, Nixon delegated the political chores to his vice president. "I had decided not to do any active campaigning in 1970. I felt confident that I would not be needed because in Ted Agnew we had the perfect spokesman to reach the silent majority on the Social Issues," Nixon wrote.[24] In 1954 Dwight Eisenhower, who liked to think himself above politics, made Nixon the de facto Republican spokesman, a role Nixon relished. Throughout the campaign Nixon attacked Democratic candidates as much as he defended Republican ones. Toward the end of the race Eisenhower finally joined Nixon on the trail, traveling over 10,000 miles in support of GOP candidates. Despite their best efforts, the results disappointed Eisenhower and Nixon as the Democrats won back both the House and the Senate.[25]

Over the next fourteen years the Democrats augmented their control of both wings of Congress. When Nixon took office in 1969 the Democrats had 57 senators to the GOP's 43. The numbers in the House stood at 243–192. The Democrats retained their majorities in the country's urban areas, as well as the South. But over the previous decade the GOP made inroads in Dixie, especially in many of the border-states. In 1970 the Republicans targeted Senate contests in Maryland, Tennessee, Kentucky, Texas, and Florida. Two years earlier Agnew campaigned heavily in those states, and his influence, the White House hoped, would help make the difference in the 1970 contests.

Agnew was especially interested in his home state. Voters in Maryland would elect a permanent gubernatorial successor, as well as fill an open Senate seat. After Agnew resigned the governorship in 1969, the Maryland legislature selected House of Delegates speaker Marvin Mandel to fill the vacancy. A Democrat, Mandel was an extraordinarily able politico, but many Republicans thought him potentially vulnerable. Still, with registered Democrats heavily outnumbering Republicans, the GOP needed a strong candidate. Agnew believed he knew such a man—his chief of staff C. Stanley Blair. Respected in Maryland as an able, smart, and honest man, Blair had the credentials to match Mandel. Blair had served in the Maryland House of Delegates from 1963 to 1967, and in 1967 Agnew appointed Blair as Maryland's secretary of state. Although Blair was an excellent administrator whom Agnew leaned heavily on (and perhaps the one Agnew aide whom the Nixon high command respected), Agnew advised and helped persuade Blair to enter the gubernatorial contest. With name recognition and the backing of Agnew, Blair became the presumptive front-runner for the GOP nomination.[26]

Blair resigned on May 31, 1970. Art Sohmer, who served as Agnew's chief of staff in Annapolis, took over the position. Blair's departure was the second significant departure in 1970. Earlier that year chief speechwriter Cynthia Rosenwald, unhappy that Agnew increasingly relied upon other writers, left the vice president's staff in February.[27] Agnew replaced Rosenwald with Herb Thompson, who previously served as the vice president's press secretary. The position of press secretary frustrated Thompson, a former journalist, who found the antagonistic relationship between his boss and the media too much to bear, and he happily accepted a new post.[28] Agnew also added several new staff members. John Damgard, a young advance assistant from the 1968 campaign, came aboard as Agnew's scheduler. Agnew hired David Keene as an executive assistant.[29] Keene, a passionate conservative, was to play a substantive role in the off-year elections, as were other right-wingers, such as Pat Buchanan. The choices show Agnew's evolving ideological views. As time went on he sought out the advice of conservative intellectuals and ideologues, a clear indication of his emerging conservatism. Since many of them distrusted Nixon, and were aghast at many of his domestic policies, they naturally sought out Agnew.[30]

During the summer, Nixon and his aides solidified their campaign plans. Given Agnew's popularity with the rank-and-file GOP, his fund-raising abilities, and his unique talent at garnering headlines, it was no surprise that he figured prominently in their plans. At the same time, the opposition also intended to use Agnew as a campaign weapon. The president's daily news summary from August 1970 included this item: "(The) Democrats are planning to make a campaign issue of the words and views of VP Agnew this fall . . . Gov. Dempsey said the Democratic campaign plan amounts to making Agnew the issue in some states." Nixon welcomed the idea, writing, "great! *for us*" on the margins.[31]

Nixon had great expectations for the fall campaign. On September 8, Nixon summoned Haldeman, Bryce Harlow, Pat Buchanan, William Safire, White House counselor Donald Rumsfeld, a former member of the House of Representatives and his long-time political advisor Murray Choitner to the Oval Office for a political planning session. Agnew was not invited. The snub might well have had to do with an item Nixon read in the September 7 Daily News Summary. The report included a story by Carl Leubsdorf of the Associated Press, which detailed a rift between the president and the vice president. According to Leubsdorf, some of Nixon's aides were upset over Agnew's popularity, while Agnew was chafing over some assignments that Nixon delegated to him.[32] During the meeting Nixon offered advice and a host of quips for Agnew, "all the stuff he'd like to say but can't," Haldeman noted. Nixon wanted a forceful aggressive campaign, one tarring administration's critics as "left-wing radical liberals."[33] Tagging their opponents was a primary goal of the White House campaign. Nixon, like many politicians and politicos, had read Richard Scammon and Ben Wattenberg's treatise, *The Real Majority*. The two authors, both Democrats, argued that cultural and social issues were increasingly eclipsing economic concerns as the primary factor in voting. For either party to win a real majority, they argued, it needed to address their concerns, such as crime, drugs, and permissiveness. If the Republicans could co-opt the Democrats on the social issues, Nixon believed, they could make huge strides in winning over white, middle and lower-middle-class voters.[34]

Nixon saw an opening and intended to take it, with Agnew as the instrument. Throughout the meeting Nixon peppered his aides with advice on how to handle Agnew, advice that demonstrated Nixon's ambivalence toward his vice president. "There's a realignment going on," Nixon proclaimed, and "Agnew can be a realigner."[35] At the same time, Nixon warned his staff about Agnew's shortcomings, principally, Agnew's supposed laziness. "Now, about Agnew himself. Not many people have the energy for the kind of grueling campaign you remember in '68. Don't work him too hard. Give him a chance to look and feel good."[36]

The meeting finalized both tactics and strategy. The strategy was to have Agnew handle the bulk of campaigning until mid-October when Nixon hit the trail. Although Nixon cautioned his aides not to overextend Agnew, Republicans across the country were eager for his services given Nixon's unavailability. Two months earlier Murray Chotiner, Nixon's earliest campaign advisor, prepared a memo listing the states where Republicans asked for an Agnew appearance. Chotiner spoke directly with senators and House members, such as California's George Murphy, who was up for reelection; Connecticut's Lowell Weicker, who was running for an open Senate seat; and John Erickson, who was challenging Wisconsin incumbent William Proxmire—all of whom wanted Agnew in their states.[37] At the September 8 meeting, Bryce Harlow surprised and pleased Nixon with the news that Nelson Rockefeller wanted Agnew's help in upstate New York.[38] However, not all Republicans were as enthusiastic about Agnew. Senator Robert Taft pointedly asked that Agnew not visit Ohio. Nixon had Harlow call Taft, letting him know Nixon did not care for the statement, but Taft hung up on Harlow.[39]

The 1970 off-year elections were memorable, not so much for the outcome, but for the harsh rhetoric, violent protests, and mostly because the elections witnessed the themes that soon became Republican staples. Nixon decided that he and his surrogates were going to present themselves as guardians of law and order, public virtue, the military, and patriotism, while painting the opposition as soft on crime, weak on defense, and enablers of radicals. Nixon stayed mostly silent on economic issues because both the inflation and unemployment rates had risen since January 1969.[40] Nixon was criticized (and still is) for campaigning on "wedge" issues that divided the public and cast aspersions on liberals. But he was also addressing legitimate concerns. The 1960s was a decade of almost unprecedented levels of violence, in urban areas and on the nation's campuses. Crime ranked as the number-one concern of Americans in 1970, and Nixon's championing of law and order, while later exposed as hypocritical, was a response to Americans' genuine fear over lawlessness. Nixon also had a duty as commander-in-chief to defend the military in the face of cries by anti-war protestors of "baby killers" leveled against returning GIs. Many Americans were frightened over the proliferating drug culture and disgusted by the increasing permissiveness of American culture, and Nixon tackled both those issues. If he failed in his ultimate goal of bringing people together, the blame should rest on his tactics, not his aim of curbing violence, restoring pride in the armed forces, and attempting to halt the drug trade. In Agnew, Nixon had a kindred spirit for his crusade. Both men were squares. Both despised the hippies, the flag-burners, and the drug-pushers. Nixon and Agnew suffered through the Depression, fought in World War II, and rose to the pinnacle of their profession. They believed in the American Dream because they lived it. They were genuinely aghast at what they saw as an assault upon America, and they were determined to defend all that was good about their country.

So too were members of the Nixon staff. Agnew might have been *persona non grata* with the White House Palace Guard, but Bryce Harlow, Pat Buchanan, Bill Safire, and Martin Anderson willingly cast their lot with Agnew. Joined by Agnew aides Art Sohmer and John Damgard, the travelers began their crusade in high spirits. Recognizing a good story, many of the media's big guns requested spots on the vice president's plane, including such luminaries as Stewart Alsop and Robert Novak.[41] In a rare instance of Agnew helping the Fourth Estate, his campaign mischievously announced that it was carrying along an unabridged dictionary that would add some color to their stories.[42] The campaign kicked off in Springfield, Illinois, on September 10. Speaking on behalf of Republican senatorial candidate Ralph Smith, Agnew delivered a fiery address that foreshadowed the rhetoric characterizing the 1970 elections. Agnew began by tearing into the nation's "elite":

> Here in Illinois, and across America this fall, there is occurring a second critical phase in the historic contest begun in the fall of 1968—a contest between the discredited elite that dominated national policy for forty years and a new national majority, forged and led by the President of the United States—a contest to shape the destiny of America.[43]

Moving on, Agnew denounced the "radical-liberal" elements of liberalism, the first of his many famous catch phrases of the campaign. In the next paragraph Agnew let loose with another blast, the first of his many alliterations, a Pat Buchanan creation, one aimed at the "pusillanimous pussyfooting" of the ultraliberals.[44] Turning to Vietnam, Agnew praised Nixon's efforts in bringing peace, reminding his audience of his recent visit to Saigon, and attacking the "caterwauling critics" of the administration's Vietnamization policies. Agnew also assailed the "troglodytic leftists who dominate Congress now." Those trolls, Agnew claimed, cared nothing for the "Forgotten Man of American politics," the blue- and white-collar workers whom the Left shafted over the years. He savaged the liberals for being soft on crime, lauded the police, and urged tougher measures against the spread of pornography. At the conclusion, Agnew blasted his favorite target—the media. "If any of you are regular readers of the Liberal Eastern press—the organ grinder of the old elite—you will probably read on your editorial pages tomorrow 'That terrible Mr. Agnew has done it again.'" No matter, Agnew said, "Let them run right up the wall. We are going to be out with the other 'happy warriors' on the campaign trail this fall—roasting marshmallows along the way."[45]

So began Spiro Agnew's "Happy Warrior" campaign. For nearly two months Agnew garnered national attention; thrilled conservative audiences; angered liberals, including liberal Republicans; and added lasting phrases to the country's political lexicon. Agnew loved every minute of it. Initially, the White House was elated with Agnew's performance. The speech made headlines and led off the networks' nightly newscasts, and for once, the media's coverage pleased the administration's news watchers. The President's Daily News Summary included these plaudits: "ABC had an *excellent* two minute report opening with footage of cheering crowds"; "A top drawer report" from the AP's Steve Geer, who wrote, "'if the truth be told' never has there been as 'effective campaigner as the man whose name is now a household word' "; and a "favorable" story from CBS's Bruce Morton.[46]

The response from most Republicans was equally favorable. "All I have to do is mention Agnew's name and the crowd goes wild," Ralph Smith happily noted.[47] But those on the receiving end of Agnew's barbs were less than thrilled. Democratic National Committee chair Lawrence O'Brien got in a dig of his own. Playing upon Agnew's troglodyte remark, O'Brien countered that Agnew was a caveman, and that since the administration had no housing policy, "we'll all be living in caves."[48]

After a visit to Casper, Wyoming, the next stop was in San Diego, California, where Agnew made an appearance for incumbent senator George Murphy, a former movie actor, elected to the Senate in 1964. As much as any speech in Agnew's career, Agnew's address to the Republican State Convention captured the nation's attention and seared into millions an unforgettable alliteration. The talk began as nothing more than the usual run-of-the mill campaign stuff. After praising Governor Ronald Reagan and endorsing George Murphy, Agnew cut to the chase. His "target" for the night, he told the assembly, was "The Professional Pessimist." This man, Agnew intoned, "has been called the prophet of gloom and doom, the troubadour of trouble, the disciple of despair." Just

> a couple of years ago he was sitting pretty. He could point to the steadily climbing rise in the cost of living. He could point to high casualties in a war that had no end in sight. He could point to ever-increasing rates of crime, and a government that had lost confidence of the people.[49]

But times had changed and "the heyday of the professional pessimist is past." All the good news only made him look harder—"when he sees defense plants humming with activity, he denounces the military-industrial complex, and when he sees a defense plant close down as a war comes to an end, he blames the peacemakers for a rise in unemployment." Agnew had a name for them: "In the United States today we have more than our share of the nattering nabobs of negativism. They have formed their own 4-H Club—the 'Hopeless, Hysterical, Hypochondriacs of History.' "[50]

He continued: Their fears of an economic recession and an accompanying "inflation psychology" were unjustified as the economic indicators pointed upward. Agnew ridiculed the "Pew red-faced economists," who "staked their reputation on the need for price controls, ignoring the rationing, black markets and strangulation of free enterprise that would surely have followed." Next Agnew needled those hypochondriacs who predicted that the passage of the ABM system would doom arms negotiations between the United States and the Soviet Union: "Well, now we have an ABM. And largely because we do, the SALT talks have been moving forward. Do you hear any of the doomsayers standing up and saying, 'Well, I guess I was proven wrong about that.' Hardly." He then went on to taunt the pessimists for their inaccurate estimations about the effect of Vietnamization; in fact Agnew argued, "Vietnamization, to the anguish of the prophets of doom, is working and working well."

The crowd roared its approval after hearing one of the hardest-hitting, bombastic, and memorable speeches ever delivered by a vice president. Republicans loved what they heard, while many Democrats predictably reacted with disgust at Agnew's words. Still, Democrats recognized the power of the Agnew effect. Even Agnew's true nemesis—the media—took to Agnew, if only because the press could not resist a great story. "Agnew has the press shilling for him," one congressman told *Newsweek*. "When you can do that, you're really on to something."[51] The alliterations sent reporters "scurrying for their dictionaries."[52] Agnew's long love of big words, coupled with his speechwriters' talents at coining phrases, made for sound bites, but not especially transparent ones. Newspapers and weeklies provided translations for their readers.[53] The dictionaries were needed, as Agnew was just getting started with his colorful phrases.

A day after his San Diego speech, Agnew held an impromptu news conference. The first two questions concerned the highjacking of an airplane in the Middle East and the possibility of a "peace offensive" in Vietnam. The reporters then interrogated Agnew over just what, and who, was a radical-liberal. One reporter wanted to know if Republican senator Charles Goodell of New York fit the definition. Agnew deflected the question but added, "I probably will make some judgments about that particular senator somewhere along the campaign trail."

When constituted a "radical-liberal?"

Agnew responded, "A radical liberal is a person, generally I'm referring to the legislative types and the people in Government, who seem to find a great necessity for applauding our enemies, castigating our friends, running down the process of American Government, attempting to overthrow tradition regardless of whether it's been proven effective and workable or not."

His own party, Agnew stated, was not "immune" from these radicals.

Was Senator "Al Gore" of Tennessee one?

Agnew was not ready to hazard an opinion, but added, "Maybe Mr. Gore's horses are radical-liberals."

"How many radical-liberals" were in the Senate?

There were "probably somewhere in the area of ten to fifteen," Agnew guessed.

"Is there anything that they can do between to now and election day" that could save them, a reporter inquired.

"Resign."

"Was that your hand in the nattering *nabobs of negativism*?"

"I've been known to natter occasionally."[54]

The session ended with a few more questions on Vietnam. Agnew spent the rest of the day at Bob Hope's estate in Palm Springs before getting back on the road. The first leg of the campaign tour ended in Michigan on September 16, when he finally named names. While at an airport hangar in Saginaw, touting Lenore Romney's (wife of George Romney, secretary, Housing and Urban Development) candidacy for the Senate, Agnew blasted her opponent, Senator Phillip Hart, as one of the Senate's "radic-libs." The event turned ugly, as a few hundred protestors shouted one of their favorite mantras, "One, two three, four, we don't want your fucking war." Never one to be daunted, Agnew shouted back, "You're pathetic." The confrontation shook Lenore Romney, who by that point was in tears. At the end of the rally, over the objections of the Secret Service, Agnew went and shook hands with supporters. All the while the demonstrators continued their screaming, with one young man yelling, "You could've killed me when I was in Vietnam."[55]

The episode might have garnered headlines, save that a bigger event took place the same day. While Agnew was in Michigan, Nixon was at Kansas State University to deliver the Alf Landon Memorial Lecture. The event attracted nationwide attendance—the networks all covered it live. The audience of some 15,000 at the university's basketball gymnasium was mostly friendly, but there were a few dozen protestors up in the rafters. During Nixon's speech, they chanted some anti-war slogans, temporarily interrupting the president. Ever the master at scoring political points, Nixon used the shouts to his advantage. "Destructive activists of our universities and colleges are a small minority, but their voices have been allowed to drown out," he said pausing momentarily, "my text at this point reads: 'The voices of the small minority have been allowed to drown out the responsible majority.' That may be true in some places, but not at Kansas State."[56]

The line prompted deafening applause. "Huge success," Haldeman wrote that night.[57] A week into the campaign, the White House believed that their strategy of pitting the Silent Majority against the Loud Minority was paying dividends. On September 24 Nixon gathered Agnew, Harlow, and Safire in the Oval Office for another political session. After Agnew gave his assessment of the Senate races, Nixon launched one of his interminable monologues. He urged Agnew to press on with the attacks, not to worry about assassination attempts—"if anybody is going to shoot you, he'll shoot you"—and to "blast the hell out the Scranton Commission Report."[58]

Until early October Agnew remained the political point man. From mid-September through early October, Nixon concentrated on foreign policy issues. In mid-September a small war erupted between Syria and Jordan, and surveillance photos indicated that the Soviets were building a nuclear submarine base in Cuba. For about ten days Nixon immersed himself in the flare-ups; then he departed on a nine-day trip abroad. Before leaving for Europe, Nixon believed "we actually had a chance to pull off an upset victory and pick up some seats."[59] By the time he returned the tide was turning—"we had peaked too early on the Social Issue"—Nixon claimed.[60] Over the next month Nixon campaigned heavily throughout the country. While still using social issues, Nixon invoked his Vietnam policies as his weapon, arguing that he was going to win the peace in Vietnam. At almost every stop anti-war protestors accosted him, usually shouting obscenities and accusing Nixon of being a war criminal. Toward the end of the campaign demonstrators pelted Nixon with eggs and rocks; the San Diego police thought it an "Act of God" that Nixon made it out alive.[61]

The violence was indicative of the extreme polarization of the American electorate, and it also demonstrated the depths to which the campaign fell. Both sides hurled invectives at each other, and the shrillness of the attacks only further divided the country. With the president on the campaign trail Agnew played second fiddle, but he nonetheless stayed in the headlines. He garnered the most publicity over his unremitting assaults on New York Republican senator Charles Goodell. Agnew's alliterations were mostly tongue-in-cheek, and his speeches, while at times over the top, were not demagogic; but when it came to Goodell, Agnew crossed the line. Agnew launched the "near-psychopathic crusade" as one magazine put it, in late September.[62] On September 30 Agnew said that Goodell's record—he had voted against Clement Haynsworth and Harrold Carswell for the Supreme Court, and voted for Hatfield-McGovern—disqualified him as a Republican, and that Goodell had become one of "those awful radical liberals."[63] A week later, Agnew was the featured speaker at a private dinner for conservative candidate James Buckley. According to those in attendance, Agnew essentially endorsed Buckley.[64] Ignoring pleas by New York Republicans, especially his old hero Nelson Rockefeller, Agnew pressed on. At a press conference in New Orleans Agnew compared Goodell to the first man in the United States to undergo successful sex change operation: "If you look at the statements Mr. Goodell made during his time in the House and compare them with some of the statements I have been referring to, you will find that he is truly the Christine Jorgensen of the Republican Party."[65]

The reference, a creation of Bill Safire's, concerned Goodell's political transformation from a conservative and somewhat hawkish representative to a mildly liberal but vocally dovish senator. Throughout it all Goodell showed considerable restraint, a good deal of class, and a great sense of humor. In the days following Agnew's endorsement of Buckley, Goodell sported a Spiro Agnew wristwatch, a popular kitsch item of the day. After the Jorgensen quip, Goodell smiled and asked, "What next from the Vice President, who knows?"[66] He never responded in kind to the *ad hominem* attacks; instead the senator challenged the vice president to a debate. Agnew demurred.[67]

Although Rockefeller asked Nixon's help in silencing Agnew, Nixon simply shied away from the conflict. Since he wanted a more ideologically intune Senate instead of a Republican Senate, his silence implied consent. One area that Nixon encouraged Agnew's outspokenness concerned the President's Commission on Campus Unrest. Chaired by former Republican governor William Scranton, Nixon established the committee after Kent State and almost immediately regretted it. Agnew had already criticized one member of the committee, and given his response to the Kerner Commission Report (that blamed urban disorders on racism, a charge Agnew vociferously condemned). The Scranton committee issued its report in October 1970 and the members concluded that the National Guard was mostly responsible for the violence at Kent State. Agnew publicly led the charge against its findings. Egged on by Nixon, though it is doubtful that he needed much goading, Agnew dismissed the conclusions as "Pablum for the Permissivists."[68]

On October 16, a grand jury investigating the shootings at Kent State handed down indictments. The grand jury indicted twenty-five students for disrupting the peace but issued no indictments for the National Guardsmen. The findings pleased the White House, but that was about the only good piece of news for the administration. Toward the end of the campaign the White House realized that its goal of winning seats in the House and changing the ideological dynamics of the Senate was dissipating. Never one to quit, Nixon redoubled his efforts, as did Agnew. Speaking somewhat tongue-in-cheek, Agnew announced, "No more Mr. Nice Guy. . . . I will try to switch off my low-key approach and start calling a spade a spade. It's time to take the gloves off."[69] The president and the vice president toured the country, hitting the Democrats and liberals even harder than before, but with varying degrees of success. On the weekend before the election, CBS News ran a special on the election. According to Bruce Morton, who traveled with Agnew throughout the fall, the vice president's "negative, hostile, and divisive" probably backfired, attracting Republican support but alienating many others.[70]

Election day fell on November 3. Agnew voted in Towson, and then watched the results from his apartment suite. The results were, at best, mixed. In Maryland incumbent governor Marvin Mandel easily defeated Agnew's former chief of staff Stanley Blair. On a brighter note Glenn Beall narrowly bested Joseph Tydings for a Maryland Senate seat. Perhaps the best news Agnew received all night was from New York, where Conservative

James L. Buckley held a narrow lead over Charles Goodell. But the White House goal of fundamentally altering the balance of the Senate fell short. The GOP picked up a total of just two seats. The Democrats had fifty-five seats, the Republicans forty-three, with two independents, Buckley and Harry Byrd of Virginia. In the House the Democrats gained nine seats, far less than the average for an opposition party in an off-year contest, but still an addition to their solid majority. The Republicans suffered a net loss of eleven governorships. Overall the GOP fared marginally well. However, given the intense, almost unprecedented campaigning by Nixon and Agnew, the outcome was disappointing.

Nixon later wrote, "It was particularly gratifying to me that some extreme liberals were among those senators retired by the voters."[71] They included Goodell, Tydings, and Albert Gore of Tennessee. Agnew targeted the trio as "radical-liberals" and could take some satisfaction in their defeats. In a lengthy postelection memo to Haldeman, Nixon urged Agnew to "de-escalate the rhetoric without de-escalating the substance of his message."[72]

Publicly Nixon said little about Agnew's role in the campaign, a sharp turnaround an earlier strong vote of confidence. On the Sunday before the election Nixon met with Agnew and mentioned his delight with his performance. Nixon also promised there would be, "No second-guessing of the campaign."[73] That tune abruptly shifted, as Nixon engaged in weeks of second-guessing, and his praise of Agnew disappeared. The deafening silence irked Agnew, and the bitterness remained with him. A decade after the elections, he expressed his anger:

> The press said that we had poor results because I was so divisive and had alienated the people. At that point, the President should have said: "That's ridiculous—we lost less than is usually lost by the President's party in an off-year election, and certainly less than we would have if the Vice-President had not been out there fighting. "[74]

Nixon's reticence increased speculation that Agnew might be dumped in 1972. Throughout the fall reporters pressed Nixon about Agnew's future. Nixon defended his vice president as "one of the greatest campaigners of all history" but refused to issue an endorsement.[75] Agnew himself brought up the subject at a meeting on November 1. He inquired about the 1972 ticket. Nixon brushed the question aside, stating that he could not say anything yet about 1972. He assured Agnew that he was "delighted" with his campaigning, but only wanted that information put out "indirectly."[76] The president's November 5 Daily News Summary reported, "The political future of VP Agnew remains a question mark."[77] The authors of the News Summary, principally Pat Buchanan, found the news distressing. Later on Buchanan lauded Agnew's role in the campaign, "He carried out his assignments to the letter," and argued that the Republicans fared quite well *because* of Agnew's "out-spokenness."[78] A day after the election Buchanan prepared a memo for Nixon, "Media Coverage, Predominantly TV, During the Last 10 Days of Campaign."

> He (Agnew) got very negative treatment overall for the final two weeks. . . . In almost every commentary on the election itself, the networks either inferred or said the campaign was hostile, divisive, and bitter—and the Vice President was charged with being a prime offender in this regard.[79]

The results of the 1970 elections were mixed but the long-term ramifications were far more consequential. Beginning in 1970 the Republicans began to use social issues as weapons against the Democrats. The GOP would increasingly paint the Democrats as soft on crime, weak on defense, and panderers to minorities. The Republicans made gains among voters who had traditionally supported Democratic candidates. Nixon's strategy of tearing apart the former Franklin Roosevelt coalition began to bear fruit in 1970.

Agnew took part in the campaign and at least in 1970 was in the forefront of the attack. His former approach of moderation was jettisoned in favor of a muscular conservatism. He was veering right at a time when many in the country were expressing dissatisfaction with the liberalism of the 1960s. His attacks on liberals resonated with many, but none more so than the GOP's conservative flank. Although he infuriated millions with his white-hot rhetoric, he also won as many fans. By the end of 1970 he was a hero to the party's right-wing, even as they were increasingly exercising more power and influence.

Chapter 7

Survival and Vindication

Spiro Agnew entered the third year of his vice presidency with questions surrounding his future. Despite his high profile and his unparalleled fund-raising abilities, Agnew's political fortune remained uncertain. One man alone could have squashed all the speculation about Agnew, but that individual had grave reservations about the vice president. Richard Nixon had strained relationships with everyone, but few were more complex than his ties with Agnew. Never friends, the pair failed to develop a rapport. As time went on, philosophical differences between the two grew. Agnew blanched at many of Nixon's policies, particularly détente with the Soviets and the opening of diplomatic relations with China. Even though Nixon was aware of Agnew's misgivings, his unease with Agnew stemmed less from policy disputes than mere personal emotional issues. Nixon thought Agnew intellectually shallow; and parochial in his thinking. His initial enthusiasm for Agnew, expressed by Nixon's exclamation in 1968, "He's got it" (the "it" being that intrinsic quality some politicians possessed), immediately evaporated. Nothing Agnew did, or even said, fully redeemed him in Nixon's eyes. Nixon's ambivalence toward Agnew sparked the most talk about Agnew's role in 1972, and his silence throughout 1971 only heightened the speculation that Agnew might not be on the 1972 ticket. Nixon's reticence about Agnew partially stemmed from concerns about his own political fate. Whereas Agnew needed only Nixon's approval, Nixon needed the backing of the American public, and even his own political party. In early 1971 he could not count on much support from either group. During 1969 and 1970 Nixon's approval ratings remained fairly steady. By 1971, however, with the war in Vietnam not over and the unemployment rate rising, his approval ratings fell below 50 percent.[1] The results were not lost on the consummate politician of the era. His own survival was at stake. When Nixon told a national television office that he "rather be a one-term president" than quit and run in Vietnam, he was lying. More than ending the war in

Vietnam, or establishing better relations with communist nations, Nixon wanted to win reelection. If Agnew in anyway harmed Nixon's chances, he would easily and quickly cast him aside.[2]

The biggest single factor against dumping Agnew was his status among the party's conservative flank. By the early 1970s the conservatives were growing increasingly powerful inside the GOP, and increasingly dissatisfied with Nixon. They had never fully trusted Nixon and his domestic policies confirmed their fears. Nixon's support for tougher environmental legislation and calls for a guaranteed national income, expansion of Medicare, Medicaid, and Social Security benefits angered the Right.[3] A number of prominent conservatives hoped to deny Nixon the Republican nomination in 1972. Nixon worried he might be vulnerable to a potential challenger. Although Nixon never said so privately or publicly, his decision to keep Agnew as his running mate was very likely a calculated move to keep the right-wing of the GOP placated.

Part of the reason the conservatives loved Agnew was for the enemies he made—especially in the media. After his fire and brimstone attacks in the fall of 1969, Agnew shied away from direct assaults upon the press, but in the waning days of the 1970 campaign Agnew issued a warning that more volleys were on the way: "When the campaigning is done, I expect to say more about these Monday morning quarterbacks."[4] Agnew opened the second round of media attacks with a letter to the *New York Times*. Ever since the *Times* ran stories questioning his probity and fitness for the vice presidency, Agnew had waged an intermittent war against the paper's editorial page. Nothing raised Agnew's ire more than critical editorials and op-ed pieces from the Old Gray Lady—even when the editorials did not directly bear upon him. On February 3, 1971, the paper published a blistering letter from Agnew to the *Times*. A few weeks earlier CBS News commentator (and frequent Agnew critic) Eric Sevareid published a piece arguing Nixon should hold frequent news conferences to ensure that he was held accountable for his actions. Agnew challenged Sevareid to appear on CBS's "Face the Nation" and answer questions concerning Sevareid's political views.[5]

Later that month Sevareid's network ran an investigative story, "The Selling of the Pentagon." The documentary focused primarily on the Pentagon's public service campaigns. The piece showed clips from a "propaganda" film made by Congressman F. Edward Hebert (D-LA), Chair of the House Armed Services Committee for the Pentagon, children being shown weapons and industrialists watching war games. The network estimated that the military spent as much as $190 million a year in its public affair campaigns.[6]

The "disreputable program" as Agnew described it, caused a political uproar with Agnew leading the charge against the network's conclusions. He castigated the network for selective editing, impugned the motives of the network and forcefully defended the military—"thank God we had the Pentagon during a couple of crucial times in our history."[7] CBS denied the substance of Agnew's charges, but of course, that failed to deter Agnew from revisiting the documentary. At a press conference on March 19 Agnew accused CBS of refusing to air a rebuttal from the Pentagon, but according to the network, "The fact is that CBS has received no request from the Department of Defense or from anybody directly or indirectly representing the Department for time to rebut the broadcast."[8] The accusations and counter-accusations went back and forth for the next few weeks, with Agnew giving no inch.

He continued his verbal assault on the national media at a speech in Jackson, Mississippi, on May 18. During his speech Agnew revisited some major themes. Two years earlier in Jackson he thundered:

> For too long the South has been the punching bag for those who characterize themselves as intellectuals. Actually they are consistently demonstrating the antithesis of intelligence. Their reactions are visceral, not intellectual; and they seem to believe that truth is revealed rather than systematically proved.

Reiterating the theme, Agnew claimed that the "Southern Strategy" was no more than a figment of the Left's fertile but dangerous imagination: "It is a political phenomenon that is born in the suspicious minds of the liberal pundits and flung at an unsuspecting public via tons of newsprint and network rhetoric whenever a national administration attempts to treat the South on equal terms with other regions of this country." He went on to eviscerate the "Seaboard Media," for excusing violent protestors, lauding communist dictatorships, and being in bed with academia and the Democratic Party.[9]

Columnists Rowland Evans and Robert Novak reported that the "gripping fact" about Agnew's offensive is that it "came without direction from or even significant consultation with the White House."[10] By that time Agnew was essentially a free agent whose contract might not be renewed in 1972. Nixon had all but decided to rid himself of his Agnew problem, and the White House's silence about Agnew's media criticisms spoke volumes. No longer did Nixon ask his vice president to perform important political tasks. Recognizing that giving Agnew a platform as the administration's political point man raised Agnew's stature within the GOP ranks, Nixon simply stopped handing his vice president any substantial chores.

Nixon wanted another man on the ticket in 1972, and if he ever approached Agnew and asked him to step aside, Agnew most likely would have graciously complied. On any number of occasions Agnew stated that he would have gladly stepped aside if Nixon so desired. At a March 8 news conference, a reporter inquired about Agnew's candidacy in 1972. Agnew responded that he had not yet made up mind about it and he would certainly play the loyal soldier. "But I have said, in response to previous questions on this subject—and I mean this very sincerely—that I would have no misgivings about removing myself from the ticket if, in the mind of the President, he could find someone who could lend more strength to his candidacy."[11]

Nixon had found such a man. After the off-year elections, Nixon made major changes in his administration. Over the next several months Nixon forced out Secretary of the Interior Walter Hickel and Secretary of Agriculture

Clifford Hardin. Most importantly, Nixon replaced Treasury Secretary David Kennedy with John Connally. Kennedy's resignation was expected and came as no surprise but the appointment of Connally sent shockwaves around the political world. The LBJ protégé, former governor of Texas, and staunch Democrat (though a conservative one) seemed an unlikely choice for the Nixon cabinet. Apart from his partisan affiliation, Connally nearly denied Nixon the presidency in 1968. Many political observers attributed Hubert Humphrey's narrow victory in Texas to Connally's shrewd political skills. Finally, Connally had ties, albeit tragic ones, to John F. Kennedy. In Dallas, on November 22, 1963, Connally, along with his wife Nellie, rode in front seats of the presidential motorcade. One bullet struck Connally in the neck.

Despite their differences, and their pasts, Nixon and Connally quickly bonded. Almost every observer commented on the awe that Connally inspired in Nixon. "The boss is in love," Nixon's people said, somewhat laughingly.[12] Tall, athletic, and handsome, Connally exuded confidence and charm. Nixon began thinking of Connally as his successor and replacing Agnew with Connally in 1972. On April 7, 1971, during one of his long, rambling talks with Haldeman, Nixon even raised the possibility of Agnew resigning and replacing him with Connally.[13] For his part Connally wanted the vice presidency but was shrewd enough not to campaign openly for the job. Agnew was by no means unaware of Nixon's infatuation with the Texas Democrat (Connally did not become a Republican until April 1973). But Agnew treated Connally cordially. Shortly after Connally came on board Agnew hosted a dinner party for Connally and the rest of the cabinet.[14] The two men never became friends but they mutually respected each other. Even after he left the vice presidency Agnew spoke highly of Connally. "I think he's a very capable, energetic man, a spellbinder as a speaker. He has great ability to project himself; he has charisma."[15]

There was a direct correlation between Connally's rise in power and Agnew's fall: "I noticed that he (Nixon) became more remote towards me as his attachment to Connally grew."[16] Agnew was correct, as a Haldeman diary entry shows. In a meeting with Haldeman on July 20, 1971, Nixon raised his Agnew problem and conjured up a solution—Agnew's resignation. Musing about his own mortality, Nixon speculated that he might die in office, which raised "the question of whether Agnew is somebody that we're willing to see become P." Nixon thought not, and launched into a diatribe about all of the man's shortcomings: "he's dogmatic, (has) his hidebound prejudices, (is) totally inflexible, and that he sees things in miniscule terms." After stating Agnew's shortcomings, Nixon and Haldeman "talked about what to do to get him out." The only solution, Nixon averred, was to have Agnew quit, and "the sooner he resigns, the better."[17]

The media picked up on the intrigue in the White House and ran stories on the strange possibility of a Democrat being on the Republican ticket in 1972. The rumors grew louder as the year went on and Agnew constantly had to address questions about the succession crisis. In August 1971, on ABC's "Issues and Answers," Howard K. Smith, the show's host, pressed

Agnew about his fate. Agnew insisted that he had not made his plans for 1972, and pleaded ignorance as to Nixon's thinking. Smith asked about the alleged feud between the vice president and the secretary of the Treasury. Agnew quickly disclaimed any rivalry, "he is one of the most capable cabinet people I have ever known," and as for being replaced by Connally, Agnew expressed no alarm, "Realistically I think many things would have to happen before I would become concerned about the possibility of a person of the other party receiving the nomination for vice president in my party."[18]

During the interview Agnew dissembled a bit. Queried about a recent *Time* magazine story that relations between him and Nixon were "chillier," Agnew replied, "That is entirely false. My relations with the President have remained consistent and entirely benign."[19] Consistent yes; benign no. The distance between the two men widened after the midterm elections, and since Nixon and Agnew were already estranged, this separation all but isolated Agnew inside the White House. Nevertheless, Agnew retained a staunch following in his own party. Republicans continued to flood the vice president's office with speaking requests. Despite his war with the major news outlets, the media continued to cover his speeches and report on his activities. If his stature within the Nixon administration fell, his public image, at least among his ardent backers, remained high.

Yet Agnew remained an outsider in the administration; Agnew was not aware that Nixon had reached out to the Chinese about establishing diplomatic relations. After two years of contacts, the Chinese government sent word that it would accept a presidential envoy. Nixon picked Henry Kissinger for the mission, but kept word of it secret:

> I felt that in order for the initiative to have any chance of succeeding, it would have to be kept totally secret until the final arrangements for the presidential visit had been agreed upon. With advance warning conservative opposition might mobilize in Congress and scuttle the entire effort.[20]

Kissinger traveled to China in early July 1971 and laid the groundwork for a presidential visit. After his return, Nixon went on national television and announced that he would be traveling to China in 1972. The announcement stunned the nation, pleasing Nixon's enemies in the liberal establishment, and irking conservatives. Fittingly, Agnew was out of the country at the time. Shutting Agnew out of the key foreign policy decisions, Nixon dispatched him on diplomatic missions to areas that Nixon cared little about. At the time, Agnew was in Africa on a ten-nation, thirty-two-day diplomatic tour that included stops in South Korea, Saudi Arabia, Kuwait, Ethiopia, Zaire, and the Congo. According to published reports, Agnew was "pleased" with the China news.[21] However, Agnew had grave reservations about the opening of relations with China and he suspected that he had been sent away precisely because Nixon knew about his objections. After leaving office, Agnew published his memoir of his time in the Nixon administration,

Go Quietly ... or else. In the book he wrote about why he might have been sent out of the country when Kissinger traveled to China:

> I presume that my firm opposition to the policy of cozying up to Communist China was the main reason the White House froze me out of the Nixon decisions in that area. In mid-1971, while I was making a goodwill trip around the world, some of Mr. Nixon's aides put out the word that I was sent out of the country so as not to be in Henry Kissinger's way when he made his secret journey to China—the journey which paved the way for the President's visit there by the following February. Then they compounded the felony by not notifying me until after the story broke in the press. I was in Kinshasa, then the capital of Congo (now Zaire), when the story broke. Mr. Nixon certainly had no reason to believe that I would have leaked the story, because he knew so well that I never leaked anything—although I had access to much secret information through the National Security and daily C.I.A. briefings. But some of his assistants were aware of my sentiments about courting the Red Chinese, so they left me out.[22]

Aware that Agnew opposed the opening to China, Nixon kept the vice president entirely out of the loop. Unhappy and unwanted, Agnew publicly urged Nixon to consider his re-nomination in a "cold, hard, practical political way," and privately weighed voluntarily stepping aside.[23] Nixon would have been thrilled if Agnew quit, but not so many conservatives. At their 1971 convention, the right-wing student organization Young Americans for Freedom (YAF) endorsed Agnew for the presidency in 1972.[24] While the move expressed the conservatives' displeasure with Nixon as much as it did their happiness with Agnew, the endorsement nonetheless demonstrated the culmination of a long political journey for Spiro Agnew. His top political aide, David Keene, a former national chair of YAF, described Agnew as having undergone a "philosophical reinvention" while in office. Keene observed as Agnew studied issues, consulted with intellectuals from conservative think tanks such as the Manhattan Institute, held seminars with his staff, and discussed public policy issues with a range of individuals from Irving Kristol to Sydney Hook.[25]

In his early political career, Agnew had disdained ideology, but by 1971, Agnew was an ideological conservative. As he journeyed rightward, Agnew grew increasingly unhappy with the direction of the administration. He was particularly bothered by Nixon's foreign policy decisions. Until the very end of his time as vice president, Agnew supported an aggressive American policy in Vietnam. He felt frustrated with what he considered the dovish Vietnam policies Nixon pursued and he bitterly opposed the steps Nixon and Kissinger took to ease Cold War tensions with the Soviet Union and China. Agnew's opposition to détente grew out of his travels abroad. During his trips to South Korea, Japan, and Taiwan, Agnew listened as the leaders of those countries expressed fear about Nixon's foreign policy. Afraid that the United States would no longer protect them against communist aggression, they impressed upon Agnew the idea that the United States needed to be the bulwark against communism. Agnew developed a particular attachment toward Taiwan, and his opposition to the China initiative resulted in his open affection for "a loyal ally whose hardworking and creative citizens have made their country a model success story for the capitalistic free-enterprise system."[26]

Agnew's growing ideological estrangement with Nixon was no secret. It was also well-known that Agnew's future with Nixon was in doubt. Agnew alluded to this in a handwritten note he sent to Nixon on November 13, 1971. After thanking Nixon for some kind remarks he had made about Agnew, Agnew concluded with opaque references to his political future, references that seemed to imply both resignation that he might not be on the ticket in 1972 and a plea that Nixon keep him: "As you know, you can always depend on my loyalty and my total support of your final decisions. However, I won't promise not to play the advocate while you are still undecided."[27]

By the end of 1971, Agnew was unsure of his future but he had millions of supporters within the Republican Party who wanted him on the ticket in 1972. Even though Nixon was the leader of the party he could not ignore their sentiments. Many of the party's leading conservatives were unhappy with Nixon as it was, and alienating them further would have hurt Nixon politically. Agnew had a base that could not be ignored. He had shrewdly cultivated support from influential conservatives and his own ideological metamorphosis solidified his standing among the party's right-wing. In the end, that support would pay dividends in 1972, as Nixon geared up for his final campaign.

On January 5, 1972, Nixon notified the chairman of his New Hampshire campaign committee that he was seeking reelection.[28] Since no one ever doubted that Nixon would run again, the pro forma announcement came as no surprise. The real interest centered upon who would be his Democratic opponent, and whom Nixon would choose as his running mate. Because Nixon remained mum on the matter, Spiro Agnew's fate remained a question mark.

Three days earlier, on January 2, Nixon had sat down for a rare prime time interview with CBS News White House correspondent Dan Rather. The newsman asked Nixon, "Mr. President, can you give us assurances categorically and unequivocally that if you are a candidate that you want to run again with Vice President Agnew and that he will be your running mate, if you have anything to do with it?" Nixon could have ended all the speculation right then and there by giving a direct answer; instead he offered some backhanded praise but shied away from offering an outright endorsement: "I believe that the Vice President has handled his difficult assignments with dignity, with courage. He has, at times, been a man of controversy, but when a man has done a good job in a position, when he has been part of a winning team, I believe that he should stay on the team." Then Nixon added a caveat, "That is my thinking at this time."[29]

Nixon clearly wanted Agnew off the ticket. Bob Haldeman's diaries are replete with entries in which Nixon ranted about the vice president's shortcomings. Nixon worried that Agnew jeopardized his own reelection chances, but there were serious political risks in shoving Agnew aside. His tempestuous relationship with the right-wing of the GOP actually deteriorated during his presidency. Angered over Nixon's affirmative action initiatives, environmental programs, big budgets, and détente, the conservatives made noise about withholding their backing for this reelection bid. The movement's godfather William F. Buckley announced that he was "suspending" his support for Nixon and searching for an alternative.[30] As noted, at a mock convention, the YAF endorsed Agnew for the presidency. John Ashbrook, a conservative Republican member of Congress from Ohio, entered the New Hampshire primary (as did liberal Republican congressman Peter McCloskey).[31]

While conventional political wisdom dictated that the Right had nowhere else to go, Nixon knew better. A decade earlier when he ran for governor of California, Nixon found himself in a fierce battle for the GOP nomination against Joe Shell, the Republican minority leader of the California assembly. Although Nixon won the nomination, Shell captured 35 percent of the vote. During the primary and in the general election Nixon disclaimed any support from the extremist John Birch Society, a move that alienated many of the state's conservatives. In the November election, incumbent Pat Brown bested Nixon by 297,000 votes out of six million cast. The lesson, as Nixon saw it, was, "You can't win the election just with these people (conservatives). But you can't win the election without these people, as I learned."[32]

Given that sentiment Nixon treaded carefully with the Agnew question. Top conservatives warned of the perils of dumping Agnew. The president's December 2, 1971 Daily News Summary included an item about California governor Ronald Reagan. "Gov. Reagan says the Veep has discussed with him the possibility of steeping down to take a judicial or cabinet post. The VP didn't tell Reagan whether he or RN had made a decision on the '72 VP slot but Reagan says RN (Nixon) will have a political problem if the Veep is dropped."[33] A poll taken by the *Los Angeles Times* in February 1972 showed that 54 percent of registered Republicans wanted Agnew as Nixon's running mate in 1972, while just 32 percent preferred another candidate.[34]

One of the hurdles confronting Nixon was his personal choice for the vice presidency: John Connally. A registered Democrat, he had no support within the GOP. Certainly the conservatives would not accept an apostate. Still, Nixon kept dreaming. On a number of occasions he met with Connally and discussed the vice presidency but Connally always demurred. Nixon talked with John Mitchell, who was resigning his cabinet post to take over the president's campaign committee. "I told him bluntly that I thought Connally should be President in 1976 and that I was weighing the possibility of giving him a head start, if he wanted it, by making him my running mate," Nixon recalled. But Mitchell argued against it. Connally's party affiliation, Mitchell told Nixon, would backfire with the "New Majority Republicans and Democrats," that Nixon so needed for his reelection. The move would be especially damaging in the South, Mitchell intoned, where Agnew was a folk hero (though a Lou Harris poll taken in autumn 1971 showed Connally with more support in the South than Agnew).[35] Mitchell pressed Nixon to commit to Agnew, if only because the longer Nixon delayed the stronger became Agnew's position. "Besides, I feel sorry for him. He's having some financial problems, and he needs to be able to plan his future," Mitchell told the president.[36]

More than any other man, John Mitchell was responsible for Spiro Agnew being the vice presidential nominee in 1968. He pushed hard for Agnew and his opinion carried great weight with Nixon at that time. Mitchell and Agnew became close friends, and apparently Agnew shared with Mitchell his concerns about the future, including his alleged financial constraints. Agnew had never been shy about lamenting the paltry salaries he earned as a public servant, though that never stopped him from seeking and holding offices. Of course throughout his tenure as Baltimore County executive, governor of Maryland, and vice president—it was later revealed—he supplemented his income with kickbacks and favors from his rich friends, something he did not share with Mitchell. It seems likely, however, that Agnew discussed with Mitchell the vice presidential nomination. Nixon respected Mitchell's judgment but made no commitment; instead he remained silent on the matter, hoping somehow that he could still rid himself of Agnew.

In the meanwhile, political considerations took a backseat to foreign policy. In February 1972, Nixon departed for this historic trip to China. For eight days the American public watched in fascination as the old Cold Warrior huddled with Mao Zedong and Zhou Enlai and other leaders of the communist state. During the trip Nixon toured the Great Wall, visited the Forbidden City, and attended lavish banquets where he heaped praise upon his hosts. At the end, the Americans and the Chinese issued a communiqué. The thorniest issue involved concerned Taiwan. The negotiations were intense, as Nixon and Kissinger fought for a statement that included Taiwan's independence, whereas Chou wanted Taiwan recognized as part of China. The final document, called the Shanghai Communiqué, recognized the differences between the two nations on the question of Taiwan, and offered no settlement of the island's future.[37]

When Nixon arrived back at Andrews Air Force Base in Maryland, the entire cabinet greeted him, including the vice president. Agnew spoke for the cabinet and delivered a rousing tribute.

> For more than a week we have witnessed through the miracle of satellite television, the sights and sounds of a society that has been closed to Americans for over two decades. We have been made aware of many new things in our society, Mr. President. We have witnessed what you have done with feelings of pride and pleasure, and immense curiosity that has certainly not been diminished by the amount of attention paid by the media to the visit ... I think I can close by simply saying that we are glad to have you back, and we feel easier tonight because of the trip that you took.[38]

Agnew's private thoughts on the rapprochement with China differed greatly from his public statements. A few weeks before Nixon's visit, Agnew appeared on NBC's *Today Show*. Asked about his skepticism over the opening, Agnew denied opposing the initiative. "The truth is that I approved mightily of the President's trip to China."[39] Agnew was being disingenuous; he opposed the visit, as did a key member of his staff. On the morning Nixon returned, David Keene, Agnew's top political aide and the most conservative member of the staff, wrote a memo "saying exactly what I thought of the whole thing."[40] After Agnew got back to his office, he read the memo and called a staff meeting. He defended the trip and told Keene that Nixon was correct in opening relations with China. Keene, never shy about expressing his opinions, fired back: "You know, Mr. Vice President, if you really believe that you're a lot dumber than I thought you were when I went to work for you." Figuring that his time on the vice president's staff was over, Keene went back to his office and started packing his belongings when the phone rang. Agnew was on the line. "When I went out Andrews (Air Force Base)," Agnew asked, "do you know what I thought when they opened that door? I wondered if he was going to be carrying an umbrella."[41]

Comparing Richard Nixon to the umbrella-toting Neville Chamberlain of Britain and his appeasement of Hitler highlighted the depths of Agnew's anti-communism and his anger at Nixon for abandoning Taiwan. Shortly after his selection in 1968 Agnew told the *New York Times* that under extraordinary circumstances, such as a deep policy disagreement, the vice president could and should resign.[42] In 1832, Vice President John Calhoun quit the office over differences with Andrew Jackson, principally over Jackson's opposition to Calhoun's theory of nullification. Calhoun's resignation came with only three months left in the term, and following the election when Jackson and the Calhoun's replacement, Martin Van Buren, won the presidential contest. Agnew had nearly a year left in office, and the likelihood of his leaving (a wish Nixon frequently expressed) was almost nil. Yet, if he remained true to his principles, he could have voluntarily taken himself out of the running for reelection in 1972.

Instead, Agnew remained in the administration. As much as he disagreed with Nixon's policies, he still believed in Nixon the man and he truly wanted Nixon reelected, especially in light of the direction the opposition took in 1972. For much of his vice presidency, Agnew vilified the radical-liberal element of the Democratic Party. In the 1970 mid-term election, he directed many of his barbs at the "radiclibs" in the U.S. Senate. That year he focused his attention on the members of that club who were up for reelection, which did not include South Dakota's George McGovern. The two-term senator was one of the most vocal critics of the Vietnam War, and in 1970 co-sponsored the McGovern-Hatfield Amendment, which called for the removal of all American troops from the country. Afraid that passage of the amendment would cripple efforts to maintain a viable South Vietnamese government, the Nixon administration fought hard against it, and Nixon delegated to Agnew the responsibility of leading the attack. Agnew agreed and at the August 7, 1970, address before the Veterans of Foreign Wars, Agnew hit McGovern hard, calling him an isolationist and blasting the amendment as "a blueprint for the first defeat in the history of the United States—and for chaos and Communism for the future of South Vietnam."[43]

As the primary season began in February 1972 McGovern trailed front-runner Edmund Muskie of Maine, Agnew's vice presidential opponent in the 1968 campaign. The White House feared Muskie, since for nearly two years most polls showed Muskie either tied or just ahead of Nixon. Worried the Maine senator might defeat Nixon, the president's men launched their own campaign against him. So, with Nixon's approval, members of the Committee to Reelect the President (CREEP) infiltrated Muskie's campaign, spied on him, and coordinated a host of dirty tricks against him. While Nixon was in China, a letter sent to the conservative *Manchester Union Leader* by "Paul Morrison" accused Muskie of calling French Canadians "Canucks." The following day the *Union Leader* ran a front-page story that accused his wife of being a drunk. A tearful Muskie appeared in front of the newspaper's offices and denounced the paper. The event damaged Muskie's already floundering campaign, and he struggled to win the New Hampshire primary, taking only 48 percent of the vote.[44] Finishing third was former conservative Alabama governor George Wallace. Four years earlier Wallace ran as an independent in the general election but remained a registered Democrat. In 1968 Nixon captured most of the border Southern states but lost the Deep South to Wallace and, though the White House was pleased with the havoc he was wreaking in the Democratic field, Nixon knew that Wallace posed a serious threat to his reelection bid. Although Wallace polled strongly in New Hampshire and swept the Florida primary, he stood no real chance of taking the Democratic nomination. Instead he would almost certainly run again on a third-party ticket, which would draw votes away from Nixon.[45]

With Muskie's candidacy imploding, and Wallace winning the most conservative voters of the party—in stepped George McGovern. Dismissed as nothing more than a protest candidate because he based his campaign on an immediate end of the Vietnam War, McGovern finished second behind Muskie in New Hampshire. But as Muskie faded, and Hubert Humphrey's candidacy went nowhere, McGovern picked up traction. Taking advantage of new rules in the Democratic Party, rules that his supporters drafted, McGovern won a series of primaries in March and April by capturing women and minority delegates. McGovern's surprising strength elated the White House. His liberalism and his strident anti-war position helped in the primary season, but at the same time alienated many moderate and conservative Democrats. During the primary season Agnew hit McGovern hard, accusing the senator, along with Muskie, Ted Kennedy, and New York mayor John Lindsay (whom Agnew termed the "flashy flugleman of Fun City") of making vicious attacks upon the United States. "Who is right?" Agnew asked a crowd. "Is Richard Nixon right when he says this is a good country? Or are they right when they say or imply that it isn't?"[46]

Meanwhile, Nixon's own political star waxed. The China trip boosted his approval ratings, as did an upturn in the economy. He also had a summit in Moscow scheduled for May—an event like the visit to China, which would hold the nation's attention for days and show Nixon as a statesman. The only lingering problem was the war in Vietnam, which still dragged on. By May 1, 1972, only 69,000 American combat troops remained, but bombing raids continued. The South Vietnamese government was stable, but Viet Cong forces still operated in the South, and on March 30, the North Vietnamese launched a full-fledged invasion across the demilitarized line that divided the countries. Some 200,000 troops, equipped with Soviet tanks and artillery, came within sixty miles of Saigon.[47] Nixon viewed the assault as a "sign of desperation" but still ordered a massive aerial attack on the North.[48] Kissinger believed that North Vietnamese offensive not only threatened the viability of South Vietnam but also the entire "design of our foreign policy."[49]

Over the next few weeks American B-52s bombed the southern parts of North Vietnam. The bombings proved effective in stalling the offensive, but toward the end of April, the communists opened another front and drove deep into South Vietnam. Believing that dramatic action was needed, Nixon weighed his options, including the mining on harbors off the coast of Hanoi. Nixon made the decision to mine the harbors, and on Monday, May 8, he held a National Security meeting to inform the participants of the upcoming action. The meeting lasted three hours, with Defense Secretary Melvin Laird opposing the mining, while Secretary of State William Rogers equivocated, saying that he would support the mining so long as it worked. Nixon noted in his diary, "Connally and Agnew predictably took a very strong position for it."[50] Agnew rarely spoke up at cabinet meeting, but on this occasion he voiced his opinion. According to Kissinger, Agnew argued that losing South Vietnam "would have disastrous international consequences, especially in the Middle East and around the Indian Ocean. We were 'handcuffing ourselves' by being 'compulsive talkers'; the President really didn't have an option."[51] After informing congressional leaders, Nixon went on national television and announced that he had ordered the mining of North Vietnamese ports.

Later that night Nixon held another cabinet meeting at which Agnew praised the president, telling him that he could count on the entire cabinet's support.[52] Following the meeting, Agnew composed a short note to the president expressing his wholehearted support. It was brief and poignant. "Dear Mr. President," he began, "However this comes out, I am very proud today to be a member of your team, with deep respect, Ted."[53]

Polls taken in the speech's immediate aftermath showed that an overwhelming majority of Americans shared Agnew's opinion. But reaction from liberal quarters was apocalyptic. Ted Kennedy called the mining a "futile military gesture taken in desperation."[54] Other critics bellowed the action would inevitably result in the cancellation of the Moscow summit, a result that Nixon and Kissinger considered a possibility.[55] But the Soviets never canceled the summit, even after a Soviet seaman was killed when a bomb hit a Soviet ship.[56]

Nixon arrived in Moscow on Monday, May 22, becoming the first sitting president since Franklin Roosevelt in 1945 to visit the Soviet Union. In the spirit of détente the principles pledged a goal of "peaceful coexistence." Nixon and Soviet Premier Leonid Brezhnev also signed the Strategic Arms Limitation Treaty. The pact restricted the number of antiballistic missile sites each country could have to two and the number of offensive missiles was frozen.[57]

On the day Nixon left for his summit he held a forty-minute meeting with Agnew. Afterward Agnew fielded questions from the White House press corps. The questions focused on his future. Earlier that week John Connally announced his resignation from the cabinet. Nixon praised Connally and his words only increased speculation that he would replace Agnew with Connally, but Agnew discounted the rumors. "I don't understand how anyone could seriously believe that a man who is registered as a Democrat in the middle of May could turn Republican and be nominated as Vice President," Agnew told the press.[58]

Still, the possibility of such a move was not out of the question given Nixon's political standing. At the beginning of the year Nixon worried about his reelection chances but by early June 1972 his reelection seemed nearly assured. Following the Moscow summit, the China opening, and the winding down of the Vietnam War, Nixon's poll ratings rose. At home the economy was strong, with inflation having dipped to 2.7 percent by the summer.[59] The Democrats were terribly divided. Nixon's fortunes were further boosted when George Wallace, the man Nixon feared could derail his reelection, was seriously wounded in an assassination attempt in April. One of the bullets struck Wallace in the neck, paralyzing him and rendering his third-party candidacy unlikely. In July Wallace officially announced that he would not run for the presidency, but by that point Nixon was in such a strong position that even a Wallace candidacy would not have jeopardized his reelection.

Yet some of the president's men were taking no chances. While Nixon was in Moscow, seven members of CREEP broke into the headquarters of the Democratic National Committee (DNC) at the Watergate Hotel in Washington, DC. Acting without any explicit orders from their superiors, though possibly with the knowledge of CREEP director John Mitchell, the burglars rifled through some files and planted listening devices on the phones. By mid-June, the bugs were no longer working, so the conspirators planned another trip. In the early morning hours of Saturday, June 17, 1972, James W. McCord, a former CIA operative, and four others attempted to enter the DNC offices. Guided by G. Gordon Liddy, CREEP's counsel, who was across the street at a Howard Johnson hotel communicating with them by walkie-talkie, McCord and the others successfully entered the DNC office. However, a security guard at the Watergate tracked their movements, called the police, and caught them. The men were arrested and charged later that day.[60]

So began the Watergate scandal. At first, the incident was dismissed by most as a stupid and bizarre prank. White House press secretary Ron Ziegler described it as a "third-rate burglary." At the time of the break-in Richard Nixon was vacationing in Florida. He first learned of the crime on Sunday, June 18, while he was perusing the front page of the *Miami Herald*. After looking over a story on troop withdraws from Vietnam Nixon noticed a headline, "Miamians Held in D.C. Try to Bug Demo Headquarters." Nixon claimed that the news left him nonplussed and that he went and called Bob Haldeman. During the conversation, Nixon later wrote, the Watergate break-in never came up.[61]

By the time Nixon returned to the White House, news stories tied the burglars to the White House. The accounts listed James McCord as a CREEP employee. The FBI linked the burglars to E. Howard Hunt, another ex-CIA official and also a former aide to Charles Colson. What seemed originally a bizarre incident was growing into a potential scandal, and the White House reacted quickly to quell any further revelations. At CREEP Gordon Liddy spent the weekend shredding documents. On Monday, June 20, Haldeman, Ehrlichman, Mitchell, Colson, and White House counsel John Dean tried vainly to figure out who exactly was involved and how to proceed. Confusion reigned at the White House, as the president's men sought to find ways to limit the fallout and protect themselves from any criminal liability.[62]

The president's men, and the president himself, had good reason to worry about the Watergate affair. The break-in was but a piece of a series of illicit and illegal actions undertaken over the previous three years. As early as March 1969 Nixon had ordered wiretaps placed on journalists—and members of his own staff. Over the 1971 Labor Day holiday, Liddy, Hunt, and the Cubans broke into Daniel Ellsberg's psychiatrist's office. Ellsberg, a one-time Pentagon employee, leaked to the press documents about the origins of American involvement in Vietnam. The "Pentagon Papers," as the documents became known, traced America's role in the war back to the Truman administration. Although Nixon's name was not even mentioned in the papers, their release infuriated Henry Kissinger, who once taught a seminar class to Ellsberg at Harvard. Kissinger goaded Nixon into action, who ordered John Ehrlichman to do something about Ellsberg. Ehrlichman handed the assignment to Liddy, who organized the burglary of the office. The burglars never found Ellsberg's file, and in an effort to hide their deed, they destroyed the office, and took pictures for souvenirs. Ehrlichman then shut down the operation, but failed to report the crime.[63]

The actions, what John Mitchell called the "White House Horrors," placed dozens of Nixon administration officials in a precarious legal position. One man who had no cause for concern was Spiro Agnew. Throughout the vice presidency Agnew lamented his exclusion from the White House inner circle, but his isolation actually (for a very brief time) benefited him. He partook in none of illegal activities, knew nothing of the crimes, and had no involvement in the cover-up of the Watergate scandal. Like many, Agnew thought the attempted burglary itself foolish. On the caper he later commented, "I must say here that I think the break-in incident was overblown and the shock expressed largely phony. I don't condone it, but the major parties have been penetrating and spying on each other for years."[64]

But the episode intrigued him. Late Monday afternoon, June 19, Agnew aide John Damgard called deputy director of CREEP, Jeb Magruder, asking if Magruder could join the vice president in a tennis match. Magruder, who was supposed to meet with Mitchell at Mitchell's Watergate apartment, accepted the invitation. As Magruder recalled, Agnew had often mentioned that they should play tennis sometime, but that night was the first time they actually did, and Magruder discovered why: Agnew wanted to ask him about Watergate. At the end of match Agnew took Magruder aside and asked, "Jeb, what the hell is going on?" Magruder responded honestly, "It was our operation. It got screwed up. We're trying to take care of it." The news struck Agnew, who frowned and looked away. "I don't think we ought to discuss it again, in that case," he told Magruder.[65]

While Agnew was through talking about Watergate, Nixon was not. The next day, Tuesday, June 20, at 11:26 A.M. Nixon met with Haldeman and discussed the background of the crime and its potential ramifications. The tapes that Nixon installed in the Oval Office recorded the conversation (though 18½ minutes of the tape were erased under mysterious circumstances). Haldeman took notes of the meeting, and it seems that he debriefed Nixon on Operation GEMSTONE. The bizarre scheme was the product of former White House assistant and general counsel of CREEP's Finance Committee G. Gordon Liddy's fertile mind. Liddy presented the plan to John Mitchell in January 1972 (when Mitchell was still serving as attorney general). It called for the kidnapping of wives of prominent Democrats and holding them for ransom, blackmailing Democrats, sabotaging the air-conditioning system at the Democratic National Convention, and break-ins. Mitchell puffed his pipe and listened as Liddy described the operation. When Liddy finished Mitchell responded, "It's not quite what I had in mind." Liddy scaled down the project. Liddy retained the wiretapping option and led the break-ins at the Watergate.[66]

Haldeman informed Nixon of the various black-bag operations and in the following day John Ehrlichman suggested pinning all the blame on Liddy, whom they all hoped would accept responsibility and remain quiet about everything else. Then, on Friday June 23, White House counsel John Dean told Haldeman of a plan that might solve the Watergate problem. Early that morning Dean called Haldeman and told him that he, Dean, had spoken with John Mitchell (Dean was lying; he had not talked with Mitchell). Dean claimed the FBI thought the break-in might be a CIA job. According to Dean, Mitchell agreed to a solution that would have CIA director Richard Helms inform acting FBI Director L. Patrick Gray that the Watergate burglary was a CIA operation and that the FBI was to drop its investigation. Haldeman relayed the scheme to Nixon, who approved it. He instructed Haldeman to sit in on the meeting and tell Gray, "'Don't go any further in this case', period!"[67]

That conversation would end Nixon's presidency, but at the time Nixon thought he had put the Watergate affair behind him, and concentrated on the election. There was but one final decision to be made—the choice of a vice president. Most prominent Republicans rallied behind Agnew. In early 1972 a group of Republicans formed the Americans for Agnew, an organization dedicated to ensuring that Agnew remained on the ticket in 1972 (actor John Wayne served as the group's spokesman).[68] A survey of Republican leaders taken in April showed widespread support for Agnew. According to a report in the *Portland Herald*, eighty-seven of ninety-two Republicans polled expected Agnew to be the vice presidential choice, and such support made it "increasingly difficult for RN to choose another running mate, should he so desire."[69] As the decision day neared, a number of prominent Republicans endorsed Agnew. Barry Goldwater, Agnew's strongest supporter in the Senate, issued a ringing defense of Agnew: "The Vice President has built himself into a national figure with courage enough to say things that should be said. Any suggestions about dumping him at this time will alienate the Republican workers across the country."[70]

How much Goldwater's support, along with that of other leading Republicans, influenced Nixon's final decision is not known. Nixon later wrote that he made the final decision on June 12. On that day:

> I asked John Mitchell to tell Agnew that I had made the decision definitely to have him on the ticket again as my running mate. I said that we would not announce it until after the Democratic convention. This would generate interest by creating suspense; it might also lead the Democrats to soft-pedal their attacks on him at their convention just in case I decided to choose someone else.[71]

But Nixon added a caveat limiting what Agnew could ask for. "Agnew is the candidate," Haldeman noted in his diary, "but we should work on a deal with him and make sure we've got things split up right without letting him develop a high price for taking the job."[72]

During an Oval Office meeting on July 21, Nixon asked Agnew to be his running mate and Agnew accepted.[73] The next day Ron Ziegler officially announced the decision. Before his departure on a campaign swing to the West Coast and Alaska, Agnew told reporters that he was "extremely gratified." Admitting that at times he felt insecure about Nixon's intentions, "I never felt like I was in deep trouble." He then foreshadowed the lines the Nixon campaign would use against the Democratic nominee George McGovern: "The Democratic Party is presently controlled by an ideological elite," he told reporters and mentioned McGovern's policies on amnesty for draft evaders, McGovern's vow to beg Hanoi for the release of American prisoners, and his "thousand-dollar giveaway," a reference to McGovern's pledge to give welfare recipients a thousand dollars each.[74]

Republicans and conservatives hailed the selection. Reagan and Conservative Party senator James Buckley of New York both described themselves as "delighted" with the choice.[75] The Democrats predictably criticized Agnew, but reaction from the press was mixed. Just prior to the announcement the editors at *Life* and the *Detroit News* called upon Nixon to dump Agnew.[76] The *Chicago Tribune*, the country's foremost Republican newspaper, issued a mild endorsement, writing, "On balance, the political positives of Mr. Nixon's decision outweigh the negatives."[77] The editors at the *New York Times* were far less generous. The editorial, "Mr. Agnew Again," was as harsh as it was unsurprising.

> He has shown himself to be a man without comprehension of the American tradition of civil liberties or the meaning of the First Amendment. As an emissary abroad, he has been a jet-propelled embarrassment . . . If he has learned anything about the nation's serious domestic problems, Mr. Agnew has kept that knowledge to himself.[78]

The *Times* also wrote, "Vice President Agnew is a campaigner able and willing to take the partisan low road while Mr. Nixon remains not only above the battle but also beyond accountability."[79] The paper correctly divined Nixon's strategy. Immediately after the 1970 elections Nixon decided that in 1972 he would stay above the fray as long as possible. In a postelection mortem John Mitchell criticized Nixon's intense involvement in the campaign, saying that Nixon acted as if he was running for local sheriff. Determined not to repeat the mistake, Nixon delegated the task of attacking McGovern to his subordinates, his campaign committee, and elected Republicans.

Some of the burden fell on Agnew. In June, Bob Haldeman sent a memo asking staffers what role Nixon should assume before the convention. Dwight Chapin, the president's scheduler, recommended that Nixon "continue non-political approach" and allow Agnew to "bang around McGovern."[80] Nixon had his own ideas about Agnew's role, and it was a small role at that. "No important duties," he told Haldeman.[81] In July he gave Agnew a detailed talking points list that included, among other things: "no attacks on press *at all*"; "attack McGovern only on issues, never personally"; "sell the positive side of the President especially on foreign policy, plus domestic issues"; "don't let yourself become the issue, stay non-controversial, avoid cute phrases—not needed"; "no discussion or comment on '76."[82]

In the talking points Nixon instructed Agnew to "totally ignore Eagleton."[83] As it turned out, the advice was unnecessary. At the Democratic National Convention in mid-July, McGovern threw the selection of the vice president to the delegates. After a fierce floor fight where the delegates jokingly nominated Mao Zedong, television persona Archie Bunker, and John Mitchell's high-profile wife Martha, the convention settled on Senator Thomas Eagleton of Missouri. The choice satisfied most but thrilled no one. A freshman senator, Eagleton was almost as unknown nationally as Agnew had been in 1968. Because of the short time between his selection and the nomination, McGovern only conducted a perfunctory background check on his running mate—and Eagleton offered no information about his medical history.[84]

McGovern paid for the oversight. Just ten days after the convention ended, Eagleton held a news conference. The media was checking on rumors about his mental health, and Eagleton tried to control the potential damage by releasing his medical records. He admitted suffering from depression and also receiving electric shock therapy and taking tranquilizers. The news rocked the campaign, but George McGovern, who stood beside Eagleton at the press conference, defended his running mate and stated that he would not ask him to quit. The following day McGovern defiantly announced that he was "1000 percent behind Eagleton." However, the drumbeat for Eagleton's removal grew with each passing hour, and on Monday, July 31, eighteen days after he was picked, Eagleton officially dropped out of the race.[85]

The episode further damaged the floundering McGovern campaign. Over the next few days McGovern added to his troubles by almost begging Hubert Humphrey, Ted Kennedy, and other top Democrats to accept the nomination, but they all turned him down. The hapless McGovern finally found a taker in Sargent Shriver, Ted Kennedy's brother-in-law and former director of the Peace Corps. Shriver brought even less to the ticket than Eagleton, but the McGovern campaign was so far beyond repair that the selection probably did not matter.

For the most part Agnew remained silent throughout the Eagleton affair. He had followed Nixon's instructions and ignored Eagleton, and Nixon ordered him to likewise not engage Shriver. As always, Nixon conveyed his wishes through a subordinate, in this case Haldeman. On August 14, he sent Haldeman a memo outlining Agnew's schedule for the fall. "I think it is very intriguing to explore the possibility of his (Agnew) following McGovern, not in every appearance McGovern makes, but once or twice a week in major cities that McGovern may visit." Nixon thought Agnew would outdraw McGovern, and in the resulting publicity, Agnew could hit McGovern hard "on points that he may have made that need to be corrected." Nixon also thought Agnew could arrive at stops a day or two earlier than McGovern and raise questions about the Democrat's stance on issues. "The more we can get Agnew engaged in a debate with McGovern the better," Nixon thought. But at no point should Agnew allow himself to get dragged in a debate with Shriver: "It is also very important to emphasize to Agnew again that he should ignore Shriver."[86]

The advice was pure Nixon: tough, cynical, and politically shrewd. So too was the tactic of avoiding any unnecessary personal contact with Agnew. Whenever possible, which was virtually always, Nixon used intermediaries instead of speaking directly with Agnew. Throughout the remainder of the campaign Nixon and Agnew had virtually no contact. Nor did Agnew have any real substantive role in the reelection effort. Two years earlier Nixon leaned heavily upon Agnew in the fall elections. The results from that campaign were mixed, but Nixon had another reason for keeping Agnew out of the limelight. Reluctantly Nixon kept Agnew as his running mate, but he was determined that Agnew would not succeed him in 1976.

Yet many Republicans saw Agnew as the party's future. As he arrived at the Republican Convention in Miami, the delegates welcomed Agnew as a hero. Four years earlier Agnew landed in Miami as an obscure border governor. After his surprise selection a cry of "Spiro Who" ran through the convention, but as Eric Sevareid, CBS's chief commentator and frequent target of Agnew's volleys, noted, the Republican delegates cheered him as their hero.[87] And Agnew had at least the support of one Nixon family member—the First Lady. When asked what she thought of Agnew in 1976 Pat Nixon gave an enthusiastic endorsement: "I'm for him. I think he has done a marvelous job as Vice President and that he would do the same job as President."[88]

The Republican Convention opened in Miami on Monday, August 21, the same place where the Democrats held their convention a month earlier. The mood on the floor was one of contentment more than excitement. Nixon held an almost insurmountable lead over McGovern, and with Nixon already having announced his support of Agnew, there was no suspense over the vice presidential selection. The real battle during the convention concerned the nomination in 1976. On August 3, David Keene and J. Roy Goodearle sent Agnew a memo warning him that Jacob Javits and other liberal Republicans "were preparing for a major fight at the convention on the various rules changes that will come before the delegates. He (Javits) has, of course, described the effort as the first step in a 'Stop Agnew in '76' campaign." The liberals wanted to change the allocation of delegates so that more urban states would gain more representation and also mandate a quota system so that half of the delegations would be female and a quarter would be minorities.[89] At the convention the proposal's changes were easily voted down by a vote of 910 to 434, demonstrating the waning influence of the moderate northeastern bloc of the GOP and the growing power of the conservative South.[90]

For the third time Republicans nominated Richard Nixon for the presidency, while Agnew was renominated for the vice presidency. Agnew gave what the *New York Times* described as a "calm, low-keyed acceptance speech."[91] A reflective, humorous, and subdued address, the talk had none of the invective or alliterations that made Agnew so politically charged. Agnew went through a litany of Nixon accomplishments and attacked McGovern for supporting school busing and quotas, and over his promise to "beg" for the release of American prisoners of war.[92]

Nixon likewise offered a forgettable speech (notably, he did not quote any parts of the address in his memoir).[93] So began the Nixon-Agnew reelection effort. In their respective political careers Nixon and Agnew had battled in nasty campaigns, but their finale was remarkably quiet. The year 1972 was a race that never was. The Gallup Poll taken in the days after the convention showed McGovern trailing Nixon by thirty-four points.[94] Four years earlier Nixon led Hubert Humphrey by fifteen points, but the race narrowed and it turned into one of the closest contents in American history. The year 1968 also had the wildcard of George Wallace, but Wallace withdrew from the race after being shot and paralyzed. In the 1970 elections, Nixon and Agnew waged a tough, at times ferocious, fight for their fellow Republicans (save a few Republicans dubbed "radiclibs" by Agnew). But in his final presidential contest Nixon conducted a "Rose Garden" campaign, where he never mentioned his opponent by name, refused to debate him, and avoided the stump until October. Although Nixon claimed to be seeking a political realignment, or a "New Majority," the only majorities he cared about in 1972 were his own. Despite their fervent pleas, Nixon ignored helping Republican candidates. Believing that campaigning for his fellow Republicans would cost him votes among Democrats and independents, Nixon sought a personal victory, in the process hurting the GOP's chances to gain seats in the House and Senate.[95]

For his part, Agnew adopted a new tone. As he prepared to leave Miami and hit the campaign trail Agnew told reporters that he was seeking a new image. "I was distressed at the generalized identity that I received as the vice presidential candidate and as a campaigner in 1970. I'd like to obliterate that. And so to that extent, if I am conciliatory, it's because I am." He also pledged not to attack McGovern personally but to stick to the issues. In contrast to Nixon, Agnew stated that he would vigorously campaign for Republican candidates.[96]

Although Nixon largely allowed Agnew freedom in the campaign he still used him as a surrogate in attacking McGovern. Nixon took the high road, but his magnanimity extended only so far. He wanted an all-out assault on McGovern and turned to White House special counsel Charles Colson to lead the war. It was a task perfectly suited for Colson, who once jokingly bragged that he would run over his grandmother to get Nixon reelected. But it was not a situation that Agnew welcomed, since throughout the fall Colson bombarded Agnew with strategy memos.[97] Agnew loathed Colson, and he chafed at taking marching orders from him. Early on in the campaign, aide David Keene recalls, Colson went to Agnew and barked, "I'm in charge of the message and the surrogates and I want to be able to get to you and tell you." The remark infuriated Agnew. "Well, first of all, Chuck," he replied, "I'm not a surrogate. I'm the Vice President of the United States. And if I hear you call me a surrogate again there's going to be hell to pay, because I'm going to the president."[98]

Agnew could not take his cause to Nixon, and Colson continued to send unsolicited advice. Nevertheless, he stayed on message by hitting McGovern hard on the issues. Frustrated that Nixon ignored him, McGovern tried to bait Nixon by leveling wild and reckless charges at the president and the administration, at one point comparing Nixon to Adolf Hitler. McGovern's rhetoric infuriated Nixon but he maintained his policy of staying silent in face of the attacks. While most of McGovern's verbal attacks were demagogic and the cries of a desperate man, one attack garnered national attention. In early October, McGovern charged Nixon as being the leader of the "most corrupt administration in history."[99] A day later, on October 4, speaking in

McGovern's home state of South Dakota, Agnew took the gloves off. Their home senator, Agnew bellowed to a crowd of 1,500, was a "desperate candidate who can't seem to understand that the American people don't want a philosophy of defeat and self-hate put upon them."[100] As the crowd cheered Agnew departed from his original text and fired away more shots. McGovern, he told the audience, "is stirring the basic hates and suspicions of people and relying solely on a campaign of smear and innuendo."[101]

Just because the Watergate scandal essentially ratified McGovern's assertion does not mean that Agnew was incorrect in his judgment of McGovern's campaign. McGovern had won the Democratic nomination almost by default. Dozens of prominent Democrats deserted him and endorsed the Republican ticket. His proposals—an immediate bombing halt, providing a $1,000 income grant to every American, amnesty to draft dodgers, decriminalizing marijuana, and cutting the defense budget by $31 billion—put him far outside the mainstream of the country. Nevertheless, McGovern's charges of corruption were grounded in reality. Throughout the summer and fall the news media, especially the *Washington Post*, ran stories tying CREEP to a slew of questionable campaign tactics. Because Nixon refused to answer McGovern directly, it fell to Agnew and other to address the Watergate matter. During a campaign swing through Illinois, Agnew held a press conference where he told the press that he was not at all concerned about the moral issues raised by Watergate. "I'm not bothered by them because I know they don't extend into the White House," he said. Agnew also expressed his firm belief that Nixon had nothing to do with Watergate, because, well, Nixon had said as much: "An investigation has been made by the President, and he's made the statement that it doesn't (reach into the White House) and I have confidence that he's telling the truth."[102]

In the end, Watergate never materialized as much of an issue in the election. The only real drama in the election was Vietnam. By the fall American military operations were winding down. Negotiations between the North Vietnamese and the Americans were proceeding apace, and on October 31, National Security Advisor Henry Kissinger announced to the nation, "Peace is at hand." In fact, peace was not "at hand," and the parties would not sign an agreement until late January, but the statement dominated news coverage and provided Nixon with cover that he was the man best suited to end the war.

With Nixon coasting toward reelection, and without any major political developments erupting from late August onward, the political class naturally speculated on 1976, and much of their focus was on Spiro Agnew. Quietly but effectively Agnew used the campaign as a stepping-stone for his own presidential ambitions. At campaign stops supporters waved "The Spiro of '76" signs.[103] In 1972 Nixon angered Republicans when he refused to campaign for GOP candidates, kept his massive campaign funds for his own election effort, and even covertly backed Democratic candidates who had supported his Vietnam policies. But Agnew earned respect and political chips with his energetic support of his fellow party members. Republicans across the country were already grateful for his fund-raising abilities, his attacks on the liberal establishment, and his willingness to assume the mantle of party spokesman. Although he mostly toned down his rhetoric in 1972, he still was active on the trail and helped his party as much as he could, and his efforts did not go unnoticed. One party official said, "Republican candidates in states with high Democratic registration felt that they were being jettisoned by the Democrats for Nixon (an organization headed by John Connally). They appreciated that Agnew, at least, extended a helping hand."[104]

Election day fell on November 7, 1972. Nixon and Agnew won a resounding landslide. They took forty-nine states (losing only Massachusetts and the District of Columbia), becoming the first ever to win that many states. Of all voters, 60.7 percent (47,169,841 total) cast their ballots for the Republican ticket, while McGovern and Shriver received just 37.5 percent and 29,172,767 votes. More people voted for the winning ticket than in any previous election, and Nixon and Agnew took the second largest number of electoral votes, 520, at that time in history.[105]

The results were partially a repudiation of George McGovern, but mostly an affirmation of Richard Nixon's policies. The only discordant notes came in the congressional elections. Despite the landslide, Nixon's coattails were remarkably short. Even though Democratic candidates were saddled with an extremely unpopular presidential ticket, they still fared quite well. The Democrats actually gained two Senate seats, thereby increasing their majority to fifty-eight to forty-two. The GOP picked up twelve seats in the House, but the Democrats still retained an overwhelming majority.

Still, the voters ratified Nixon's handling of the Vietnam War, the détente, moving the federal courts in a rightward direction, and his economic policies. Four years earlier the country was bitterly divided. A wave of violence struck across the country's urban centers and on the nation's college campuses. By 1972, the discord had dissipated. By voting so overwhelmingly for Richard Nixon and Spiro Agnew, the voters placed their hopes, and their trust, in the two men.

Shortly after midnight, Nixon and Agnew appeared together at Washington's Shoreham Hotel. Nixon praised Agnew for his efforts in the campaign.[106] The next day Agnew sent Nixon a handwritten note that was touching. "Dear Mr. President," he began, "On this morning after your resounding victory, may I take the opportunity to thank you for your support and thoughtfulness during my first term." In actuality Nixon was extremely ungracious and extended almost no support, but on that morning Agnew displayed a great deal of magnanimity. "Your generous remarks at the end and your kind letter at the tough stage were comforting." He closed with a prediction: "Four more years of Nixon leadership will be the best possible strengthening of our Republic as it approaches its 200th birthday."[107]

Chapter 8

President Agnew?

Spiro Agnew celebrated his fifty-fourth birthday on November 9, 1972, at a ballroom in Agnews' residence, Washington's Sheraton Park Hotel. Hosted by I. Harold "Bud" Hammerman, Agnew's childhood friend, the gathering celebrated the vice president's birthday and his political future. Three-hundred guests attended, including wife Judy, their three daughters, Frank Sinatra, tennis star Rod Laver, and Vince Lombardi's widow Marie. The theme of the gala was the "The Spiro of '76."[1]

The revelers were justifiably excited about a President Agnew. In four years Agnew went from "Spiro Who?" to a household word to a leading contender, if not the front-runner, for the Republican presidential nomination in 1976. Throughout the 1972 campaign Agnew disavowed any talk of his prospects, but he and his supporters (and his detractors) were looking ahead. Agnew's political future seemed bright. He had been part of the most successful Republican reelection team in the country's history. The rank and file of the GOP loved him for his attacks on the liberal establishment and spirited defense of the country's traditional values. He earned the gratitude of the party's leadership through his prodigious fund-raising abilities and energetic support of Republican candidates. Should he run for the presidency Agnew had name recognition, a base of supporters, and access to money, and he held a position that gave him an advantage over his potential rivals—that of free publicity.

All of those elements gave Agnew a solid chance of capturing the Republican nomination. But Agnew faced an important barrier, one that could derail his efforts even before the campaign commenced. Richard Nixon was determined that Agnew not succeed him in. Nixon disliked Agnew and thought him unsuited for the presidency. Nixon wanted John Connally to succeed him. Given Nixon's overwhelming reelection, he was in a strong position to determine the next Republican candidate for president.

The week after the election, Nixon, along with Haldeman and Ehrlichman, flew to Camp David. Isolated at the presidential retreat in the Catoctin Mountains of Maryland, the trio plotted to put into motion what Nixon described as the "New American Revolution." Part of the revolution involved a thorough reorganization of the federal bureaucracy and the White House staff. Nixon also wanted a political realignment. "I intended to revitalize the Republican Party along New Majority lines," he wrote in his memoirs.[2] If Nixon had his way Agnew would not be part of it. On November 14, Nixon huddled with Haldeman and Ehrlichman and discussed Agnew's future. Ehrlichman took notes and Haldeman dictated the contents of the conversation in his diary. According to Haldeman, Nixon felt "that we need to keep our leverage over him, so we shouldn't break it off now, but we do not further his interests politically for '76."[3] Ehrlichman wrote that Nixon ticked off three areas where Agnew fell short: "Energy—likes to play golf. Leadership. Consistency—he's all over—he's not really a conservative."[4] After finishing with his shortcomings Nixon devised a strategy on how to handle Agnew. "Benign neglect—yes, that's our strategy," Ehrlichman quoted Nixon as saying.[5]

Nixon's opposition might effectively end Agnew's candidacy before it began. That seems to have been Nixon's goal. Writing about Nixon's post-election mood, Henry Kissinger observed, "Victory seemed to have released a pent-up hostility so overwhelming that it would not wait even a week to surface; it engulfed colleagues and associates as well as opponents."[6] Nixon targeted Agnew as if he was an opponent. Always calculating, Nixon conjured up a plan for the vice president: putting him in charge of the bicentennial celebration. Agnew rejected the idea as beneath him.[7]

During the next few weeks, Nixon was almost entirely occupied with Vietnam. Finally, after more than a decade of fighting, the parties signed the Paris Peace Accords on January 27, 1973. The terms included most of the provisions included in the October agreement. It called for an immediate cease-fire, the withdrawal of the remaining 27,000 American troops, the return of the American POWs (both within sixty days after January 27), and the establishment of a National Council on Reconciliation and Concord to carry out general elections. The 160,000 communist troops stationed in the South were allowed to stay, but Nixon covertly promised Thieu that he would provide military assistance, including bombing raids, if the North violated the terms of the pact.[8]

To reassure the skeptical Thieu, Nixon arranged for Agnew to travel to South Vietnam in late January to ease Thieu's concerns about the recently concluded settlement. Agnew departed for Asia on January 30 for a eleven-day, eight-nation trip. He first visited South Vietnam where he huddled with the South Vietnamese leader. Agnew assured a "skeptical President Nguyen Van Thieu that until the South Vietnamese people decided otherwise in a free election, our government would continue to recognize his as the only legitimate regime in South Vietnam; and that if the North Vietnamese violated the pact, we would react against them with force."[9]

Agnew left behind "a somewhat reassured but still uneasy President Thieu," and made an unannounced stop in Cambodia. The visit had been kept secret from the traveling press corps because of security concerns. The Khmer Rouge, the communist insurgents battling Lon Nol's government, was closing in on the capital of Phnom Penh. *Air Force Two* landed and its occupants quickly deplaned. An armed motorcade escorted the vice presidential party into the country's capital, where Agnew met with Lon Nol. Agnew "was shocked to see what a toll his recent stroke had taken physically." Lon Nol thanked Agnew for the show of support but his position was just as shaky as Thieu's. American bombing would soon end, though Agnew told him that the administration would still send military aid.[10]

From Cambodia Agnew stopped at Thailand, followed by Laos, Singapore, Indonesia, Malaysia, and the Philippines. Agnew flew back on February 9, and Nixon greeted Agnew at the "Western White House" in San Clemente, California. "I would say that the Vice President's trip served a very important purpose at this point in terms of building the structure of peace in not only the Indochina area but the whole area of Southeast Asia," Nixon told reporters. When Agnew began speaking, Nixon quickly interrupted him. Agnew tried again, but Nixon interjected. Finally, when Agnew said a few words, Press Secretary Ronald Ziegler ushered the press away. For ninety minutes Agnew briefed Nixon and Deputy National Security Advisor General Brent Scowcroft.[11]

On Friday, February 16, Agnew reported on his trip to the cabinet. Haldeman dictated:

> He did a pretty good job, taking about a half-hour to paint the overall picture. Regarding Thieu, he said he's in pretty good shape, positive, would win, with an 85 percent vote on an election held today, a much better position than his image in the United States shows, and the VP urged him to try and improve his image in the United States.[12]

Agnew's optimism hardly reflected reality. Perhaps Agnew was blind to the situation in Vietnam, where Thieu was in a precarious position. But his blindness resulted from his sense of loyalty, not ignorance or stupidity. Agnew had visited Thieu three times in Vietnam and he developed a friendship with him. Agnew also believed that the United States should protect the stability and security of South Vietnam and Cambodia, and that meant fully backing Thieu and Lon Nol. Unlike Nixon, who abandoned Thieu after the Paris Peace Accords, Agnew remained committed to the embattled president.

Thieu visited the United States in early April. By that time the White House was engulfed in the Watergate scandal, and Nixon later wrote Thieu "must have been concerned about the effect the domestic drain of Watergate would have on my ability to act forcefully abroad."[13] Thieu must also have noticed the lack of support he received from others in the administration. When he left the United States, he departed at Andrews Air Force Base. The only member of the Nixon administration on hand to see him off was

Spiro Agnew. The gesture demonstrated that whatever his flaws, Spiro Agnew possessed one trait often lacking among the president's men—loyalty.

Throughout the entire first term, Nixon kept Agnew at arm's length. Being shut out of power frustrated Agnew, but ironically, the separation had its advantages. As he put it, "I also knew that I was completely in the clear on the Watergate scandal. Having been frozen out of the inner circle at the White House, I knew absolutely nothing about Watergate and nobody ever claimed that I was tainted by it."[14] As of February 1973, few accused Richard Nixon of having any involvement in the scandal, but only because Nixon and his aides had successfully covered up their actions. But the wall the White House constructed began crumbling. On February 7, the Senate voted seventy to zero to create a select committee to probe the 1972 election. Senator Sam Ervin, a Democrat from North Carolina, was named chair of the committee.[15]

The Justice Department's own investigation proceeded apace. In late January a jury found Gordon Liddy and James McCord guilty of burglary. The five Cubans, along with Hunt, had already pled guilty. The presiding judge, John Sirica, an Eisenhower appointee, expressed frustration over the prosecutors' inability to crack open the case fully. When Howard Hunt entered his plea, he stated that he knew of "no higher ups" who were involved in the crime.[16] Hunt, it turns out, was lying, and he had been paid generously for his lies. After being caught in Democratic National Committee headquarters, the burglars remained silent. In exchange for their silence White House counsel John Dean, who had directed much of the cover-up, sent monies from the coffers of the Committee to Reelect the President (CREEP), to the burglars' attorneys and families. The hush money ensured their cooperation, but a personal tragedy threatened the scheme. In December 1972, Hunt's wife died in an airplane crash, and the news devastated him. Charles Colson warned the president that Hunt might cooperate, and the threat hovered over Nixon for the next three months.[17]

The Watergate cover-up began to come apart in March 1973. James McCord started talking with the federal prosecutors as did Howard Hunt. As they began implicating members of the White House staff, Nixon's men scrambled to save themselves. Agnew watched the events unfold from a distance. Insulated from the scandal, but intensely interested in its ramifications, Agnew correctly judged the political winds. After a state dinner on April 17, Agnew stopped by a small party being hosted by Frank Sinatra. Earlier in the day Nixon announced that he was waiving claims of executive privilege for his aides, so they would testify before the Ervin Committee. Nixon called Kissinger and asked his opinion about the statement, but Kissinger said he could not comment on it since he had not seen it. Nixon abruptly asked if he should fire Haldeman and Ehrlichman. Again Kissinger demurred. As Kissinger put down the telephone, Agnew strode into the room and asked Kissinger for his opinion of Nixon's comments. Kissinger claimed he "could not assess its impact." Agnew had his own thoughts on the matter. According to Kissinger, Agnew, in an "unfeeling manner," remarked "that Nixon was kidding himself if he thought he could avoid firing Haldeman and Ehrlichman. He would be lucky if he could save himself."[18] In his memoirs, Kissinger wrote that Agnew "was not exactly heartbroken over the prospect that his tormentors on the White House staff would now be taken down a peg."[19]

Nixon's April 17 statement was one of a series of desperate measures to stem the bleeding, but it failed. Watergate had completely engulfed his administration. Calls for Haldeman's and Ehrlichman's resignation increased. Nixon was also under pressure to explain his own involvement in the scandal. Nixon had assured the public that he had not known of the burglary (which was true) and that he had not participated in any cover-up (which was not true). Forcing out his praetorian guard jeopardized his own future. Since Haldeman and Ehrlichman were acting under instruction from Nixon, if they turned on him Nixon could lose all. As of late April there was no direct evidence of Nixon's participation in a plot to obstruct justice. For the most part John Dean's testimony to the prosecutors focused on Haldeman, Ehrlichman, and John Mitchell. And though Dean had spoken with the president over a dozen times, Dean had no records, no notes, nor any secret tape recordings of the conversations.[20]

Still, Nixon could not escape Watergate. In the face of all the sordid revelations, Nixon's protestations of innocence rang hollow. As public confidence in him eroded, even many Republicans backed away from him but he had a defender in Spiro Agnew. On April 26, Agnew issued a ringing defense of his embattled chief. Agnew prepared a brief statement for the press that he delivered in a conference room adjoining his office in the Executive Office Building. It took just ninety seconds and afterward Agnew walked away before reporters could ask questions. "At the outset, I want to make it very clear that I have full confidence in the integrity of President Nixon and in his ability to resolve the Watergate matter to the full satisfaction of the American people."[21]

The *New York Times* ran an editorial mocking that it was necessary for Agnew to proclaim his belief in the president. Perhaps Agnew was exacting a bit of revenge, the editors opined, "by subtly denigrating his chief while ostensibly supporting him."[22] Nixon's old torturer Herblock, the *Washington Post*'s editorial cartoonist, ran a sketch that harkened back to Nixon's first great crisis. Twenty-one years earlier, Nixon faced questions about a political fund operated by some of his supporters. Running as the vice presidential nominee with General Dwight Eisenhower, Nixon went on national television and successfully defended himself against charges of malfeasance. During the "Checkers Speech" that saved his career, Nixon detailed his financial holdings and challenged the Democratic nominee, Adlai Stevenson, and his running mate, Senator John Sparkman, to issue full financial disclosures. In the process he subtly asked the same of Eisenhower. While watching the speech at an auditorium in Cleveland, Eisenhower tapped a pencil on a pad. When Nixon said "something to hide" a visibly agitated Eisenhower snapped the pencil on the pad. The commander of the Normandy landing had received a generous tax rebate for his war memoir, *Crusade in Europe*, a fact that the cynical and shrewd Nixon was more than aware of. The sly dig angered Ike, and he did not forget it. The day after the address, Nixon met Eisenhower at the airport in Wheeling, West Virginia. As the plane door opened, Eisenhower walked up the steps, greeted Nixon, and announced, "You're my boy!"[23] The condescending remark echoed throughout Nixon's career, and Herblock could not pass up the opportunity to use it against Nixon. He drew a sketch that ran on April 26. A visibly taller and grinning Agnew had his hand on the slouching Nixon. The caption read, "You're My Boy."[24]

Agnew's expressions of support for Nixon were noble. Instead of steering clear of the crisis, Agnew risked much politically by standing by the beleaguered president. As vice president, Agnew had to say something in support of the president, but Agnew went beyond the minimum required of him. Just a week earlier Agnew told Kissinger he doubted if Nixon could survive Watergate, which would have made Agnew president. By remaining mum and distancing himself from Nixon, Agnew could have, if all the pieces fell together for him (and fell apart for Nixon), taken office free of any taint of Nixon and Watergate. But that was not Agnew's way. He was loyal to Nixon. Even though Agnew undoubtedly gained a measure of revenge in watching Nixon's plight, Nixon was still the president and Agnew stood by him. Agnew was but one of many officials urging Nixon to break free of Watergate. On Monday, April 30, 1973, Nixon announced from the Oval Office that he had accepted the resignations of Bob Haldeman and John Ehrlichman. He also said that John Dean had resigned, as had Attorney General Richard Kleindienst.[25]

As with every step Nixon took throughout the scandal, the April 30 speech only added to his travails. Although he accepted the onus for Watergate, Nixon denied that he was in any way implicated in the cover-up. Yet in accepting the resignations, Nixon allowed that the highest-ranking members of his administration acted in illicit and illegal ways. Nixon's vague and transparently misleading statement about his own involvement in Watergate led to more questions. With the media going after the story, with a select committee preparing an investigation, and with a special prosecutor appointed just after April 30, Nixon could not escape the metastasizing scandal.

Nixon knew his peril and could easily foresee the trouble he faced. As Watergate overtook his presidency Nixon asked several of his aides if he should resign. It is doubtful that Nixon, the man who spent his political life lusting after the presidency, really considered resigning, but he raised the subject on a number of occasions. Each time he broached the topic Nixon got the answer he expected—and wanted: don't.[26]

On April 30, while at Camp David, Nixon spoke with speechwriter Ray Price. During the talk Nixon actually accepted the responsibility for Watergate, telling Price, "the boss can never pass it on." Yet the problem, Nixon mused, was "that if you go too far in terms of saying, well, I take all the blame, and I don't blame these poor fellows and all that, then you think well, Christ, this poor damn, dumb President why didn't he resign? Which might not be a bad idea. The only." Price interrupted the thought by laughing; the idea was too comical, frightening to contemplate:

Nixon: "is—the only problem, is I mean you get Agnew. You want Agnew?"

Price: "No, I think—I think we'll be going around on this."[27]

Price claims that Nixon asked him three times that day if he should resign. "No" Price, answered, since "Vice President Agnew—whatever his other qualities—simply was not up to carrying forward the delicate diplomatic maneuverings that the United States was engaged in, in its effort to prevent war and preserve the peace."[28]

Price and the others told Nixon what he wanted to hear. It is a sad commentary that Richard Nixon had so little regard for the man he who stood a heartbeat, or a conviction, away from the presidency. His sneering tone toward Agnew is as striking as it is dangerous. In a nuclear age, when the president of the United States had the capacity to order the use of nuclear weapons, the vice presidency assumed a greater importance. After John F. Kennedy's assassination on November 22, 1963, the United States was without a vice president until Hubert H. Humphrey was inaugurated as vice president on January 20, 1965. There was no constitutional procedure allowing the president to choose and Congress approve a vice presidential nomination when a vacancy occurred. Nor was there any mechanism to allow a vice president to assume the powers of the presidency when and if the chief executive became incapacitated. Given the stakes of the Cold War, Congress passed, and the states ratified, the 25th Amendment. Section 1 of the amendment spelled out the line of succession: "In case of the removal of the President from office or his death or resignation, the Vice President shall become President." Section 2 provided for the selection of a vice president: "Whenever there is a vacancy in the office of the Vice President, the President shall nominate a Vice President who shall take office upon confirmation by a majority vote of both Houses of Congress." Sections 3 and 4 vested the powers of the office in the vice presidency if the president states himself or is declared unable to discharge his duties by the vice president and the majority of cabinet officers. The amendment was ratified in 1967. Nixon had testified before Congress in support of it. He, as much as anyone, knew the importance of the vice presidency and having someone in the office whom he, Nixon, believed was qualified to succeed him. If Nixon truly cared about the country, if he truly cared about the office of the presidency, he should have asked Agnew to not be his running mate in 1972.

Years later, when interviewing Nixon, the journalist Michael Kramer tried asking Nixon about Agnew. Nixon, in a rare display of humor, shot back, "Who?" When Kramer pressed, Nixon snorted: "Agnew was nothing."[29] Since Nixon disdained Agnew so much, he assumed that so too did everyone else. He thought of Agnew as his insurance policy, both against impeachment or calls for his resignation. So long as Agnew remained vice president, Nixon believed, even his worst enemies would think long and hard about removing him from office. "What the hell, you know. People say impeach the President. Well, then they get Agnew. Is that all right?" he asked Attorney General Richard Kleindienst. "There's not going to be anything like that," Kleindienst assured him.[30]

For his part Agnew deflected any talk of his ascension. He continued to publicly support the president, but Nixon still wanted more. During a conversation with newly appointed chief of staff Alexander Haig, as Nixon railed about "the little asshole John Dean," he wondered who might lead an attack on Dean. Nixon's former counsel had turned against him and was cooperating with the prosecutors. Dean knew enough to possibly end Nixon's presidency and he wanted an all-out assault on him. "Agnew?" he wondered aloud. "Connally? Connally won't? I don't know. I don't know. Agnew may," he thought. Haig concurred. "I think Agnew would want to and he'll do it." Later on Nixon turned toward Agnew and became furious. "What the hell's Agnew doing?" he bellowed, "He's never spoken up once on this Goddamn thing."[31]

Agnew had defended Nixon, and would continue to do so, and he also offered Nixon advice that could have saved Nixon's presidency. The Senate Select Committee, chaired by Senator Sam Ervin, a Democrat from North Carolina, began hearings in May 1973. The committee heard from former White House counsel John Dean, who testified that the president was deeply involved in the Watergate cover-up. H. R. Haldeman and John Ehrlichman mostly contradicted Dean's testimony, leaving open the question of who was being more forthright. On Monday, July 16, 1973, the committee heard from Alexander P. Butterfield, Haldeman's former assistant, who revealed that Nixon had been taping his conversations. The Senate Committee voted to subpoena the tapes, as did Archibald Cox, the special prosecutor.[32]

The battle over Watergate—and the future of Nixon's presidency—became a fight over the tapes. The night before Butterfield testified about the tapes, Nixon was taken to Bethesda Naval Hospital in Maryland, suffering from pneumonia. By the middle of the week he was well enough to have visitors. Agnew came by and told Nixon, "you've got to have a bonfire, and right now."[33] Nixon ignored Agnew's advice. He kept the tapes, but refused to surrender them. By July 1973, Nixon's approval ratings had fallen, and he faced the prospect of impeachment. *Time* magazine reported in its June 4, 1973, edition that Agnew was keeping his distance from Nixon. It was well that he should, since the magazine noted "Agnew might suddenly find himself President."[34]

Chapter 9

August 1973

As Spiro Agnew prepared for his second term in office, the U.S. attorney for Maryland, George Beall, brother of Maryland Republican senator J. Glenn Beall, opened an investigation of corruption in Baltimore City and Baltimore County. A federal grand jury was impaneled beginning on December 5, 1972. Beall's chief target was Baltimore County executive Dale Anderson, a Democrat who succeeded Agnew in the job. Beall heard rumors that Anderson was accepting kickbacks from contractors doing business with the county. With the help of his assistants, Beall issued subpoenas for companies and individuals who were awarded contracts by the county. By January rumors swept through the Baltimore metropolitan area that the U.S. Attorney's Office was hot on the trail. Early that month the prosecutors issued a subpoena to Lester Matz, a partner in the engineering firm of Matz, Childs, and Associates, that had done business with Baltimore County for over a decade. Matz quickly made an appointment with Baltimore lawyer Joseph H. H. Kaplan, a former assistant U.S. attorney who specialized in litigation matters. Matz met with Kaplan on January 15, 1973. He showed Kaplan the subpoena and Kaplan assured Matz the prosecutors were not really after him. All Matz needed to do, Kaplan advised, was cooperate with the investigators and provide the names of public officials whom he had bribed. In return Beall would provide Matz with immunity from prosecution. Matz asked Kaplan if he had to tell U.S. Attorney's Office everything he knew. Yes, because withholding information from the prosecutors would nullify the plea bargain agreement, he was told. Matz said he would not cooperate. Kaplan asked why.

"Because I have been paying off the Vice President."[1]

For years rumors about Spiro Agnew's ethical shortcomings abounded in Maryland, and for just as long journalists and partisan political operatives could find no concrete evidence to support the allegations. After Nixon surprised the country by choosing Agnew as his running mate, swarms of investigators descended upon the Baltimore area looking for some dark spot on Agnew's record. The *New York Times* ran a piece questioning Agnew's investment in a real estate partnership that invested in land where the state considered building a second Chesapeake Bay Bridge. The story was old news in Maryland, and the *Times* uncovered nothing that suggested any illegal activity by Agnew.[2]

Over the next four years a number of reporters tried to find some dirt about Agnew. Joseph Albright, a *Washington Post* investigative reporter, spent three years digging into Agnew's background. In 1972 he published a critical, and at times scathing, portrait, *What Makes Spiro Run? The Life and Times of Spiro Agnew*. Much of the work focused on Agnew's cozy friendships with his benefactors. Albright probed Agnew's business transactions and his political fund-raising and interviewed scores of Agnew's friends and associates, dug through public records, and read everything he could about his subject. He portrayed Agnew as a cunning individual who skirted the law but never quite broke it. Agnew sat down with Albright and fielded the sharp questions Albright hurled his way. "The biggest red herring that I ever had to contend with," Agnew said in response to questions about the Bay Bridge. Albright pressed Agnew about his relationship with J. Walter Jones, a real estate executive who also served on the board of the Chesapeake National Bank. Jones and Agnew had been friends for over two decades and, as county executive, Agnew had the county's deposits placed in Jones's bank. Agnew took umbrage at any suggestion that his dealings with Jones as represented any conflict of interest.[3]

Albright's work came and went and inflicted no damage on Agnew. Another reporter, Jerry Landauer of the *Wall Street Journal*, had been spending time in Maryland pursuing the hints about Agnew's improprieties. But Landauer came up empty. If Agnew had anything to hide, anything to fear, not even his fiercest political opponents had found it. From 1968 through 1972 Agnew had been under as much scrutiny as any public figure and yet no one had exposed any corruption on his part. "He's clean," an unidentified Maryland figure told Albright.[4]

As far as most knew, Agnew was above reproach. Despite the many investigations into his financial dealings, nothing had been produced to tie Agnew to any wrongdoing. That was about to change, and Agnew knew it. On July 18, 1973, two weeks before his scandal exploded, Agnew sat down for an interview with *Newsweek* columnist Stewart Alsop. "All I'm saying," he told Stewart Alsop, in response to questions about the swirling federal investigation (the one he was, unknown to Alsop, a target of), "there's been a certain permissiveness that's run through the financing of politics over the years, and suddenly the rules are changed in the middle of the game, so that people," presumably Agnew himself, "who have become accustomed over the years to financing political campaigns in certain ways are suddenly—this is no longer permissible—it's morally reprehensible and it's suddenly jerked up."[5]

Agnew was laying the groundwork for his defense. I did it, but everyone else did it, so what I did was not wrong. But he clearly recognized his perilous position, hence the diatribe about the rules being changed during the game. By late July the U.S. attorneys were aiming right at him, and he needed to formulate an answer to the barrage of questions he would soon face from the grand jury, the media, and the public.

Agnew first learned of the grand jury investigation after he returned from his trip to the Far East.

> On February 3, 1973, my attorney, George White, telephoned me from Maryland. He was extremely agitated. His voice was strained, and he sounded like a man under tremendous pressure. He said he had to speak to me immediately about a matter that was too dangerous to discuss over the telephone. I agreed that he should fly out at once and tell me the whole story.[6]

White flew out to California and met the vice president at Frank Sinatra's Palm Springs estate. "George White told me an incredible tale—of a federal investigation in Maryland that threatened to involve me," Agnew wrote. According to White, two of Agnew's friends and political contributors, Lester Matz and Jerome B. Wolff, were targets of the federal grand jury probe. Both men visited White while Agnew was in Asia and related their worries about the investigation. Agnew claimed that White told him that the men were frantic and wanted Agnew's help in derailing the probe. If Agnew refused, then Matz and Wolff might "say things that were very embarrassing to me." Agnew asked White what the men were referring to:

"They will say they made kickback payments to you."

Agnew denied the allegation. He admitted receiving campaign contributions from the men, but the money did not go to him personally. White pressed him: "This is very serious. I want you to level with me about it." Agnew assured White that he was telling the truth. Matz, he told White, was not a close friend and Wolff was always having money trouble. Whatever the men might say, Agnew stated that he was innocent.[7]

That is the story Agnew related in *Go Quietly*. George White, however, recalled the conversation differently. Eight years after Agnew left office, the state of Maryland brought a lawsuit against him, demanding that he return the money he took as governor. The lawsuit came after the publication of *Go Quietly*. White believed Agnew libeled him in *Go Quietly* by suggesting he, White, knew of illegal activities taking place in Maryland but failed to report the crimes, as he was required to do as an attorney. He won the case and Agnew wrote him a letter of apology. In the wake of the suit, the presiding judge in the civil action ruled that lawyer–client privilege no longer held, and he ordered White to testify about what Agnew had told him. Under oath, White stated Agnew admitted taking bribes, and said that this type of corruption had been going on for "a thousand years."[8]

Jerome Wolff served as Agnew's science and technology advisor from February 1969 to May 1970. According to journalists Jules Witcover and Richard Cohen, authors of the definitive work on the Agnew scandal, *A Heartbeat Away: The Investigation and Resignation of Spiro T. Agnew*,

Agnew apparently discharged Wolff after White House counsel John Dean ruled that Wolff had a conflict of interest because he kept a stake in two engineering companies.[9] Agnew made no mention of this in his memoirs. He wrote that Wolff quit because he needed more money than his government salary paid. Agnew agreed to retain Wolff as a consultant to the Marine Council at the rate of $100 per day.[10] At the time Agnew greatly admired Wolff. The two had worked together for eight years. Before going to Washington, Wolff worked as director of Maryland's State Roads Commission. As the director, Wolff awarded consulting contracts. He oversaw the contracting for two of the biggest projects, the building of a parallel Chesapeake Bay Bridge and a crossing bridge in outer Baltimore harbor. The state approved a $200 million bond issue to finance the two projects, and significant portions of the monies went to Lester Matz's firm, Matz, Childs, and Associates.[11]

On February 6, George Beall informed Attorney General Richard Kleindienst that Agnew was not under investigation. Kleindienst called Beall back three days later and said Agnew had complained that the investigation could embarrass him. Agnew had no cause for worry, Beall replied. There was no evidence against him, and further, since Beall and his team were focusing on malfeasance in Baltimore County, any wrongdoing committed by Agnew as county executive was protected by the statute of limitations. Agnew had also expressed worry about one of the prosecutors, Barnet Skolnik, who had briefly worked for Edmund Muskie's presidential campaign. Beall expressed confidence in Skolnik's professionalism but added that for the time being Skolnik would adopt a lower profile. After speaking with Kleindienst, Beall informed his staffers, Barnet Skolnik, Russell Baker, and Ronald Liebman, about Agnew's conversation with the attorney general. Baker, alone among the four, thought Agnew was "acting like a guilty man."[12]

Agnew's concern about the prosecutors ran deeper than Skolnik's partisanship. Agnew believed the Justice Department team, headed by George Beall, was out to get him. Beall, Agnew argued, carried a grudge against him dating back to 1968. Both men attended the 1968 Republican National Convention in Miami. Agnew went as a favorite son; Beall went as a Rockefeller delegate. Agnew tried persuading Beall, along with other delegates, to switch to Nixon; but Beall held out as long as he could. Agnew didn't forget the episode. He later wrote:

> When Beall's recommended appointment as a federal prosecutor for Maryland came to my attention—every Maryland appointment went across my desk and was subject to my approval when I was Vice President—I remember holding it a couple of days and thinking, "George Beall was as stubborn as a mule at the convention and he is not on our team, so why should we make him the U.S Attorney?"

But Beall's friends interceded and Agnew let "bygones be bygones" and approved the nomination.[13]

For the rest of his life, Agnew believed that George Beall had destroyed him. Whatever the merits of Agnew's charge, he was clearly afraid of where the investigation was going. During February and March the investigation proceeded apace and Agnew was kept abreast of the investigation via his new attorney Judah Best. On April 10, Agnew approached Bob Haldeman. "I gave Bob Haldeman a complete summary of the Maryland problem, assured him of my innocence, but expressed concern that I could, nevertheless, be seriously harmed by false charges," Agnew recalled.[14] Could Haldeman help? Haldeman recorded in his diary:

> The VP called me over today and said he had a real problem, because Jerome Wolff, who used to work for him back in Maryland, was about to be called by the United States Attorney who was busting open campaign contribution cases and kickbacks to contractors. It seems that Wolff kept verbatim records of meetings with the VP and others, back over the years, concerning fund-raising, and has a lot of quotes about how much we ought to get from a certain contractor, and so on, who has good jobs. It wasn't shakedown stuff, it was merely going back to get support from those who benefited from the Administration, but the way it's worded, the VP feels it sounds bad. He made the point that (U.S. Attorney) George Beall is (Maryland Senator) Glenn Beall's brother, and that if Glenn Beall would talk to him, he could straighten it out. The VP's tried to get him, but apparently not successfully, so he wanted me to talk to Glenn Beall, which, of course, I won't do, in order to verify a White House awareness and concern. He feels that publication of this stuff would finish the VP, because Wolff was with him for so long and is very much concerned.[15]

In retrospect, the April 10, 1973, entry is damning for Agnew. Agnew later claimed he never explicitly tried to stop George Beall's probe; only that he attempted to alert Haldeman, and Nixon, that the investigation might embarrass the administration. But Haldeman's notes suggest otherwise. Further, Agnew told Haldeman that Wolff's records "could finish" him.[16] Unless someone intervened and blocked the probe, Agnew knew that his political career was over and he admitted as much to Haldeman.

Haldeman had some advice for Agnew—that he contact former White House assistant Charles Colson, who had left the White House and was working in the law firm of Colson and Shapiro. Agnew took the advice, even though he and Colson disliked one another. Colson suggested Agnew retain his partner Judah Best as his criminal defense attorney. "So Best became my liaison with the prosecutors in Baltimore."[17]

Best spoke with George Beall shortly thereafter and Beall assured Best that Agnew was not a target of the investigation. But that quickly changed. From January through April, Lester Matz, along with his business partner John Childs, engineers in the firm of Matz, Childs, and Associates, refused to cooperate with the federal prosecutors. So too did Jerome Wolff, former Roads Commissioner of Maryland, who had served as Agnew's science and technology advisor from 1969 to 1970. All three men were represented by attorney Joseph Kaplan. But on Friday, May 18, 1973, Kaplan called Russell Baker and told Baker that Matz, Childs, and Wolff might be willing to cooperate, and that they could finger Agnew in the kickback schemes. While the revelation was a bombshell, Baker cautiously noted that the statute of limitations ruled out any indictment of Agnew since he ceased being county executive in 1966. Then Kaplan informed the prosecutor that the payments continued while Agnew served as governor—and as vice president.[18]

It was on May 18, 1973, that Richard Nixon's and Spiro Agnew's problems began to dovetail. That day the new attorney general Elliot Richardson appointed a special prosecutor, Archibald Cox, to lead the Watergate investigation. Richardson saw Cox as the perfect choice for the post given Cox's reputation and standing in legal circles. A professor of constitutional law at Harvard, Cox had served as solicitor general for President John F. Kennedy. Nixon viewed the appointment differently. Cox was a Kennedy man, a member of the liberal establishment that hated Nixon.[19]

Try as he might, Nixon could not make Watergate go away, and Cox's pronouncement dominated news coverage that day. Agnew's own problems were kept from public view. In late May through early August, the Baltimore prosecutors tried to keep the story under wraps that the vice president was a target of their probe. Meanwhile, Beall and his team went back and forth with attorneys Joseph Kaplan and Arnold Weiner, who was also representing Jerome Wolff. The lawyers for the engineers wanted full immunity but Beall and his staff held out and the negotiations dragged on through June.[20]

On June 12, George Beall sat down with Attorney General Elliot Richardson. Twenty-six years later Beall recounted the meeting: "I seized the opportunity to brief my new boss on our expanding Baltimore investigation of the Vice President. The Attorney General, confronted with the increasing vulnerability of President Nixon to the Watergate entanglement, responded with remarkable equanimity." Richardson, according to Beall, "confirmed that principle mattered more than politics in federal criminal law enforcement, a sentiment I shared."[21]

The plea bargain arrangements made by Matz and Wolff ratcheted up the pressure on Agnew. Matz informed the prosecutors he and his business partner John Childs "welcomed Mr. Agnew's candidacy for Baltimore county Executive because they believed that his election would present them with an opportunity to be a member of the small group of engineers that, they believed, would inevitably form around his administration and receive most of the substantial county engineering work." After Agnew's victory, a figure that the prosecutors called the "close associate" (J. Walter Jones) allegedly contacted Matz and told Matz "that the two of them were going to make a lot of money under the Agnew administration." Shortly afterward, Jones approached Matz and inquired how much money engineers should kickback from county contracts. Matz said 5 percent and provided Jones with a chart that projected the profits from expected contracts, how much he figured to make, and what percentage he would pay to Agnew. The final arrangement included a 5 percent fee on engineering contracts and 2½ percent on surveying contracts. Jones, according to Matz, said that the payments were not "political contribution" but "payments made in return for contracts."[22]

Between January 1967 and the summer of 1968, Matz made no payments to Agnew, but "sometime in late June or early July 1968, Matz calculated that he owed Governor Agnew approximately $20,000 on the basis of 5% of fees that his company had already received from the state." In a complicated maneuver, Matz generated the $20,000 in cash and handed it to Agnew, just before Agnew was named the Republican vice presidential nominee. But according to Matz's own estimate he owed Agnew an additional $10,000. In early 1969, Matz met with Agnew at the White House. He gave the vice president a yellow legal sheet with his calculations and then handed Agnew an envelope that contained the $10,000, which Agnew put in a drawer.[23]

In the future Matz was to call Agnew's secretary and tell her that Matz had "information" for the vice president. According to Matz, upon his return from Washington, he told Childs of the payment and how the payoff to the vice president left him "shaken." Apparently Matz was not shaken enough to hope that Agnew might help him win federal contracts. But Agnew had limited control over such matters and Matz reportedly received one contract (Agnew tried unsuccessfully to land him more). Jones, claimed Matz, requested that Matz contribute $10,000 to the Nixon-Agnew reelection campaign, but Matz declined. When pressed again by Jones, Matz complained directly to the vice president, who "told Matz to say that he gave at the office."[24]

Jerome Wolff claimed that his illicit dealings with Agnew also stretched back a decade. Wolff recalled that while Agnew served as county executive, "friends in the consulting business asked Wolff, while Mr. Agnew was County Executive, how much Wolff was paying for the engineering work that he was receiving from Baltimore County. They seemed to assume that he was paying," the prosecutors wrote. Wolff confirmed the assumptions. He recalled making roughly four payments to Agnew through Jones. Wolff, like Matz, contributed to Agnew's gubernatorial campaign and Agnew appointed him director of State Roads Commission: "Over the course of the subsequent 18 to 20 months that Agnew served as Governor of Maryland, the scheme agreed to by Mr. Agnew, Hammerman, and Wolff was fully implemented," according to Wolff and Hammerman. With Hammerman serving as the middleman, engineers kicked the money up to Agnew, with Wolff taking in his share. A meticulous man, Wolff kept a detailed record of every single transaction. Wolff contended he never openly discussed the illicit dealings with Agnew, but that, at one point during Agnew's gubernatorial days, Agnew warned Wolff: "Look after yourself but be careful."[25]

Allen Green related that he first met Agnew in 1963. At the time Green's engineering firm "did a small amount of business in Baltimore County" and Agnew "inquired why Green and Associates had not more aggressively solicited County business." A little while later Green visited Agnew who said that Green's company "would be considered for county work." Impressed by Agnew, Green stated that he arranged an introduction for

Agnew with Maryland Senator J. Glenn Beall, Sr. ("It is ridiculous for him to assert that," Agnew argued. "How could two of the best-known and important Republicans in the state of Maryland—where you can count Republican officeholders on your fingers—not know each other?")[26] Green and Associates were awarded a few contracts, but Green told the U.S. attorneys, "I believe that neither I nor my company made any cash payments to him or to anyone in his administration." When Agnew ran for governor he asked for Green's support and Green willingly agreed because "I genuinely admired the man and believed that he would make an excellent Governor." Green also believed "that he would be grateful for my support, and I anticipated that he would express his gratitude by giving my company state work if he were elected."[27]

Green told investigators when he and Agnew met in the governor's Baltimore office in 1967, Agnew wailed about the financial burdens. As the "titular leader of the Republican Party," Agnew complained of having to raise substantial monies for the Maryland GOP. He lamented "that it was extremely difficult for a person in his limited financial situation to bear the personal expenses of high public office, in that his new position would require him, he believed, to adopt and maintain a life style that was beyond his means." A sympathetic Green told Agnew that he understood the problems and would like to help: "I believed that it would be possible for me to make periodic cash payments to him." Agnew, Green testified, "replied that he would appreciate such assistance very much."[28]

Between 1967 and 1968, Green approximated that he met with Agnew six times a year. At every visit Green handed Agnew envelopes containing $2,000–$3,000. Agnew, Green recalled, placed the envelopes in a drawer or in a coat pocket. Green alleged he kept a written list of the payments, but destroyed the paper when the grand jury subpoenaed his company's financial records. However, after Agnew's election in 1968, Jerome Wolff presented Green with a list of the state contracts he received during the Agnew administration. Shortly thereafter, Green met with Agnew and discussed Wolff's records. Agnew mentioned that he was glad Green's firm had done so well and "then reiterated that he had been unable to improve his financial situation during his two years as Governor," and though Agnew would make more money as vice president, "he expected that the social and other demands of the office would substantially increase his personal expenses." Given these burdens Agnew hoped that his friend "would continue the financial assistance that I had been providing to him over the preceding two years." Green took the hint; the two men had a "tacit understanding" between them. Green estimated that he still owed Agnew money from existing bids and would make good on his debts.[29]

From 1969 through December 1972, Green visited Agnew a few times a year and made his contribution. Agnew's new station and environs awed and disturbed Green: "I recall the first occasion upon which I paid money to Mr. Agnew in his offices in the Executive Office Building. I was quite impressed with his office and with his position and felt very uncomfortable about the transaction that was about to occur" (that testimony was partially untrue. Green claims that his first payment occurred in the February 1969 at Agnew's EOB office. However, in February 1969 Agnew's office was in the West Wing). He also feared that the room might be wiretapped and so Green thereafter said little other than that he was making his usual political contribution. These "contributions" included $2,000 payments in February, July, October, and November 1969. Over the four years Green calculated that he gave Agnew a total of $28,000.[30]

Their last meeting occurred in May 1973 at a luncheon where Green presented Agnew with a watch. During the lunch Agnew brought up the grand jury investigation but indicated to Green that neither had any cause for concern. Green informed Agnew that his corporate records had been subpoenaed. If the U.S. attorney wanted his records going back more than three years Green told Agnew that he would take the Fifth Amendment.[31]

I. H. "Bud" Hammerman held out until August. Hammerman and Agnew grew up together in Baltimore but they had drifted apart. They reestablished contact after Agnew won election as Baltimore County executive. By that time Hammerman was a successful real estate developer and banker. Following Agnew's victory, Hammerman called and offered his congratulations and asked for a meeting. During their talk Hammerman "told Mr. Agnew that he knew all campaigns had deficits, and he offered Mr. Agnew a post-election contribution of $10,000. Mr. Agnew refused, but told Hammerman that he would expect a contribution three times as large when he ran for office again."[32]

Hammerman claimed that during Agnew's county executive days, the pair "developed a close, personal friendship." Agnew confided in Hammerman, often bewailing about his tight financial situation. Hammerman took pity on Agnew, introducing him to wealthy friends and showering Agnew with gifts. And Hammerman made good on his promise to aid Agnew's political career. In the 1966 election many of Hammerman's friends pressured him to support the Democratic candidate, but Hammerman stayed loyal to Agnew. Hammerman served as one of Agnew's financial chairmen, gave $25,000, and "raised an even larger amount in campaign contributions."[33]

The trio's "system" worked well, and across Maryland, "It was soon generally understood that among engineers that Hammerman was the person to see in connection with State Roads engineering contracts." Most of the time the engineers approached Hammerman and inquired whether the state had any jobs and Hammerman would "see what he could do." There was never any mention made of a shakedown since "the engineers clearly indicated that they knew what was expected of them." Wolff alerted Hammerman of which company received a bid and Hammerman called the company and issued congratulations: "These congratulations were intended as signals that a cash 'contribution' was due, and the engineer would then meet with Hammerman and bring the money." Agnew would periodically call Hammerman and inquire how many "papers" Hammerman had for him. According to their code, "paper" signified $1,000. Hammerman would then collect the money from a safe-deposit box and deliver it to the governor.[34]

By July 1973 the U.S. Attorney's Office had the outlines of the corrupt practices from Matz, Wolff, and Green (Hammerman began cooperating in late August). On July 3, the four prosecutors, Beall, Skolnik, Baker, and Liebman, sat down with Elliot Richardson and outlined the case against Agnew. The meeting lasted for three hours. The prosecutors provided the details and Richardson peppered them with some probing questions. Beall and his staff argued forcefully that Nixon should be kept in the dark. Telling Nixon, they contended, meant telling his aides, and the nature of the allegations would inevitably get to the vice president. Richardson concurred. He was already having enough trouble with Nixon as it was, and he did not want any more headaches.[35]

Nixon knew much more about Spiro Agnew's legal problems than Richardson or the Baltimoreans suspected. After Agnew spoke with Haldeman on April 10, Haldeman dutifully told Nixon about the conversation. Nixon sympathized with Agnew's plight "but in view of all the other problems and our strained relations with Capitol Hill, I did not see how we could do anything to help him."[36] When Nixon replaced Chief of Staff Bob Haldeman with Alexander Haig, Nixon knew from Haldeman of Agnew's request to halt the probe. Haig first learned of Agnew's problems in June when Elliot Richardson informed him of the investigation.[37]

Richardson told Haig that Agnew might have taken money while vice president. The day before Wolff agreed to cooperate, on July 9, Agnew's attorney, Judah Best, called George Beall and inquired about the state of the probe. Beall told Best that he could not discuss the matter over the phone and suggested that Best arrange a meeting. When Best followed up on July 10, the same day that Wolff was revealing his secrets, Beall informed Best that he could no longer speak with Best.[38]

Spiro Agnew was now a target of the investigation. His oldest and closest associates were all turning state's evidence against him. Allen Green, a man Agnew had "come to know and like," entered into negotiations on July 17. Soon afterward Elliot Richardson informed Alexander Haig that the Justice Department was zeroing in on Agnew. On August 1, 1973, Judah Best arrived at the U.S. Attorney's Office in Baltimore. George Beall handed Best a letter that Agnew later noted, "made me the first (sitting) Vice-President in United States history to be officially placed under criminal investigation."[39]

"Dear Mr. Best," the letter began,

> This office is now conducting an investigation of allegations concerning possible violations by your client and others of federal criminal statutes, including but not limited to Section 371 (conspiracy), Section 1951 (extortion), and Section 1952 (extortion and bribery) of Title 18, United States Code, and certain criminal provisions of the tax laws of the United States (Title 26, United States Code).

The letter's purpose, Beall wrote, was "to invite your client, or his authorized representative, to produce and deliver to this office ... the following materials"—which included bank records, canceled checks, check books, and his state and federal tax returns from January 1, 1967 to the present. "I felt frustrated and helpless," Agnew wrote in his memoirs. "I was beset by an ideologically attuned group of people who were all against me on the basis of my beliefs and the way I was conducting my public responsibilities, and most of them would profit by my destruction. They wanted to wreck my life."[40]

The same day that Judah Best received official word from Beall, Attorney General Elliot Richardson contacted Chief-of-Staff Alexander Haig, telling Haig that he needed to see him right away. Haig listened as Richardson detailed the charges. A former state prosecutor in Massachusetts, Richardson said that he had never seen "as open-and-shut a case of multiple crimes."[41] Haig described Richardson's tone as "one of cold contempt" and he told the chief of staff an indictment could come as soon as six weeks. When Haig alerted Nixon about the gravity of the charges Nixon asked that J. Fred Buzhardt and Leonard Garment, both White House counsels, meet with Attorney General Richardson. Hosting Buzhardt and Garment at his home in Alexandria, Virginia, on Sunday, August 5, Richardson argued Agnew should resign.[42]

Buzhardt and Garment agreed and they informed Nixon. In his memoirs, Nixon wrote, "after their meeting Richardson, Buzhardt and Garment sent back gloomy evaluations: they agreed with Richardson that this was one of the most solid cases that they had ever seen."[43] On Monday, August 6, Nixon conferred with Richardson in the Oval Office. Richardson laid out the case against Agnew with "irrefutable documents" pointing to Agnew's complicity. As he reported the shocking details, Richardson was struck by Nixon's impassivity. All Nixon could muster was a cynical observation that Marylanders politicians were "all like that."[44] But Nixon's seemingly blasé manner masked his inner feelings: "Objectively I recognized the weight of Richardson's evidence, but emotionally I was still on Agnew's side. I wanted to believe him." Nixon ordered Richardson to take over complete responsibility of the investigation, and to prevent Agnew from being railroaded by the Baltimore prosecutors and the press. He also requested that Assistant Attorney General Henry Petersen be brought in to offer an independent examination of the evidence.[45]

Later that afternoon Agnew and Richardson met face-to-face. When Nixon appointed Richardson as attorney general, Agnew praised his "impeccable reputation."[46] That view had changed. Agnew wrote, "at 3:15 that Monday afternoon, the Attorney General strode into my suite in the Old Executive Office Building. He seemed even more stiff and starchy than I had remembered him from previous encounters. The proper Bostonian was definitely hostile."[47]

Richardson was blunt, telling Agnew he was there "because the President asked me to come." Agnew then introduced his attorneys, including two New Yorkers, Jay H. Topkis and Martin London of the firm of Weiss, Rifkind, Wharton & Garrison. The two new lawyers were liberal Democrats, but they set aside their philosophical differences and vigorously defended their client. Richardson proceeded to outline the charges while Agnew "listened to this farrago of lies with rising indignation." As Richardson ticked off the specifics, Agnew let loose with a barrage against the accusers and the prosecutors. Governors picked engineers for state commissions; that was part of the job. And those same engineers made political contributions. As for one of those engineers, "Matz is crazy," he exclaimed. Beall and his associates were out to get him. Agnew requested that they be removed from the investigation.[48]

Then Agnew's lawyers took over. Judah Best also complained about the "Gang of Four." Word had reached Best that Russell Baker had bragged at a cocktail party, "We're breathing down Agnew's neck." Topkis weighed in on the same subject. The investigation cried out for a special prosecutor, one without any vested interest in the case. Martin London asked for the specifics of the charges. Throughout the session Richardson brushed off all questions and requests. He defended Beall and the other U.S. attorneys. Afraid of leaks, at least those that did not emanate from his office, Richardson would not go into further details about the case. But Richardson agreed that he would contact Henry Petersen and have Petersen review the matter.[49]

"The Attorney General had failed in his mission," Agnew claimed.[50] Although Nixon ignored the Richardson–Agnew meeting, its purpose apparently was to have Richardson present the facts, and Agnew, seeing the damning evidence, would come to the conclusion that he would have to resign. Following the meeting Agnew asked to see Nixon, but Nixon had flown to Camp David. That evening Agnew sat in his office with his chief-of-staff Art Sohmer, hoping to hear from Nixon. As they waited, Sohmer informed Agnew that the *Wall Street Journal* had broken the story.[51]

Sohmer also had more news. Nixon would not speak with Agnew; instead he was sending a delegate, Bryce Harlow, knowing Agnew trusted Harlow and would listen to him. Harlow was a former House member who had served as legislative director in the Eisenhower and Nixon administrations. He was widely respected and he and Agnew had a good relationship. Harlow arrived at 9:15, accompanied by Alexander Haig. When could he see the president, Agnew asked? Without responding directly, Haig told Agnew that Nixon was "floored by the news" and so sent Haig and Harlow as emissaries. Haig did most of the talking, but mostly danced around the purpose of the visit. Frustrated by Haig's evasiveness Agnew asked, "What are you here to tell me? What do you want?"

Haig said bluntly, "We think you should resign."

"Resign? Without even having a chance to talk to the President?"

"Yes, resign immediately." Haig replied.

Agnew asked if the men were conveying Richard Nixon's wish. Yes, Haig told him. Agnew began pacing the floor in his office. He would not quit, he yelled back, not until "I see the President. I want to see him just as soon as I can."[52]

Then Art Sohmer, who had sat quietly throughout the meeting, came to his boss's defense. He exchanged "harsh words" with Haig and Harlow. Finally, Agnew escorted the two out. "I was seething with rage, frustration, and despair," he wrote. Since first being alerted of the inquiry, Nixon and his men all assumed Agnew was guilty. But not once did Nixon, Haig, Harlow, or anyone else on the staff ask Agnew if he was guilty. Without hearing his side, they demanded his resignation. The process struck Agnew as blatantly unfair, and if he had contemplated resigning, now he dug in. A proud and willful man, Agnew resisted, hating taking orders from anyone, including the president. And he certainly would not take orders from two staff members, so he held on.[53]

As the night ended, news of the investigation crossed the newswires. The floodgates opened on Tuesday, August 7. For years *Wall Street Journal* reporter Jerry Landauer had doggedly pursued rumors that Agnew was on the take. Although Landauer never found anything incriminating, his determination paid off in one respect. He knew of the grand jury probe and he broke the story. On the front page of the country's leading financial sheet, a banner headline proclaimed: "Vice President Spiro Agnew was formally notified by the Justice Department last week that he is a target of a far-ranging criminal investigation by the U.S. attorney's office in Baltimore. The allegations against him include bribery, extortion, and tax fraud."[54]

Finally, Agnew had his opportunity to tell his side of the story to Nixon. The two met in Nixon's hideaway office in the Executive Office Building. Agnew, Nixon recalled, "walked into my office with the same, easy stride that he always had and began our conversation by declaring that he was totally innocent of the charges."[55] Agnew remembered the beginning of the meeting differently: "He greeted me warmly at the door and led me to an easy chair, talking all the while about inconsequentials [*sic*] so as not to allow the gaps in the conversation he found so uncomfortable. When we were seated the monologue continued."[56]

By that time Nixon had removed the White House taping system so there is no way to determine whose version of the meeting is more accurate, but their respective versions agree in that Agnew questioned the integrity and motives of the Baltimore prosecutors. In *Go Quietly*, Agnew also wrote that he detailed the shortcomings of the investigation and the fact that the case boiled down to a he-said-he-said contest, with his accusers having been offered immunity for their testimony. "I don't think that I'm getting a fair shake out of Richardson. I want an independent review of the case." Nixon, who had his own concerns about Richardson, said that he would have Assistant Attorney General Henry Petersen look into the matter. The comment seemed designed to allay Agnew's fears about being railroaded, and it did—somewhat.

> Because Richardson had mentioned Petersen at the meeting in my office the day before, I was a little surprised that Nixon acted as if the thought had just struck him. However, I desperately wanted to believe the President had been persuaded I was not being treated fairly and that he wanted to rectify that.

As Agnew departed, he mentioned that he was planning on holding a press conference the next day. Nixon warned Agnew about making any statements that could come back and haunt him. Agnew ignored the advice.[57]

Chapter 10

"Damned Lies"

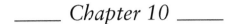

On August 8, 1973, at 3:15 EST, Spiro T. Agnew strode into the auditorium in the Old Executive Office Building. The room was packed with reporters waiting for the vice president of the United States to answer questions about his involvement in the Maryland scandals. The news conference was televised live on all three networks.

At times he was brazen. At times he was defiant. At times he was defensive. At times he was aggressive. Sometimes he told the truth. Sometimes, as the facts later proved, he lied. Sometimes he was forthright. At times he was circumspect. He answered questions. He dodged questions.

He read a prepared statement:

> Ladies and gentleman, I have a very short statement to make, following which I will take your questions.
>
> Because of the defamatory statements that are being leaked to the news media by sources that the news reports refer to as close to the Federal investigation, I cannot adhere to my original intention to remain silent following my initial statement a few days ago which asserted innocence and which indicated I would have nothing further to say until the investigation is completed.
>
> Under normal circumstances, the traditional safeguard of secrecy under such proceedings would protect the subject, but apparently this protection is not to be extended to the Vice President of the United States.
>
> Well, I have no intention to be skewered in this fashion, and since I have no intention to be so skewered, I have called this press conference to label as false and scurrilous and malicious these rumors and accusations that are being circulated, and to answer your questions regarding them, and any other questions that I might be able to answer concerning the general situation.

This is when the barrage of questions came from the reporters who packed the auditorium.

"If you are invited or subpoenaed by the Grand Jury of Baltimore County, how would you respond?"

He would wait for advice of his attorneys.

"Whose idea was it to hold the news conference?"

It was his own idea.

A reporter asked if the charges made by Jerome Wolff were true, specifically the allegation reported in that morning's papers that Wolff had paid Agnew $1,000 a week.

That charge, like many made over the next two months, was baseless, as it turned out. In their zeal to cover the story, some journalists had lost their sense of skepticism and rushed to print nearly every rumor, no matter what the source and no matter how damaging to Agnew personally.

"Do you deny the charges?"

"I am denying them outright and I am labeling them—and I think a person in my position at a time like this might be permitted this departure from normal language—as damned lies."

The forceful denial did not satisfy the reporters in the room, as another journalist wanted to know about Jerome Wolff's $1,000-a-week payoffs.

That story, Agnew noted, had been "attributed to him," but cautioned that everyone must "draw a distinction between rumor and fact."

Unfortunately for Agnew, few made the distinction. Whatever the truth of the case against him, from the very beginning Agnew was buried underneath an avalanche of allegations, innuendo, and in some cases, smears. He expressed indignation about the media's coverage of the matter, and justly so.

But not all the allegations were unfounded. "Mr. Vice President, have you ever received money for your personal use from any person, contractor, or company doing business with the State of Maryland or with the Federal Government?"

"Absolutely not," he shot back.

He was lying. For over a decade engineers had paid him more than $200,000, all for his personal use.

Had Agnew "considered stepping down temporarily until the matter is cleared up"?

"I have not."

Would he consider resigning "to protect public confidence"?

No, Agnew said, because "I have no expectation of being indicted, and I am not going to face any kind of contingent thinking in that respect at this time."

"Mr. Vice President, prior to the time your counsel told the U.S. Attorney that you were not trying to impede the investigation, were any contacts made with the U.S. Attorney, either authorized by you or encouraged by you with the U.S Attorney?"

Throughout most of the conference Agnew answered all questions directly, but he evaded this one: "Not to my knowledge. Not to my knowledge." In fact, Agnew tried on several occasions to halt the investigation. In one instance he requested the intervention of George Beall's brother, Senator Glenn Beall, to halt the investigation.

Why was Agnew holding the press conference when Nixon had not held one for months?

"The best answer that I can give you to that is that President Nixon hasn't received a letter from the United States Attorney telling him he is under investigation."

On July 16, 1973, former White House assistant Alexander Butterfield had told the Senate Select Committee on Campaign Practices (the Ervin Committee) that for over two years, Nixon had been tape-recording his conversations. A reporter wanted to know if Agnew had recorded any of his conversations since first being alerted to the probe in February.

"No."

The second part of the next question concerned "the Watergate atmosphere." Had that atmosphere contributed to the investigation?

"Now, the second part of your question concerning the Watergate atmosphere: If I said I thought I was involved in this, I would have to say—if I were in your position—that that would be a very self-serving declaration. I leave it to your judgment whether it is or not."

Was Agnew satisfied with the president's "grudging expression of confidence in you?" a reporter wondered.

Agnew turned that question around. He reiterated his "total confidence" in the president. He then added: "I think the Vice President of the United States should stand on his own feet. It really isn't that important what a President says, although I welcome the President's support, and as I would reassert, he has given it to me unequivocally."

"Mr. Vice President, could you speak to the specifics of the charges against you?"

"I could not," he answered, "because I am not aware of the specifics."

That was another half-truth. Two days earlier Agnew met with Elliot Richardson and the attorney general provided some concrete information. While Agnew, or his lawyers, did not know all the specifics, they knew more than Agnew was letting on.

"Mr. Vice President, before that, had anyone either directly or indirectly threatened to drag you into this unless you helped kill the Baltimore County investigation?"

Agnew dodged the question. In his account of the events, Agnew wrote that in fact Lester Matz and Allen Green issued several veiled and several not-so-veiled threats that they would implicate him unless he shut down the probe. But at the time Agnew sidestepped the matter. "I am not going to respond to that question at this time because it is premature for me to make such judgments. If you say with a direct contact, to me I would say no."

"Did anyone ask you to kill the investigation in Baltimore County?"

Agnew later wrote that sometime in the spring of 1973, real estate developer Bud Hammerman handed him a letter from Lester Matz. "The letter," Agnew claimed, "was a cry of anguish with an undertone of threats." Agnew alleged that he told Hammerman, "I wish I hadn't seen this letter." Wolff then asked what he should tell Matz. "You can't tell him anything." Hammerman insisted that Agnew had to intervene to halt the investigation. "There's nothing I can do to stop it. I could easily be charged with obstructing justice."[1]

But at his press conference that day, Agnew categorically stated, "No, no one asked me to do it" (stop the investigation).

The last question concerned just how much he would cooperate with the investigation.

"As I said before, I have nothing to hide. I will make available at the appropriate time and in the appropriate way to the appropriate parties as determined after consultation with my counsel whatever records, or my own body, for interrogation, whatever is needed, but I am not going to make those judgments at this time. As you know, there are certainly highly unprecedented constitutional questions that must be considered so I am not foreclosing any result in that respect. I will just not be able to reach that at this time."[2]

Agnew had achieved a remarkable, albeit brief, victory. For over an hour he stood at the podium and fielded tough, at times, hostile questions. Throughout the entire interrogation Agnew never flinched. He shot down the accusations, or at least most of them. The contrast with Richard Nixon could not have been greater. The day after the story broke, Agnew called a news conference. When Watergate imploded, Nixon dodged the media as much as possible. Whereas Agnew appeared candid, Nixon seemed evasive.

Agnew's performance railed public support behind him. His office was flooded with telegrams and telephone calls congratulating him on his spirited defense. Even some of his harshest critics, especially those in the media, lauded him. Agnew adopted "an admirable posture" in declaring that he had nothing to hide, wrote the editors at the *New York Times*.[3] R. W. Apple, a columnist at the paper, contrasted Agnew's performance with Nixon's and wrote, "To reporters at the news conference or watching on television, Mr. Agnew seemed in complete control of the situation—relaxed after a bit of initial nervousness, direct, unpretentious and self-confident."[4] The *Los Angeles Herald Examiner* argued that the charges against Agnew "were perpetuated by the same gang of Nixon-haters who specialize in innuendo, vague 'official sources' and who care nothing of what happens to the country as long as they can get the President." The paper praised Agnew's "self-assurance, his concise answers, and his command of the English language." The paper expressed confidence that Agnew would be vindicated.[5]

The night before, Nixon took a cruise down the Potomac River on the presidential yacht *The Sequoia* with speechwriter Ray Price. Over drinks Nixon ruminated about the Agnew case. "He was clearly troubled, and clearly torn" about the matter, Price recalled. Suspicious about the motives and the politics of the Baltimore prosecutors, Nixon was unsure how we would proceed. He also wondered if Elliot Richardson's "own judgment might be warped by his political differences—and potential direct political rivalry—with Agnew." As he spoke with Price, Nixon grew emotional. He told Price he "was damn well not going to stand for having the Vice President of the United States pilloried unless the case against him was solid."[6] Nixon did not watch the news conference. White House chief-of-staff Alexander Haig and White House counsel Fred Buzhardt reported to him that they believed Agnew had scored a "short-term political triumph." However, given their view of the evidence against Agnew, both men concluded that Agnew had achieved a pyrrhic victory. Buzhardt wondered how Agnew could have made such declarative statements that could not, in his view, hold up.[7]

One prominent Republican quickly came to Agnew's defense. Barry Goldwater announced his belief that Agnew was "not guilty of anything" and stated that he still supported Agnew for president in 1976.[8] Yet many elected Republicans chose to stay silent. The news came as another shock to Republicans already reeling from the sordid Watergate revelations. Republicans who had defended Richard Nixon and the White House against charges of a cover-up looked foolish as the scandal unfolded. Although Agnew had been untouched by Watergate, he felt its effect on the body politic. Republicans were understandably wary of sticking their necks out again and few rushed outwardly to his defense.

As for the prosecutors, Agnew's ringing declaration of innocence gave them no pause. As requested by President Nixon, Richardson brought in Assistant Attorney General Henry Petersen for an independent review of the probe. On Thursday, August 9, Petersen met with Agnew's attorneys Jay Topkis and Martin London. During the meeting Topkis and London hammered away at the credibility issue. They argued that both the witnesses against Agnew and the prosecutors pursuing the case lacked it. Topkis and London assured Petersen of Agnew's full cooperation. Agnew, Topkis stated, would hand over all the necessary documents and might even agree to a grand jury appearance.[9]

The Justice Department suffered a brief setback when J. Walter Jones refused to cooperate with the investigation. The prosecutors fingered Jones as the middleman in the payoffs from the engineers to Agnew, and they were eager to enlist him. Jones rebuffed their overtures, or as Agnew put it, "He flatly refused to sell me out."[10] Jones was the proverbial big fish. Unlike Lester Matz or Allen Green, he was not a target of the investigation, and the Justice Department had unearthed no evidence that he had engaged in illegal activity. Given his impeccable reputation, and that he would not have been testifying against Agnew to save his own skin, Jones would have been a perfect witness for the prosecution. Jones was Spiro Agnew's main benefactor. An enormously rich man, Jones owned a 68-foot yacht and an estate in Riva, Maryland. After World War II, Jones established the J. Walter Jones & Company, and by the 1960s it was the largest real estate firm in Baltimore County. A wine connoisseur (he paid for the installation of a wine cellar in the basement of the governor's mansion), Jones stored his vast collection in three separate cellars.[11]

When Agnew ran for county executive, Jones was one of Agnew's biggest fund-raisers, and he served on Agnew's gubernatorial finance committee in 1966.[12] A generous man, Jones clearly tried to help his friend, but as the

New York Times noted, "[M]ost of Mr. Jones's investment suggestions appear to have brought Mr. Agnew more political controversy than profit."[13] Whatever the results of their financial agreements, the two men stayed close, and when the storm erupted in 1973, Jones vigorously defended Agnew. According to the *Times*, Jones's word counted for much in Maryland: "Mr. Jones's exculpatory judgment of Mr. Agnew as not 'that type of man' has been received in Maryland as well-informed, even expert testimony. For no one has been closer to Mr. Agnew than Mr. Jones."[14]

Five years earlier, when Richard Nixon picked the relatively obscure Maryland governor as his running mate, reporters descended upon the state, looking for dirt on Agnew. Try as they could, no journalists could uncover any evidence of wrongdoing by him. In August 1973 the media again flocked to the Old Line State. Towson, the seat of Baltimore County, attracted considerable attention. In recent months, criminal charges had been filed against the state attorney in Towson, against the deputy in the County Executive's Office, and charges were looming against the current County Executive Dale Anderson. The flurry of indictments and the speculation about Spiro Agnew's future did not generate much interest, let alone indignation, in the county. "The people I talk to are more interested in what the Orioles are doing today than what the grand jury might do in the future," a county judge told the *New York Times*.[15]

While many Marylanders took the news accounts in stride, the scandals reverberated across the state's legal community. Maryland's Federal District Court had nine judges. One of the nine was C. Stanley Blair, Agnew's former chief of staff. After losing his bid for the governorship in 1970, Blair was appointed by President Nixon to serve on the District Court of Maryland. Blair impaneled the grand jury in December 1972, but when the allegations against Agnew became public, Blair immediately recused himself from presiding over any parts of the investigation. In mid-August, the chief judge of the Ninth Circuit, Edward S. Northrop, announced that he and the seven other judges were disqualifying themselves from the matter. Citing the vice president's "unique relationship" with the Maryland bench, Northrop stated that he would ask Chief Judge Clement Haynsworth of the Fourth Circuit Court of Appeals to appoint an official from outside Maryland to handle all issues relating to Agnew. Soon afterward, Haynsworth appointed Judge Walter E. Hoffman, also of the Fourth Circuit, to preside over the case.[16]

At times it seemed that Hoffman's role was unnecessary, since the prosecutors seemingly wanted to try the case in the media, not the courts. Beginning on August 7, when news of the investigation was made public, a daily barrage of stories about the case appeared in the newspapers with most of the leaks coming directly from the Justice Department. In an effort to prevent information about the case from becoming public, and to keep a leash on the Baltimore team, Elliot Richardson required all contacts between outsiders and anyone in the Justice Department involved in the Agnew case be reported—except for contacts with journalists.[17] The exemption provided cover for everyone in the department to speak freely with the media, and nearly everyone did. Agnew suspected that the first damaging, and blatantly false allegation, charging that Agnew accepted $1,000 a week in bribes from Jerome Wolff, came directly from one of the prosecutors, Barnet Skolnik.[18]

But Beall, Skolnik, Russell Baker, and Ronald Liebman were not solely to blame for the cascade of "revelations" that the press reported. Instead of employing customary caution, such as checking on sources and confirming accounts, many journalists rushed stories into print or on the air, and the result was an avalanche of rumor and innuendo. The resulting publicity rankled those who actually cared about due process and the rights of the accused. The American Civil Liberties Union called for an immediate halt to the leaks and demanded that Elliot Richardson intervene. Charles W. Morgan, the director of the ACLU's national office, wrote Richardson a letter warning, "The release of this information (the leaks) raises serious questions about the due process being accorded the Vice President and the others whose names have been mentioned." Morgan admitted that the ACLU could not "determine the source of the leaks with any certainty." Still, it seemed beyond doubt that some of the information "could only have come, directly or indirectly, from law enforcement officials." Given that fact, Morgan agued to Richardson, "The responsibility must be yours: to stop such leaks before they occur."[19]

The leaks also raised concerns from the editors at the papers in which the stories appeared. Richard Nixon noted this bizarre fact in his memoirs: "By August 8 the newspapers and the networks had begun reporting a series of leaks and attacks on Agnew that became so irresponsible that the New York *Times* and the Washington *Post* ended up criticizing on their editorial pages what was being done on their own newspages."[20]

Following the publication of the article in *Time*, where the details of the case against Agnew were laid out and the prosecutors predicted an indictment, Agnew demanded that Elliot Richardson put a halt to the leaks. Appearing on ABC's *Issues and Answers*, Richardson claimed to be disturbed by the leaks but stated that he was satisfied that the "Gang of Four" was not the perpetrators.[21] Richardson later claimed: "So far as we could find out, the critical leaks had come from Agnew's own staff."[22]

Richardson did not offer any evidence to back that claim, and it seems unlikely that Agnew's lawyers were providing damning evidence about their client to the media. The Justice Department's leaks damaged Agnew's right to a fair trial and took away any presumption of innocent until proven guilty. Keeping quiet for a while, between August 9 and August 17, Agnew mostly stayed out of the public view and allowed his attorneys to handle the case. Still, the flood of information stemming from the investigation harmed his public image and he fought back. On August 18 a "tanned and fit" Agnew appeared at a campaign rally for State Senator Robert Bauman, who was running for a special election for Maryland's vacant First Congressional District.[23] After delivering some opening remarks, he added an understatement, "1973 has been a rather tough year for Republicans everywhere." Bauman, he promised the crowd, would help Republicans, and the country, by working for his constituents and not playing the "Watergate game." His election to the House would help end the "masochistic pleasure that some people take out of constantly looking at everything they can find that's wrong with our country." Agnew added, "I want to make clear that I do not speak of my own immediate problems when I say that. There seem to be experts in abundance on that subject. And they all seem to use the same alias—they call themselves 'informed reliable sources close to the investigation', and they don't have any hesitancy at all about violating my civil rights or constitutional rights. But I'm going to have more to say about that later. Just let me say today that I intend to fight and establish my innocence of any wrongdoing."[24]

Three days later, on August 21, Agnew held his second news conference in less than two weeks. His tone was less forceful, but he was still combative. In his prepared statement, Agnew zeroed in on the leaks: "I can only assume that some Justice Department officials have decided to indict me in the press whether or not the evidence supports their position. This is a clear and outrageous attempt to influence the outcome of possible grand jury deliberations." Agnew also read from a letter he sent to George Beall, which included a swipe at those who suggested that Agnew and his attorneys were the culprits: "Let me dispose of one rumor—that I have encouraged this stream of leaks as part of my 'defense strategy'. This is malicious nonsense. Indeed, in view of the prejudicial character of the leaks and their regular attribution to Justice Department sources, the rumor is inherently absurd."[25]

On Wednesday, August 22, 1973, Nixon held his own news conference. All three networks carried the event live from Nixon's summer White House residence at San Clemente, California. Most questions concerned Watergate, but when asked about Agnew, Nixon came to his defense. "The concerted press attack against Agnew caused me to reconsider my belief in the dependability of the investigation going on in Baltimore," he wrote. At the news conference Nixon said that he ordered Richardson to track down the sources of the leaks and promised that anyone at the Justice Department who leaked information would be "summarily dismissed." Nixon then expressed his confidence in his embattled vice president and said any talk about Agnew's resignation would be "inappropriate."[26]

An appreciative Agnew called Nixon later that day and thanked him for the show of support. According to Agnew, Nixon let loose with a diatribe against Richardson, calling the attorney general "that little Ivy League pipsqueak s.o.b."[27] Both Agnew and Nixon had come to detest Richardson. Their real problem with Richardson was that he was doing his job. Richardson had not asked to be appointed attorney general; he had just been named secretary of defense before Nixon asked him to take over the Justice Department in April. Nixon selected Richardson in part because Richardson was an Ivy Leaguer with impeccable credentials among the "Eastern Establishment."

Yet as the *National Review* (a conservative magazine created by William F. Buckley as a counter-weight to the Eastern Establishment) pointed out when the Agnew scandal broke, Richardson had earned Nixon's trust. He was, the conservative journal opined, "a team player. While in the State Department, Richardson defended the 1970 Cambodian invasion. As Secretary of Health, Education, and Welfare he cooperated with the Administration efforts against forced busing. And he was a solid supporter of the President during the Christmas bombing in Hanoi."[28]

But Richardson had never liked or respected Agnew. He had taken part in the last-minute effort to block Agnew's nomination in 1968. David Keene, Agnew's top political aide, believed Richardson disdained Agnew: "The fact of the matter was that if you put yourself in the position of a Brahmin from Massachusetts," Keene said, "as he was and is, and think about his political career and then you have him look at Spiro Agnew, he would be disgusted by Agnew—before he knew what Agnew did or didn't do. This is a group of people who wouldn't hire the Irish, let alone a bunch of Greeks."[29] Richardson also harbored presidential ambitions of his own and as long as Agnew stayed a heartbeat away, and remained a darling to the party's rank-and-file—he stood in Richardson's path. *Time* reported that many on Agnew's staff believed "that the Attorney General sees himself as a prime contender for the G.O.P. presidential nomination in 1976 and would like nothing better than to have Agnew knocked out of the running by a scandal."[30]

Richardson's hostility toward Agnew partially explains his aggressive handling of the case. Once informed of the charges against Agnew, Richardson did all he could to force Agnew from office. He also did nothing to prevent the out-of-control prosecutors from running roughshod over Agnew's constitutional rights. And he reveled in taking down a sitting vice president. As detailed in Richard Cohen and Jules Witcover's *A Heartbeat Away*, Richardson "was beginning to enjoy the chase, the thrill of closing in on a man and bringing him to his terms." His feelings about Agnew were ably summarized in his declaration to the other Agnew haters at Justice—"Get the Bastard."[31]

The investigators did. The Justice Department launched a massive investigation into Agnew's past finances. He later wrote, "[S]warms of federal agents went forth, snooping into my private affairs. They went to everybody I had ever had any financial contact with, trying to find that imaginary cash. They interviewed merchants, charitable organizations, business associates, the Kiwanis Club. They checked a store where I had bought two ties for a little over six dollars." The agents checked Agnew's royalties from the popular Spiro Agnew wristwatch (he donated the proceeds to two charities, one, the families of prisoners of war and the other, an organization aiding the education of Native American children). They also spoke with Joseph Rash, an executive with the company Fair Foods, Inc., whole foods distributor from Baltimore who supplied Agnew with turkeys and hams.[32]

Despite their best efforts, the Justice Department and the Internal Revenue Service could never locate any huge sums of hidden money. The lack of a money trail left them unfazed; the prosecutors came up with the idea that Agnew was simply "cheap."[33] With the financial probe ongoing, the prosecutors turned their attention to the feasibility of indicting Agnew. They concluded that there was sufficient evidence to go to the grand jury. By late August, Allan Green and Bud Hammerman had both provided statements, and their testimony, along with that of Matz and Wolff, was enough for Richardson and Beall.

As August 1973 drew to a close, Spiro Agnew's future remained in limbo. He was facing an indictment. He was getting hammered daily in the media, with leaks sprouting up every day. Few Republicans were coming to his defense. President Nixon, who had more than his own share of problems, was keeping a safe distance. But Spiro Agnew had not climbed to the vice presidency of the United States by just taking punches. He was a fighter who could throw roundhouse rights. Since the story of the investigation broke, he had come out swinging, and as August turned to September, he kept punching away.

But the charges against Agnew cost him political capital. A Gallup Poll taken between August 17 and 22 showed Agnew's support eroding among Republicans. Gallup asked Republicans whom they preferred as the GOP's presidential nominee in 1976. Agnew tied California Governor Ronald Reagan for the lead with 22 percent. Four months earlier Agnew commanded a solid plurality with 35 percent compared to Reagan's 20 percent.[34]

Given the severity of his plight, Agnew asked to meet with Nixon, who in late August was holed up at the Western White House in San Clemente. When the White House announced that Nixon was flying in from California to see Agnew, the media immediately speculated that Nixon was trying to force Agnew to quit.[35] The suddenness and rarity of the meeting excited intense speculation and "the atmosphere of the meeting surrounding their get-together resembled a summit between the chiefs of two not-terribly friendly nations, rather than a chat between a President and his two-term Veep," *Newsweek* commented.[36]

Despite all the rampant speculation and the intense scrutiny the announcement caused, the purpose of the meeting was far more mundane. Agnew simply wanted to give Nixon an update on the proceedings. The two men had talked a couple of times on the telephone since their last meeting on August 7, but they had not seen each other since and Nixon noticed a sharp change in the vice president. "The strains were beginning to show." During the meeting Agnew repeated many of the same themes he first discussed a month earlier. Agnew expressed bitterness over the Justice Department's tactics, how the testimony against him was tainted, and how he had done nothing wrong. As Nixon listened he "felt genuinely sympathetic to Agnew." Yet at the same time Nixon urged Agnew to examine the matter from a legal perspective: "Only then would he be able to make decisions in his own best interest."[37]

In his mind Agnew was viewing the case as a lawyer and he determined that he could not receive a fair trial. All criminal defendants are entitled to a fair trial with a jury of their peers, but Agnew believed that the circumstances of his case precluded any such process. "I told Nixon that I despaired of finding any court in the Washington area or in Maryland that could possibly treat me fairly, since the minds of most people had been poisoned against me by the outrageous propaganda emanating from the Justice Department and being featured in such sensational fashion in the Washington area and by the national news media." The people of Baltimore, Agnew argued, should not be allowed to judge him, since they could not understand the problems inherent in raising political funds, and further, Agnew had made many enemies in the city following his attack on the state's black leadership in April 1968. Agnew had a solution. He proposed that the House of Representatives hear his case: "I believed that if a congressional committee would hear the witnesses on both sides, their session would be televised across America. I would make my defense—not to the congressmen alone but to the American people, who would be watching the drama on television, just as they had been staring at their TV sets during the Watergate hearings that summer."[38]

The meeting lasted two hours. Unfortunately for history, Nixon had removed the tape recording system in his offices, so there is no transcript of their conversation. But in his memoirs, Nixon writes that he came to understand "the manner in which he had come to think about his actions as governor." Agnew had only a paltry salary and yet many social calls. The funds from the engineers and contractors were not kickbacks or part of a quid pro quo but legitimate campaign contributions. The funds covered the expenses he incurred as a public citizen. Nixon had not only noticed the strain upon Agnew but also came away with the feeling that Agnew "was no longer as sure as he had been in our first meeting that the charges against him were not provable in court."[39]

Nixon was vague about what Agnew meant by "his actions as governor," but it seems that Agnew admitted to Nixon that he took money from contractors. If Nixon's version is correct, it corresponds with what Agnew's lawyer, George White, claimed—that Agnew said he accepted kickbacks. White also testified that Agnew told him "everybody" did it, and Nixon hints at the same thing. It was a brazen defense, but by that point in time he knew that Lester Matz, I. H. "Bud" Hammerman, and Allen Green were providing evidence to the Justice Department that showed his malfeasance. When Nixon wrote that Agnew was no longer confident he could be acquitted in a trial, Agnew was likely thinking of the evidence the prosecutors had. Unable to honestly claim he did not take any money, Agnew resorted to attacking the Justice Department's credibility and arguing that since everyone in Maryland did it, he wasn't guilty of anything. Other Maryland politicians used the same argument. Joseph Alton, the Republican county executive of Anne Arundel County, was indicted in 1974 on many of the same charges facing Agnew. Following his indictment, a defiant Alton said that while he might have broken the law, he had not done anything wrong.[40]

Agnew was making the same case. But his argument has no merit. Corruption was undoubtedly pervasive in Maryland, but that was no excuse for Agnew to take part in it. He violated the public's trust by extorting money from firms doing business with Baltimore County and the state of Maryland. Some of the participants in the scheme told the federal prosecutors Agnew continually complained that his government salary was not enough for his family. Agnew was at fault for that, since he made the decision to enter politics. He knew what the salary was and he willingly stayed in public office for over a decade.

Agnew continued to take money while he was vice president. It is difficult to explain why he believed his actions would never become public. While he may have believed he wasn't doing anything ethically or morally wrong, when he learned of the federal investigation into corruption in Baltimore, he tried to halt it. His public protestations of innocence were far different then his private acts. He knew that he was not just fighting to save his political career; he was also battling to stay out of prison.

Fearing a jury would find him guilty of corruption, Agnew pinned his hopes on a trial in the House of Representatives. All politicians needed funds and all politicians dealt with unscrupulous wheelers and dealers like Matz, Hammerman, Wolff, and Green. The politicians in the House, Agnew believed, would readily understand the grubby nature of political fundraising and be automatically sympathetic to his plight. So Agnew saw the House of Representatives as his best hope. To bypass the federal grand jury, Agnew needed to persuade House members that they could hear his case. Agnew initially broached the idea with Nixon, who was hardly receptive to the idea. Throughout the summer Nixon had taken a beating of his own. The Watergate hearing severely damaged his political standing and his approval ratings dropped to near record lows for a president. Although he faced questions about his involvement in the criminal cover-up, the House of Representatives had not yet begun an impeachment inquiry and Nixon did not want the House using Agnew as a dry run.

At the time, however, Nixon made no response to Agnew's claim that the House should hear his case. The meeting between the two men settled nothing. Nixon's spokesman Gerald Warren and Agnew's press secretary J. Marsh Thomson released few details about the talk, with Thomson offering that his boss "was as calm and relaxed as I've ever seen him." Afterward Agnew flew with his wife and daughter Susan to Ocean City, Maryland, for the Labor Day weekend. Nixon went up to Camp David.[41]

Elliot Richardson spent the Labor Day weekend relaxing at his vacation home in Cape Cod. When reached by reporters, he would not say whether he had decided to proceed with charges before the grand jury.[42] The same weekend, William Ruckelshaus, Richardson's deputy, convened a meeting with Henry Petersen and the Baltimore prosecutors at his home in Rockville, Maryland. Alexander Haig had called Ruckelshaus and told him that Nixon wanted to confer with Richardson, so Ruckelshaus wanted to prepare Richardson for the talk. While the men were speaking, Richardson telephoned and asked Ruckelshaus how much longer the investigation would take. Sixty days, he was told. Richardson told Ruckelshaus to bring the evidence against Agnew to the grand jury. The men then discussed what Richardson should tell Nixon. Fearful of more leaks, at least those not coming directly from them, they decided that Richardson should provide Nixon with a copy of the indictment.[43]

Agnew was not immediately made aware that Richardson had given the go-ahead for an indictment. His attorney Judah Best had requested that he be given advanced notice of any move before the grand jury, but his appeal for information was denied. But Agnew and his attorneys learned that the lawyers at the Justice Department viewed the matter of an indictment and ultimately a conviction as inevitable. With Nixon's urging and Agnew's consent, J. Fred Buzhardt, who essentially acted as the go-between with Nixon and Agnew, sat down with Agnew and two of his attorneys, Jay Topkis and Judah Best (Alexander Haig was also present), on Monday, September 10, in Agnew's EOB office.

The "stormy meeting" as Agnew described it, began with Buzhardt delivering a "cold, clinical, pessimistic analysis of the case" against Agnew. "Then Haig moved in saying 'Richardson has a hard case. He wants to throw it to the grand jury, with witnesses testifying under oath.' " Haig warned Agnew about taking the case to Congress. Richardson, Haig told him, would send the House the grand jury records, and "you'll be playing a high-risk ball." Both Buzhardt and Haig mentioned that the prosecutors had witnesses who would testify against him.

When they finished, Agnew went on another diatribe against Justice Department. "This matter is not in the hands of fair-minded people," he complained. As for the witnesses against him, "They're hostile to me. They've been made to understand that if they don't testify against me, the prosecutors will be angry and take it out on them."

"I am *not* guilty," he protested. And he could produce witnesses of his own who could verify his honesty and integrity. "I can put on the witness stand fifty contractors who did business with the county and state and who will testify that I never directly or indirectly made any improper approach to them."

The president's aides mentioned that Henry Petersen had interviewed the accusers and believed their stories. The news left Agnew angry since "I thought Petersen would get all the facts and then render an impartial opinion. He did not."

Why, Agnew inquired, was Haig opposed to taking the case before the House?

Nixon opposed the idea, Haig replied, and added, "The President may not back you."

Shouldn't the president wait until all the evidence was in before making any judgment?

Yes, Haig answered, but in the meantime Agnew might face "impeachment and indictment, the worst of both worlds."

"Can't the President tell Richardson to send it to the House?" Agnew asked.

"Not until they finish taking testimony under oath," Haig said.

Agnew argued that Nixon was "being emasculated by his own Attorney General."

Buzhardt told Agnew that Richardson feared "that if the evidence presented to the House doesn't stand up, he will be criticized."

The back-and-forth ended without settling anything. Haig wanted Agnew's resignation, but Agnew "stubbornly refused."[44]

Still, Nixon believed that some good had come from the session: "The gravity of Haig and Buzhardt's report must have had some effect. Within days, Agnew's lawyer, Judah Best, had made the first tentative overtures toward negotiations with the Justice Department."[45] But Agnew was not ready to throw in the towel. A day later, Jay Topkis called Elliot Richardson. Agnew's attorneys wanted a sit-down with him. The request brought some excitement at Justice; perhaps for all his denials, Agnew accepted his guilt, and his fate, and was looking for a deal. Richardson, Petersen, several top aides, along with George Beall, prepared a list of points that Agnew needed to agree to in order to reach a settlement. He would have to resign, and the facts of the case must be made public.[46]

On Wednesday, September 12, Jay Topkis, Judah Best, and Martin London gathered in Elliot Richardson's office at the Justice Department to discuss their client's case with the attorneys general, Henry Petersen and George Beall. Topkis quickly disabused them of any notion that Agnew wanted to plea bargain. Topkis informed them that his research suggested that a sitting vice president could not be indicted.[47] Richardson replied that his own research indicated otherwise, "We feel it is clear that the grand jury should take testimony and there is no constitutional obstacle to indictment." If the vice president took the case to the House, would that change Richardson's mind?, Topkis inquired. No, answered Richardson. Topkis claimed that the nub of the issue concerned which body, a grand jury or the House of Representatives, would "less likely incapacitate the Vice President." Topkis thought the House, but Richardson opposed the idea and wondered if impeachment proceedings were to begin, "are we to forget about the grand jury?" Yes, Topkis replied.[48]

The meeting lasted an hour. Judah Best made the short trip back to the White House, where he conferred with Agnew. At 6:05, Agnew and Best met with Haig and Buzhardt. "I thought we'd better get together tonight ... The President wants to do what's right," Haig said. Buzhardt then proceeded with an overview of the charges. Agnew, still defiant, declared, "I'll fight this."

Haig quickly jumped in, "Richardson thinks it's a strong case." Asking the House to take the case would accomplish nothing, Haig said, since Richardson would ask Speaker of the House Carl Albert for a delay in impeachment proceedings and Albert would acquiesce. "The President has lost his ability to exercise any power," Haig continued. "The House action will take six months. There will be a clamor for a trial." Haig then demanded Agnew's resignation.

The confrontation grew so heated that Best asked to talk alone with Haig. Agnew stepped out the room. Once Haig and Buzhardt left, Agnew went back and spoke with Best. Perhaps, Best thought, it was time to think about entering into negotiations with the White House.

Agnew agreed. "I was so worn out and frustrated after seven months in this pressure cooker, and so fearful about the harm which the controversy was causing my wife and family that I said wearily, 'Well, let's explore what terms we can get.' "[49]

Despite his protestations of innocence, his ringing declarations that he would fight to clear his name, Agnew decided to quit. He justified his decision on the basis of protecting his family and the fact that he was under extraordinary duress. Writing of his decision later, he explained, "Since my trusted friend and attorney, George White, had warned me in February that Matz and Wolff were threatening to implicate me in their troubles, I had been under constant fire from all quarters—the U.S. Attorney's office in Baltimore, the Justice Department, the White House, the news media." He went on: "Although I knew I had done nothing more than every politician charged with the responsibility for raising campaign funds had done, I was being painted every day by the press as a solicitor of bribes and an extortioner."[50]

He was being portrayed as such because as Baltimore County executive, governor of Maryland, and vice president of the United States, Agnew solicited bribes. For nearly a decade he accepted cash-filled envelopes from friends and associates who received government contracts for their payments.

Agnew was certainly correct that many stories appearing in print and on newscasts were blatantly false. He was justly angry at the Justice Department for violating his civil rights by leaking what should have been secret and confidential information to the media. And he had good reason to be bitter toward a White House whose only concern was minimizing damage to the president, even if it meant unfairly jettisoning his vice president.

None of those factors exculpated Spiro Agnew. He had violated the public trust, his oaths of office, and the law by accepting kickbacks from contractors and engineers. Undoubtedly some of the testimony against him was tainted and his accusers were potential felons (though the Justice Department never bothered to prosecute them). He was in a similar situation with his boss. Nixon was not the first president to wiretap his political opponents or use the powers of the executive branch to harass his enemies, just as Agnew was not the first to extort money. Yet they were both guilty of crimes. The evidence against them was as overwhelming as it was conclusive.

Realizing that the Justice Department had sufficient evidence to indict him, Agnew asked his legal team to begin plea bargaining negotiations with the federal prosecutors. On September 12, Elliot Richardson received word that Judah Best wanted to speak with him directly. Richardson agreed to hear Best out, and Best visited the Justice Department for the second time that day. Best told Richardson they both shared a major problem that needed resolution and Best wanted to arrange a deal for his client.[51]

The negotiating began in earnest the next morning. Best insisted that Agnew be spared a jail sentence, which, according to Agnew, enraged the two. "They went crazy at that," Best told Agnew. Best also asked that the case be dropped solely in return for Agnew's resignation, but Richardson squelched the idea. Then Best proposed an alternative—Agnew would resign and plea *nolo contendere* (no contest) to a single charge and ask for a recommendation from the Justice Department that Agnew serve no jail time.[52]

Richardson would not commit. When Best left, he called the Baltimore team and asked them to come to Washington. Earlier that day Beall had begun grand jury proceedings and the "Gang of Four" hoped to keep the case in their hands. But Richardson informed them of the talk with Best and all concerned began trying to find a resolution that forced Agnew from office and demonstrated that Agnew had committed crimes that warranted his resignation and a plea agreement.[53]

Later that night Spiro informed Judy of his decision. "I'll never forget the circumstances if I live to be a hundred," he later wrote. After having dinner with Judy's mother and their daughter Susan, he and Judy went upstairs to the bedroom. As they got into the dressing robes, Ted said that the deck was stacked against him and he had little chance of winning. So he was considering resigning. When he finished she slumped to the floor. He rushed to her side and placed her on the bed. Judy then began crying. After a while she looked at her husband and said, "It's such a shock but it's not the end of the world. You still have us, and we believe in you."[54]

Agnew spent the weekend of September 15–16 in "prayerful thought." On Monday, September 17, he told Judah Best that he was willing to enter a plea bargain. He would plead no contest to one charge of underpaying his taxes.[55]

While Agnew was close to the end, he still held out hope "that somehow the President would see what was happening and come to my defense."[56] It was a false hope. He not only wanted Agnew out but realized that Agnew could never survive. On September 19, Nixon sent Haig to talk with Agnew. Haig, according to Agnew, told him the prosecutors were going to seek an indictment and then make the facts of the case public. When that happened, "the President will call for your resignation." The threat unnerved Agnew, who still naively believed that Nixon might come to his defense. He shot back: "The President is not going to give me the same presumption of innocence that I gave him on Watergate. I want to talk to the President. I insist upon seeing him now."[57]

Agnew's bombast worked as he and the president conferred the following day, September 20. It was their third talk in six weeks. Nixon noticed a sharp change in Agnew's attitude and demeanor. "He had come a long way since the first session six weeks earlier at which he had protested his complete innocence. Now he asked what I thought he should do and talked poignantly about the problems of going away and starting a new life."[58]

Agnew remembered the session quite differently. "I have not misused the public trust," he told Nixon. "I believe you," he had Nixon saying.

Agnew claimed that he asked if Nixon would support him. Nixon "hedged" and responded, "You must do what is best for you and your family." Agnew said that he would resign, plead no contest to a misdemeanor charge of tax evasion, and "end this whole miserable business." But if Richardson fought him, Agnew pledged that he would fight.[59]

Agnew left the meeting convinced that Nixon understood that he would "fight all the way if Richardson did not come around to my terms for resignation."[60] It is difficult to see how Nixon could have understood Agnew's supposed tough stance. Agnew was already thinking about his life after the vice presidency. His lawyers were already negotiating with the Justice Department, and the haggling concerned only the points of the deal, not the end result. Richardson was in a far stronger position than Agnew, and he could, as Nixon well knew, control the terms of a settlement. Eventually Agnew would have to accept an agreement that the Justice Department concluded was fair. Agnew perhaps was trying to put his own spin on past events. Nixon was not going to fight for him.

The lawyers at the Justice Department watched the political machinations from a distance. For several days Richardson argued back and forth with the Baltimore prosecutors about the terms of any settlement. Some of the prosecutors wanted a jail term, but Richardson countered that the public interest was best served by a quick resolution, and since Agnew would fight any efforts to put him in prison, Richardson would allow him to escape a prison sentence. The prosecutors presented a united front when they sat down for negotiations with Best, Topkins, and London on September 19 and 20. During the meetings the attorneys on each side wrangled over a statement Agnew would make, whether he would plead guilty or no contest, and other matters. The haggling went on and on for hours but produced no agreement.[61]

The back-and-forth between Agnew's lawyers and the Justice Department masked the crucial fact that Agnew was seriously weighing resignation and holding out for the best terms possible. Although he still proclaimed his innocence, he no longer fought to keep his job. By Friday, September 21, a deal appeared close. Nixon later wrote, "Buzhardt reported to me he thought there had been a breakthrough. Richardson and Best had reached agreement on language that would not commit Agnew to a 'knowing' acceptance of money for preferential treatment, while still acknowledging that others would allege it. Agnew was going to think about it over the weekend, so Monday would be the day of decision."[62]

On Monday, Agnew decided he was going to fight the charges. Ever since the story about Agnew first broke in early August, the prosecutors at the Justice Department had continually violated their charge of keeping information secret. They had leaked evidence against Agnew to the press, then piously decried the leaks, but denied any culpability in trashing Agnew. The leaks outraged Agnew, his defenders, and even some of his critics. However, the lawyers at the Justice Department continued their campaign to destroy Agnew through the media. Over the weekend CBS News reported Henry Petersen as saying, "We've got the evidence. We've got it cold."[63]

The Petersen quote infuriated Agnew. "I decided to break off the bargaining sessions then and there, and fight it out—in Congress, or in the courts, if necessary."[64] Agnew's stance set the stage for a potential constitutional crisis. He decided that his only recourse was to take the fight to the House of Representatives. Under Article I, Section 2, of the Constitution, the House of Representatives has the sole power of impeachment. Under Article 2, Section 4, "The President, Vice President and all civil Officers of the United States, shall be removed from Office on Impeachment for, and Conviction of, Treason, Bribery, or other high Crimes and Misdemeanors."

On Tuesday, September 25, Nixon met with Elliot Richardson and Henry Petersen. The latter repeated to Nixon what he said to the media, that it was "an open and shut case." Richardson informed Nixon that he was ready to begin presenting the case to the grand jury. Nixon asked that the Justice Department "prepare an opinion on the question of whether it would be constitutional to indict a Vice President while he was still in office."[65]

Minutes after Richardson and Petersen departed, Agnew entered the Oval Office. Again he protested his innocence. Richardson, he complained, "was determined to wreck me with tainted testimony," and he defiantly stated, "I'm going to take my case to the House leadership early this afternoon."[66] Nixon wrote that Agnew would only consider resigning if he was granted immunity from prosecution. Then, according to Nixon's account, Agnew's "manner changed, and in a sad and gentle voice he asked for my assurances that I would not turn my back on him if he were out of office."[67] Agnew claimed that he suggested Nixon "go on television and tell the people that I could not have a fair trial in view of the countless leaks against me."[68]

Nixon hardly ever went on television to defend himself, so there was little chance that he would go before the cameras for his vice president. Still, Nixon released a statement calling upon Americans to afford Agnew the presumption of innocence.[69] He also encouraged Republicans on Capitol Hill to support Agnew's request that the House hear his case.[70]

Later that afternoon Agnew arrived at Capitol Hill. He came with a letter for the Speaker of the House, Democrat Carl Albert of Oklahoma. The two men spoke for a while, with Agnew complaining about the Justice Department's handling of his case and the pressure from the White House to force his resignation.[71]

The letter Agnew gave Albert asked that the House of Representatives take over the investigation. The letter began with the request: "I respectfully request that the House of Representatives undertake a full inquiry into the charges which have apparently been made against me in the course of an investigation by the United States Attorney for the District of Maryland." His lawyers, Agnew wrote, "have advised me that the Constitution bars a criminal proceeding of any kind . . . against a President or Vice President while he holds office. In these circumstances," the letter continued, I believe, it is the right and duty of the vice president to turn the House.[72]

After Albert read the letter, Agnew spent the next thirty minutes pleading his case. Although Agnew and Albert were from opposing parties, they shared a mutual respect. Reminiscing about the talk a few years later, Albert described Agnew as a "very articulate, attractive looking fellow that really made a good impression on you." Agnew, according to Albert, was friendly and personable—"he was a pretty sharp individual."[73] Agnew reciprocated, "A man of small stature but great integrity," he wrote of the speaker. He told Albert that the Justice Department was running amok, that the White House was trying to force him out, so the only place he could turn was the House, where he hoped that Albert would appoint a select committee.[74]

Agnew and Albert were joined by House Majority Leader Tip O'Neill of Massachusetts; Peter Rodino, D-NJ, chairman of the House Judiciary Committee; Majority Whip John McFall, D-CA; House Minority Leader Gerald Ford, R-MI; Minority Whip Leslie Arends, R-IL; Edward Hutchinson of Michigan, the ranking Republican on the Judiciary Committee; and Lew Deschler, the House parliamentarian. (Ford later said he was there out of courtesy to Agnew and also Bryce Harlow, who asked him to attend.)[75] Some of the participants discussed the meeting in their respective memoirs. Agnew dictated a "recollection of events" later that day and cited it in *Go Quietly*. "Albert," he claimed, "seemed sympathetic." Albert asked Deschler for his views, but Deschler "did not seem too receptive to the idea." Deschler suggested that the leaders of the House come in, and as they filed into the office, they were handed copies of Agnew's letter. "There was a great deal of conversation about the letter; and the leadership, with the exception of O'Neill, seemed to approve of the idea of the House doing something about my request. Rodino was immediately and outwardly hostile." After some further discussion, the group agreed that Albert would read the letter to the full House. The meeting broke up after thirty minutes. Before Agnew departed, Tip O'Neill expressed concern over Agnew's travails and said, "Pal it's a damn shame."[76]

O'Neill expressed no such sympathy as he detailed the meeting, "I didn't like the idea," and thought the matter should stay in the courts.[77] Gerald Ford, who remembered Agnew as being "very matter-of-fact," agreed that Albert seemed "sympathetic." Ford wrote that Peter Rodino was "cautious and noncommittal" and O'Neill "was skeptical." As Ford left the meeting, he said, "I had the distinct impression that Tip would prevail."[78] In his account, Albert claims he was not sympathetic to Agnew's request. Calling it a "bolt from the skies grayed by the Watergate investigations," Albert "knew instantly that the House must not involve itself in a nearly completed criminal investigation before the federal courts." Albert spoke with Rodino, who agreed. Rodino "offered to check the Calhoun precedent and report to me the next morning."[79]

The "Calhoun precedent" concerned the investigation of Vice President John Calhoun in 1826, which Agnew references in his letter to Albert. The charges against Calhoun stemmed from his tenure as secretary of war during the James Monroe administration. Calhoun's opponents claimed that as secretary of war he had illegally profited from a defense contract. In a day when a man's honor was as important as his life, Calhoun vigorously denied the allegations and requested that the House of Representatives investigate the matter. The House duly agreed and created a Select Committee. After just six weeks the committee issued a report exonerating Calhoun of any wrongdoing.[80]

Thirty-six years later, Vice President Schuyler Colfax also found himself under an ethical cloud. In the waning days of the 1872 election, the *New York Sun* published an exposé on the questionable financial practices of the Credit Mobilier Company. The federal government subsidized the building of the transcontinental railroad and gave a contract to Union Pacific, a railroad company, to build part of the line. Instead of hiring an outside firm, Union Pacific created their own construction company, Credit Mobilier, and awarded the government contracts to themselves. When in the late 1860s, Congress made noises about investigating the company, the directors of Union Pacific tried to thwart any probe by bribing members of Congress with stocks in Credit Mobilier. Some refused, but evidence suggested that Colfax, then speaker of the House, purchased some of the stock at a reduced price.[81]

In 1873, the House formed a Select Committee, the Poland Committee as it became known, to look into the charges against Colfax and members of Congress. Colfax denied ever purchasing any stock and receiving any dividends from the alleged transaction. He willingly testified before the committee and confronted his main accuser, Representative Oakes Ames of Massachusetts, who claimed that he gave Colfax $1,200 and was still holding the stock for Colfax. The hearings went on for weeks, with Colfax cross-examining his accusers and the accusers questioning the vice president. Eventually the committee ruled that the House could not impeach a vice president for conduct that occurred before he became the vice president, but since Colfax had not run for reelection with Ulysses S. Grant in 1872, and his term was set to expire a few days before the committee issued its conclusion, the point was moot.[82]

Both precedents offered Agnew some glimmer of hope. In the Calhoun case, the House accepted responsibility for investigating the charges (and the Select Committee also cleared him of any wrongdoing). In the Colfax case, the committee ruled that the House could not impeach Colfax for any illegal acts prior to his becoming vice president. Yet Agnew's lawyers contended that since the grand jury was probing kickbacks he allegedly received from 1969 to 1972, the House could assert its jurisdiction. But both cases were silent on the crucial issue of whether a sitting vice president could be indicted while in office.

After looking into the Calhoun case, Peter Rodino told Albert "that the cases were not at all similar."[83] Later that morning, Wednesday, September 26, Albert spoke with the House leadership and informed them that he was rejecting Agnew's request. He called in the media and issued a terse statement: "The Vice President's letter relates to matters before the courts. In view of that fact, I, as Speaker, will not take any action on the letter at this time."[84]

> Minority Leader Gerald Ford argued that the House should get involved. He released a statement that read in part: "I believe deeply in the American principle that a man should be presumed to be innocent unless proved to be guilty. I favor a House investigation of the charges against Vice President Agnew because fairness dictates that he should be permitted this opportunity to defend himself in open hearings." Ford stated that because of all the leaks, Agnew could not possibly get a fair trial. And Agnew's letter convinced him that the House could and should take over the investigation: "In my view, the House should act as soon as possible on the Vice-President's request and should act affirmatively, in line with the Calhoun case of 1826–1827. The Calhoun case established a precedent which should guide us now."[85]

Reaction in the rest of the House fell mostly along partisan lines.[86] Agnew learned of Albert's decision while he was at the Capitol lunching with a group of moderate and liberal Republicans, the same types he excoriated on the campaign trial in 1970. But now, under fire and needing all the help he could get, Agnew accepted an invitation from Oregon Senator Mark Hatfield to join him and thirteen others for lunch. Over roast beef, chicken, and ham sandwiches, Agnew shared his state of mind with the "Wednesday Group," pledging that he would fight the charges. Hatfield, admitting that he and the other Republicans had strong philosophical differences with Agnew, came away impressed by Agnew's determination. "This man is going to stand his ground and fight," he told the news media.[87]

On Friday, September 28, Agnew flew to California, where he met up with Frank Sinatra, who had been especially encouraging throughout the ordeal. Agnew and Sinatra had developed a very close friendship and Agnew leaned on his friend during the crisis. Of Sinatra, Agnew later wrote: "As does every Vice President, I met a lot of celebrities during my years in office . . . Most of them were fine people . . . Francis Albert Sinatra, however, falls in a special bracket, a bracket of one."[88]

No stranger to adverse publicity, Sinatra counseled Agnew and even made his own personal attorney Mikey Rudin available for consultation. After hitting the links, Agnew and Sinatra retreated to the entertainer's Palm Beach home, where Sinatra cooked pasta for Agnew, Judy, and several staff members. Following dinner they talked about the case, with Sinatra urging a full-frontal attack. Retiring late, Agnew "spent a restless night—confused, angry, and hurt by my inability to do anything about a steadily deteriorating situation."[89]

While Agnew golfed, his lawyers filed papers with the Federal District Court in Baltimore asking for a temporary stay enjoining the Justice Department and federal grand jury from investigating any further. His lawyers contended that a vice president could not be indicted until first impeached and removed from office. In separate documents the lawyers accused the Justice Department of misusing "their offices in an immoral and illegal attempt to drive the Vice President from the office to which he was elected and to assure his conviction." While R. Stanley Mortenson, an associate in Topkis and

London's firm filed the papers, Topkis, London, and Best were in Norfolk, Virginia, for a closed session with Judge Walter Hoffman, where they were joined by Henry Petersen and another Justice Department attorney. After an hour-long meeting, Hoffman announced he would hold a formal hearing on Agnew's motions on October 12. Hoffman also ruled that the grand jury could continue to hear evidence, but the Justice Department indicated that it would hold off calling important witnesses until Hoffman reached his decision.[90]

Hoffman's ruling gave the sides two weeks of preparation. Agnew had no comment on the matter, but he had plenty to say about the case the following day, Saturday, September 29. He was scheduled to address the National Federation of Republican Women. In the days before the talk, Agnew's aides prepared a typical speech devoid of any mention of Agnew's troubles, but after the late-night session with Sinatra, Agnew awoke in a fighting mood. With his wife, Sinatra, and some top aides, Agnew flew from Palm Beach to Los Angeles. During the flight Agnew jotted down some notes.[91]

Anticipation ran high in the auditorium and all three networks broke away from their regularly scheduled broadcasting to cover the address live. As Agnew entered the speaker's platform, 2,000 women gave him a thunderous ovation. Some waved signs, "Spiro is my Hero." As the applause wore down, Agnew began his speech.

Ever since Agnew learned of the investigation in Maryland, he privately and publicly declared his innocence. He saw himself as a victim of malicious prosecution. His accusers, he believed, were liars. His allies, especially those in the White House, had deserted him. He was angry, he felt betrayed, and he took out his frustration on those whom he saw as most responsible for his troubles—the lawyers in the Justice Department.

"In the past several months I have been living in purgatory. I have found myself the recipient of undefined, unclear, and unattributed accusations that have surfaced in the largest and most widely circulated organs of our communications media. I want to say at this point—clearly and unequivocally—I am innocent of the charges against me."

The women exploded in cheers. Agnew continued: "I have not used my office, not abused my public trust as county executive, as governor, or as Vice-President, to enrich myself at the expense of my fellow Americans."

He then targeted Henry Petersen. Petersen's comment, "We've got him cold," infuriated Agnew more than any other aspect of the whole investigation and he let loose on his nemesis:

> I say this to you, that conduct of high officials in the Department of Justice, particularly the conduct of the chief of the criminal investigation division of that department, is unprofessional and malicious and outrageous, if I am to believe what has been printed in the newsmagazines and said on the television networks of this country, and I have no denial that this is not the case.

Petersen, Agnew claimed, was still stung from the criticism he received over his handling of the Watergate scandal. Accused of not probing deeply enough after the break-in, and charged with being cowed by the White House, Petersen was removed from direct responsibility for investigating Watergate by Special Prosecutor Archibald Cox. Petersen and his cohorts at the Justice Department, Agnew bellowed, were "trying to recoup their reputation at my expense. I'm a big trophy."

Because of Petersen's ineptness, Agnew claimed, "he needs to reinstate his reputation as a tough and courageous hard-nosed prosecutor. Well, I'm not going to fall down and be his victim, I assure you."

He finished with a fierce and rousing conclusion that brought his audience to its feet:

> I want to make clear another thing so clear that it cannot be mistaken in the future. Because of these tactics which have been employed against me, because small and fearful men have been frightened into furnishing evidence against me—they have perjured themselves in many cases, it's my understanding—I will not resign if indicted. *I will not resign if indicted!*[92]

Chapter 11

Resignation

"I will not resign if indicted."

So declared Spiro Agnew on September 29, 1973. His thunderous statement wowed his audience of female partisans, but the speech hardly went over as well in other quarters, as he later wrote, "My speech not only evoked roars of enthusiasm from the Republican women and an echoing surge of support from people across the country, it touched off a wave of anger and fear in the White House."[1]

Undoubtedly the salvo irked the White House, but it caused more frustration than fear. Huddled up at Camp David with a few advisors, Nixon spent that last weekend in September worrying about Special Prosecutor Archibald Cox's subpoenas of his tapes. Nixon believed that his Agnew problem would soon be behind him, and with it, possibly his Cox problem. Nixon believed that getting rid of Agnew meant he could fire Cox. Agnew's defiance rattled Nixon and threw a wrench in his plans. Over the weekend he and his counselors plotted their next move. According to Agnew, "General Haig evidently feared that I was declaring war, not only on the Justice Department but on the entire administration." So, at Haig's "instigation," the White House and the Justice Department "leaked out a false story that I had a phased escalation plan for a four stage assault." The plan was to attack Henry Petersen, George Beall, Elliot Richardson, and finally, Nixon.[2]

Agnew denied ever hatching up a plot and blamed Haig for spreading the rumors. By that point Agnew distrusted and hated Haig ("totally self-centered, ruthless and ambitious," Agnew wrote of Haig).[3] Given their respective personalities, and to say nothing of their very different interpretation of the evidence, clashes between the two were inevitable. From the beginning Haig feared the prospect of a "double impeachment" and pushed mightily for Agnew's resignation. Unlike Nixon, Haig thrived on confrontation. A career military man who had served under Douglass MacArthur, commanded battalions in two tours of duty in Vietnam, and had risen to the rank of four-star general, Haig possessed a forceful personality and embraced battles with a gusto reminiscent of his old boss MacArthur. When confronting Agnew, Haig acted like a general giving orders to a private. In characteristically blunt language, Haig ordered Agnew to quit. The message and the messenger infuriated Agnew and left him, for a time, undaunted. An equally strong figure, Agnew time and time again ignored the general's commands.

At that point in time Agnew viewed Haig as an enemy, not an emissary, for Agnew still held out hope that Nixon might somehow intervene on his behalf. Publicly at least Nixon had supported Agnew, or at least had not undermined him. But during an October 3 news conference, Nixon sent out signals that suggested he was backing away from Agnew. When Clark Mollenhoff, a former aide in the Communications Office who helped Agnew with his attacks on the media, wondered if Nixon thought "there is any substance to Mr. Agnew's charges that this is a frivolous investigation, that it is a frame-up, and that it is in fact a smear," Nixon minced no words. The charges "are serious and not frivolous." In a follow-up, Mollenhoff asked if Nixon still had confidence in Henry Petersen's "handling of the investigation." Nixon's answer, Agnew believed, signaled "the end of White House neutrality."[4] Nixon forcefully replied: "If I did not support Mr. Petersen's handling of the investigation, he would have been removed at this time."[5]

Nixon knew full well the impact of such a statement. On national television, in front of millions of viewers, Nixon had severely undercut Agnew's main line of defense—that he was being hounded by unscrupulous prosecutors. Ironically, Nixon felt the same way about Archibald Cox, but Nixon liked and respected Petersen, as he made known publicly and privately. After Agnew leveled his charges against Petersen, Nixon called Elliot Richardson and told the attorney general that he backed Petersen. Although relations between Nixon and Richardson were strained, Richardson appreciated the call, since the fury of Agnew's remarks took everyone at the Justice Department by surprise. Petersen himself did not respond to Agnew's allegations, "I'm not going to be able to say anything."[6]

The attack on Petersen was a public relations problem, but the lawyers at Justice faced a new legal issue when Judge Walter Hoffman summoned the prosecutors and Agnew's attorneys to the Baltimore courthouse. In their brief to halt the grand jury proceedings, Jay Topkis, Judah Best, and Martin London argued that the leaks had damaged their client so deeply that he could not receive a fair trial. Judge Hoffman sent a letter to Topkis (along with a copy to Henry Petersen) that demonstrated that Hoffman took the matter seriously: "Gentleman: Relating solely to the publicity question raised by the applicant, unless the brief of the Department of Justice persuades me to the contrary, I am presently inclined to the belief that the applicant would at least be entitled to an evidentiary hearing on his charges that the prosecution was responsible for the allegedly prejudicial (leaks)."[7]

On October 3, the same day Nixon held his news conference and expressed his support for the Justice Department, Hoffman gathered the attorneys and informed them of the supplemental charge that he would make to the grand jury later that day. It read, in part, "We are rapidly approaching the day when the perpetual conflict between the news media ... and the judicial system, charged with protecting the rights of persons under investigation for criminal acts, must be resolved." George Beall protested that the grand jury was the domain of the prosecution, but after noting Beall's objection, Hoffman read the letter he wrote to Topkis. Martin London then said that they would like to begin interviewing witnesses immediately, and Hoffman accepted Topkis's list, which began with Richardson, Petersen, and Beall and followed with members of the media.[8]

The next day's front page of the *New York Times* had a photo of a beaming Topkis, London, and Best leaving the courthouse.[9] They had achieved a remarkable legal victory. The focus of the case shifted from whether Agnew took bribes into whether the Justice Department had violated his civil rights. If the investigation could uncover any substantive evidence that the leaks came directly from Richardson or his associates, Agnew stood a chance of beating the charges against him.

From the beginning of the case, in an ironic twist, a great number of members of the media came to Agnew's defense. Agnew later cited a few of the columnists who decried the use of leaks against him, including some surprising allies such as Tom Wicker of the *New York Times* and William Raspberry of the *Washington Post*. In his piece, "Hanged Without a Trial," Raspberry wrote, "Unless you are either totally devoid of feeling or totally convinced of his guilt, you have to have at least a little sympathy for Vice President Agnew." Agnew was dead, having "drowned in a dambreak of leaks."[10] Nick Thimmesch, a syndicated columnist, ran a column blasting the Justice Department's "cruel sieve of rumors" and criticizing the flood of stories that Agnew was resigning, which were based on nothing more than speculation.[11]

Since the scandal first broke, Agnew directed most of his ire toward the investigators, blaming them more for leaking harmful (and he thought false) information than the press for printing it. Agnew also noticed that many of his former targets, especially the editorial page writers of the *New York Times* and *Washington Post*, were taking his accusations of prosecutorial misconduct seriously. But when the *Post* ran a story on October 2 that partially absolved Henry Petersen of the responsibility in telling CBS "We've got Agnew cold," Agnew struck back. Agnew dashed off a letter to the *Post*, appearing in the pages of the *New York Times* on October 3, but not the *Post* until October 4. Its tone was alternately snide, angry, and indignant. "On Tuesday, October 2," it began, "your staff writer, Mr. John P. MacKenzie, spread forth a cute little vignette critical of my attributing to Assistant Attorney General Petersen the quote, 'We've got the evidence. We've got it cold'. Mr. MacKenzie refers to CBS News as reporting the quotation from 'a source close to the negotiations' and not from Mr. Petersen. He goes on to say how the story changed a little in the retelling."[12]

Quoting the *Post*, the *Times*, the *Baltimore Sun*, and the *Washington Star-News*, Agnew cited how each paper originally, in his opinion, named Henry Petersen as the direct source of the line, "We've got the evidence." Now, without offering any proof, Agnew charged that "the Justice Department is now making the assertion that the leak of Mr. Petersen's comment came from my attorneys." His lawyers, he claimed, "are willing to sign affidavits that they did not discuss anything concerning the meeting with the news media. Mr. Graham of CBS (legal correspondent Fred Graham) should be decent enough to confirm that his source was not my attorneys." The bigger problem as Agnew saw it was "that four newspapers of considerable circulation left the distinct impression with their readers that Mr. Petersen made this improper, unprofessional and highly prejudicial comment." The truth of the matter would come out: "The American people are not going to be confused by Mr. MacKenzie's tricky attempt to make it look as though I was trying to create a misimpression. The point remains that the Justice Department is wrong and has not denied it was wrong."[13]

The *Post* responded the same day. In an editorial "F.Y.I.," the paper answered Agnew in a measured tone. Citing the CBS story from September 22, the editors surmised, Agnew "abandoned his confidence in the criminal justice system" and the story also "formed the basis of his extraordinary assault against Mr. Petersen." In those attacks Agnew had "leveled a heavy charge against a public official, especially when coupled with the implicit suggestion that Mr. Petersen and other high Justice Department officials bungled the Watergate case and were trying to recoup their reputations at Mr. Agnew's expense." The editors concluded that a careful examination of the CBS report demonstrated that Petersen was not the direct source of the quote and "therefore it could not be regarded, on the available evidence, as part of a plot by Mr. Petersen to prosecute Mr. Agnew in the press by publicly advertising the strength of the government's case."[14]

Agnew had good cause to be angry over the "We've got it cold" statement, regardless of the source. The First Amendment provides for freedom of the press, and any media outlet had the right to print it. Agnew had no reason, therefore, to blame the media, but he was justly furious that a member of the prosecution damaged his standing through the media. Regardless of any individual's culpability in a crime, the justice system in this country is supposed to protect everyone's right to a fair and impartial trial. Because of the systematic attacks in the media, Agnew had no real hope for such a result. Even his critics in the media came to his defense and blasted the leaks as unjust.

Though Agnew argued his constitutional rights had been violated, he decided to quit. In his memoirs he offered an explanation as to why: "I have kept this secret for six years but now it must be told: Not long before our scheduled departure time from Chicago on October 4, I received an indirect threat from The White House that made me fear for my life."[15]

Agnew got word of the "threat" from his military assistant General Michael Dunn. Arthur Sohmer alerted Agnew that Dunn wanted a meeting with Agnew and Sohmer. When Agnew asked why Dunn had not come to him, "Sohmer made motions that revealed that he feared my office was bugged." Agnew and Sohmer met with Dunn at the general's military suite, where Dunn took them inside the office of Agnew's pilot. In the office a "grave and tense" Dunn "recounted a shocking story."

Dunn related a conversation he had that day with Haig. The chief of staff requested a meeting with General Dunn and the two sat down in Haig's office. According to Dunn's memorandum of the conversation (which Agnew cites in his book), Haig "began by stating that he had been briefed on the evidence against STA and it was massive." The Justice Department believed it had an "ironclad case for conviction." Haig then warned: "[T]he clock is running—it will be too late once an indictment is obtained to do this gracefully." There was no use of fighting since Haig "knows of every phone call made by STA [Agnew]. Conversations were also not unknown."

According to Dunn, Haig also implied that he could shut down Agnew's legal defense fund. In late September, W. Clement Stone, a Chicago businessman who made billions selling insurance, agreed to chair the Agnew Defense Fund. A philanthropist who preached the power of positive thinking, Stone viewed the Republican Party as one of his favorite charities. He gave $2 million to Nixon's reelection effort, and despite the adverse publicity stemming from the contribution, Stone remained close to Nixon, and by extension, with the chief of staff, who relayed to Dunn that "Stone was specifically awaiting a call from Haig at that very moment."

There were more threats: "Once 'facts' are made known to people, further support from Nixon impossible." Agnew should not trust his New York attorneys; they were merely "using him to get at Nixon." When Dunn asked what Haig wanted of him, Haig responded that he desired that someone on Agnew's staff deliver Agnew a message. As he departed, Haig said that he would speak with Fred Buzhardt, but he was still convinced that regardless of Agnew's culpability, he would be found guilty in a court of law.

After speaking with Dunn, Agnew realized "with a sickening shock, that I had finally lost the last slim thread of hope that the President would help me in my fight. On the contrary, he had turned against me and become my mortal enemy."

It got worse. The IRS had stepped up the net worth investigation, and since the Agnews signed joint tax returns, Judy also faced a possible jail sentence. "It was the lowest blow of all."

On top of threatening Judy, Dunn also claimed that Haig raised the stake of assassination. "The President has a lot of power—don't forget that."

"His remark sent a chill through my body. I interpreted it as an innuendo that anything could happen to me; I could have a convenient accident."

While later admitting that he might have overreacted, Agnew believed Haig's "directive was aimed at me like a gun at my head. That is the only way I can describe it. I was told, 'Go Quietly—or else.' "[16]

The entire episode had a surreal feel. For his part Agnew undoubtedly accepted Dunn's tale as fact; hence the title *Go Quietly . . . or else.*

While Agnew believed it, there is no reason that anyone else should. Agnew did himself no favors by including this absurd story in his retelling of what happened. Certainly Haig spoke with Dunn and, in his characteristic fashion, tried to lay out the facts in the hopes of forcing Agnew's resignation. Since August, Haig had spoken with Agnew, Sohmer, and other aides, but his efforts were in vain. Perhaps he was rough with Dunn, and perhaps he even raised the specter of Judy Agnew's possible peril. But he did not threaten Agnew's life (Haig joked with his wife that in the event of his death she should look for his body in bridge pilings in Maryland.)[17]

Despite his fears Agnew awoke alive and well on Friday, October 5. That same day his attorneys served subpoenas to reporters and news organizations. The list included Richard Cohen of the *Washington Post*, Ron Nessen of NBC, and Fred Graham of CBS.[18] The subpoenas called upon the news organizations to release all information about contacts their reporters had with government officials involved with the Agnew case. The news companies quickly announced that they would fight the subpoenas. Through a spokesperson the *New York Times* said, "The *Times* believes this attempt to force disclosure of confidential sources and information to be in violation of the First Amendment."[19]

As the media and the prosecutors revved up for a fight, Agnew threw in the towel. Late Friday evening he contacted Judah Best and asked Best to meet with Fred Buzhardt. After two months of furiously declaring his innocence, and less than a week after shouting he would not resign if indicted, Agnew gave up. He wanted a deal and requested that Topkis negotiate the terms with Buzhardt. "Go speak to Buzhardt. See what can be done."[20]

Agnew claimed his decision resulted from Nixon's betrayal and Haig's threats. He contended he had no chance of being acquitted and his only recourse was resignation. There might well have been a more deciding factor, as the "White House" (presumably Buzhardt) told Richardson that the plea bargaining resumed because Agnew could not bear the strain and potential revelations of the IRS net-worth investigation.[21]

During the sweeping, exhaustive, and intrusive probe, the investigators unearthed some embarrassing details about Agnew's private life. For several years Agnew had an extramarital affair with a member of his staff. The Justice Department discovered that some of Agnew's benefactors had bought his mistress a sports car for a Christmas present. If Agnew continued his fight, if the case against him became a matter of public record, the details about his adultery might well have become public. Since Agnew prided himself as a man of virtue, and since he drew his support from those who admired his apparent honesty, integrity, and championing of old-fashioned values, any hint that he acted improperly would have destroyed whatever credibility he had left. And he had to consider the damage to his family. While they had always supported his career, Judy and the children had never welcomed the spotlight and the fallout from the details of Agnew's relationship would have proved devastating. Agnew, of course, made no mention of any affair, but it likely played a large role in his choice to resign.[22]

As Judah Best and Fred Buzhardt were arranging Agnew's resignation, Arab forces in the Middle East were launching a surprise attack against Israel. A coalition of Egyptian and Syrian armies attacked on early Saturday morning, Yom Kippur, the holiest day of the Jewish calendar, catching the Israel, as well as the United States, off-guard. At the time President Nixon was in Key Biscayne obsessing over his Watergate problems, while Henry Kissinger, just recently confirmed as secretary of state, was in New York preparing for the opening of the UN session.

With the very future of Israel at stake, and the possibility that the United States and the Soviet Union would be drawn into the conflict, Elliot Richardson fretted about the security and stability of the government. The cataclysmic events convinced him that Agnew needed to go as quickly as possible. Over the weekend Richardson huddled with his associates and talked about the need for resolving the Agnew crisis in an expeditious manner.[23] Remarkably, there were no leaks about the endgame. Given the momentous stakes, all parties must have recognized the gravity of the situation. On Monday, October 8, Judah Best contacted Agnew and provided an outline of the final negotiations. Agnew instructed Best to tell Haig and Buzhardt there would be no deal unless "Richardson and the Department of Justice assure us there will be *no* incarceration." Without that guarantee Agnew thought he "might as well take my chances with White House threats and a Baltimore jury, prejudiced and biased as it might be, rather than resign the vice presidency and be railroaded to prison despite my innocence."[24]

Exactly two months earlier Agnew stood before the nation, declared his innocence, and promised to fight to clear his name. Now he was begging for mercy. He was still the vice president, still a heartbeat away from the presidency. He had all the trappings of power, the planes, the Secret Service agents, the staffers at his beck and call. But for all the pomp and circumstance, he was about to be exposed as the emperor without any clothes.

All that remained were the final details of the plea bargaining. On Tuesday, October 9, Agnew spent his last full day at the White House. Though hardly a typical day, Agnew stuck mostly to his routine—meeting with staffers—and making no reference to his impending resignation. He provided a clue when he canceled a meeting scheduled for the next morning on Capitol Hill. A couple of supporters in the House, Republicans Sam Devine of Ohio and Bill Dickinson of Alabama, had organized a breakfast for Agnew in order to revise the push for a congressional impeachment inquiry, unaware that Agnew no longer was going to try and fight the charges. At the last moment Agnew called it off, but never said why.[25]

During the day Agnew spoke with attorneys. The final deal essentially followed the original offer six weeks earlier—Agnew would plead no contest to a single charge of tax evasion, pay a fine, receive a suspended sentence, and of course, resign from the office. The pact complete, Agnew sat down and prepared two letters: one for Secretary of State Henry Kissinger and one for President Nixon. To Kissinger, Agnew wrote simply: "I hereby resign the office of the Vice Presidency effective immediately."

Having signed off on the plea arrangements, and tendered his resignation, Agnew had one final duty—to formally relay his decision to President Nixon. At 6:00 P.M. he walked out of his suite in the Old Executive Office Building and made way to the West Wing of the White House where Nixon awaited him in the Oval Office. Over the preceding four years and ten months, Nixon and Agnew had very few private meetings. Not until Agnew's legal troubles surfaced did Nixon grant Agnew much of an audience. Now they came together for the last time.

It was an emotional and historic meeting. For only the second time in the nation's history, a living vice president was leaving the office before his term ended. According to Nixon, they shook hands and sat down in front of the fireplace. Nixon spoke first, telling Agnew how sorry he was and expressing his concern for Agnew's family. Agnew later wrote that Nixon's sympathy seemed genuine: "My eyes filled at his solicitous words."

As the meeting ended, Agnew claimed Nixon put his arm on Agnew's shoulders, shook his head, and expressed his sorrow. Nixon recalls that he shook Agnew's hand and told him that he could always count on him as a friend. Agnew sensed that at that point, "I suddenly had the feeling that he couldn't wait to get me out of there."[26]

They never spoke again.

The next morning, Agnew left his office in the Old Executive Office Building and departed the gates of the White House just after 1:30 in the afternoon for Baltimore, Maryland. Born in that city 55 years earlier, the son of a Greek immigrant, Agnew rose from his humble beginnings to the vice presidency of the United States. Where his life began his political career would end, and all for less than $200,000 in alleged kickbacks.

Arthur Sohmer accompanied Agnew. For over a decade Sohmer worked side-by-side with Agnew. Although Sohmer's competence was often called into question, his loyalty and his integrity were not. Other aides had come and gone, but Sohmer remained, and just as Sohmer was with Agnew when he launched his political career, he was there at the end. As the limo traveled up Interstate 95, Agnew and Sohmer sat in quiet contemplation. With the tension as "thick as a London fog" Agnew tried to wax philosophical, quoting from Shakespeare's *As You Like It*, "All's the world a stage." In a poignant moment, Agnew saw Sohmer wiping away tears. The sight brought a "surge of emotion" in Agnew and he turned away "for fear of crying." Steadying himself, Agnew "focused on the idea that this was just a play and I must perform my part credibly."[27]

Along with Sohmer and Secret Service agents, Agnew entered Baltimore's old Federal Building shortly after 2:00 P.M. EST. His attorneys were already present in courtroom number three. At 2:04 Judge Walter Hoffman entered the courtroom. The bailiff asked all to rise, and after calling the court into session, Judah Best came in. As he took his place at the defendant's table, Best whispered, "Your letter of resignation has been delivered to the Secretary of State as you directed."

Agnew nodded. As the proceedings continued, Agnew focused on Judge Hoffman, who was speaking with Jay Topkis. Most of those assembled in the courtroom expected a hearing on the leaks, but Topkis informed the spectators that the court was making a criminal determination against his client. When Topkis finished, a brief murmur swept through the room, followed by a deafening silence.[28]

With the full weight of the moment sinking in, Agnew steeled himself. "I was numb—outside myself looking down on the scene as though it were a dream," he recalled. "Grief and sorrow were held in a secret cage to be released later." And there was another emotion: anger. As he sat he thought of his opponents, who, he surely knew, would revel in his downfall. At the hour of his political death, Agnew resolved that he would not give them any additional pleasure: "I only knew that I must not break in public. I could not give my enemies that satisfaction."[29]

Just a few feet away sat some of those men, Elliot Richardson, Henry Petersen, and George Beall. While Agnew watched, Beall handed Judge Hoffman a copy of the charge against Agnew. During the proceedings Richardson cast a glance at the vice president, but Agnew never looked his way.[30]

Then it came time for the formal plea bargain. Agnew, dressed in a light blue suit, white shirt, and striped tie, rose and answered affirmatively when Hoffman asked if Agnew was waiving his right to a jury trial and that he understood he was pleading no contest to a felony count.

Once the questioning ended, Agnew read aloud a prepared statement. "Thank you, your honor," he began. Steeling himself, Agnew looked down upon the paper. Speaking, as always, in a deliberate tone, he expressed his "appreciation for the courtesy and cooperation extended to me through my counsel in their deliberations with the prosecutors and throughout the consultation on this matter."

Quickly turning to the charges, Agnew justified his decision to enter the deal because "the public interest requires a swift disposition of the problems which are facing me. I am advised that a full legal defense of the probable charges against me could consume several years. I am concerned that intense media interest in the case would distract public attention from important national problems, to the country's detriment."

"I am aware," he went on, "that witnesses are prepared to testify that I and my agents received cash payments from consulting engineers doing business with the State of Maryland during the period I was Governor."

"With the exception of the admission that follows, I categorically deny the assertions of illegal acts on my part made by government witnesses."

In what must have been the most painful few seconds of his life, Agnew announced before the court his crime. "I admit that I did receive payments during the year 1967 which were not expended for political purposes and that therefore these payments were income, taxable to me in that year, and that I so knew."

With that short statement, thirty-six words in total, Agnew ended the fight of his life and admitted that he broke the law.

There was another admission: "I further acknowledge that contracts were awarded by state agencies in 1967 and other years to those who made such payments, and that I was aware of such awards. I am aware that government witnesses are prepared to testify that preferential treatment was accorded to the paying companies pursuant to an understanding with me when I was Governor. I stress, however, that no contracts were awarded to contractors who were not competent to perform the work, and, in most instances, state contracts were awarded without any arrangement for the payment of money by the contractor."

Although Agnew admitted accepting kickbacks, he denied "that the payments in any way influenced my official actions." Agnew also stated that "my acceptance of contributions was part of a long-established practice of political fund-raising in the state. At no time have I enriched myself at the expense of the public trust."

"In all the circumstances, I have concluded that protracted proceedings before the grand jury, the Congress, and the courts, with the speculation and controversy inevitably surrounding them, would seriously prejudice the national interest."

"These, briefly stated, Your Honor, are the reasons that I am entering a plea of nolo contendere to the charge that I did receive payments in 1967 which I failed to report for the purposes of income taxation."

His statement over, Agnew listened as Judge Hoffman summarized the case. At the end Hoffman stated the government's forty-page exposition of evidence, along with Agnew's denial, was not germane to the matter at hand. It would have been his "preference to omit these statements and end the verbal warfare as to this tragic event in history."

Turning to the defendant, Hoffman asked if Agnew had anything else to say.

"I have no further comments," Agnew answered.

Judge Hoffman then handed down his ruling: "It is the judgment of this court that imposition of any sentence be suspended for three years, conditioned that you, Spiro T. Agnew, at all times will be of uniform good behavior, that you will not violate the laws of the United States or any state; that as a further condition of this probation, you are to pay a fine in the sum of ten thousand dollars within forty days from this date, or otherwise stand committed for nonpayment of said fine; and that you shall not be required to be under the supervision of the probation officer of this court unless otherwise ordered by the court."[31]

And then it was over. The entire proceeding had lasted but forty minutes. Now the former vice president, Agnew slipped out of the courtroom by a side door. Most of the media expected Agnew to leave via the main exit on Calvert Street, so as he walked out of the building, there were only a few cameras. Turing to the microphones Agnew noticed a few more faces and silently nodded. He made a brief statement, saying only that he had resigned in order "to spare my family from a brutalizing court fight that could have lasted two years."[32]

Epilogue

For the rest of his life, Agnew toiled away in obscurity. Unlike Richard Nixon, he was largely content to stay out of the spotlight. Agnew had none of Nixon's demons and none of Nixon's desire to shape history. He devoted most of his time to write two books and to pursue various business endeavors, while largely eschewing politics.

His resignation did not mean an end to his problems. When Agnew awoke on Thursday, October 11, the full weight of his plight had sunk in. "I wanted nothing more than to pull the covers over my head and withdraw from the human race. The terrible emptiness had returned and had brought an unwelcome companion, self-pity," he recalled.[1] But he could have been excused for hoping to escape from his nightmare. Thanks to the plea bargain, he had escaped the most terrifying of all possibilities—prison time—but his legal difficulties were far from over. That morning's *New York Times* reported that an official spokesman for the Internal Revenue Service (IRS) claimed the agreement between Agnew and the Justice Department did not prohibit the IRS from bringing new charges against Agnew based on all unreported income from the bribes he took.[2] Agnew also owed money to his attorneys, and though his legal defense fund was still operating and had raised over $80,000, he told Clement Stone that he would return checks to anyone requesting or demanding their money back.[3]

With pressing debts, Agnew turned to singer Frank Sinatra for help. Throughout the time of troubles, Sinatra was Agnew's biggest supporter, offering counsel, and solace. Far from feeling betrayed by Agnew, Sinatra stuck by him. The day after Agnew resigned, Sinatra sent him $30,000. When the IRS demanded that Agnew pay $150,000 in back taxes, Sinatra stepped in and loaned him $200,000. By 1978, Agnew had made enough money to pay Sinatra back. A grateful Agnew dedicated *Go Quietly ... or else* to Sinatra.[4]

Agnew earned his living as a consultant, founding Pathlite. Inc., a business that helped American companies invest in foreign markets. Agnew had held out a glimmer of hope that he would be able to practice law, but soon after his plea bargain, the Maryland State Bar Association began proceedings to disbar him. Realizing that the bar would take some action against on the account of his no-contest plea, Agnew hoped that he would only receive a suspended sentence. Not only was the law his only profession, he professed a deep respect for the "orderliness of the law, its rote and unhurried logic."[5] On December 18, the state bar convened a hearing consisting of a three-member special panel, Shirley Jones, Ridgely P. Melvin, and William H. McCuliogh, all circuit court judges. Agnew, accompanied by his lawyers and Secret Service agents, arrived early at the Anne Arundel Courthouse. Mobbed by reporters and television cameras, Agnew walked past them all without making any comment. The proceeding began at 10:40 A.M. and lasted over two hours. Alfred P. Scanlan, one of the attorneys for the bar association, argued Agnew's actions merited disbarment. "It is now the court's burden to see the house swept clean," Scanlan told the court. Dale Adkins, one of Agnew's lawyers, countered that precedent suggesting that Agnew's license should be temporarily suspended. Adkins also asked for compassion. " 'Is there really no limit to the penance that society requires?' " he asked. Speaking on his part, Agnew admitted that his actions warranted a penalty, but that the "correct determination in my case would not be to strip me of my livelihood, not to impose the ultimate sanction, but to find some suitable suspension as the result of which I could remain away from practice . . . and perhaps come back at a future date, resume my practice and attempt to bring credit upon my state and upon the legal profession." A month after the hearing, the judges voted unanimously to strip Agnew of his license. Claiming that he was "unfit" to be an attorney, the judges urged the Maryland Court of Appeals to disbar him. Agnew's lawyers filed an appeal, but the judgment was upheld and Agnew was permanently disbarred.[6]

The plea bargain, resignation, and disbarment took their toll on Agnew. "The first two years (after his resignation) were very painful; the wound was raw and easily inflamed by new irritations."[7] His family helped him get through the worst of times. Judy was a "tower of strength" for him throughout the crisis. As Spiro and Judy rode home in the limousine the night of his resignation, he "took my wife's hand. She held on very tight. Somehow that made it better." The four Agnew children held up remarkably well. They loved and supported their father. Susan, the second daughter, lived with her parents during the ordeal, and remembers that she and her siblings simply went on with their lives. If they suffered any slights, they never let on to their father. "They set an example," he wrote, "that made it possible for me to survive the abrupt slide from top to bottom."[8]

Agnew also made it through the tough times with the help of former staff members. During his public career, Agnew developed friendships with staffers, and quite a number said he was the best boss they ever had.[9] In interviews, letters, and memoirs, a number expressed how they believed Agnew was a good man and important historical figure and that history should not overlook his accomplishments. Agnew inspired loyalty in almost all of them, and he kept in touch with many of his former staff members and even his Secret Service agents.[10]

Shortly after leaving the vice presidency, Agnew decided to write a novel. He began shopping around for a publisher, but was rejected by several major companies before settling on *Playboy Press*. In early 1974 the *Ladies Home Journal* announced that it would serialize parts of the novel, for which Agnew received a hefty fee of $100,000.[11] The finished work, *The Canfield Decision*, published in 1976, followed the exploits of Vice President Porter Newton Canfield, a Democrat from Pennsylvania, serving under the Walter Hurley administration. Set in 1983, the book centers on Porter Canfield's presidential prospects for 1984 and his growing estrangement with the Hurley administration, principally over Middle Eastern affairs. When it was released in mid-1976, the novel quickly shot up the best-seller lists; reviews were mixed. Reviewing it in the *New York Times*, economist John Kenneth Galbraith wrote that it "might not be a great novel" but commended Agnew for offering some sharp insights on Washington parlor games and how the vice presidency worked.[12]

Agnew wrote a novel because, at the time, he "was not ready to write the real story of resignation." After a few years, Agnew started working on a memoir about the events leading to his resignation. Published in 1980, *Go Quietly . . . or else* tells Agnew's side of the story. An unapologetic account, *Go Quietly* attempts to exonerate Agnew of all wrongdoing. The first sentence of the book makes this clear: "I am writing this book because I am innocent of the allegations against me which compelled me to resign from the vice-presidency of the United States in 1973."[13]

Agnew paints himself as a victim of a conspiracy designed to bring him down. "I am a man who was judged out of court on the basis of false testimony abetted by those who sought my political ruin." Agnew denies all the charges against him. He pled guilty and resigned; he writes in order to spare his family any more agony, and because of the alleged threat Al Haig made against him. According to Agnew, Haig told Agnew's military aid, General Mike Dunn, "The president has a lot of power—don't forget that." That message "sent a chill through my body," Agnew wrote. "I feared for my life."[14]

The absurd tale of an assassination threat, along with Agnew's denial he did not break the law, renders *Go Quietly* very suspect. Had Agnew admitted his crimes, he might have made a much more convincing case that he was the victim of overzealous prosecutors who, with the help of a hostile media, trampled on his civil rights and essentially precluded any chance of his ever receiving a fair trial.

In the memoir, Agnew makes it perfectly clear he believes Richard Nixon betrayed him. As for Agnew and Nixon, they never spoke. Nixon tried a couple of times to contact Agnew, but Agnew refused to take his calls. After the publication of *Go Quietly*, Agnew all but disappeared from public life.

When Nixon passed away in April 1994, his daughter Tricia contacted Agnew and asked if he would come to the funeral. Deciding to put away his bitterness, Agnew agreed. At the ceremony, Agnew sat just in front of G. Gordon Liddy.

Agnew returned to Washington, D.C., in May 1995. Every vice president had a bust in the capital—except Agnew. Finally, after two decades, a bust was commissioned, and Agnew, Judy, and his children came to Capitol Hill for the unveiling. About 300 attended, including Tricia Cox, former staffers, and about a dozen senators. Agnew delivered a brief speech, where he acknowledged, "I'm not blind or deaf to the fact that some people feel that this is a ceremony that should not take place," He said, "I would remind those people that, regardless of their personal view of me, this ceremony has less to do with Spiro Agnew than with the office I held, an honor conferred on me by the American people two decades ago."[15]

Always physically active, Agnew continued to golf and play tennis into his mid-seventies. In September 1996, while staying in Ocean City (where he and Judy owned a co-op), he scheduled a tennis match with a friend for Wednesday, September 17, 1996. But the night before, Agnew fell ill in his condo. Judy found him lying prostrate on the floor. She immediately called an ambulance, but by the time the ambulance arrived, he was already dead. The cause of death was acute leukemia, which had gone undiagnosed. He was 77.[16]

Word of the death became public on September 18. The nightly newscasts each ran a story on Agnew, but in a sign of how much he had faded into obscurity, the stories aired last on the programs. In some papers, Agnew's obituary was on the front page, but in many others it was buried in the back. Almost all the stories focused on Agnew's resignation, with some coverage given to his famous speeches and alliterations.

The funeral was a small affair, attended by Judy, the children, and grandchildren. But some of Agnew's old friends and associates came to pay their respects, including Pat Buchanan and some of the Secret Service agents who guarded him, who asked to be there for a man they admired. Spiro T. Agnew was laid to rest in Timonium, Maryland. His small grave reads simply, "Spiro T. Agnew: 1918-1996."[17]

Spiro Agnew was not a tragic figure. His story is that of a politician who got caught taking kickbacks and was forced from office. Despite his steadfast denials, the evidence against him was clear and overwhelming. He accepted a plea of no contest because the facts were against him. His resignation ended his political career and cost him any chance at the presidency.

That Richard Nixon never conducted a background check on Agnew in 1968 is a testimony to a problem that has consistently plagued the American political process. The office of the vice presidency is an essentially powerless institution, yet nine times in the nation's history a vice president has succeeded to the presidency following the death or resignation of the chief executive. During Watergate, Nixon's failure to probe Agnew's background added to the crisis already facing the nation. The country faced the specter of the president and the vice president being removed from office at the same time for their crimes. Fortunately Agnew quit, which allowed Nixon to appoint the untainted Gerald Ford to the vice presidency. Still, Nixon was derelict in not looking into Agnew's past and making the selection as an afterthought. Nixon's poor decision did not lead to immediate change. In 1972 George McGovern was unaware of Thomas Eagleton's bouts with depression and shock therapy. Sixteen years later, George H. W. Bush picked Dan Quayle, an obscure Indiana senator, who faced questions about his maturity, competence, and intelligence and whether he dodged the draft. In 2008 John McCain shocked nearly everyone by selecting Alaska governor Sarah Palin, who, like Agnew, had been a governor for just two years. The decision set off a storm of protest and ridicule and almost certainly hurt McCain's election chances.

The vice presidency has grown in importance over the previous several decades. Since 1952 Richard Nixon, Hubert Humphrey, Walter Mondale, George H. W. Bush, and Al Gore have all gone on to win their party's nomination to the presidency. Although he disavowed any interest in the presidency and did not seek the Republican nomination in 2008, Vice President Richard Cheney wielded considerable influence in the George W. Bush administration. Agnew never came close to having any such power, but he did use the office to advance his views and in the process burnished his conservative credentials.

Agnew's shift to the right explains his larger significance. During the 1960s the Republicans engaged in a battle over the future of their party. It was by no means clear which faction would emerge as the strongest. Barry Goldwater's nomination in 1964 did not mean the conservatives had won the struggle; for two years liberal and moderate Republicans scored victories in a number of key congressional and gubernatorial races. These included Ed Brooke in Massachusetts, Charles Percy in Illinois, Winthrop Rockefeller in Arkansas, and Spiro Agnew in Maryland. Agnew had won in part by presenting himself as a moderate, one who eschewed ideology in favor of pragmatism. That approach worked for him, and at that point in time Agnew hoped the GOP would stay in the middle of the political spectrum.

In just a few years Agnew had shifted to the right, as had the Republican Party. By 1972 the conservatives were in the ascendancy. A number of factors explain this trend. First, Agnew like millions of other Americans believed that the Great Society had done as much, if not more than, harm as good. During the late 1960s, crime in America exploded. Drugs use was widespread. Young adults were protesting Vietnam and burning their draft cards. To Agnew and many likeminded people, the changes were the result of liberalism's excesses. In 1964 Lyndon Johnson's liberalism had crushed Barry Goldwater's conservatism. By 1968 liberalism was in decline.

The 1968 election signaled the shifting political winds. Richard Nixon and George Wallace took 58 percent of the vote, while Hubert Humphrey won 42 percent, a full 20 percent less than LBJ four years earlier. A number of reasons account for the change, but race was a critical factor. Once the Civil Rights and Voting Rights Act passed, many white Americans believed the fight for racial equality had been achieved. But beginning in the summer of 1965, riots erupted in the nation's cities, striking fear in the hearts of middle- and lower-middle-class white Americans. There was also a feeling that the federal government and the leadership of the Democratic Party favored minorities over whites.

All these feelings led to the fall of liberalism across the country and the decline of moderation in the Republican Party. Spiro Agnew's political career is emblematic of the change occurring during that time. In 1964 Agnew opposed Barry Goldwater's nomination. Eight years later, Goldwater helped ensure that Agnew would stay on the presidential ticket. Agnew had become a conservative and a hero to the right. His career came to a crashing halt but that same career helps explain the transformation of American politics.

Notes

INTRODUCTION

1. Spiro T. Agnew, *Go Quietly . . . or else* (New York: William Morrow, 1980), 10.

2. For an excellent overview of the end of the solid South, see Kari Frederickson, *The Dixiecrat Revolt and the End of the Solid South, 1932–1968* (Chapel Hill: University of North Carolina Press, 2001).

3. Robert David Johnson, *All the Way with LBJ: The 1964 Presidential Election* (New York: Cambridge University Press, 2009).

4. Lewis L. Gould, *1968: The Election that Changed America*, 2nd edition (Chicago: Ivan R. Dee, 2010).

5. Leo P. Ribuffo, "Why Is There So Much Conservatism in the United States and Why Do So Few Historians Know Anything About It?," *The American Historical Review* 99, no.2 (April 1994): 438–449.

6. Mary C. Brennan, *Turning Right in the Sixties: The Conservative Capture of the GOP* (Chapel Hill: University of North Carolina Press, 1995).

7. Geoffrey Kabaservice, *Rule and Ruin: The Downfall of Moderation and the Destruction of the Republican Party, From Eisenhower to the Tea Party* (New York: Oxford University Press, 2012); Rick Perlstein, *Before the Storm: Barry Goldwater and the Unmaking of the American Consensus* (New York: Hill and Wang, 2001).

CHAPTER 1: THE RISE OF SPIRO AGNEW

1. "Agnew Reminisces over Family Album," *Baltimore Sun Magazine*, January 19, 1969, 9.

2. In the Agnew papers at the University of Maryland there is a letter to an Agnes Birnbaum, the editorial director of the book department of Universal Publishing. In 1970 the company published a biography of Agnew by Jim Lucas. In the work Lucas claimed that Agnew's father arrived in the United States in 1902 and then spent several years in Boston. But in the letter to Birnbaum it is stated that he came to America in 1902 and "settled in Schenectady, New York (not Boston), after his ship docked in New York." The letter is dated June 12, 1970, but was unsigned or

the next page was missing. The letter can be found in the "Articles, Books, and Booklets Written about the Vice President and His Family 1970," folder 3, box 90, subseries 3.5, series 3, Spiro T. Agnew Papers, Special Collections, University of Maryland Libraries, College Park, Maryland (hereafter "Agnew MS").

3. Spiro T. Agnew to C. J. Harkader, November 25, 1969, folder 1, box 15, subseries 3.1, series 3, Agnew MS.

4. Paul Hoffman, *Spiro!* (New York: Tower Publications, 1971), 36.

5. Jules Witcover, *White Knight: The Rise of Spiro Agnew* (New York: Random House, 1972), 34.

6. Witcover, *White Knight*, 33.

7. "Spiro Theodore Agnew Scholarship Fund Dinner," December 10, 1969, folder 49, box 2, subseries 3.7, series 3, Agnew MS.

8. "Spirostyle," undated article, file A, box 2, Joseph P. Albright Papers, Western Heritage Center, University of Wyoming, Laramie.

9. As Agnew climbed the political ladder a legend grew that he changed his name, party affiliation, and religious denomination in an effort to assimilate. Although Agnew always wanted to be one of the crowd, he had never been a member of the Greek Orthodox Church, as he explained in a letter in 1976, "I have never changed my religion. My mother was an Episcopalian. I was raised in the Episcopalian Church and am still a member of that Church." Agnew to the *Baltimore Sun*, May 30, 1976, Spiro Agnew Vertical File, Enoch Pratt Library, Baltimore, Maryland.

10. Hoffman, *Spiro!*, 34–36.

11. Agnew quit smoking after a few years. See *Baltimore Sun*, January 9, 1969, 12.

12. *Baltimore Sun*, December 16, 1962, 1.

13. For the quote and the further information see, Agnew to Office of the Registrar, Johns Hopkins University, January 3, 1945; Irene Davis to Agnew, February 2, 1945, Office of the Registrar, Record group 13.010, subgroup 1, series 2, the Ferdinand Hamburger Jr. Archives of the Johns Hopkins University Library, Johns Hopkins University, Baltimore, Maryland.

14. *Baltimore Sun*, December 16, 1962, 1.

15. *Parade*, August 9, 1970, 5.

16. "Agnew's Service Record," folder 6, box 90, subseries 3.5, series 3, Agnew MS.

17. Agnew to Robert J. Dodds Jr., June 24, 1969, folder 1, box 9, subseries 3.1, series 3, Agnew MS.

18. *Baltimore Sun*, January 19, 1969, 12.

19. John S. Hunter to Agnew, April 12, 1968, Civil Rights folder, MSA-SC, 1041–1713, Governor, General File, Maryland State Archives, Annapolis, Maryland.

20. "Agnew's Service Record."

21. "Biography of Judy Agnew," folder 18, box 1, subseries 2.4, series 2, Agnew MS.

22. Witcover, *White Knight*, 39; "History Blanks for Instructors," February 21, 1955, box 4, series XX, University of Baltimore Collection, University of Baltimore Library, Baltimore, Maryland. In his application for a position at the law school Agnew under "Teaching experience and subject taught," wrote "Army 1943–1944," but did not specify exactly what he taught.

23. "Agnew's Service Record."

24. Witcover, *White Knight*, 40–41.

25. "Agnew's Service Record."

26. Agnew to Davis, February 2, 1945, Office of the Registrar, JHU.

27. *Where He Stands: The Life and Convictions of Spiro T. Agnew* (New York: Hawthorne Books, 1968), 12. The book was a document out together by the Nixon–Agnew campaign staff shortly after Agnew's selection as Richard Nixon's vice presidential running mate in 1968.

28. Theo Lippman, Jr., *Spiro Agnew's America: The Vice President and the Politics of Suburbia* (New York: W.W. Norton & Company, 1972), 29; Jules Witcover, *White Knight: The Rise of Spiro Agnew,* 43.

29. *Baltimore Sun*, May 30, 1976.

30. Years later Agnew tried to help Barrett's son Don Barrett obtain a job in the State Department. In April 1969 he wrote to Secretary of State William Rogers to help Barrett. I was unable to determine if the intervention was successful. Agnew to William Rogers, April 21, 1969, folder 1, box 34, subseries 3.1, series 3, Agnew MS.

31. Witcover, *White Knight*, 44.

32. *Today's Health*, July 1971, 69.

33. *Baltimore Sun*, December 16, 1962, A1.

34. George C. Callcott, *Maryland and America, 1940–1980* (Baltimore: Johns Hopkins University Press, 1985), 213.

35. Jim C. Lucas, *Agnew: Profile in Conflict* (New York: Award Books, 1970), 13.

36. Callcott, *Maryland and America*, 213.

37. *Baltimore Sun*, February 22, 1994, 1B.

38. Neal A. Brooks, Eric G. Rockel, and William C. Hughes, *A History of Baltimore County* (Towson: Friends of Towson Library, 1979), 410–412.

39. *Baltimore Sun*, May 14, 1962, B2.

40. *Baltimore Evening Sun*, May 16, 1962, A1.

41. *Baltimore Evening Sun*, May 16, 1962, A28.

42. "Baltimore County at a Glance," folder 2, box 1, subseries 1.6, series 1, Agnew MS; Brooks et al., *A History of Baltimore County*, 370–371.

43. "Baltimore County at a Glance, 1964–1965," folder 2, box 1, subseries 1.6, series 1, Agnew MS; Brooks et al., *History of Baltimore County*, 371.

44. Callcott, *Maryland and America*, 20–21.

45. *Baltimore Evening Express*, August 28, 1991, D6; *Easton Express*, April 21, 1967, 18.

46. "American Institute for Political Communication," *The New Methodology: A Study of Political Strategy and Tactics* (Washington, DC: American Institute for Political Communication, 1967), 100–101.

47. *Baltimore Sun*, August 28, 1962, 28C.

48. DeFilippo went on to serve as press secretary to Marvin Mandel, Agnew's successor as governor. He got to know Agnew and grew to dislike him. "He was difficult to like. He was a relentlessly middlebrow kind of guy, standoffish. He didn't like to work," DeFilippo told the *Washington Post* two days after Agnew died. *Washington Post*, September 20, 1996, 2A.

49. *Baltimore News Post*, September 26, 1962, 2C.

50. Joseph Albright, *What Makes Spiro Run: The Life and Times of Spiro Agnew* (New York: Dodd, Mead, 1972), 90.

51. "Transcript of Remarks on Station WFBR Radio," undated, box 8, MSA SC 4804–01.

52. "Fact Sheet on Spiro T. Agnew," box 13, Franklin L. Burdette Papers, Special Collections, University of Maryland, College Park.

53. *The Pittsburgh Press*, March 5, 1972, B17.

54. Newspaper clip, *Baltimore Sun*, November 6, 1962, folder 3, box 1, subseries 1.6, series 1, Agnew MS.

55. "The Relationship between Mr. Agnew, I. H. Hammerman, II and Jerome B. Wolff," 2, sub-series 1, series 1, Baltimore County/Spiro T. Agnew investigation, Personal Papers of the Beall Family, J. Glenn Beall Archives, Lewis J. Ort Library, Frostburg State University, Frostburg, Maryland (hereafter "Beall Papers").

56. Richard M. Cohen and Jules Witcover, *A Heartbeat Away: The Investigation and Resignation of Vice President Spiro T. Agnew* (New York: Viking Press, 1974), 35–36; *Los Angeles Times*, October 11, 1973, 1; *Washington Post*, February 20, 1963, A1.

57. "The Relationship between Mr. Agnew and Lester Matz," 1, sub-group 6, series 1, subseries 1, Beall Papers.

58. For the amount that Matz gave in 1962, see "The Relationship between Mr. Agnew and Lester Matz," 1, Beall Papers.

59. "The Relationship of Mr. Agnew, I. H. Hammerman, II, and Jerome B. Wolff," 1–4, Beall Papers.

60. "Exposition of the Evidence against Spiro T. Agnew Accumulated by the Investigation in the Office of the United States Attorney for the District of Maryland as of October 10, 1973," 31, Beall papers.

61. "Biography of Judy Agnew," Agnew MS.

62. "Spiro Agnew: Life with Father," box 16, Papers of Nick Thimmesch, MSC 709, Special Collections Department, University of Iowa Libraries, Iowa City, Iowa.

63. *Baltimore Sun*, March 7, 1993, 1A.

64. *Sports Illustrated*, June 21, 1971, 72; "Spiro T. Agnew: Suburban Man, Colts Fan, Unruffled Politician," *Washington Post*, October 17, 1966.

65. Brooks et al., *A History of Baltimore County*, 390.

66. Thomas Borstlemann, *The Cold War and the Color Line: American Race Relations in the Global Arena* (Cambridge: Harvard University Press, 2001); Mary C. Dudziak, *Cold War Civil Rights: Race and the Image of American Democracy* (Princeton: Princeton University Press, 2000), 167–168.

67. Dudziak, *Cold War Civil Rights*, 168.

68. *Washington Post*, May 13, 1963, A16.

69. "New Releases—Civil Rights, 1963–1964," folder 4, box 1, subseries 1.3, series 1, Agnew MS.

70. Ibid.

71. Brooks et al., *History of Baltimore County*, 391, "Agnew-Civil Rights, 1963," folder 3, box 1, subseries 1.2, series 1, Agnew MS.

72. The information from this paragraph and the following paragraphs are from various newspaper clippings found in "Publications about Agnew, 1953–1966" folder 3, box 1, subseries 1.6, series 3, Agnew MS.

73. Ibid.

74. Ibid.

75. Ibid.

76. Ibid.

77. Ibid. In *Griffith et al. v. Maryland*, the Supreme Court ruled that the state's trespass law violated the 14th Amendment and vacated the convictions. See *United States Reports* Vol. 378 (Washington: Government Printing Office, 1965), 130–138.

78. Ibid.

79. Ibid.

80. Ibid.

81. Ibid.

82. Richard Walsh and William Lloyd Fox, *Maryland: A History, 1632–1974* (Baltimore: Maryland Historical Society, 1974), 836.

83. Laura Jane Gifford, *The Center Cannot Hold: The 1960 Presidential Election and the Rise of Modern Conservatism* (DeKalb, IL: Northern Illinois Press, 2009); Richard North Smith, *On His Own Terms: A Life of Nelson Rockefeller* (New York: Random House, 2014).

84. Barry M. Goldwater, *The Conscience of a Conservative* (Shepherdsville, KY: Victor Publishing Company, 1960).

85. Agnew to Thomas Kuchel, June 18, 1963, folder 1, box 1, subseries 1.1, series 1, Agnew MS.

86. "Statement by Spiro T. Agnew, Baltimore County Executive," July 30, 1963, folder 3, box 1, subseries 1.1, series 1, Agnew MS.

87. Kuchel to Agnew, August 1, 1963; Agnew to Kuchel, August 17, 1963, folder 15, box 1, subseries 1.3, series 1, Agnew MS.

88. *Baltimore Sun*, December 7, 1962, 1.

89. "Political Philosophy," January 6, 1964, folder 22, box 1, subseries 1.2, series 1, Agnew MS.

90. Agnew to Dwight D. Eisenhower, July 25, 1963, and Robert Schulz to Agnew, July 29, 1963, folder 3, box 1, subseries 1.2, series 1, Agnew MS.

91. Agnew noted this in his endorsement of Kuchel.

92. John Steffey to Agnew, November 6, 1963, and Agnew to Steffey, November 12, 1963, folder 4, box 1, subseries 1.1, series 1, Agnew MS.

93. George D. Wolff, *William Warren Scranton: Pennsylvania Statesman* (London: A Keystone Book, 1981), 94–95; *Washington Post*, June 13, 1964, A1.

94. *Baltimore Sun*, June 13, 1964, 17.

95. *Washington Post*, July 15, 1964, A4.

96. Lee Edwards, *Goldwater: The Man Who Made a Revolution* (Washington, DC: Regnery, 1995), 265.

97. *Baltimore Sun*, July 17, 1964, 1.

98. "Goldwater Endorsement Reservations," July 24, 1964, folder 4, box 1, subseries 1.2, series 1, Agnew MS.

99. "Civil Rights," folder 22, box 1, subseries 1.2, series 1, Agnew MS.

100. Ibid.

101. Dan T. Carter, *The Politics of Rage: George Wallace, the Origins of the New Conservatism, and the Transformation of American Politics* (New York: Simon & Schuster, 1995), 208–211.

102. Stephen Lesher, *George Wallace: American Populist* (Reading: Addison-Wesley Publishing, 1993), 296.

103. Jody Carlson, *George C. Wallace and the Politics of Powerlessness* (Brunswick: Transaction Books, 1981), 34.

104. Agnew to Jay T. Cloud, May 14, 1964, folder 4, box 1, subseries 1.1, series 1, Agnew MS.

105. Witcover, *White Knight*, 103.

106. Carter, *The Politics of Rage*, 213.

107. Newspaper clip, *Baltimore News American*, July 18, 1964, folder 3, box 1, subseries 1.6, series 1, Agnew MS.

108. Agnew to Arthur I. Bell, March 18, 1965, folder 5, box 1, subseries 1.1, series 1, Agnew MS.

109. *Baltimore News American*, March 7, 1993; Lippman, *Spiro Agnew's America*, 72.

110. Lippman, *Spiro Agnew's America*, 72–73.

111. On February 3, 1966, Agnew wrote to his friend Al Shuger about his decision: "Because of our warm friendship over some years, I want you to be the first to know that I have made a final decision to run for governor," folder 5, box 1, subseries 1.1, series 1, Agnew MS.

112. Callcott, *Maryland and America*, 215.

113. Newspaper clip, *Washington Evening Star*, folder 3, box 1, subseries 1.6, series 1, Agnew MS.

114. "Agnew, December 3–December 5, 1966," folder 2, box 1, subseries 1.6, series 1, Agnew MS.

115. Lucas, *Agnew*, 35–36; *Washington Post*, October 17, 1966.

116. Newspaper clip, *Central Maryland News*, March 24, 1966, folder 3, box 1, subseries 1.6, series 1, Agnew MS.

CHAPTER 2: AGNEW AND THE POLITICS OF RACE

1. "Agnew files for Republican Gubernatorial Nomination," *Annapolis Evening Capitol*, April 21, 1966, 1, 19.

2. "Agnew Offers a Spur," *Baltimore Sun*, April 17, 1966, 12.

3. George C. Callcott, *Maryland and America, 1940–1980* (Baltimore: Johns Hopkins University Press, 1985), 215.

4. *Where He Stands: The Life and Convictions of Spiro T. Agnew* (New York: Hawthorne Books, 1968), 27–28; Dave Halberstam, "The Luck of Spiro Agnew," in *New York Stories: Landmark Writing from Four Decades of New York Magazine* (New York: Random House, 2008), 540–542.

5. In a "Fact Sheet on Spiro T. Agnew" the authors noted, "Agnew is reputed to have an active distaste for the public functions and appearances required in politics, and to lack a genuine liking for mixing with voters." "Fact Sheet on Spiro T. Agnew," 3, Franklin Burdette Papers, Special Collections, University of Maryland Libraries, College Park, Maryland (hereafter "Burdette MS"). Accessed on February 16, 2015.

6. *Baltimore Sun*, July 8, 1966, A8, C9; Theo Lippman, Jr., *Spiro Agnew's America: The Vice President and the Politics of Suburbia* (New York: W.W. Norton & Company, 1972), 78–80.

7. *Baltimore Sun*, July 8, 1966.

8. "Fact Sheet on Spiro T. Agnew," Burdette MS; *New York Times*, October 22, 1968, 29.

9. "Fact Sheet on Spiro T. Agnew," Burdette MS.

10. For the "chronic campaigner" quote, see Stephen E. Ambrose, *Nixon: The Triumph of a Politician, 1962–1972* (New York: Simon & Schuster, 1989), 96.

11. "George Percy Mahoney," folder 21, box 3, subseries 2.4, series 2, Spiro T. Agnew Papers, Special Collections, University of Maryland Libraries, College Park, Maryland (hereafter "Agnew MS").

12. James T. Patterson, *Grand Expectations: The United States, 1945–1974* (New York: Oxford University Press, 1996), 588.

13. David Burner, *Making Peace with the 60s* (Princeton: Princeton University Press, 1996), 34.

14. Robert Dallek, *Flawed Giant: Lyndon Johnson and His Times, 1961–1973* (New York: Oxford University Press, 1998), 223.

15. David Danzing, "Conservatism after Goldwater," in *Politics 1968*, ed. Francis M. Carney and Frank Way Jr. (Belmont: Wadsworth Publishing Company, 1967), 59.

16. One critic was the former baseball player Jackie Robison who wrote a piece, "New Order Spotlights Kennedy's Courage," *Chicago Defender*, December 1–7, 1962, 14.

17. James S. Giglio, *The Presidency of John F. Kennedy* (Lawrence: University Press of Kansas, 1991), 172.

18. Hugh Davis Graham, *The Civil Rights Era: Origins and Development of National Policy, 1960–1972* (New York: Oxford University Press, 1990), 259.

19. Giglio, *The Presidency of John F. Kennedy*, 172.

20. By 1964, eighteen states and forty-two cities had passed open laws. See, Kaye Sizer Noe, "The Fair Housing Movement: An Overview and Case Study" (M.A. Thesis, University of Maryland, 1965), 65.

21. The fact did not go unnoticed by Southern legislators. Senator Sam Ervin, a Democrat from North Carolina who led the charge against the bill, commented, "It should be most interesting to watch the politics or the debate now that others' oxen are being gored." Graham, *The Civil Rights Era*, 262.

22. Edward L. Schapsmeier and Frederick H. Schapsmeier, *Dirksen of Illinois: Senatorial Statesman* (Urbana: University of Illinois Press, 1985), 184–186.

23. Stephen B. Oates, *Let the Trumpet Sound: The Life of Martin Luther King Jr.* (New York: Harper & Row, 1982), 412.

24. For an excellent study of Mahoney and the 1966 election, see Richard Hardesty, " 'A Veil of Voodoo': George P. Mahoney, Open Housing, and the 1966 Governor's Race," *Maryland Historical Magazine* 104, no. 2 (Summer 2009).

25. Newspaper clip, "Miles and Lane Won't Support Mahoney," folder 21, box 3, subseries 2.4, series 2, Agnew MS.

26. *Washington Post*, September 18, 1966, 1.

27. *Washington Post*, September 15, 1966, 4.

28. Mary C. Dudziak, *Cold War Civil Rights: Race and the Image of American Democracy* (Princeton: Princeton University Press, 2000), 130.

29. "The Polls: Speed of Integration," *Public Opinion Quarterly* (Fall 1968), 514–515.

30. Timothy N. Thurber, *Republicans and Race: The GOP's Frayed Relationship with African Americans, 1945–1974* (Lawrence: University Press of Kansas, 2013).

31. "The Significance of a Symbol in Relation to a Presidential Campaign," folder 21, box 3, subseries 2.4, series 2, Agnew MS.

32. "Remarks by Spiro T. Agnew," September 17, 1966, box 9, Burdette MS.

33. "The GOP Loves You, George Mahoney," Newspaper clip, *Washington Post*, November 26, 1968, C1, folder 21, box 3, subseries 2.4, series 2, Agnew MS.

34. "Mahoney Sets Essex Greeting," folder 21, box 3, subseries 2.4, series 2, Agnew MS.

35. *Annapolis Evening Capitol*, October 7, 1966, 1.

36. "Mahoney Gallops into Montgomery," undated message, folder 21, subseries 2.4, series 2, Agnew MS.

37. Thurber, *Republicans and Race*, 229–238, 260–263

38. *Annapolis*, July 18, 2003; *Hagerstown Morning Herald*, October 14, 1966, 1.

39. *Baltimore Sun*, October 18, 1966, B20.

40. *Cumberland Evening Times*, October 15, 1966, 16.

41. *Baltimore Sun*, October 16, 1966, 26.

42. Dean Acheson to the *Baltimore Sun*, October 19, 1966, 16.

43. *News American*, October 16, 1966, 2F; *New York Times*, October 12, 1966, 42; "Ted-A-Gram: Agnew for Governor," folder, series 2, Agnew MS.

44. "The Political Picture in Maryland," October 1966, box 4, Apfelbaum Collection, Administrative papers of Arthur Sohmer, Maryland State Archives Special Collections, 4804.

45. Ibid.

46. Ibid.

47. Ibid.

48. David S. Broder and Stephen Hess, *The Republican Establishment: The Present and Future of the G.O.P.* (New York: Harper & Row, 1967), 63–64.

49. "Ted-A-Gram to the Baltimore NAACP," October 17, 1966, box 1, Apfelbaum Collection, MSA 4804; *Baltimore Sun*, October 6, 1966, A20; *Hagerstown Morning Herald*, October 24, 1966, 24.

50. *Washington Post*, September 12, 1966, B1.

51. Michael S. Hatfield, "The 1966 Maryland Gubernatorial Election: The Political Saliency of Open Occupancy" (M.A. Thesis, University of Massachusetts, 1975), 11–19.

52. "Open Housing: Model Community," folder 22, box 1, subseries 1.2, series 1, Agnew MS.

53. In one speech he told an audience, "Everybody believes and knows that your house is your castle." *Baltimore Sun*, C10, October, 1966.

54. Theodore R. McKeldin Jr., Oral History 8202, July 25, 1977, 21, Maryland Historical Society, Baltimore, Maryland; *Baltimore Sun*, October 23, 1966, 30; Lippman, *Spiro Agnew's America*, 83.

55. *Cumberland Evening Times*, October 26, 1966, 14. After the election, Agnew asked Thompson to serve as his press secretary. During the campaign Thompson came away as "very impressed with Agnew," though he found the candidate to be a "little on the shy side." Author interview with Herb Thompson, February 12, 2003.

56. *Baltimore Sun*, October 27, 1966, C20.

57. *Baltimore Sun*, October 29, 1966, B20.

58. "Quality in Government," Alumni Association, October 1966, box 4, series XX, University of Baltimore Collection, University of Baltimore Library, Baltimore, Maryland.

59. *New York Times*, October 30, 1966, 76.

60. *Hagerstown Morning Herald*, November 2, 1966, C24.

61. *Baltimore Sun*, November 3, 1966, C20.

62. *Baltimore Sun*, November 4, 1966, C24.

63. In the story on the gubernatorial race, the *New York Times* wrote, "Few informed persons here regard Mr. Mahoney as a committed segregationist." *New York Times*, October 30, 1966, 76.

64. *Washington Post*, November 5, 1966, A1.

65. *Baltimore Sun*, November 8, 1966, C10.

66. *Baltimore Sun*, November 9, 1966, A12; D. P. Campbell to Agnew, November 10, 1966, folder 12, box 1, subseries 2.4, series 2, Agnew MS.

67. *Baltimore Sun*, November 9, 1966, A1.

68. Ibid; Jules Witcover, *White Knight: The Rise of Spiro Agnew* (New York: Random House, 1972), 149.

69. Thurber, *Republicans and Race*; Jonathan Darman, *Landslide: LBJ and Ronald Reagan at the Dawn of a New America* (New York: Random House, 2014); Matthew Dallek, *The Right Moment: Ronald Reagan's First Victory and the*

Decisive Turning Point in American Politics (New York: Free Press, 2001). All three of the authors argue that 1966 was a watershed moment in American politics when the GOP and conservatives seized upon the racial backlash and began forging an electoral majority.

CHAPTER 3: GOVERNOR AGNEW

1. Ann Pinchot, *Where He Stands: The Life and Convictions of Spiro T. Agnew* (New York: Hawthorne Books, 1968), 16.
2. *Baltimore Sun*, November 11, 1966, C26.
3. *Baltimore Sun*, September 9, 1967, C20; November 2, 1967, C20.
4. *Baltimore Magazine*, January 1968, 27.
5. Jules Witcover, *White Knight: The Rise of Spiro Agnew* (New York: Random House, 1972), 150–151.
6. *Baltimore Sun*, November 11, 1966, C26.
7. *New York Times*, January 26, 1967, 20.
8. *Washington Post*, January 4, 1967, A1, 5.
9. Newspaper clip, *Baltimore Afro-American*, June 17, 1967, folder 3, box 1, subseries 2.2, series 2, Spiro T. Agnew Papers, Special Collections, University of Maryland Libraries, College Park, Maryland (hereafter "Agnew MS"); Lucas A. Powe Jr., *The Warren Court and American Politics* (Cambridge: Belknap Press, 2000), 285–286.
10. Robert J. Bruegger, *Maryland, a Middle Temperament: 1634–1980* (Baltimore: Johns Hopkins University Press, 1996), 621; "Statement on Signing Senate Bill 237 and Senate Bill 173," April 21, 1967, *Addresses and State Papers of Spiro T. Agnew*, Governor of Maryland, 1967–1969 (Annapolis: State of Maryland, 1975), 158–159; "Civil Rights Accomplishments of the Agnew Administration," Governor (General Files), box 14, MSA SC 1041–1713.
11. "Mitchell Bares Rights Pledge by Governor," *Baltimore Evening Sun*, March 8, 1967, C28.
12. *Baltimore News American*, April 22, 1967, 1; *Addresses and State Papers*, 158–159.
13. "News Release on Legislation for People's Advocate," February 27, 1967, *Addresses and State Papers*, 68–69.
14. Newspaper clipping, *Baltimore News American*, February 28, 1967, "Agnew-editorials for," folder 3, box 1, subseries 2.2, series 2, Agnew MS.
15. All the quotes from clippings folder 3, box 1, Agnew MS.
16. *New York Post*, January 20, 1970, 41.
17. "Judge Harry Cole" Oral History 8103, Maryland Historical Society, Baltimore, Maryland.
18. Agnew to Gilbert Ware, undated memo, Governor (General File), box 14, MSA SC 1041–1713.
19. "Transcript of joint press conference with Roy Wilkins, executive director of the NAACP, following their meeting in Annapolis," July 19, 1967, *Addresses and State Papers*, 344–355.
20. Quoted in Peter B. Levy's "Civil War on Race Street: The Black Freedom Struggle and White Resistance in Cambridge, Maryland, 1960–1964," *Maryland Historical Magazine*, 89 (Fall 1994), 292.
21. Clayborne Carson, *In Struggle: SNCC and the Black Awakening of the 1960s* (Cambridge: Harvard University Press, 1981), 244; PeterLevy, *Civil War on Race*

Street: The Civil Rights Movement in Cambridge, Maryland (Gainesville: University of Florida Press, 2003), 139.

22. "Analysis of the Cambridge, Maryland Disturbance, Office of the Assistant Deputy Director for Research," Summer 1967, Governor (General File), Cambridge related information folder, box 14, MSA SC 1041–1713.

23. Ibid.

24. Transcription of H. Rap Brown's Speech in Cambridge on July 24, 1967, accessed March 14, 2015, http://msa.maryland.gov/megafile/msa/speccol/sc2200/sc2221/000012/000008/html/00000001.html.

25. George C. Callcott, *Maryland and America, 1940–1980* (Baltimore: Johns Hopkins University Press, 1985), 163; *New York Times*, July 26, 1967, 1.

26. Levy, *Civil War on Race Street*, 5.

27. Callcott, *Maryland and America*, 164; Bruegger, *Maryland*, 618–621; *Baltimore Sun*, July 21, 1967, A1, 6; "News Conference," July 26, 1967, *Addresses and State Papers*, 369–370.

28. See for example, Callcott, *Maryland and America*, 163; Carson, *In Struggle*, 256. Not everyone agreed with this assessment, however. Jim C. Lucas, an aide to Agnew and later a critical biographer, argued that the turning point came a year later in the Bowie State incident. Jim C. Lucas, *Agnew: Profile in Conflict* (New York: Award Books, 1970), 54.

29. Agnew to Rebecca R. Sadin, August 22, 1968, Governor (General File), Cambridge Related information folder, box 14, MSA SC 1041–1713.

30. Levy, *Civil War on Race Street*, 154.

31. *Washington Post*, July 30, 1967, 1.

32. *New York Times*, July 25, 1967, 34.

33. *New York Times*, July 26, 1967, 1, 19.

34. "Statement on Civil Rights and Rioting," July 30, 1967, *Addresses and State Papers*, 369–371.

35. Witcover, *White Knight*, 164–165; *New York Post Daily Magazine*, January 21, 1970, 1; Gary Wills, *Nixon Agonistes: The Crisis of a Self-Made Man* (New York: Houghton Mifflin, 1970), 287.

36. "Executive Proclamation," box 14, MSA SC 1041–1713; *Annapolis Evening Capitol*, April 5, 1968, 1.

37. *Annapolis Evening Capitol*, April 6, 1968, 1.

38. Ibid; *Washington Post*, April 8, 1968, A16.

39. "Comment on the Killing of Dr. Martin Luther King Jr.," *Addresses and State Papers*, 753–754.

40. *Washington Post*, April 11, 1968, A1, 6.

41. Patterson, *Grand Expectations*, 656–658.

42. Ware to Agnew, March 6, 1968, box 14, MSA SC 1041–1713.

43. Ibid.

44. Agnew to Nelson Rockefeller, November 4, 1967; Rockefeller to Agnew, December 20, 1967, box 1, record group 4, Nelson A. Rockefeller Papers, The Rockefeller Archive Center, Tarrytown, New York.

45. *Annapolis Evening Capitol*, April 5, 1968, 6.

46. Alex Csicsek, "Spiro T. Agnew and the Burning of Baltimore," in Jessica I. Elfenbein, et al., eds., *Baltimore '68: Riots and Rebirth in an American City* (Philadelphia: Temple University Press, 2011), 71.

47. *Washington Post*, April 9, 1968, A1; Lippman, *Spiro Agnew's America*, 109–110.

48. Csicsek, "Spiro T. Agnew and the Burning of Baltimore," 72.

49. "Statement at conference with civil rights and community leaders," April 11, 1968, *Addresses and State Papers,* 758–762.

50. "Statement at conference with civil rights and community leaders," April 11, 1968, *Addresses and State Papers*, 758–762.

51. *Baltimore Afro-American*, April 13, 1968, 1.

52. Kenneth Durr, "Why We Are Troubled: White-Working Class Politicians in Baltimore, 1940–1980" (Ph.D. Dissertation, American University, 1998), 284; Paul Hoffman, *Spiro!* (New York: Tower Publications, 1971), 26.

53. Joseph Albright, *What Makes Spiro Run: The Life and Times of Spiro Agnew* (New York: Dodd, Mead, 1972), 191.

54. Mary Muzette Ogle Ray to Agnew, April 11, 1968, folder 15, box 1, subseries 2.1, series 2, Agnew MS; All other letters from MSA SC 1041–1713. There are seven boxes full of letters of support to Agnew about his speech.

55. *Washington Post*, April 13, 1968, A6.

56. *New York Times Magazine*, October 29, 1972, 17.

57. Willie Adams, Oral History 8210, Maryland Historical Society, Baltimore, Maryland.

58. *Baltimore Afro-American*, April 13, 1968, 4.

59. *Report of the National Advisory Commission on Civil Disorders* (Washington, DC: Government Printing Office, 1968), 5.

60. *Addresses and State Papers*, 924–930.

61. Rick Perlstein is the author of two works that reduce Nixon's and Ronald Reagan's success to race. This reductionist approach renders much of those works suspect. See Rick Perlstein *Nixonland: The Rise of a President and the Fracturing of American* (New York: Scribner, 2008); *The Invisible Bridge: The Fall of Nixon and the Rise of Reagan* (New York: Simon & Schuster, 2014).

62. Matthew Lassiter offers a nuanced examination of how white suburbanites voted in his work, *The Silent Majority: Suburban Politics in the Sunbelt South* (Princeton University Press, 2007).

CHAPTER 4: NIXON, AGNEW, AND THE 1968 CAMPAIGN

1. George Herring, *From Colony to Superpower: U.S. Foreign Relations since 1776* (New York: Oxford University Press, 2008), 752.

2. Lewis L. Gould, *1968: The Election that Changed America* (Chicago: Ivan R. Dee, 2010).

3. *Where He Stands: The Life and Convictions of Spiro T. Agnew* (New York: Hawthorne Books, 1968), 16; Newspaper clip, *Baltimore Sun*, January 28, 1968, Spiro T. Agnew vertical file, Enoch Pratt Library, Baltimore, Maryland.

4. "News conference," April 25, 1967; *Addresses and State Papers of Spiro T. Agnew, Governor of Maryland, 1967–1969* (Annapolis: State of Maryland, 1975), 174.

5. "News conference," September 14, 1967, *Addresses and State Papers*, 406–407.

6. Ibid.

7. Joseph Albright, *What Makes Spiro Run: The Life and Times of Spiro Agnew* (New York: Dodd, Mead, 1972), 162–163.

8. Rockefeller to Agnew, November 15, 1963; Agnew to Rockefeller, November 20, 1963, folder 3, box 1, subseries 1.1, series 1, Spiro T. Agnew Papers,

Special Collections, University of Maryland Libraries, College Park, Maryland (hereafter "Agnew MS").

9. *New York Times*, October 18, 1967, 1, 29.

10. "News conference," April 25, 1967, *Addresses and State Papers*, 176.

11. Author interview with Herb Thompson.

12. Spiro T. Agnew, *Go Quietly . . . or Else* (New York: William Morrow, 1980), 60–61.

13. "News conference," January 3, 1968, *Addresses and State Papers*, 590–591.

14. "Formation of a Citizens Committee for Rockefeller," January 9, 1968, folder 10, box 3, subseries 2.3, series 2, Agnew MS.

15. Theodore H. White, *The Making of the President 1968* (New York: Atheneum Publishers, 1969), 70.

16. Richard Norton Smith, *On His Own Terms: A Life of Nelson Rockefeller* (New York: Random House, 2014), 345.

17. Michael Kramer and Sam Roberts, *I Never Wanted to be Vice President of Anything: An Investigative Biography of Nelson Rockefeller* (New York: Basic Books, 1976), 328.

18. Smith, *On His Own Terms*, 514–515; *Washington Post*, March 11, 1968, A1, 4.

19. Agnew, *Go Quietly*, 61.

20. Ibid.

21. "Remarks on the Rockefeller Announcement," March 21, 1968, folder 69, box 3, subseries 2.3, series 2, Agnew MS.

22. Author interview with Herb Thompson; Theo Lippman, *Spiro Agnew's America: The Vice President and the Politics of Suburbia* (New York: W.W. Norton & Company, 1972), 121.

23. Agnew, *Go Quietly*, 61–62.

24. Jules Witcover, *White Knight: The Rise of Spiro Agnew* (New York: Random House, 1972), 198; Smith, *On His Own Terms*, 516–517.

25. "News conference," March 21, 1968, *Addresses and State Papers*, 731.

26. Witcover, *White Knight*, 193.

27. Stephen E. Ambrose, *Nixon: The Education of a Politician, 1913–1962* (New York: Simon & Schuster, 1987), 384.

28. Milton S. Eisenhower to Agnew, March 26, 1968, folder 12, box 1, subseries 2.1, series 2, Agnew MS.

29. Agnew to Eisenhower, April 1, 1968, Agnew MS.

30. Eisenhower to Agnew, April 24, 1968, Agnew MS.

31. Richard Nixon, *RN: The Memoirs of Richard Nixon* (New York: Touchstone, 1978), 300.

32. Richard J. Whalen, *Catch the Falling Flag: A Republican's Challenge to His Party* (Boston: Houghton Mifflin, 1972), 203.

33. Stephen E. Ambrose, *Nixon: The Triumph of a Politician, 1962–1972* (New York: Simon & Schuster, 1989), 153.

34. "News conference," May 3, 1968, *Addresses and State Papers*, 786.

35. Smith, *On His Own Terms*, 516.

36. Nixon, *RN*, 303.

37. *Washington Post*, May 17, 1963, A1; Witcover, *White Knight*, 207.

38. Nixon, *RN*, 335.

39. Ibid., 312.

40. Ibid., 265–266.

41. W. J. Rorabaugh, *The Real Making of the President: Kennedy, Nixon, and the 1960 Election* (Lawrence: University of Kansas, 2009), 115–116, 166.
42. Albright, *What Makes Spiro Run*, 209–210.
43. Jonathan Aitken, *Nixon: A Life* (Washington, DC: Regnery Publishing, 1993), 251–352.
44. "News conference," July 18, 1968, *Addresses and State Papers*, 924.
45. *New York Times*, August 5, 1968, 1.
46. *Washington Post*, August 7, 1968, A14.
47. Lippman, *Spiro Agnew's America*, 128.
48. Hebert Klein, *Making It Perfectly Clear* (New York: Doubleday, 1980), 156.
49. Agnew, *Go Quietly*, 62.
50. Nixon, *RN*, 309.
51. Author interview with Herb Thompson.
52. Agnew, *Go Quietly*, 62.
53. "Agnew Nominating Nixon," August 7, 1968, folder 1, box 1, subseries 3.7, series 3, Agnew MS.
54. The conclusions about how Agnew's speech went over with the crowd are based on my viewing of the speech.
55. Nixon, *RN*, 310.
56. Ibid., 311–312; Jules Witcover, *Very Strange Bedfellows: The Short and Unhappy Marriage of Richard Nixon and Spiro Agnew* (New York: Public Affairs, 2007), 26–27.
57. Nixon, *RN*, 312–313.
58. Nixon, *RN*, 313.
59. Ibid.
60. *Time*, August 16, 1968, 19.
61. For a list of Nixon's qualifications, see the *Washington Post*, August 9, 1968, Q1, 17.
62. Robert Caro, *Means of Ascent: The Years of Lyndon Johnson* (New York: Alfred A. Knopf, 1990). For a summary of Caro's work, see Jack Shafer, "The Honest Graft of Lady Bird Johnson," *Slate Magazine*, accessed March 12, 2015, http://www.slate.com/articles/news_and_politics/press_box/2007/07/the_honest_graft_of_lady_bird_johnson.html.
63. James Hite, *Second Best: The Rise of the American Vice Presidency* (San Diego: Cognella Academic Publishing, 2013).
64. Klein, *Making It Perfectly Clear*, 158; "Press conference," August 8, 1968, folder 18, box 8, subseries 3.8, series 3, Agnew MS.
65. Nixon, *RN*, 313.
66. *Time*, August 16, 1968, 19.
67. Gerald R. Ford, *A Time to Heal: The Autobiography of Gerald R. Ford* (New York: Harper & Row, 1979), 85–86.
68. *New York Times*, August 9, 1968, 19.
69. Witcover, *Strange Bedfellows*, 26–29.
70. William Safire, *Before the Fall: An Insider View of the pre-Watergate White House* (New York: Belmont Tower Books, 1975), 56.
71. Tom Wicker, *One of Us: Richard Nixon and the American Dream* (New York: Random House, 1991), 225; Nixon, *RN*, 276.
72. *New York Times*, August 10, 1968, 1.
73. Author interview with David Keene, July 19, 2004.

74. A Gallup Poll taken after the convention had Nixon leading Humphrey 45–29. Nixon, *RN*, 316.

75. Lippman, *Spiro Agnew's America*, 156.

76. Jody Carlson, *George C. Wallace and the Politics of Powerlessness* (Brunswick: Transaction Books, 1981), 81; *New York Times*, August 10, 1968, 11.

77. *New York Times*, July 27, 1967, 18.

78. Evan Thomas, *Robert Kennedy: His Life* (New York: Simon & Schuster, 2000), 370.

79. Robert Mason, *Richard Nixon and the Quest for a New Majority* (Chapel Hill: University of North Carolina Press, 2004), 20.

80. The first question asked, "What do you think is the most important problem facing the country today?" Vietnam garnered 42 percent, while race relations received 25 percent, followed by crime and lawlessness at 15 percent. Gallup Poll, vol. III, 2128.

81. White, *The Making of the President 1968*, 407.

82. Dean Kotlowski, *Nixon's Civil Rights: Politics, Principle, and Policy* (Cambridge: Harvard University Press, 2002).

83. Peter B. Levy's "Civil War on Race Street," *Maryland Historical Magazine* (Fall 1994): 153; Patrick J. Buchanan, *The Greatest Comeback: How Richard Nixon Rose from Defeat to Create the New Majority* (New York: Crown Forum, 2014). Buchanan offers an insightful rebuttal to the idea that Nixon employed a "Southern Strategy." Buchanan was part of Nixon's inner circle and would be in a position to know if Nixon ever adopted such a strategy. Buchanan shows this piece of political lore is largely a myth.

84. Michael Nelson, *Resilient America: Electing Nixon in 1968, Channeling Dissent, and Dividing Government* (Lawrence: University Press of Kansas, 2014), 136–176.

85. See for example, *New York Times*, August 31, 1968, 32.

86. In his memoirs, Nixon wrote that "Muskie was a strong addition to the ticket." Nixon, *RN*, 317.

87. Gould, *1968*; Nelson, *Resilient America*, 192–193.

88. Newspaper clip, "Agnew Wanted to Quit Race," *Baltimore News American*, February 18, 1970, folder file A, box 2, Joseph Albright Papers, Western Heritage Center, Laramie, Wyoming.

89. *Washington Post*, September 7, 1968, A1; *Baltimore Sun*, September 7, 1968, A4.

90. *Baltimore Sun*, September 9, 1968, A1, 4.

91. Lippman, *Spiro Agnew's America*, 157.

92. *Baltimore Sun*, September 10, 1968, A1.

93. *Baltimore Sun*, September 13, 1968, A1. Agnew's words angered Ford to no end. In his memoirs he called the allegations "ridiculous" and noted that he "got word to Agnew and urged him not to make that kind of mistake again." Ford, *A Time to Heal*, 86–87.

94. *Washington Post*, September 15, 1968, B6.

95. *Washington Post*, September 11, 1968, A18.

96. *Baltimore Sun*, September 12, 1968, A1.

97. *Baltimore Sun*, September 14, 1968, A14.

98. Witcover, *Very Strange Bedfellows*, 43.

99. Klein, *Making It Perfectly Clear*, 160; Thompson interview with author.

100. "Transcript of speech of the Honorable Spark M. Matsunaga," September 23, 1968, speeches file, Spark M. Matsunaga Papers, Hawaii Congressional Papers Collection, Manoa Library, University of Hawaii, Manoa, Hawaii.

101. "Remarks on Ethnic Slurs," September 23, 1968, *Addresses and State Papers*, 974.

102. Ibid.

103. Ibid.

104. Humphrey easily won Hawaii, taking 59 percent of the vote.

105. Warren Kozak, *LeMay: The Life of General Curtis LeMay* (Washington, DC: Regnery Press, 2009), 341; Nelson, *Resilient America*, 205–206.

106. "Vice Presidential Campaign Staff," Vice Presidential folder, Governor (General File) MSA SC 1041-1711.

107. Newspaper clip, *Baltimore News American*, undated, box 2, Joseph Albright Papers, American Heritage Center, University of Wyoming, Laramie, Wyoming.

108. Author interview with Keene, July 17, 2003. After speaking with Keene, Evans and Novak agreed to retract the story, one of the few times the pair ever took back a story. For the columns, see the *Washington Post*, June 7, 1970, and June 14, 1970.

109. See Buchanan memo to Agnew in Klein, *Making It Perfectly Clear*, 163–164.

110. Newspaper clip, *Washington Star*, folder 8, box 7, subseries 3.8, series 3, Agnew MS.

111. "VP Staff," vice presidential folder, MSA SC 1041-1711.

112. Gould, *1968*, 112–113, 135–141.

113. Newspaper clip, *Washington Star*, folder 7, box 3, subseries 3.8, series 3, Agnew MS.

114. For the crowds' estimates, see, *Washington Post*, September 22, 1968, A4. For the campaign schedule, see "1968 V.P. campaign itinerary," folder 20, box 6, subseries 3.8, series 3, Agnew MS.

115. *Washington Post*, October 17, 1968, A4.

116. Klein, *Making It Perfectly Clear*, 161.

117. Nelson, *Resilient America*, 192.

118. *New York Times*, October 22, 1968, 29.

119. Ibid.

120. *New York Times*, October 26, 36.

121. "Press release, Nixon-Agnew Campaign Committee," October 29, 1968, news release folder, box 3, Albright MS.

122. *New York Times*, October 30, 1968, 46.

123. White, *The Making of the President 1968*, 414–418.

124. Kent G. Sieg, "The 1968 Presidential Election and Peace in Vietnam," *Presidential Studies Quarterly* (Fall: 1996), 1064.

125. Nixon, *RN*, 326–329.

126. Robert D. Schulzinger, *U.S. Diplomacy since 1900* (New York: Oxford University Press, 2008), 248; Ken Hughes, *Chasing Shadows: The Nixon Tapes, the Chennault affair, and the origins of Watergate* (Charlottesville: University of Virginia Press).

127. Ambrose, *Triumph of a Politician*, 215.

128. Hughes, *Chasing Shadows*. Hughes argues Nixon was guilty of treason but exonerates LBJ of any wrongdoing.

129. Witcover, *Very Strange Bedfellows*, 52; Catherine Mary Forslund, "Woman of Two Worlds: Anna Chenault and Informal Diplomacy in US-Asian relations, 1950–1990" (Ph.D. dissertation, Washington University, 1997), 226.

130. Ibid.

131. Agnew, *Go Quietly*, 106. Ken Hughes contends LBJ did not tap Nixon's phones. Hughes, *Chasing Shadows*.

132. White, *The Making of the President 1968*, 458–459.

133. Nixon, *RN*, 334–335.

134. Nelson, *Resilient America*, 221–223.

135. Newspaper clip, "Agnew Viewed as Key to Victory," *Washington Daily News*, November 8, 1968, "Editorials-Good," folder 17, box 7, subseries 3.8, series 3, Agnew MS.

136. Newspaper clip, "Spiro T. Asset," *Dallas Morning News*, November 10, 1968, Editorials-Good, Agnew MS.

137. Nixon, *RN*, 365–366.

CHAPTER 5: BECOMING "NIXON'S NIXON"

1. For Nixon's troubled relations with conservatives see, Sarah Katherine Mergel, *Conservative Intellectuals and Richard Nixon: Rethinking the Rise of the Right* (Basingstoke: Palgrave Macmillan, 2010).

2. John P. Judis, *William F. Buckley: Patron Saint of the Conservatives* (New York: Simon & Schuster, 1988), 329.

3. *Washington Post*, November 10, 1968, A1. Bryce Harlow, a former Eisenhower assistant, urged Nixon to give Agnew that office. Bob Haldeman objected, since he had his eyes on that suite, but Nixon sided with Harlow. Bob Burke and Ralph G. Thompson, *Bryce Harlow: Mr. Integrity* (Oklahoma City: Oklahoma Heritage Association, 2000), 185.

4. "Agnew Staff Members as of December 2, 1968," box 2, MSA SC 4804; Newspaper clip, *Philadelphia Inquirer*, November 28, 1968, Agnew staff folder, folder 8, box 7, subseries 3.8, series 3, Spiro T. Agnew Papers, Special Collections, University of Maryland Libraries, College Park, Maryland (hereafter "Agnew MS").

5. "The Office of the Vice President of the United States of America," Jean Spencer Papers, University of Maryland, Special Collections, Hornbake Library, College Park, Maryland (hereafter "Spencer Papers").

6. James Hite, *Second Best: The Rise of the American Vice Presidency* (San Diego: Cognella Academic Publishing, 2013).

7. *New York Times*, November 11, 1968, 95; November 15, 1968, 33; *Washington Post*, December 24, 1968, A2.

8. "The Office of the Vice Presidency of the United States," Agnew biography folder, box 2, Spencer Papers; *New York Times*, November 20, 1968, 29.

9. Undated news clip, Judy Agnew vertical file, Pratt Library.

10. Richard M. Cohen and Jules Witcover, *A Heartbeat Away: The Investigation and Resignation of Vice President Spiro T. Agnew* (New York: Viking Press, 1974), 129–130; "The Agnew-Hammerman-Wolffe Scheme," Beal MS. Agnew did not specifically address this meeting but argued that every time he met Green, it was at Green's insistence. Spiro T. Agnew, *Go Quietly ... or else* (New York: William Morrow, 1980), 99.

11. Blair to Agnew, February 20, 1969, folder 76, box 17, subseries 3.5, series 3, Agnew MS.

12. "C. Stanley Blair Biography," folder 76, box 17, subseries 3.5, series 3, Agnew MS.

13. *Baltimore Evening Express*, August 28, 1991, D6; *Easton Express*, April 21, 1967, 18. In *Go Quietly*, Agnew details how Sohmer rode with him to the courthouse in Baltimore where Agnew resigned. Sohmer was in tears.

14. John Osborne, *The Nixon Watch* (New York: Liveright, 1970), 122.

15. Author interview with Thompson; *Baltimore Sun*, June 10, 2011.

16. Theo Lippman, Jr., "Nearby, Spiro T. Agnew Says None of . . .," *Baltimore Sun*, July 13, 1991.

17. *Baltimore Sun*, December 5, 1968, 23.

18. *National Review*, October 27, 1972, 1183.

19. "Frank DeCosta biography," folder 81, box 17, subseries 3.5, series 3, Agnew MS.

20. For the information in this paragraph I also consulted an organizational sheet dated April 21, 1969, in Arthur Sohmer's Papers, box 12, MSA SC 4804.

21. Agnew, *Go Quietly*, 36.

22. H. R. Haldeman, *The Haldeman Diaries: Inside the Nixon White House* (New York: G.P. Putnam's Sons, 1994), 27.

23. Agnew, *Go Quietly*, 31.

24. Ibid., 32.

25. "Executive Order Establishing an Office of Intergovernmental Relations," February 14, 1969, box 17, MSA SC 4804.

26. Nixon to Reverend Theodore Hesburgh, February 24, 1969, *Public Papers of the President of the United States: 1969* (Washington: Government Printing Office, 1971), 72.

27. Haldeman, *Haldeman Diaries*, 52.

28. Ibid., 53.

29. John Ehrlichman, *Witness to Power: The Nixon Years* (New York: Simon & Schuster, 1982), 145.

30. Agnew, *Go Quietly*, 23.

31. Richard Nixon, *RN: The Memoirs of Richard Nixon* (New York: Touchstone, 1978), 383.

32. Agnew, *Go Quietly*, 27.

33. Ibid., 36.

34. Osborne, *The Nixon Watch*, 129.

35. John Ehrlichman Notes, September 5, 1969, folder id 9/5/69, box 1, John Ehrlichman Papers, Hoover Institution, Stanford University, Stanford, California (hereafter "EP").

36. Nixon, *RN*, 402.

37. Ibid.

38. Haldeman, *Haldeman Diaries*, 99.

39. *New York Times*, October 15, 1969, 1, 16.

40. "Citizens Testimonial Dinner," October 19, 1969, folder 27, box 2, subseries 3.7, series 3, Agnew MS.

41. Ibid.

42. *Washington Post*, October 20, 1969, 1; Theo Lippman, *Spiro Agnew's America: The Vice President and the Politics of Suburbia* (New York: W.W. Norton & Company, 1972), 188.

43. *New York Times*, October 21, 1969, 46.

44. "Inside the Nixon White House," *Look*, October 17, 1971,40.

45. According to Pat Buchanan, Nixon described the "Buckleyites" as "more dangerous than the Birchites." Patrick J. Buchanan,*Right from the Beginning* (Washington: Regnery, 1988), 322.

46. *National Review*, August 18, 1972, 898.

47. *Jackson Advocate*, October 25, 1969, 1.

48. "List of Major Speeches Given by Vice President Agnew since January 20, 1969," staff responsibilities folder, box 1, Spencer Papers.

49. "Jackson, Mississippi," October 20, 1969, folder 28, box 2, subseries 3.7, series 3, Agnew MS.

50. Ibid.

51. *Time*, October 31, 1969, 12.

52. Folder id 10/27/1969, box 1, EP.

53. Nixon, *RN*, 408.

54. Ibid., 409.

55. Ibid., 409–410.

56. Lippman, *Spiro Agnew's America*, 191.

57. Haldeman, *Haldeman Diaries*, 106.

58. Agnew, *Go Quietly*, 28.

59. Blair to Rosenwald with Rosenwald's Comments, November 12, 1969, folder, box 2, series 3, Agnew MS.

60. Haldeman, *Haldeman Diaries*, 107.

61. "Mid-west Regional Republican Committee Meeting," November 13, 1969, folder 40, box 2, subseries 3.7, series 3, Agnew MS.

62. Ibid.

63. Matt K. Lewis, "How Spiro Agnew Helped Invent Conservative Punditry," *Daily Caller*, May 20, 2014, accessed March 18, 2015, http://dailycaller.com/2014/05/20/how-spiro-agnew-helped-invent-conservative-punditry.

64. Buchanan, *Right from the Beginning*, 230.

65. Lewis, "How Spiro Agnew Helped Invent Conservative Punditry."

66. Agnew, *Go Quietly*, 28–29.

67. Haldeman, *Haldeman Diaries*, 107–108.

68. *New York Times*, November 16, 1969, 78.

69. *New York Times*, November 14, 1969, 24.

70. *New York Times*, B14, July 3, 2012.

71. *New York Times*, November 15, 1969, 15.

72. *New York Times*, November 16, 1969, 78.

73. " 'News Bias' as Howard K. Smith Sees It," Republican Congressional Committee Newsletter, March 9, 1970, White House Special Files, Staff Member and Office Files: H. R. Haldeman: Box 148: HRH-Political 1970 Political. Richard Nixon Presidential Library and Museum, Yorba Linda, California.

74. Edith Efron, *The News Twisters* (Los Angeles: Nash Publishing, 1972), 47.

75. Ibid., 135.

76. Ibid., 136.

77. *New York Times*, March 13, 1995.

78. The results were analyzed in a 1988 article in *Channels* magazine, "Network News, 15 Years after Agnew." The authors Michael Robinson and Maura E. Clancy disputed the charge of a liberal bias in the television networks.

79. Agnew, *Go Quietly*, 35.

80. Author interview with Keene.

81. See Buchanan memo to Stanley Blair, folder 43, box 2, subseries 3.7, series 3, Agnew MS.

82. Stephen E. Ambrose, *Nixon: The Triumph of a Politician, 1962–1972* (New York: Simon & Schuster, 1989), 248–249.

83. Benjamin C. Bradlee, *Conversations with Kennedy* (New York: W.W. & Norton, 1984); Evan Thomas, "Why Nixon Hated Georgetown," *Politico*, June 4, 2015, accessed July 6, 2015, http://www.politico.com/magazine/story/2015/06/richard-nixon-georgetown-set-118607_Page2.html#.VZsK-_mumcw.

84. "Address by the Vice President," November 20, 1969, folder 43, box 2, subseries 3.7, series 3, Agnew MS.

85. Ibid.

86. Ibid.

87. Ibid.

88. *New York Times*, November 21, 1969, 22.

89. *Washington Post*, November 21, A7.

90. Memo, Haldeman to Buchanan, November 21, 1969, WHSF: SMOF: H. R. Haldeman: Box 54, Memos/Pat Buchanan (November 1969), NL.

91. Memo, Nixon to Haldeman, November 24, 1969, WHSF: President's Personal File: Box 1: Memos (November 1969), NL.

92. "News Summary," November 27, 1969, WHSF: President's Office File: Box 31: News Summaries (November 1969), NL.

93. Ibid.

94. "News Summary," undated (the Godfrey story ran on November 29), WHSF: POF: Box 31: News Summaries (November 1969), NL.

95. News Summary, November 29, 1969: WHSF: POF: Box 31, News Summaries (November 1969), NL.

CHAPTER 6: "NATTERING NABOBS OF NEGATIVISM"

1. Spiro T. Agnew, *Go Quietly … or Else* (New York: William Morrow, 1980), 27.

2. Henry Kissinger, *White House Years* (Little, Brown, and Company, 1979), 491.

3. Jeffrey Kimball, *Nixon's Vietnam War* (Lawrence: University Press of Kansas, 1998), 203.

4. Richard Nixon, *RN: The Memoirs of Richard Nixon* (New York: Touchstone, 1978), 452–453.

5. Agnew, *Go Quietly*, 30.

6. Nixon, *RN*, 454.

7. Ibid., 454–455.

8. Agnew to Harry Byrd et al., June 24, 1969, folder 21, box 3, subseries 3.4, series 3, Spiro T. Agnew Papers, Special Collections, University of Maryland Libraries, College Park, Maryland (hereafter "Agnew MS").

9. John Ehrlichman Notes, folder id 5/20/70, John Ehrlichman Papers, Hoover Institution, Stanford University, Stanford, California (hereafter "EP").

10. *Washington Post*, May 4, 1970, A2.

11. *Washington Times*, May 5, 1970, A3.

12. For the original speech, see, "Idaho Republican Dinner," May 8, 1970, folder 31, box 3, subseries 3.5, series 3, Agnew MS.

13. *New York Times*, May 9, 1970, 1.

14. See the May 6 and May 7 entries in H. R. Haldeman, *The Haldeman Diaries: Inside the Nixon White House* (New York: G.P. Putnam's Sons, 1994), 161–162.

15. Ibid., 170.

16. Bruce Oudes, ed. *From the President: Richard Nixon's Secret Files* (New York: Harper & Row, 1989), 136.

17. Roger Morris, *Richard Milhous Nixon: The Rise of an American Politician* (New York: Henry Holt, 1989), 620.

18. "Midwest Regional GOP Meeting Dinner," folder 40, box 2, subseries 3.7, series 3, Agnew MS.

19. Agnew to Mano Swartz, May 14, 1970, box 1, MSA SC 4804.

20. "Republican Congressional Newsletter," March 16, 1970, WHSF: SMOF: H. R. Haldeman: Box 134: HRH-Political-1970 Political, NL.

21. Republican Congressional Newsletter, SMOF.

22. Ibid, "Illinois GOP Dinner," February 12, 1970, folder 31, box 129, subseries 3.5, series 3, Agnew MS.

23. William Safire, *Before the Fall: An Insider View of the pre-Watergate White House* (New York: Belmont Tower Books, 1975), 318.

24. Nixon, *RN*, 491.

25. Stephen E. Ambrose, *Nixon: The Triumph of a Politician, 1962–1972* (New York: Simon & Schuster, 1989), 356–357.

26. "Biography of Blair," Agnew MS.

27. *New York Times*, February 26, 1970, 15.

28. Author's interview with Thompson. The task of handling media relations temporarily fell to J. Roy Goodearle. "Memorandum for All Members of the Vice President's Staff," June 30, 1970, Office of the Vice President folder, box 1, series 2, Jean Spencer Papers, University of Maryland, Special Collections, Hornbake Library, College Park, Maryland (hereafter "Spencer Papers").

29. Author interview with Keene, July 17, 2003.

30. For example, in January 1971, R. Emmett Tyrrell, the editor and founder of the *Alternative*, a conservative weekly, wrote Agnew requesting a meeting with the man Tyrrell praised profusely in his paper (Agnew agreed to a meeting). Tyrrell eventually moved to Washington DC and renamed his journal *The American Spectator*. Tyrrell to Agnew, January 25, 1970, Executive 1970, folder 41, box 1, subseries 3.1, series 3, Agnew MS.

31. "News Summary" undated, WHSF: POF: Box 32: News Summaries—August 1970, NL. While there is no specific date on the paper, I found the item in the "August" folder.

32. Memo, John R. Brown to Bryce Harlow, September 8, 1970, WHSF: SMOF: H. R. Haldeman: Box 148, Haldeman-Political-Vice President.

33. Haldeman, *Haldeman Diaries*, 192.

34. Nixon, *RN*, 491.

35. Safire, *Before the Fall*, 316.

36. Safire, *Before the Fall*, 321.

37. Memo, Murray Chotiner to Haldeman, July 7, 1970, WHSF: SMOF: H. R. Haldeman: Box 134, Haldeman-Political-Vice President, NL.

38. Safire, *Before the Fall*, 319.

39. Bob Burke and Ralph G. Thompson, *Bryce Harlow: Mr. Integrity* (Oklahoma City: Oklahoma Heritage Association, 2000), 215.

40. In October 1970, the unemployment and inflation rates both hovered at 6 percent. Ambrose, *Triumph of a Politician*, 390–391.

41. "Telecon W/Art Sohmer, News People Requesting to Travel on Vice President's Campaign Plane," September 5, 1970, WHSF: SMOF: H. R. Haldeman: Box 148: Haldeman-Political-Vice President, NL.

42. Safire, *Before the Fall*, 323.

43. "Address by the Vice President," September 10, 1970, WHSF: SMOF: H. R. Haldeman: Box 148: Haldeman-Political-Vice President.

44. For Buchanan's contribution, see Safire, *Before the Fall*, 323.

45. "Address by the Vice President," WHSF, SMOF.

46. "News Summary," September 11, 1970, folder 10, box 5, subseries 3.13, series 3, Agnew MS.

47. *Newsweek*, September 28, 1970, 26.

48. "News Summary," September 11, 1970, folder 10, box 5, subseries 3.13, series 3, Agnew MS.

49. "Speeches—San Diego," September 11, 1970, folder 6, box 4, subseries 3.7, series 3, Agnew MS.

50. Prior to the address, Bill Safire offered Agnew a choice of using either the "nattering nabobs" or "hysterical hypochondriacs." "Hell, let's use them both," Agnew decided. Safire, *Before the Fall*, 322.

51. *Newsweek*, September 28, 1970, 26.

52. "News Summary," September 12, 1970, folder 10, box 5, subseries 3.13, series 3, Agnew MS.

53. See for example, "Leaves from a Lurid Lexicon," *Newsweek*, September 28, 1970, 24.

54. "Press Conferences," Palm Springs, California, September 12, 1970, folder 35, box 15, subseries 3.7, series 3, Agnew MS.

55. *New York Times*, September 17, 1970, 29.

56. Ambrose, *Nixon: Triumph of a Politician*, 375–377; Haldeman, *Haldeman Diaries*, 194.

57. Haldeman, *Haldeman Diaries*, 194.

58. Safire, *Before the Fall*, 324. On September 16 Grand Rapids police arrested a man on charges of violating the city's firearms law. The man reportedly threatened Agnew's life. *New York Times*, September 17, 1970, 29.

59. Nixon, *RN*, 491.

60. Ibid.

61. Ibid., 492–493.

62. *Commonweal*, October 23, 1970, 83–84.

63. Theo Lippman, *Spiro Agnew's America: The Vice President and the Politics of Suburbia* (New York: W.W. Norton & Company, 1972), 216.

64. *New York Times*, October 6, 1970, 1.

65. Jules Witcover, *White Knight: The Rise of Spiro Agnew* (New York: Random House, 1972), 378–379.

66. *New York Times*, October 9, 1970, 17.

67. *New York Times*, October 10, 1970, 10.

68. *Life Magazine*, October 16, 1970, 30.

69. "News Summary," undated, folder 17, box 5, subseries 3.13, series 3, Agnew MS.

70. "CBS-TV Election Special," November 1, 1970, folder 17, box 5, series 3, subseries 3.13, Agnew MS.

71. Nixon, *RN*, 494–495.
72. Ibid., 495.
73. Ehrlichman Notes, folder id 11/1, 1970, box 1, EP.
74. Agnew, *Go Quietly*, 37.
75. "News Summary," undated, folder 17, box 5, subseries 3.13, series 3, Agnew MS.
76. Ehrlichman Notes, folder id 11/1/70, box 1, EP.
77. "News Summary," November 5, folder 17, box 6, subseries 3.13, series 3, Agnew MS.
78. "News Summary," undated, folder 15, box 6, subseries 3.13, series 3, Agnew MS.
79. Buchanan to Nixon, November 4, 1970, folder 1, box 6, subseries 3.1, series 3, Agnew MS.

CHAPTER 7: SURVIVAL AND VINDICATION

1. Nixon described the first few months of 1971 as "the lowest point of my first term as President." Richard Nixon, *RN: The Memoirs of Richard Nixon* (New York: Touchstone, 1978), 497.
2. In his biography of Nixon, newspaper magnet Conrad Black contends that Nixon's Watergate problems stemmed in large part from his loyalty to his own people. It is not a persuasive argument. See Conrad Black, *Richard M. Nixon: A Life in Full* (New York: Public Affairs, 2007).
3. Donald T. Critchlow, *The Conservative Ascendancy: How the Republican Right Rose to Power in Modern America* (Lawrence: University Press of Kansas, 2011), 94–97.
4. News Summary, undated, folder 17, box 5, subseries 3.13, series 3, Spiro T. Agnew Papers, Special Collections, University of Maryland Libraries, College Park, Maryland (hereafter "Agnew MS").
5. *New York Times*, February 9, 1971, 38.
6. For this information I relied on the *New York Times* review of the documentary published a day after it aired. *New York Times*, February 24, 1971, 83.
7. "Press Conferences" March 8, 1971, folder 52, box 15, subseries 3.7, series 3, Agnew MS.
8. "CBS News Release," March 19, 1971, box 1, Theodore F. Koop Papers, Special Collections Department, University of Iowa Libraries, Iowa City, Iowa.
9. "Speeches, Mississippi Fundraiser." May 18, 1971, folder 7, box 6, subseries 3.7, series 3, Agnew MS.
10. *Washington Post*, March 25, 1971, A24.
11. "Press Conferences," March 8, 1971, folder 52, box 15, subseries 3.7, series 3, Agnew MS.
12. William Safire, *Before the Fall: An Insider View of the pre-Watergate White House* (New York: Belmont Tower Books, 1975), 497.
13. H. R. Haldeman, *The Haldeman Diaries: Inside the Nixon White House* (New York: G.P. Putnam's Sons, 1994), 268–269.
14. Ibid., 259.
15. Spiro T. Agnew, *Go Quietly . . . or else* (New York: William Morrow, 1980), 38.
16. Ibid.
17. Haldeman, *Haldeman Diaries*, 324–325.

18. Transcript, "Issues and Answers," August 22, 1971, folder 5, box 14, subseries 3.7, series 3, Agnew MS.

19. Ibid.

20. Nixon, *RN*, 550.

21. *New York Times*, July 17, 1971, 4.

22. Agnew, *Go Quietly*, 34–35.

23. *New York Times Magazine*, November 14, 1971.

24. Gregory L. Schneider, *Cadres for Conservatism: Young Americans for Freedom and the Rise of the Contemporary Right* (New York: New York University Press, 1998), 150.

25. Author's interview with Keene. For Agnew's interaction with Hook, I relied upon materials found in the Sidney Hook Papers at the Hoover Institute. Included is a letter from Agnew that began: "The enclosed article by Dr. Sidney Hook is among the most cogent and compelling documents I have read on the question of student violence." Dated September 18, 1970, folder 16, box 70, Sidney D. Hook Papers, the Hoover Institute, Stanford University, Palo Alto, California.

26. Agnew discusses his views on Vietnam and détente in *Go Quietly*, 27–35.

27. Memo, Agnew to Nixon, November 13, 1971, WHSF: SMOF: PPF: Box 5, Agnew, Spiro, NL.

28. Nixon, *RN*, 541.

29. "A Conversation with the President," January 2, 1972, *Public Papers of the Presidents of the United States: Richard Nixon, 1972* (Washington: Government Printing Office, 1974), 2.

30. Sarah Katherine Mergel, *Conservative Intellectuals and Richard Nixon: Rethinking the Rise of the Right* (New York: Palgrave Macmillan, 2010), 133–134.

31. Jules Witcover, *Strange Bedfellows: The Short and Unhappy Marriage of Richard Nixon and Spiro Agnew* (New York: Public Affairs, 2007), 221.

32. Nixon, *RN*, 239; Hebert Parmet, *Richard Nixon and His America* (Boston: Little, Brown, 1990), 415–417.

33. "News Summary," December 2, 1971, WHSF: POF: Box 37: December 2–7, 1971, NL.

34. *Los Angeles Times*, February 25, 1972, 3.

35. *Washington Post*, November 12, 1971, A19.

36. Nixon, *RN*, 674–675.

37. Ibid., 574–580.

38. "President's Arrival, Andrews AFB," February 28, 1972, folder 21, box 7, subseries 3.7, series 3, Agnew MS.

39. "Transcript of Interview the Honorable Spiro T. Agnew, Vice President of the United States," February 7, 1972, folder 7, box 14, subseries 3.7, series 3, Agnew MS.

40. Keene interview with author.

41. Ibid.

42. "Agnew Says Vice President Should Quit in a Major Rift," *New York Times*, August 25, 1968, 1.

43. "Speeches—Miami, Florida," August 17–18, 1970, folder 59, box 3, subseries 3.7, series 3, Agnew MS.

44. Rick Perlstein, *Nixonland: The Rise of a President and the Fracturing of America* (New York: Scribner, 2008), 628–629. "Paul Morrison" was actually Donald Segretti.

45. Nixon, *RN*, 542.
46. "News Summary," March 27, 1972, WHSF: POF: Box 40: March 27–31, 1972, NL.
47. Howard Jones, *The Crucible of Power: A History of American Foreign Relations since 1897* (Wilmington: Scholarly Resources, 2001), 399.
48. Nixon, *RN*, 587.
49. Henry Kissinger, *White House Years* (Boston: Little, Brown, and Company, 1979), 1098.
50. Nixon, *RN*, 604.
51. Kissinger, *White House Years*, 1184.
52. Haldeman, *Haldeman Diaries*, 456–457.
53. Memo, Agnew to Nixon, May 8, 1972, WHSF: PPF: Box 5, Agnew, Spiro, NL.
54. Nixon, *RN*, 606.
55. Richard Nixon, *No More Vietnams* (New York: Arbor House, 1985), 147.
56. Nixon, *RN*, 607.
57. Howard Jones, *The Crucible of Power: A History of American Foreign Relations since 1897* (Wilmington: Scholarly Resources, 2001), 400.
58. *New York Times*, May 20, 1972, 1.
59. Nixon, *RN*, 670.
60. Keith W. Olson, *Watergate: The Scandal that Shook America* (Lawrence: University of Kansas Press, 2003), 37–40.
61. Olson, *Watergate*, 49; Nixon, *RN*, 626.
62. Olson, *Watergate*, 47–51.
63. Olson, *Watergate*, 17–21; Michael A. Genovese, *The Watergate Crisis* (Westport, CTL Greenwood Press, 1999), 16–19.
64. Agnew, *Go Quietly*, 65.
65. Jeb Magruder, *An American Life: One Man's Road to Watergate* (New York: Atheneum, 1974), 225–226.
66. Olson, *Watergate*, 37–38, 49.
67. Stanley I. Kutler, ed., *Abuse of Power: The New Nixon Tapes* (New York: The Free Press, 1997), 67; Len Colodny and Robert Gettlin, *Silent Coup: The Removal of a President* (New York: St. Martin's Press, 1991).
68. Randy Roberts and James S. Olson, *John Wayne: American* (New York: Free Press, 1995), 604. In an interview Agnew stated that he had nothing to do with the organization, but "one cannot turn away assistance that comes to him by friends." *U.S. News & World Report*, March 13, 1972, 37.
69. "News Summary," April 6, 1972, WHSF: SMOF: POF: Box 40: April 1–11, 1972, NL.
70. Agnew, *Go Quietly*, 39.
71. Nixon, *RN*, 675.
72. Haldeman, *Haldeman Diaries*, 470.
73. Agnew, *Go Quietly*, 39–40.
74. *Chicago Tribune*, July 23, 1972, 1, 4.
75. *New York Times*, July 23, 1972, 28.
76. *New York Times*, July 23, 1972, 28; July 25, 1972, 19.
77. *Chicago Tribune*, July 25, 1972, 18.
78. *New York Times*, July 24, 1972, 26.
79. Ibid.
80. Memo, Dwight Chapin to Haldeman, June 14, 1972, WHSF: SMOF: H. R. Haldeman: Box 131: Campaign Strategy Memos, NL.

81. Haldeman, *Haldeman Diaries*, 485.

82. "Talking Points," July 21, 1972, WHSF: SMOF: PPF: Box 5: Agnew, Spiro, NL.

83. Ibid.

84. Melvin Small, *The Presidency of Richard Nixon* (Lawrence: University Press of Kansas, 1999), 259.

85. Joshua M. Glasser, *The Eighteen-Day Running Mate: McGovern, Eagleton, and a Campaign in Crisis* (New Haven: Yale University Press, 2012), 236–237, 259–271.

86. Memo, Nixon to Haldeman, August 14, 1972, WHSF: PPF: Box 4: Memos-August 1972, NL.

87. "Convention News Summary," No. 10, August 23, 1972, box 12, MSA-SC 4804.

88. *Newsweek*, September 4, 1972, 27.

89. David Keene and J. Roy Goodearle to Agnew, August 3, 1972, folder 16, box 10, subseries 3.8, series 3, Agnew MS.

90. *New York Times*, August 23, 1972, 26.

91. *New York Times*, August 24, 1972, 40.

92. Text of speech reprinted in the *Washington Post*, August 24, 1972, A18.

93. See *RN*, 678–679.

94. Ibid., 680.

95. Justin P. Coffey, "Watergate and the Committee to Reelect the President" (Master's Thesis, University of Wyoming, 1998).

96. *Washington Post*, August 25, 1972, A10.

97. The memos can be found in folder 30, box 10, subseries 3.8, series 3, Agnew MS.

98. Keene interview with author.

99. Stephen E. Ambrose, *Nixon: The Triumph of a Politician, 1962–1972* (New York: Simon & Schuster, 1989), 620.

100. *New York Times*, October 5, 1972, 97.

101. Ibid.

102. *The State Journal-Register*, October 22, 1972.

103. *New York Times*, October 3, 1972, 32.

104. *Washington Post*, November 5, 1972, A2.

105. Nixon, *RN*, 716.

106. *Washington Post*, November 8, 1972, A11.

107. Memo, Agnew to Nixon, November 8, 1972, WHSF: SMOF: PPF: Box 5, Agnew, Spiro, NL.

CHAPTER 8: PRESIDENT AGNEW?

1. *Washington Post*, November 10, 1972, B1, 15; Spiro T. Agnew, *Go Quietly ... or else* (New York: William Morrow, 1980), 22. In the work Agnew claims that the "elaborate celebration" was "insisted on, arranged, and financed by I. Harold (Bud) Hammerman, who was then my friend."

2. Richard Nixon, *RN: The Memoirs of Richard Nixon* (New York: Touchstone, 1978), 764.

3. H. R. Haldeman, *The Haldeman Diaries: Inside the Nixon White House* (New York: G.P. Putnam's Sons, 1994), 534.

4. Ehrlichman Notes, folder id 11/14/72, box 3, EP.

5. Ibid.

6. Henry Kissinger, *White House Years* (Boston: Little, Brown, and Company, 1979), 1406–1407.

7. Agnew, *Go Quietly*, 38.

8. Howard Jones, *The Crucible of Power: A History of American Foreign Relations since 1897* (Wilmington: Scholarly Resources, 2001), 404.

9. Agnew, *Go Quietly*, 23.

10. Ibid.

11. *Baltimore Sun*, February 11, 1973, A1, 3.

12. Haldeman, *Haldeman Diaries*, 580.

13. Nixon, *RN*, 812–813.

14. Agnew, *Go Quietly*, 40.

15. Keith W. Olson, *Watergate: The Scandal that Shook America* (Lawrence: University of Kansas Press, 2003).

16. Len Colodny and Robert Gettlin, *Silent Coup: The Removal of a President* (New York: St. Martin's Press, 1991), 239.

17. Olson, *Watergate*, 68; Melvin Small, *The Presidency of Richard Nixon* (Lawrence: University Press of Kansas, 1999), 276.

18. Henry Kissinger, *Years of Upheaval* (Boston: Little, Brown, and Company, 1982), 89–90.

19. Ibid.

20. Olson, *Watergate*, 101.

21. *New York Times*, April 27, 1973, 1, 34.

22. Ibid., 36.

23. Roger Morris, *Richard Milhous Nixon: The Rise of an American Politician* (New York: Henry Holt, 1989), 827–847.

24. *Washington Post*, April 26, 1973, A30.

25. Nixon, *RN*, 849.

26. Pat Buchanan describes how "Richard Nixon will telegraph the answer he expects by making a strong assertive statement, and then ending it with 'or am I wrong?' " Patrick J. Buchanan, *Right from the Beginning* (Washington: Regnery, 1988), 321.

27. Stanley I. Kutler, ed., *Abuse of Power: The New Nixon Tapes* (New York: The Free Press, 1997), 380.

28. Raymond Price, *With Nixon* (New York: The Viking Press, 1977), 155.

29. *New York Daily News*, July 23, 2002.

30. Kutler, *Abuse of Power*, 336.

31. Ibid., 420.

32. Olson, *Watergate*, 96–101.

33. Olson, *Watergate*, 101–105; Peter A. Jay, "Strands in the Tapestry of Maryland's Political Life," *Baltimore Sun*, June 1, 1995. In *Go Quietly*, Agnew wrote Nixon should have "burned the tapes," 65.

34. *Time*, June 4, 1973.

CHAPTER 9: AUGUST 1973

1. Richard M. Cohen and Jules Witcover, *A Heartbeat Away: The Investigation and Resignation of Vice President Spiro T. Agnew* (New York: Viking Press, 1974), 4–7.

2. See Chapter 4.

3. "Albright interview with Agnew," February 9, 1971, interviews folder, box 3, Joseph P. Albright Papers, University of Wyoming, Western Heritage Center, Laramie, Wyoming; Robert Marsh, *Agnew: The Unexamined Man* (New York: M. Evans Company, 1971),130.

4. Joseph Albright, *What Makes Spiro Run: The Life and Times of Spiro Agnew* (New York: Dodd, Mead, 1972).

5. "Newspaper Interviews," July 18, 1973, folder 1, box 15, subseries 3.7, series 3, Spiro T. Agnew Papers, Special Collections, University of Maryland Libraries, College Park, Maryland (hereafter "Agnew MS").

6. Spiro T. Agnew, *Go Quietly ... or else* (New York: William Morrow, 1980), 41.

7. Ibid., 42–46.

8. *Chicago Tribune*, December 9, 1981; *New York Times*, September 19, 1996; *Baltimore Sun*, November 18, 1998.

9. Cohen and Witcover, *A Heartbeat Away*, 60.

10. Agnew, *Go Quietly*, 47.

11. *New York Times*, August 15, 1973, 17.

12. Cohen and Witcover, *A Heartbeat Away*, 15–16.

13. Agnew, *Go Quietly*, 62. Herb Thompson, Agnew's press secretary, recalls that Beall held a grudge about Agnew's switch from Rockefeller to Nixon. Author interview with Thompson.

14. Agnew, *Go Quietly*, 57.

15. H. R. Haldeman, *The Haldeman Diaries: Inside the Nixon White House* (New York: G.P. Putnam's Sons, 1994), 629–630.

16. Ibid.

17. Agnew, *Go Quietly*, 58.

18. Witcover and Cohen, *A Heartbeat Away*, 80–81.

19. Stephen E. Ambrose, *Nixon: Ruin and Recovery, 1973–1990* (New York: Simon & Schuster, 1991).146.

20. Witcover and Cohen, *A Heartbeat Away*, 69–96.

21. George Beall testimony before the United State Senate Committee on Governmental Affairs, March 3, 1999, accessed March 2015, www.hsgac.senate.gov/download/?id=710d14d3.

22. "The relationship between Matz and Agnew," Baltimore County/Spiro T. Agnew investigation, Personal Papers of the Beall Family, J. Glenn Beall Archives, Lewis J. Ort Library, Frostburg State University, Frostburg, Maryland (hereafter "Beall Papers").

23. Ibid.

24. Ibid.

25. "The relationship between Agnew, Hammerman, and Wolff," Beall Papers.

26. Agnew, *Go Quietly*, 89.

27. "Statement of Allen Green," Beall Papers.

28. Ibid.

29. Ibid.

30. Ibid.

31. Ibid.

32. The information concerning Hammerman is from "The relationship between Agnew, Hammerman, and Wolff," Beall Papers.

33. "The relationship between Agnew, Hammerman, and Wolff," Beall Papers.

34. Ibid.
35. Witcover and Cohen, *A Heartbeat Away*, 105–112.
36. Richard Nixon, *RN: The Memoirs of Richard Nixon* (New York: Touchstone, 1978), 816.
37. Alexander Haig, *Inner Circles: How America Changed the World, A Memoir* (New York: Warner Books, 1992), 350.
38. Agnew, *Go Quietly*, 81; Cohen and Witcover, *A Heartbeat Away*, 117.
39. Agnew, *Go Quietly*, 92.
40. Ibid., 94.
41. Deborah Hart Strober and Gerald S. Strober, *The Nixon Presidency: An Oral History of the Era* (Washington, DC: Brassey's, 1994), 431.
42. Haig, *Inner Circles*, 352–353.
43. Nixon, *RN*, 913.
44. Jonathan Aitken, *Nixon: A Life* (Washington, DC: Regnery Publishing, 1994), 503.
45. Nixon, *RN*, 913.
46. "Transcript, Q & A with Students," May 8, 1973, folder 82, box 15, subseries 3.7, series 3, Agnew MS.
47. Agnew, *Go Quietly*, 98.
48. Agnew, *Go Quietly*, 98–102; Cohen and Witcover, *A Heartbeat Away*, 148–151.
49. Agnew, *Go Quietly*, 98–102; Cohen and Witcover, *A Heartbeat Away*, 148–151.
50. Agnew, *Go Quietly*, 101.
51. Ibid., 102–103.
52. Ibid.
53. Ibid.
54. *Wall Street Journal*, August 7, 1973, 1.
55. Nixon, *RN*, 914.
56. Agnew, *Go Quietly*, 107.
57. For Agnew's version of the meeting, see Agnew, *Go Quietly*, 107–110; for Nixon's, see Nixon, *RN*, 914.

CHAPTER 10: "DAMNED LIES"

1. Spiro T. Agnew, *Go Quietly ... or else* (New York: William Morrow, and Company, 1980), 51–52.
2. "Press Conferences-re Maryland Funds," August 8, 1973, folder 87, box 15, subseries 3.7, series 3, Spiro T. Agnew Papers, Special Collections, University of Maryland Libraries, College Park, Maryland (hereafter "Agnew MS").
3. *New York Times*, August 9, 1973, 18.
4. Ibid, 21.
5. *Los Angeles Herald Examiner*, August 9, 1973, 1.
6. Raymond Price, *With Nixon* (New York: The Viking Press, 1977), 252.
7. Richard Nixon, *RN: The Memoirs of Richard Nixon* (New York: Touchstone, 1978), 914.
8. Robert Alan Goldberg, *Barry Goldwater* (New Haven: Yale University Press, 1995), 277.
9. Agnew, *Go Quietly*, 116–117.
10. Ibid, 118.

11. *New York Times*, August 17, 1973, 17.
12. Agnew, *Go Quietly*, 117.
13. *New York Times*, August 23, 1973, 17.
14. Ibid.
15. *New York Times*, August 20, 1973, 54.
16. *Baltimore Sun*, August 16, 173, A1.
17. *New York Times*, August 9, 1973, 1.
18. Agnew, *Go Quietly*, 113.
19. *New York Times*, August 16, 1973, 27; Charles Morgan Jr. to Elliot Richardson, August 11, 1973, folder 18, box 169, Legislative Series, Carl T. Albert Papers, Carl Albert Congressional Research and Studies Center Congressional Archives, University of Oklahoma, Norman, OK.
20. Nixon, *RN*, 914.
21. Richard M. Cohen and Jules Witcover, *A Heartbeat Away: The Investigation and Resignation of Vice President Spiro T. Agnew* (New York: Viking Press, 1974), 196.
22. Elliot Richardson, *The Creative Balance: Government, Politics, and the Individual in America's Third Century* (New York: Holt, Rinehart, and Wilson, 1976), 105.
23. *Baltimore Sun*, August 18, 1973, A1. The election was called after Republican Congressman William Mills committed suicide.
24. "Speeches," August 18, 1973, folder 30, box 11, subseries 3.7, series 3, Agnew MS.
25. "Press Conferences," August 21, 1973, box 15, subseries 3.7, series 3, Agnew MS.
26. Agnew, *Go Quietly*, 134–135; Nixon, *RN*, 915.
27. Agnew, *Go Quietly*, 60.
28. *National Review*, September 28, 1973, 1034.
29. Deborah Hart Strober and Gerald S. Strober, *The Nixon Presidency: An Oral History of the Era* (Washington, D.C: Brassey's Inc., 1994), 434.
30. *Time*, September 3, 1973, 26.
31. Cohen and Witcover, *A Heartbeat Away*, 208.
32. Agnew, *Go Quietly*, 136–138.
33. *Time*, August 27, 1973, 15.
34. *The Gallup Poll Index*, Report 99, September 1973, 13.
35. In his front-page story about the meeting, Lou Cannon wrote, "Deputy Press Secretary Gerald L. Warren denounced as 'erroneous' and 'false' speculation that Mr. Nixon would seek Agnew's resignation." *Washington Post*, September 1, 1973, A1.
36. *Newsweek*, September 10, 1973, 18.
37. Nixon, *RN*, 915.
38. Agnew, *Go Quietly*, 140–141.
39. Nixon, *RN*, 915–916.
40. Cohen and Witcover, *A Heartbeat Away*, 37.
41. *Washington Post*, September 2, 1973, A6.
42. *New York Times*, September 2, 1973, 34.
43. Cohen and Witcover, *A Heartbeat Away*, 212–214.
44. Agnew wrote that his "recollections of this stormy meeting are substantiated by detailed notes which Best wrote immediately afterward." Agnew, *Go Quietly*, 141–143.
45. Nixon, *RN*, 916.
46. Cohen and Witcover, *A Heartbeat Away*, 220–221.

47. Topkis was a brilliant attorney and one well qualified to make such a judgment. He taught constitutional law for sixteen years at Columbia University.

48. Agnew, *Go Quietly*, 143–145; Jules Witcover, *Strange Bedfellows: The Short and Unhappy Marriage of Richard Nixon and Spiro Agnew* (New York: Public Affairs, 2007), 319–320.

49. Agnew, *Go Quietly*, 145–146. In his memoirs, Haig said he met with Agnew in the second week of September after Haig had talked with Richardson. The case against Agnew was "solid" and the Justice Department could prove that Agnew had taken $172,000 in illegal payments over the years. It was then that Haig claims he brought up resignation, an option that brought "genuine astonishment" from Agnew. Haig does not give a date for the meeting, nor does he mention any other participants. See Alexander Haig, *Inner Circles: How America Changed the World, A Memoir* (New York: Warner Books, 1992), 362.

50. Agnew, *Go Quietly*, 147.

51. Cohen and Witcover, *A Heartbeat Away*, 222–223.

52. Ibid.

53. Ibid., 224.

54. Agnew, *Go Quietly*, 150–151.

55. Ibid.

56. Ibid, 152.

57. Ibid, 157.

58. Nixon, *RN*, 916.

59. Agnew, *Go Quietly*, 157–158.

60. Ibid, 158.

61. Cohen and Witcover, *A Heartbeat Away*, 239–244.

62. Nixon, *RN*, 916.

63. Agnew, *Go Quietly*, 163.

64. Ibid.

65. Nixon, *RN*, 917.

66. Agnew, *Go Quietly*, 164.

67. Nixon, *RN*, 917.

68. Agnew, *Go Quietly*, 164.

69. Ibid.

70. Nixon, *RN*, 917.

71. Carl Albert with Danney Goble, *Little Giant: The Life and Times of Speaker Carl Albert* (Norman: University of Oklahoma Press, 1990), 359.

72. Agnew, *Go Quietly*, 165–168; Agnew to Carl Albert, September 25, 1973, folder 25, box 191, Legislative Series, Albert Papers.

73. "Ronald M. Peters interview with Carl Albert," May 23, 1979, Oral History Series, Albert Papers.

74. Agnew, *Go Quietly*, 171.

75. Thomas M. DeFrank, *Write It When I'm gone: Remarkable Off-the-Record Conversations with Gerald R. Ford* (New York: G.P. Putnam's Sons, 2007), 103.

76. Agnew, *Go Quietly*, 168–170.

77. O'Neill, *Man of the House*, 258.

78. Ford, *A Time to Heal*, 102.

79. Albert, *Little Giant*, 359.

80. I have a copy of a report, "Why the Calhoun Precedent Governs and the Colfax Precedent Does Not Apply," which I found in Arthur Sohmer's papers at the Maryland State Archives in Annapolis. MSA–SC 4804.

81. Jean Edward Smith, *Grant* (New York: Touchstone, 2001), 552; *Washington Post*, September 29, 1973, A4.

82. "The Calhoun Precedent," MSA–SC 4804.

83. Albert, *Little Giant*, 359–360.

84. "Agnew Letter," September 26, 1973, folder 121, box 17, Speeches Series, Albert Papers.

85. "Statement by Representative Gerald Ford," September 26, 1973, folder 1, box 22, General Correspondence Series, John H. Camp Collection, Albert Center.

86. *Washington Post*, September 26, 1973, A1, 11.

87. *New York Times*, September 27, 1973, 29.

88. Agnew, *Go Quietly*, 177.

89. Ibid.

90. *Washington Post*, September 29, 1973, A1, 10; *Baltimore Sun*, September 29, 1973, A1, 8.

91. Cohen and Witcover, *A Heartbeat Away*, 265–266.

92. Agnew, *Go Quietly*, 180. For the original text of the speech, see "Speeches-National Federation of Republican Women," September 29, 1973, folder 34, box 11, subseries 3.7, series 3, Agnew MS.

CHAPTER 11: RESIGNATION

1. Spiro T. Agnew, *Go Quietly ... or else* (New York: William Morrow, and Company, 1980), 180.

2. Ibid, 182.

3. Ibid, 190.

4. Ibid, 183.

5. "The President's News Conference," October 3, 1973, in *The Nixon Presidential News Conferences* (New York: Earl M. Coleman Enterprises, Inc., 1978), 357–360.

6. Richard M. Cohen and Jules Witcover, *A Heartbeat Away: The Investigation and Resignation of Vice President Spiro T. Agnew* (New York: Viking Press, 1974). The Petersen quote is from 270; the information about Nixon calling Richardson is on page 276.

7. Agnew, *Go Quietly*, 184.

8. Ibid, 184–185; Cohen and Witcover, *A Heartbeat Away*, 279–282.

9. *New York Times*, October 4, 1973, 1.

10. Agnew, *Go Quietly*, 173; *Washington Post*, October 1, 1973, A1.

11. *Chicago Tribune*, October 4, 1973, 18.

12. *Washington Post*, October 4, 1973, A28.

13. Ibid.

14. Ibid.

15. Agnew, *Go Quietly*, 186–190.

16. Ibid.

17. Alexander Haig, *Inner Circles: How America Changed the World, A Memoir* (New York: Warner Books, 1992), 365–366.

18. Nessen later went on to serve as White House press secretary under Gerald Ford.

19. *New York Times*, October 6, 1973, 1, 8.

20. Agnew, *Go Quietly*, 194.
21. Cohen and Witcover, *A Heartbeat Away*, 290.
22. Jules Witcover discusses the affair on page 351 in *Very Strange Bedfellows.*
23. Cohen and Witcover, *A Heartbeat Away*, 295–301.
24. Agnew, *Go Quietly*, 197.
25. Ibid.
26. For Agnew's version, see *Go Quietly*, 197–198. For Nixon's version, see *RN*, 922–923.
27. Agnew, *Go Quietly*, 14.
28. Ibid., 13.
29. Ibid., 14.
30. *Chicago Tribune*, October 11, 1973, 1.
31. Agnew, *Go Quietly*, 14–17.
32. *New York Times*, October 11, 1973, 1, 35.

EPILOGUE

1. Spiro T. Agnew, *Go Quietly ... or else* (New York: William Morrow, and Company, 1980), 21.
2. *New York Times*, October 11, 1973, 1.
3. Agnew, *Go Quietly*, 185–186.
4. Ibid., 203–204.
5. Ibid., 15.
6. Ibid., 217–218; *Baltimore Sun*, December 19, 1973, A1, 12; *Washington Post*, May 16, 1974, A14.
7. Agnew, *Go Quietly*, 223.
8. Ibid., 19–21, 215; *Los Angeles Times*, May 1, 1976, 22.
9. Herb Thompson, and David Keene told me that Agnew was the best boss they ever had. Both men remembered Agnew very fondly and expressed their gratitude to Agnew for all he did for them.
10. Agnew, *Go Quietly*, 213; Theo Lippman, "Nearby, Spiro T. Agnew Says None of the ...," *Baltimore Sun*, July 13, 1991. Lippman wrote a biography of Agnew, published in 1972. In his 1991 column, Lippman discussed a letter he received from Cynthia Rosenwald, one of Agnew's speechwriters. In the letter, Rosenwald argued that Agnew, as governor, "was pro civil rights, pushed the state toward constitutional reform and set up a cabinet system in the executive branch."
11. *New York Times*, February 6, 1974, 16; *Newsweek*, February 4, 1974, 20.
12. *New York Times Book Review*, June 6, 1976, 3.
13. Agnew, *Go Quietly*, 9.
14. Ibid., 189–190.
15. *Baltimore Sun*, May 25, 1995.
16. "Spiro T. Agnew, ex-vice president, dies in Maryland at 77," *Baltimore Sun*, September 18, 1996, 1.
17. "Agnew laid quietly to rest," *Evening Capital* (Annapolis), September 22, 1996, MSA SC 3520. Y 25, 1995.

Bibliography

MANUSCRIPT COLLECTIONS

Enoch Pratt Library, Baltimore, Maryland
Vertical Files
Frostburg State University, J. Glenn Beall Archives, Lewis J. Ort Library, Frostburg, Maryland
Personal Papers of the Beall Family
Johns Hopkins University, Ferdinand Hamburger Jr. Archives, Milton S. Eisenhower Library, Baltimore, Maryland
Office of the Registrar Series
Maryland State Archives, Special Collections, Annapolis, Maryland
Governor (General File), 1967–1968, MSA SC 1041–1713
Apfelbaum Collection, MSA SC 4804
The Richard M. Nixon Presidential Library and Museum, Yorba Linda, California
President's Personal Files
White House Special Files
White House Office Files
The Rockefeller Archive Center, Tarrytown, New York
Nelson A. Rockefeller Papers
Stanford University, Hoover Institution Archives, Stanford, California
John Ehrlichman Papers
Sidney D. Hook Papers
University of Baltimore Library, Special Collections, Langsdale Library, Baltimore, Maryland
University of Baltimore Collection
University of Hawaii, Hawaii Congressional Papers Collection, Manoa Library, Manoa, Hawaii
The Senator Spark M. Matsunaga Papers
University of Iowa, Special Collections Department, University of Iowa Libraries, Iowa City, Iowa
Papers of Theodore F. Koop
Papers of Nick Thimmesch

University of Maryland, Special Collections, Hornbake Library, College Park, Maryland
Jean Spencer Papers
Franklin L. Burdette Papers
Spiro T. Agnew Papers
University of Oklahoma Carl Albert Congressional Research and Studies Center Congressional Archives, Norman, Oklahoma
Carl Albert Collection
John H. Camp Collection
University of Wyoming, American Heritage Center, Laramie, Wyoming
Joseph P. Albright Papers

NEWSPAPERS AND PERIODICALS

Annapolis Evening Capitol
Baltimore Afro American
Baltimore Evening Express
Baltimore News American
Baltimore Sun
Channels
Chicago Defender
Commonweal
Cumberland Evening Times
Easton Express
(Hagerstown) Morning Herald
Jackson Advocate
National Review
Newsweek
New York Daily News
New York Post
New York Times
Time
U.S. News & World Report
Wall Street Journal
Washington Post
Washington Evening Star

INTERVIEWS

Herb Thompson. Interview with author, February 14, 2003.
David Keene. Interview with author, July 17, 2003.

ORAL HISTORIES

William L. Adams, Oral History 8210, August 4, 1977, Maryland Historical Society Oral History Office, Baltimore, Maryland.
Theodore R. McKeldin Jr., Oral History 8282, July 25, 1977, Maryland Historical Society Oral History Office, Baltimore, Maryland.

GOVERNMENT PUBLICATIONS

United States Reports Vol. 378. Washington, D.C.: Government Printing Office, 1965.

Addresses and State Papers of Spiro T. Agnew, Governor of Maryland, 1967–1969. Annapolis: State of Maryland, 1975.

Report of the National Advisory Commission on Civil Disorders. Washington, D.C.: Government Printing Office, 1968.

Public Papers of the President of the United States: 1969–1972. Washington, D.C.: Government Printing Office, 1971–1974.

DISSERTATIONS/THESES

Coffey, Justin P. "Watergate and the Committee to Reelect the President." Master's thesis, University of Wyoming, 1998.

Durr, Kenneth. " 'Why We Are troubled': White-Working Class Politicians in Baltimore, 1940–1980." Ph.D. Diss., American University, 1998.

Forslund, Catherine Mary. "Woman of Two Worlds: Anna Chenault and Informal Diplomacy in US-Asian Relations, 1950–1990." Ph.D. Diss., Washington University, 1997.

Hatfield, Michael S. "The 1966 Maryland Gubernatorial Election: The Political Saliency of Open Occupancy." Master's thesis, University of Massachusetts, 1967.

Noe, Kaye Sizer. "The Fair Housing Movement: An Overview and Case Study." Master's thesis, University of Maryland, 1965.

BOOKS

Agnew, Spiro T. *Go Quietly . . . or else*. New York: William Morrow, and Company, 1980.

Albert, Carl with Danney Goble. *Little Giant: The Life and Times of Speaker Carl Albert*. Norman: University of Oklahoma Press, 1990.

Albright, Joseph. *What Makes Spiro Run: The Life and Times of Spiro Agnew*. New York: Dodd, Mead, 1972.

Ambrose, Stephen E. *Nixon: The Education of a Politician, 1913–1962*. New York: Simon & Schuster, 1987.

Ambrose, Stephen E. *Nixon: The Triumph of a Politician, 1962–1972*. New York: Simon & Schuster, 1989.

Ambrose, Stephen E. *Nixon: Ruin and Recovery, 1973–1990*. New York: Simon & Schuster, 1991.

Black, Conrad. *Richard M. Nixon: A Life in Full*. New York: Public Affairs, 2007.

Borstlemann, Thomas. *The Cold War and the Color Line: American Race Relations in the Global Arena*. Cambridge: Harvard University Press, 2001.

Bradlee, Benjamin C. *Conversations with Kennedy*. New York: W.W. Norton & Company, 1984.

Brooks, Neal A., Eric G. Rockel, and William C. Hughes. *A History of Baltimore County*. Towson: Friends of Towson Library, 1979.

Brugger, Robert J. *Maryland, A Middle Temperament: 1640–1980*. Baltimore: Johns Hopkins University Press, 1996.

Buchanan, Patrick J. *Right from the Beginning*. Washington: Regnery, 1988.

Buchanan, Patrick J. *The Greatest Comeback: How Richard Nixon Rose from Defeat to Create the New Majority*. New York: Crown Forum, 2014.

Burke, Bob and Ralph G. Thompson. *Bryce Harlow: Mr. Integrity*. Oklahoma City: Oklahoma Heritage Association, 2000.

Burner, David. *Making Peace with the 60s*. Princeton: Princeton University Press, 1996.

Callcott, George C. *Maryland and America, 1940–1980*. Baltimore: The Johns Hopkins University Press, 1985.

Carlson, Jody. *George C. Wallace and the Politics of Powerlessness*. Brunswick: Transaction Books, 1981.

Caro, Robert. *Means of Ascent: The Years of Lyndon Johnson*. New York: Alfred A. Knopf, 1990.

Carson, Clayborne. *In Struggle: SNCC and the Black Awakening of the 1960s*. Cambridge: Harvard University Press, 1981.

Carter, Dan T. *The Politics of Rage: George Wallace, the Origins of the New Conservatism, and the Transformation of American Politics*. New York: Simon & Schuster, 1995.

Cohen, Richard M. and Jules Witcover. *A Heartbeat Away: The Investigation and Resignation of Vice President Spiro T. Agnew*. New York: The Viking Press, 1974.

Colodny, Len and Robert Gettlin, *Silent Coup: The Removal of a President*. New York: St. Martin's Press, 1991.

Critchlow, Donald T. *The Conservative Ascendancy: How the Republican Right Rose to Power in Modern America*. Lawrence. University Press of Kansas, 2011.

Cutler, John Henry. *Ed Brooke: Biography of a Senator*. Indianapolis: Bobbs-Merril, 1972.

Darman, Jonathan. *Landslide: LBJ and Ronald Reagan at the Dawn of a New America*. New York: Random House, 2014.

Dallek, Robert. *Flawed Giant: Lyndon Johnson and His Times, 1961–1973*. New York: Oxford University Press, 1998.

DeFrank, Thomas. *Write It When I'm Gone: Remarkable Off-the-Record Conversations with Gerald R. Ford*. New York: G.P. Putnam's Sons, 2007.

Dudziak, Mary C. *Cold War Civil Rights: Race and the Image of American Democracy*. Princeton: Princeton University Press, 2000.

Edwards, Lee. *Goldwater: The Man Who Made a Revolution*. Washington, D.C.: Regnery, 1995.

Efron, Edith. *The News Twisters*. Los Angeles: Nash Publishing, 1972.

Ehrlichman, John. *Witness to Power: The Nixon Years*. New York: Simon & Schuster, 1982.

Elfenbein, Jessica I. et al., eds., *Baltimore '68: Riots and Rebirth in an American City*. Philadelphia: Temple University Press, 2011.

Eisele, Albert. *Almost to the Presidency: A Biography of Two American Politicians*. Blue Earth, MN: Piper Company, 1972.

Emery, Fred. *Watergate: The Corruption of American Politics and the Fall of Richard Nixon*. New York: Touchstone, 1994.

Evans, Rowland Jr. and Robert D. Novak. *Nixon in the White House: The Frustration of Power*. New York: Random House, 1971.

Ford, Gerald R. *A Time to Heal: The Autobiography of Gerald R. Ford*. New York: Harper & Row, 1979.

Frederickson, Kari. *The Dixiecrat Revolt and the End of the Solid South, 1932–1968*. Chapel Hill: University of North Carolina Press, 2001.

Genovese, Michael. *The Watergate Crisis*. Westwood, CT: Greenwood Press, 1999.

Giglio, James S. *The Presidency of John F. Kennedy*. Lawrence: The University Press of Kansas, 1991.

Gifford, Laura Jane. *The Center Cannot Hold: The 1960 Presidential Election and the Rise of Modern Conservatism*. DeKalb: University of Northern Illinois, 2009.

Gifford, Laura Jane and Daniel K. Williams, eds. *The Right Side of the Sixties: Reexamining Conservatism's Decade of* Transformation. New York: Palgrave Macmillan, 2012.

Glad, Betty. *Jimmy Carter: In Search of the Great White House*. New York: W.W. Norton, 1980.

Glasser, Joshua M. *The Eighteen-Day Running Mate: McGovern, Eagleton, and a Campaign in Crisis*. New Haven: Yale University Press, 2012.

Goldberg, Robert Allen. *Barry Goldwater*. New Haven: Yale University Press, 1995.

Goldstein, Joel K. *The Modern American Vice Presidency*. Princeton: Princeton University Press, 1982.

Goldwater, Barry. The Conscience of a Conservative. Shepherdsville, KY: Victor Publishing, 1960.

Goldwater, Barry. *Goldwater*. New York: Doubleday: 1988.

Gould, Lewis L. *1968: The Election that Changed America*, 2nd edition. Chicago: Ivan R. Dee, 2010.

Graham, Hugh Davis. *The Civil Rights Era: Origins and Development of National Policy, 1960–1972*. New York: Oxford University Press, 1990.

Haig, Alexander. *Inner Circles: How America Changed the World, A Memoir*. New York: Warner Books, 1992.

Haldeman, H. R. *The Haldeman Diaries: Inside the Nixon White House*. New York: G.P. Putnam's Sons, 1994.

Herring, George. *From Colony to Superpower: U.S. Foreign Relations since 1776*. New York: Oxford University Press, 2008.

Hite, James E. *Second Best: The Rise of the American Vice Presidency*. San Diego: Cognella Academic Publishing, 2013.

Hoffman, Paul. *Spiro!* New York: Tower Publications, 1971.

Hughes, Ken. *Chasing Shadows: The Nixon Tapes, the Chennault Affair, and the Origins of Watergate*. Charlottesville: University of Virginia Press, 2014.

Johnson, Robert David. *All the Way with LBJ: The 1964 Presidential Election*. New York: Cambridge University Press, 2009.

Jones, Howard. *The Crucible of Power: A History of American Foreign Relations since 1897*. Wilmington: Scholarly Resources Inc., 2001.

Kabaservice, Geoffrey. *Rule and Ruin: The Downfall of Moderation and the Destruction of the Republican Party, from Eisenhower to the Tea Party*. New York: Oxford University Press, 2012.

Kalman, Laura. *Right Star Rising: A New Politics, 1974–1980*. New York: W.W. Norton & Company, 2010.

Kimball, Jeffrey. *Nixon's Vietnam War*. Lawrence: University Press of Kansas, 1998.

Kissinger, Henry. *White House Years*. Boston: Little, Brown, and Company, 1979.

Kissinger, Henry. *Years of Upheaval*. Boston: Little, Brown, and Company, 1982.
Klein, Herbert. *Making It Perfectly Clear*. New York: Doubleday, 1980.
Kotlowski, Dean. *Nixon's Civil Rights: Politics, Principle, and Policy*. Cambridge: Harvard University Press, 2002.
Kozak, Warren. *LeMay: The Life of General Curtis LeMay*. Washington, D.C.: Regnery Press, 2009.
Kramer, Michael and Sam Roberts. *I Never Wanted to Be Vice President of Anything: An Investigative Biography of Nelson Rockefeller*. New York: Basic Books, 1976.
Kutler, Stanley I., ed. *Abuse of Power: The New Nixon Tapes*. New York: The Free Press, 1997.
Lesher, Stephen. *George Wallace: American Populist*. Reading: Addison-Wesley Publishing, 1993.
Levy, Peter. *Civil War on Race Street: The Civil Rights Movement in Cambridge, Maryland*. Gainesville: University Press of Florida, 2003.
Lippman, Theo. *Spiro Agnew's America: The Vice President and the Politics of Suburbia*. New York: W.W. Norton & Company, 1972.
Lucas, Jim C. *Agnew: Profile in Conflict*. New York: Award Books, 1970.
Magruder, Jeb. *An American Life: One Man's Road to Watergate*. New York: Atheneum, 1974.
Mason, Robert. *Richard Nixon and the Quest for a New Majority*. Chapel Hill: University of North Carolina Press, 2004.
Mergel, Sarah Katherine. *Conservative Intellectuals and Richard Nixon: Rethinking the Rise of the Right*. New York: Palgrave Macmillan, 2010.
Morris, Roger. *Richard Milhous Nixon: The Rise of an American Politician*. New York: Henry Holt, 1989.
Nelson, Michael. *Resilient America: Electing Nixon in 1968, Channeling Dissent, and Dividing Government*. Lawrence: University Press of Kansas, 2014
The Nixon Presidential News Conferences. New York: Earl M. Coleman Enterprises, Inc., 1978.
Nixon, Richard. *RN: The Memoirs of Richard Nixon*. New York: Touchstone, 1978.
Nixon, Richard. *No More Vietnams*. New York: Arbor House, 1985.
O'Neill, Tip with William Novak. *Man of the House: The Life and Political Memoirs of Speaker Tip O'Neill*. New York: Random House, 1987.
Oates, Stephen B. *Let the Trumpet Sound: The Life of Martin Luther King Jr*. New York: Harper & Row, 1982.
Olson, Keith W. *Watergate: The Presidential Scandal That Shook America*. Lawrence: The University of Kansas Press, 2003.
Osborne, John. *The Nixon Watch*. New York: Liveright, 1970.
Oudes, Bruce, ed. *From: The President: Richard Nixon's Secret Files*. New York: Harper & Row, 1989.
Parmet, Herbert. *Richard Nixon and His America*. Boston: Little, Brown, 1990.
Patterson, James T. *Grand Expectations: The United States, 1945–1974*. New York: Oxford University Press, 1996.
Perlstein, Rick. *Before the Storm: Barry Goldwater and the Unmaking of the American Consensus*. New York: Hill and Wang, 2001.
Perlstein, Rick. *Nixonland: The Rise of a President and the Fracturing of America*. New York: Scribner, 2008.

Perlstein, Rick. *The Invisible Bridge: The Fall of Nixon and the Rise of Reagan.* New York: Simon & Schuster, 2014.
Price, Raymond. *With Nixon.* New York: The Viking Press, 1977.
Reeves, Richard. *President Nixon: Alone in the White House.* New York: Simon & Shuster, 2001.
Richardson, Elliot. *The Creative Balance: Government, Politics, and the Individual in America's Third Century.* New York: Holt, Rinehart, and Wilson, 1976.
Richardson, Elliot. *Reflections of a Radical Moderate.* New York: Pantheon Books, 1996.
Roberts, Randy and James S. Olson. *John Wayne: American.* New York: Free Press, 1995.
Rorabaugh, W. J. *The Real Making of the President: Kennedy, Nixon, and the 1960 Election.* Lawrence: The University of Kansas, 2009.
Safire, William. *Before the Fall: An Insider View of the Pre-Watergate White House.* New York: Belmont Tower Books, 1975.
Schapsmeier, Edward L. and Frederick H. *Dirksen of Illinois: Senatorial Statesman.* Urbana: University of Illinois Press, 1985.
Schneider, Gregory L. *Cadres for Conservatism: Young Americans for Freedom and the Rise of the Contemporary Right.* New York: New York University Press, 1998.
Schoenwald, Jonathan M. *A Time for Choosing: The Rise of Modern American Conservatism.* New York: Oxford University Press, 2001.
Schultz, George. *Turmoil and Triumph: My Years as Secretary of State.* New York: Charles Scribner's Sons, 1993.
Schulzinger, Robert D. *U.S. Diplomacy since 1900.* New York: Oxford University Press, 2008.
Small, Melvin. *The Presidency of Richard Nixon.* Lawrence: University Press of Kansas, 1999.
Small, Melvin, ed. *A Companion to Richard M.* Nixon. Chichester, UK: Wiley-Blackwell, 2011.
Smith, Jean Edward. *Grant.* New York: Touchstone, 2001.
Smith, Richard Norton. *On His Own Terms: A Life of Nelson* Rockefeller. New York: Random House, 2014.
Strober, Deborah Hart and Gerald S. Strober. *The Nixon Presidency: An Oral History of the Era.* Washington, D.C.: Brassey's Inc., 1994.
Thomas, Evan. *Robert Kennedy: His Life.* New York: Simon & Schuster, 2000.
Thurber, Timothy. *Republicans and Race: The GOP's Frayed Relationship with African Americans, 1945–1974.* Lawrence: The University of Kansas Press, 2013.
Walsh, Richard and William Lloyd Fox. *Maryland: A History, 1632–1974.* Baltimore: Maryland Historical Society, 1974.
Whalen, Richard J. *Where He Stands: The Life and Convictions of Spiro T. Agnew.* New York: Hawthorne Books, 1968.
Whalen, Richard J. *Catch the Falling Flag: A Republican's challenge to his party.* New York: Houghton Mifflin, 1972.
White, Theodore H. *The Making of the President 1968.* New York: *Atheneum* Publishers, 1969.
Wicker, Tom. One of Us: Richard Nixon and the American Dream. New York: Random House, 1991.

Wills, Garry. *Nixon Agonistes: The Crisis of the Self-Made Man*. Boston: Houghton Mifflin Company, 1970.

Witcover, Jules. *White Knight: The Rise of Spiro Agnew*. New York: Random House, 1972.

Witcover, Jules. *Strange Bedfellows: The Short and Unhappy Marriage of Richard Nixon and Spiro Agnew*. New York: Public Affairs, 2007.

Wolff, George D. *William Warren Scranton: Pennsylvania Statesman*. London: A Keystone Book, 1981.

Index

About the Author

Justin P. Coffey, Ph.D., is an associate professor of History at Quincy University, Quincy, Illinois. He specializes in recent American history and is the author of numerous chapters and articles, including "Nixon and Agnew," in *A Companion to Richard M. Nixon*, Melvin Small (ed.), 2011.

CPSIA information can be obtained
at www.ICGtesting.com
Printed in the USA
BVHW070037151218
535393BV00017B/335/P

9 781440 841415